Springer Texts in Business and Economics

Springer Texts in Business and Economics (STBE) delivers high-quality instructional content for undergraduates and graduates in all areas of Business/Management Science and Economics. The series is comprised of self-contained books with a broad and comprehensive coverage that are suitable for class as well as for individual self-study. All texts are authored by established experts in their fields and offer a solid methodological background, often accompanied by problems and exercises.

More information about this series at http://www.springer.com/series/10099

Maksym Ivanyna • Alex Mourmouras
Peter Rangazas

The Macroeconomics of Corruption

Governance and Growth

Second Edition

Springer

Maksym Ivanyna
Joint Vienna Institute
Vienna, Austria

Alex Mourmouras
IMF
Washington, DC, USA

Peter Rangazas
IUPUI Economics
Indianapolis, IN, USA

ISSN 2192-4333 ISSN 2192-4341 (electronic)
Springer Texts in Business and Economics
ISBN 978-3-030-67559-2 ISBN 978-3-030-67557-8 (eBook)
https://doi.org/10.1007/978-3-030-67557-8

This Springer imprint is published by the registered company Springer Nature Switzerland AG
The registered company address is: Gewerbestrasse 11, 6330 Cham, Switzerland

Contents

Introduction 1

It is clear that the government is needed to lay the foundation for economic development. Development cannot occur without a public infrastructure that establishes and facilitates markets via the provision of national defense, a transportation system, legal protection of private property and marketable ideas, education and basic research, and a stable currency. In the early stages of development, governments also establish the first banks and corporations, often in partnership with private owners. The fundamental issue of public sector economics is how to constrain the government to provide these goods and services in a way that benefits most citizens rather than the private interests of politicians and the relatively small groups of their most important supporters.

Bad behavior by governments does not always take the form illegal actions and outright corruption. The performance of governments in leading their country's economic growth is frequently disappointing despite being perfectly legal. Selfish and political motives pull resources away from investment in future productivity and toward financing current consumption of favored groups. As a result, sustained growth in many poor countries has never occurred. Previously successful economies have seen growth stall and income inequality increase. Expanding social insurance programs in rich countries have resulted in public debt trajectories that place heavy fiscal burdens on future generations, to the point of creating potential fiscal crises that could send their economies into recessions or worse.

Education policies in developed countries are misallocating human capital investments, contributing to a slowdown in economic growth and a rise in wage inequality. Partly due to selfish motives and partly due to ignorance, there is too much attention and funding focused on college and college-preparation. Despite this bias, enrollment and graduation rates at 4 year universities have not significantly improved. Standards are also slipping as both high school and college have an increasingly larger "consumption" component. College costs are rising faster than income at the same time that the skills being acquired are falling. The small minority of each age-cohort that obtains more than a four-year degree is the main reason for the high average return to college. The majority of each age-cohort does not even

M. Ivanyna et al., *The Macroeconomics of Corruption*, Springer Texts in Business and Economics, https://doi.org/10.1007/978-3-030-67557-8_1

attend or fails to graduate from a 4-year program and, because of the bias toward college preparation in high school, has acquired few productive skills to fall back on.

It has become increasingly clear that the earth's climate is changing and mostly due to human activity. The effects of climate change on the welfare of future generations are difficult to determine but economists agree that the effects will be significant and will become worse due to government inactivity. The problem of climate change and the likelihood of a prompt policy response to it bears some resemblance to the fiscal crises facing many developed countries. Both problems have been long in the making: decades of greenhouse gas accumulation for climate change and decades of population aging and expanded transfer payments to retirees for the fiscal crisis. In each case the necessary policy responses will be costly, creating an incentive for politicians to ignore the problems and shift the burden of dealing with them to future generations.

Why do governments fail to live up to their responsibilities or worse, engage in outright corruption?

1.1 Corruption

The ancient Greeks invented a democracy with perhaps more direct participation by (male) citizens than democracies today. Despite the active participation of its citizenry, they remained quite worried about the selfish motives of politicians. Aristotle was concerned that the government could assume a perverted form where rulers' decisions are dominated by private interest.[1] The ancient Greek historian Polybius focused on corruption, which he defined as the decay of government into one that fails to deliver for, and even mistreats, its citizens.[2] Thucydides saw the root of corruption as the broader human failing to avoid greed and overreach when placed in positions of wealth and power.[3]

Similar to the ancient Greeks, many analysts today define corruption broadly as government behavior that ignores the public's welfare in favor of narrow private interests.[4] This broad definition includes *rent seeking* behavior that is technically *legal* but has the potential to reduce economic efficiency by creating excessive pork barrel spending, monopoly power, and weak enforcement of justifiable regulations. Although we discuss several aspects of rent seeking, as well as simply *bad policies* carried out by selfish dictators, we define corruption more narrowly to include activities that are *illegal* within the laws of a country.

[1]Wallis (2006, p. 23).

[2]Glaeser and Goldin (2006), p. 7).

[3]Woodruff (1993).

[4]See, for example, Bueno de Mesquita and Smith (2011) and Cost (2015).

At least in principle, this conservative approach makes corruption easier to detect and measure, apart from the flaws of legal politics and policy making. However, a perfect separation is impossible. Illegal corruption is probably highly correlated with the most offensive and costly types of legal rent seeking and the worst policy abuses of dictators. In addition, selfish behavior of government officials may be technically legal, by the standards of the country's laws, but essentially equivalent to corruption in terms of economic consequences. In some places, such as Ukraine, corruption is so infused throughout the government that corruption and the government's normal day-to-day operations cannot be separated in a meaningful way.[5] All activities that are not in the national interest can distort fiscal policy away from growth, efficiency, and fairness considerations, so any attempt at perfectly clear distinction is somewhat artificial. In the end, it would perhaps be better to let corruption be defined in the eye of the beholder, independent of a particular legal definition. The methods that we develop to study corruption can also be used to study many forms of legal rent-seeking and selfish policy making.

We also make a distinction between *petty* corruption and *grand* corruption. Petty corruption involves bribing bureaucrats who are responsible for implementing and enforcing laws and regulations. If the laws and regulations of a country are counter-productive, then bribes that help avoid them can improve efficiency. For this reason, we focus on the grand corruption of high-level politicians who are responsible for setting the country's economic policy. Grand corruption has not received as much attention in the literature but we think it is more closely related to fiscal crises and more likely to undermine an economy's growth.

Our interest in economic growth leads us to examine the corruption associated with budgeting and implementing public investment projects. There is evidence that large fractions of the budgets allocated for public school investments[6] and physical capital infrastructure[7] are diverted to public officials and their supporters for private use. The diversion of funds can take the form of direct skimming of the investment budgets or through bribes that cause public officials to select over-priced bids on public projects and procurements.

Large construction projects (e.g. schools, roads, ports, dams, military complexes) are favorites in more autocratic regimes of developing countries because they create easy-pickings for dictators and their cronies.[8] However, these projects also create corruption opportunities in the democracies of developed countries. For example, corruption problems intensified during the 1980s in Greece, Italy, and Turkey as infrastructure spending rose. In Greece, much of the corruption involved collusion between government officials and foreign companies in Europe that supplied

---

[5]de Wall (2016)

[6]Reinikka and Svensson (2004).

[7]Tanzi and Davoodi (1997), Pritchett (1996, 2000), Keefer and Knack (2007), Olken (2007), Baliamoune-Lutz and Ndikumana (2008), and Haque and Kneller (2008, 2012).

[8]Bueno de Mesquita and Smith (2011), Van der Does de Willibois et al. (2011), and Chayes (2015).

equipment, defense goods, and infrastructure construction to Greece.[9] In Italy, the famous *mani pulite* trials of the 1990s exposed widespread corruption associated with public works projects that had been going on for decades.[10] In Turkey, the early eighties saw domestic market liberalization, privatization of state-run industries, and an expansion in infrastructure projects. The expansion in economic activity caused a rise in corruption associated with privatization deals and public contracting.[11]

Brazil is currently embroiled in corruption scandals that reach to the highest levels of government. One aspect of the scandals is the rigging and over-budgeting of construction contracts paid out to Brazil's two largest construction companies. This is just the most recent example of inefficient government investment made by the Brazilian government— investment made not in the national interest, but rather to maximize the bribes received by public officials.[12]

Even countries that appear clean by standard measures have significant corruption issues. Ireland has little in the way of petty corruption where bribes are offered to avoid laws and regulations or to obtain timely governments services. However, corruption played a role in Ireland's housing bubble and financial crisis, with the government heavily involved in side-deals with builders and property developers.[13] In Japan, standard corruption measures fail to capture deeply institutionalized legal political corruption.[14] The Japanese practice of *amakudari* involves systematically stockpiling assets and opportunities for the benefit of specific subgroups of public servants. Part of this system involves building infrastructure of questionable utility to support quasi-public corporations charged with operating them. The *amakudari* tradition has given Japan one of the largest collections of government-controlled physical assets. Using tax payer funds, those operating these corporations receive lucrative salaries and benefits.

It seems likely that high-level political corruption in Ireland and entrenched corruption in Japan played some role in the sharp expansion of unnecessary investment projects financed by public debt. While the role of corruption in their stories might be missed by studies using available measures of corruption, they fit the corruption-investment scenario modeled in the book. The fact that corruption and the infrastructure spending that is needed for economic growth often go hand-in-hand in *both* autocratic and democratic regimes is a major reason for our focus.

Beyond the direct consequences of corruption itself, we consider how the nature and form of fiscal policy is affected by the opportunity to divert public funds for private use (Chaps. 3, 6, 7 and 8). We link rent seeking and corruption to the level of tax rates, the composition of government expenditures, and the extent to which

[9]Zoakos (2010).

[10]Cohen and Federico (2001), Brosio and Marchese (1986), and Tanzi and Davoodi (1997).

[11]Olsson (2014, pp. 271–272) and Zurcher (2004, pp. 267, 286, and 308–309).

[12]Romero (2016) and Lyons and Luhnow (2016).

[13]Clarke and Hardiman (2012).

[14]Jones (2015).

public debt is relied on for financing. The effects of the resulting changes in fiscal policy on economic growth are then also studied.

1.2 Close Cousins: Kleptocracy, Corruption, and Rent-Seeking

Bad governance, where public officials serve themselves and close supporters at the expense of the nation as a whole, takes many forms. In strong autocratic regimes with little threat of overthrow, the dictator and his close supporters establish the rules and the resulting policies. In this setting, little effort is made to disguise the intent of the government's objectives. In less powerful autocracies and weak democracies, there is some independent rule of law or some threat of political entry by other groups.[15] Here, policy must have a broader appeal and corruption must be more subtle and discrete. In strong democracies, it is harder to be corrupt without getting caught. The bigger problem becomes legal rent seeking, which in the end often has similar effects as corruption proper.

Strong autocratic regimes tend to set tax rates to maximize revenue without regard to efficiency considerations. This causes the country to have a large government, especially relative to its stage of development. For example, several poor African countries have ratios of government purchases to GDP in excess of 30 percent, far greater than the less than 20 percent ratios found in countries such as the U.S.[16]

Table 1.1 gives examples of poor countries (1/10 of US worker productivity, denoted by y^{US}, or less) with ratios of government purchases to GDP that about double those of the US. The comparison is for 1985, a year that generates close to the largest income gaps between the U.S. and most African countries during the twentieth century.[17] Starting in the 1990s, Africa began growing faster. Most of the countries in Table 1.1 have grown between 4 and 9 percent per year since the mid-1990s. The exceptions are the Central African Republic and Comoros, whose growth rates remain low and thus have seen their income gaps expand.

We should not be viewed as picking on Africa. There are plenty examples of similar behavior outside of Africa, where the majority is heavily taxed to benefit a small minority. Consider the regimes of Milosevic in Serbia, Suharto in Indonesia, and Duvalier in Haiti. In some cases, the incentive to both benefit the coalition of supporters *and* harm opponents with high taxes is so strong that the country's tax rates *exceed* those that maximize government revenue.[18] We provide an explanation for this counter-intuitive policy choice in Chap. 6.

In Chap. 6, we also develop a growth model with endogenous fiscal policy formation. We use the model to capture the ways that autocratic regimes set their

[15]Mulligan and Tsui (2015).

[16]Das et al. (2018) and Mourmouras and Rangazas (2009).

[17]World Bank (2008, Table 1).

[18]Padro i Miguel (2007).

Table 1.1 Government size—selected low-income countries (1985)

Country	Government Purchases/GDP	$y^{US}/y^{country}$
Angola	0.36	11
Burkina Faso	0.29	33
Central African Republic	0.44	17
Comoros	0.49	10
Ethiopia	0.28	40
Gambia	0.37	17
Mozambique	0.31	33
Uganda	0.28	33
Average	**0.32**	**24**

Source: Alan Heston, Robert Summers, and Bettina Aten, Penn World Table Version 6.1, Center for International Comparisons at the University of Pennsylvania, October 2002

fiscal policy. The information in Table 1.1 is used to calibrate a parameter that captures the relative weight the government places on the welfare of private households versus its own consumption. Variation in this determinant of government quality can be used to compute different fiscal policies and their effects on economic growth.

In less strong autocracies and weak democracies of developing countries, more subtlety must be used to circumvent laws or make the redistribution of wealth less obvious. A common strategy is to label government spending as public investment, when in fact the majority of the spending is simply a transfer to government officials and supporters—a key feature of one of the models used in Chap. 6. In Egypt since the 1970s, a large portion of public funds have been used for projects that essentially create consumption benefits for the military and big businesses closely aligned with the ruling party. Public investment elsewhere in the country was consistently over-budgeted and carried out with low quality materials, providing plenty of unused cash for public officials. In Afghanistan during the 1980s, contracts were written to build hundreds of structures for drying grapes. About 20 were actually built, the rest of the funds were pocketed by public officials and favored contractors.[19] In the Philippines under Marcos, 2 billion dollars were budgeted to build a nuclear power plant that never was able to produce energy.[20] From 1996 to 2000, the government of Trinidad and Tobago rigged the bidding to select overpriced bids for the construction of an international airport. The government officials involved in the scandal went as high as the country's finance minister. In 2002, the Kenyan government awarded a contract to a fictitious company for 32 million euros to replace its passport printing system and then subcontracted it to a French company to do the job for 6 million euros.[21]

[19]Chayes (2015).

[20]Pritchett (1996).

[21]Van der Does de Willibois et al. (2011).

Several well-established democracies in richer countries have also failed to control corruption. Despite the *mani pulite* trials mentioned above, Italy has failed to establish long-term reforms capable of limiting the return and growth of corruption. Recent arrests of government officials, including several high-ranking ones, were reported in 2014 and 2015. The arrests were based on illegal involvement in public construction projects that diverted funds for private use. The more high-profile cases among these were associated with Expo 2015 in Milan, the Venice flood barrier, and high speed train rails in Florence.[22] Reflecting on these events, Antonio Di Pietro, a leading magistrate during the *mani pulite* investigations, said,

> There is nothing new under the sun. Corruption continues to exist, like back then, and nothing has been done to introduce transparency in public administration.[23]

In Chap. 7, we show that this type of corruption is connected to public debt and the fiscal crisis facing many developed countries.

In rich countries with stronger checks on corruption, the main problem is rent seeking, a topic we address in Chap. 3. Rent seeking diverts funds that could be used for investment toward transfer payments and government consumption. Rent seeking can also cause the funds that are budgeted for investment to be misallocated, as political considerations dominate economic ones. In the U.S., for example, when politicians gain positions on the committees charged with allocating investment budgets, the funds tend to be used in the politician's home districts or in areas where the politicians personally own businesses and land.[24] In Japan, standard corruption measures fail to capture deeply institutionalized legal political corruption. The legal corruption involves building infrastructure of questionable utility to support quasi-public corporations that generate lucrative salaries and benefits for public officials.[25]

When one takes the time to look around, it is easy to see that rent seeking and legal corruption are pervasive parts of modern societies. Consider public high school and universities. The public officials and teachers that run these institutions should have the interest of all young people in mind. However, they have a vested interest in protecting a status quo that, as we mentioned earlier, is clearly not working for the majority of students in many countries. The educated elite benefit from the current system and are reluctant to even consider reallocating society's human capital investment funds toward preschool or vocational training despite evidence that this may raise economic growth and reduce wage inequality.[26] Reeves (2017) begins his

---

[22]See Rueters news service reports for May 9, 2014, June 13, 2014, and March 16, 2015 on Rueters.com

[23]Rueters report, May 9, 2014.

[24]Cost (2015, Chap. 10).

[25]Jones (2015).

[26]For discussion of the college bias that serves to misallocate human capital investment see Murray (2008) and Bennett and Wilezol (2013). The potentially high returns for many students from preschool and vocational training are discussed in Heckman (2013) and Newman and Winston (2016).

book *Dream Hoarders* with a revealing account of President Obama's attempt to remove tax benefits from the 529 college saving plan in favor of tax credits that would help the broad middle class. Despite the fact that the President's proposal shifts subsidies away from high income households to ones that benefit households with average incomes and below, it was attacked by liberal Democrats and quickly withdrawn.

How different is advocating for subsidies to higher education than lobbying for subsidies to, or deregulation of, the financial industry and large corporations? Both types of interest groups can claim that the government subsidies would promote greater capital formation and economic growth. The subsidies in either case would predominately raise the welfare of high income households.

1.3 Modeling the Government

Any assessment of government must be guided by some criteria defining "good" governance. We take a pragmatic approach to this issue based on principles of good governance that are widely accepted on equity and efficiency grounds.[27] The first three of these principles are commonly cited. The fourth is less so, but we feel it also reflects a sentiment that most people share and has influenced the laws that restrain individual behavior in most societies.

1.3.1 Focus on the National Interest

The government should *not* be a vehicle to redistribute income to public officials or to a relatively small group of their supporters. Given the inherently selfish nature of people, especially when placed in positions of power, keeping the focus on the national interest could be the largest challenge of good governance.

1.3.2 Efficiency of Resource Use

Policies that maximize total output by promoting efficiency of resource use should be given a priority. The level and allocation of government investment ought to be productively efficient, directed to projects and locations where the rate of return is the highest. It also means that policy makers should seek to raise revenue in a way that minimizes any negative effects on productive activity.

[27]Besley (2007, pp. 21–25) provides a nice discussion of the issues involved in defining good governance.

1.3.3 Limit Economic Disparity

There should be a tendency to limit large disparities in consumption and to equalize opportunities for economic success. This principle can conflict with the attempt to maximize total output. The efficiency-equity tension should cause policy makers to focus on equalizing economic outcomes by investing in the productivity of disadvantaged households rather than relying heavily on simply redistributing income.

1.3.4 Value Future Generations

Finally, the temptation to redistribute wealth to current generations from unborn generations should be limited. This last principle follows straightforwardly from the notion of fairness, which is bolstered by the intergenerational altruism we feel toward our children and is evident in laws that prevent children from being legally responsible for their parents' financial debt in most societies. Some regard this principle as a crucial element of a good society.[28]

The essence of these principles can be represented by a utilitarian social welfare function. This social welfare function is simply the sum of the utility functions of individual households.[29] Chapter 2 uses the utilitarian social welfare function to think about what good policies look like in our setting. Chapters 3, 6 and 7 present positive theories of government that create deviations from good policies.

Our positive theory of government behavior assumes the government officials that determine economic policy are fundamentally no different than private households. Their behavior is motivated by a mix of public and private concerns. They have public concerns because they are members of the society like everyone else. Their private concerns arise because they are aligned with particular groups or regions or because they seek political support from those groups. They may also have opportunities to divert public funds for private use while serving, i.e. they may have opportunities for corruption. It is the private desire of public officials to favor certain groups or raise their own income that causes the government to fail to perform in the national interest.

One approach to understanding government focuses on the role of elections in disciplining the behavior of self-interested politicians. The idea is that governments behave better in stronger democracies because only politicians that create policies serving the national interest will be re-elected. While we believe elections do provide

---

[28]See, for example, Ferguson (2012, pp. 43–45).

[29]The utilitarian social welfare function is commonly used, but is also subject to criticism. Arguments in favor of making the interpersonal comparisons of utility, that are needed to make the social welfare approach logically consistent and pragmatic, can be found in Besley (2007, pp. 21–25 and Chap. 2), Binmore (2007, Chap. 19), and Stigler and Becker (1977). We view the utilitarian social welfare function as a simple way of expositing the rationale for the principles of good governance.

some discipline to officials' behavior, the discipline is weak and insufficient to guarantee good behavior of public officials and policies that are in the national interest.

Our skepticism about elections being an effective disciplining device causes us not to focus on the selection of public officials or the even precise form of government. We do not explicitly model voting or the less peaceful struggles to achieve political positions. We abstract from these details for several reasons. First, we believe that government performance is largely independent of exactly who serves—any government official faces the same influence from the more powerful groups of the society and faces the same temptations to abuse their position once in office.[30] Second, for similar reasons, we believe the exact form of government is not of first order importance. Powerful groups and individual temptation will play a major role in all types of governments. Third, while voters tend to be rational about the incentives they are directly presented with, their understanding of the economy as a whole and what policies are ultimately in their best interest is flawed. Public officials have access to much more technical expertise than voters on the effects of different policies. Voters are generally unequipped to make a rational assessment of policies.[31] Finally, trying to model more institutional details has costs. Voting, rich heterogeneity in household types, and institutional details associated with different forms of government, add complexity that makes dynamic general equilibrium macroeconomic modeling difficult. Our book is an introduction to some aspects of political economy and we purposely avoid complexity that stems from features we feel are not absolutely essential. We leave a complete analysis to more advanced treatments. Chapter 9 contains some suggestions for important extensions and further reading that directs students toward more detailed discussions of the issues we introduce.

Mulligan et al. (2004) offer some empirical support for our approach. They find that the composition of policies coming from democracies is not different from those of nondemocracies. Furthermore, while the overall size of government is smaller in democracies than in communist regimes, it is not in autocracies more generally. Instead, government size and policies are determined by economic and demographic fundamentals. For example, countries with higher per capita income have larger governments (Wagner's Law) and a smaller fraction of the budget devoted to government consumption purchases. A higher percentage of the workforce in agriculture is associated with smaller government and a smaller allocation of the government budget to social transfers.[32] An older population raises the fraction of the budget devoted to social transfers. In addition to economic and demographic fundamentals, our model attempts to capture the harder to measure influence of culture and social norms. We view culture and social norms as important

[30]See Besley (2007) for an analysis of the situation where particular politicians matter—i.e. of the situation where there are different types and where who gets selected into office makes a difference.

[31]Caplan (2007, 2009) makes a case against assuming fully rational voters.

[32]For an explanation of the connection between the relative sizes of agriculture and government, see Das et al. (2018, Chap. 8).

determinants of good governance and we treat them as endogenous variables in our model, just as we do with economic variables.

The positive theory of government in Chaps. 3, 6, and 7 assumes each public official manages a public sector investment project. They consider the possibility of diverting public funds, earmarked to finance investment projects, for their own private use. In addition, each private household considers hiding income from the government to avoid taxation. Both illegal activities are potentially costly to the individual because resources are lost in attempting to conceal the illegal actions. The stronger are the government's detection institutions, the more resources are lost in avoiding detection.

However, the empirical literature indicates tax evasion cannot be explained by the detection of illegal activity alone, tax payer guilt also plays role. To capture this result, we assume households experience a loss in utility, "guilt" from violating a social norm, when evading taxes. Furthermore, as the empirical literature also suggests, the strength of the guilt associated with tax evasion varies inversely with the average level of corruption by government officials.[33]

We assume the same social norm enters the minds of politicians who consider engaging in corruption. Similar to tax evasion, given the relatively low expected penalty, it is difficult to explain why there isn't more corruption. The average behavior of the government sets a social norm by which all individuals judge their own illegal actions, both tax evasion and corruption. In this sense, private households and government officials are the same "type." Each considers taking illegal actions when the opportunity presents itself. Each is affected by social norms when deciding on the extent of their illegal activity.

Our model follows the research focusing on the horizontal transmission of culture on preferences.[34] There are several important examples of the horizontal transmission of culture in economics. Lindbeck et al. (1999) assume that individuals receiving a pecuniary gain from welfare programs also experience a disutility from living on public transfers rather than their own work. Culture enters because the disutility or stigma from public transfers is weaker the greater is the number of individuals in the society who receive government welfare. Fernandez (2010) assumes that a women's disutility for work is a function of the mean disutility for work by women in the society. In this way a women's preference for work is affected by the labor force participation rate of women in the economy as a whole. Butler et al. (2012) argue that standard pecuniary preferences need to be augmented with a moral cost function. Based on experimental evidence, they propose a moral cost function that is a decreasing function of the deviation of an individual's behavior from what society expects.

Similar to the approach of these authors, we assume there is a disutility associated with illegal behavior. Horizontal cultural transmission enters our model because we further assume that the average amount of corruption in society influences the individual's disutility associated with their own illegal behavior.

[33]Lambsdorff et al. (2005, p. 3).

[34]Cavalli-Sforza and Feldman (1981).

1.4 Tax Evasion

Tax evasion receives a good deal of attention in some of the models. We provide some additional background material on the topic here. As mentioned, tax evasion is an illegal activity that has close ties to government corruption. One immediately thinks of the petty corruption associated with bribes to tax collectors made by households and businesses to avoid paying taxes. However, tax evasion is also connected to corruption in other ways.

Azariadis and Ioannides (2015) attempt to explain why corruption and tax evasion are currently so widespread in Greece. A key factor in their explanation is the social norm of corruption—"an individual's perception that others engage in corrupt practices may provide an incentive for him or her to also do so (p. 7)." The suggestion is that tax evasion is justified by government corruption. We agree that corruption and tax evasion are connected, at least in part, because of the cultural dimension stressed by Azariadis and Ioannides.

In the previous section we indicated that there is growing evidence about how culture alters individual attitudes and economic behavior.[35] In particular, it is well known that the standard neoclassical approach to explaining tax evasion is incomplete: the predicted levels of tax evasion are too high and the responsiveness of tax evasion to the expected penalty is too weak to explain observed behavior.[36] In addition to the deterrent from legal penalties, the personal guilt associated with the violation of social norms plays a significant role in limiting tax evasion. Furthermore, the strength of the social norm in creating the personal guilt depends on perceptions of the government's performance. Uslander (2005, p. 87), similar to Azariadis and Ioannides, argues that there is a causal connection between corruption and tax evasion—"Countries with high levels of corruption also have higher levels of theft and tax evasion. People see corrupt regimes and believe it is acceptable to steal and especially to withhold their taxes."

A culture of corruption effect is consistent with the evidence provided in Figs. 1.1 and 1.2. The figures are based on data from the World Values Survey (1980–2007). The survey asks households questions about their views on government performance and tax evasion. The public perception of government performance and the presence of corruption is plotted on the horizontal axis and public willingness to engage in tax evasion is plotted on the vertical axis. In both cases there is a positive and statistically significant correlation between the public's concerns about their government and the public's willingness to evade taxes. The correlations exhibited in Figs. 1.1 and 1.2 are consistent with studies that find a positive correlation between *actual* evasion and more objective measures of corruption based on expert opinion from outside the country being studied.[37]

---

[35]Guiso et al. (2006) and Fernandez (2010).

[36]Fischer et al. (1992), Erard and Feinstein (1994), Andreoni et al. (1998), King and Sheffrin (2002), Orviska and Hudson (2002), Slemrod (2003), and Schneider and Klinglmair (2004).

[37]Johnson et al. (1998, Figures 6–9), Uslander (2005, Table 5.3), Alm and Torgler (2006), and Buehn and Schneider (2009, Figure 2).

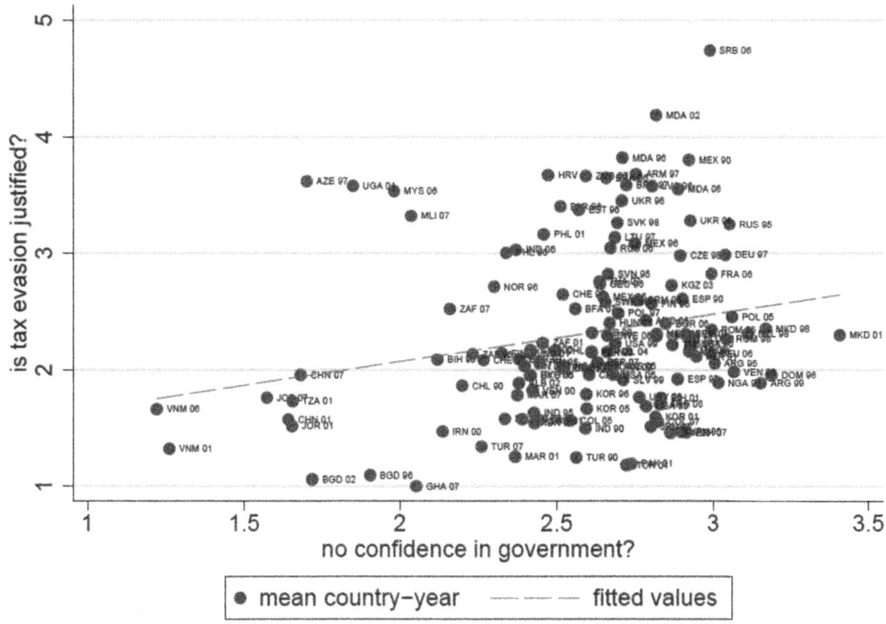

Fig. 1.1 Tax evasion vs. confidence in government. *Note* Datasource – World Values Survey, Waves 1–5 (years 1980–2007). Y-axis: country-year average individual responses on question "Do you think cheating on taxes can always be justified, never be justified, or something in between?" (answers: "1" – never justifiable, "2" ... "9", "10" – always justifiable). X-axis: country-year average individual responses on question "How much confidence do you have in government?" (answers: "1" – a great deal, "2" – quite a lot, "3" – not very much, "4" – none at all) Circles denote corresponding points in the dataset, dashed grey line is the trend line (fitted values). Slope coefficient of trend line is 0.51 (statistically significant at 1% level)

The cultural effects of corruption are not limited to tax evasion alone. There is also evidence that the *average* level of government corruption in an economy affects the willingness of *individual* government officials to engage in corruption. Experimental evidence shows that guilt affects corrupt behavior and that guilt may be influenced by cultural factors.[38] Perhaps even more convincing is the now famous natural experiment identified by Fisman and Miguel (2007, 2008 (Ch. 4)). They find that the corrupt behavior of government officials during their visits to the U.S. is highly correlated with the level of corruption in their home country. Their conclusion is that corrupt behavior is deeply engrained in culture and the standard prescriptions of economic reward and punishment may not be enough to root it out.

The cultural dimension of both tax evasion and corruption is consistent with broader findings about human behavior. Generally people care about being honest and are only dishonest when they can justify their lies. The basis for justifying

[38]Schulze and Frank (2003), Barr and Serra (2010), and Robert and Arnad (2013).

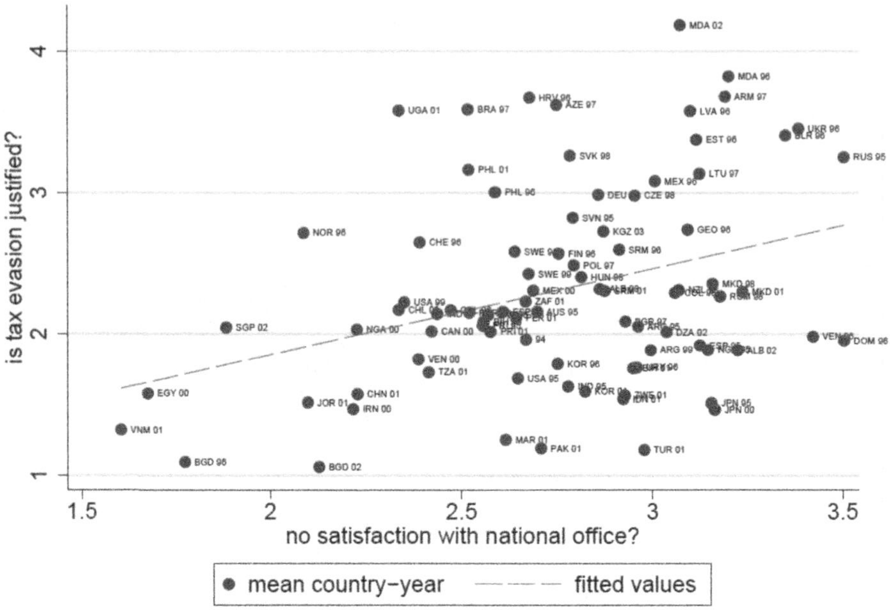

Fig. 1.2 Tax evasion vs. satisfaction with government. *Note* Datasource – World Values Survey, Waves 1–5 (years 1980–2007). Y-axis: country-year average individual responses on question "Do you think cheating on taxes can always be justified, never be justified, or something in between?" (answers: "1" – never justifiable, "2" ... "9", "10" – always justifiable). X-axis: country-year average individual responses on question "How satisfied are you with the way the people now in national office are handling the country's affairs?" (answers: "1" – very satisfied, "2" – fairly satisfied", "3" – fairly dissatisfied, "4" – very dissatisfied). Circles denote corresponding points in the dataset, dashed grey line is the trend line (fitted values). Slope coefficient of trend line is 0.61 (statistically significant at 1% level)

dishonesty is, in turn, dependent on the environment. People benchmark their dishonesty with the behavior they observe in their daily lives.[39]

Our modeling approach attempts to capture an interaction between corruption and evasion with causation running in both directions. In Chaps. 3, 6, and 7 we model a "culture of corruption" effect where the average level of government corruption affects an individual's willingness to engage in illegal behavior—in particular a household's willingness to evade taxes and an individual government official's willingness to be corrupt. Tax evasion, in turn, influences corruption by limiting the government's ability to raise funds that may be diverted for private use. Tax evasion limits the size of the budget that is managed by public officials. In our model, the fraction of the budget that is diverted for private use is increasing in the size of the budget—stealing a given *share* of the budget delivers a larger payoff, the larger is the budget. Thus, tax evasion, by limiting government

[39]Gatchter and Schulz (2016).

revenue, creates a check on corruption similar to that found in Choi and Thum (2005) and Dreher et al. (2005).

1.5 Taxation and Government Debt

Another aspect of our approach is that we look at how politics and the presence of opportunities for corruption affect the determination of fiscal policy.

1.5.1 Endogenous Tax Rates

In Chap. 3 we examine how interest group politics raises taxation. The fundamental problem of interest group politics, known as the *common pool problem*, is that the revenue used to finance transfers targeted to *specific groups* comes from a *general* tax fund. As a result, each group pushing for government benefits only pays a relatively small fraction of the tax expense. We examine how the expansion in the number of interest groups, a natural occurrence in maturing democracies, affects the level of taxation.

In Chap. 6, we study how the opportunity for corruption affects the tax policy chosen by government officials. We first calibrate a hypothetical baseline, with no corruption and no tax evasion, and then compute the optimal tax rate in this setting. We next introduce the opportunity for corruption and tax evasion and re-compute the preferred tax rate of public officials. When we set parameters to target realistic rates of corruption and tax evasion, we find the tax rate is significantly higher than in the baseline case. Despite the limiting factor of greater evasion, politicians with corruption opportunities will increase budgets by raising tax rates. As mentioned, a stylized fact about currently developing countries is that many of them have unusually large governments, especially for their stage of development. One explanation for this could be their inability to control corruption.

1.5.2 Endogenous Government Debt

We also study the effects of politics and corruption on government debt in developed countries. There is growing concern over historically high debt-to-GDP ratios in Western democracies. The debt ratios are just the tip of the iceberg. Unfunded liabilities associated with the pay-as-you-go financing of social insurance dwarf the official debt numbers. The totality of government liabilities represents a large fiscal burden on future generations.[40]

[40]Kotlikoff (2003), Kotlikoff and Burns (2004, 2012), Hubbard and Kane (2013) and Ferguson (2012).

Parts of Chaps. 2, 3, and 5 offer possible explanations for the widespread increase in debt ratios and the expansion in transfer programs that redistribute wealth across generations. One explanation for the rise in debt financing begins with a theory of why special interest groups tend to accumulate in prosperous economies with secure democracies, offered by Olson (1982). The lack of significant aggregate threats to the nation's economy increases the attempts by different domestic groups to get a piece of the large economic pie. Politicians respond to the interest groups for political support. The political response results in more spending and a larger and more complex government where advantages and favors to special interest groups are less transparent. Winning support with government favors puts pressure on government finances, especially because expanding tax loopholes is one way of benefiting particular interest groups.

Beyond interest group politics, other recent changes in economic fundamentals have also worked to generate broad support for government debt. The lack of growth in median real income since the 1970s in many developed countries, along with the increase in the relative price of education and health investments, has reduced the standard of living in middle class families. This has caused the broad middle class to favor an expansion in intergenerational redistribution, as they seek funding from their adult children as a means to relieve the current constraint on family consumption and investment.

Another economic fundamental is the opening of economies in the last quarter of the twentieth century that increased the international flow of funds across borders. High saving rates in growing Asian economies help keep the cost of funds low for stable governments looking to borrow. The combination of an expansion in interest groups politics, the tightening budget constraints of the middle class, and the glut of saving around the world created the motivation and the external funding to expand spending in excess of taxes. The rise in public debt created by these forces is projected to continue throughout the twenty-first century. The debt projections are not fully appreciated because traditional government accounting does not track the fiscal consequences of the expanding pay-as-you-go social insurance programs and the aging of the developed world's population.

Much of the expansion in public debt is due to intensified rent seeking and the increasing polarization of political interests of national representatives. However, the growing size, role, and complexity of governments also opened the door for illegal government corruption in less diligent democracies, creating further incentives to issue debt. The increased infrastructure spending and corruption in Greece, Italy, and Turkey, mentioned above, was associated with an increase in government borrowing.[41] In 1981, public debt in Greece was only 23 percent of GDP. A decade later, it was 71 percent. In 1970, debt as a fraction of GDP in Italy was only 31 percent. By the time the *mani pulite* investigations were held in the early 1990s, it was well over 100 percent. Turkey, behind Greece and Italy in economic development, didn't see a sustained increase in its public debt ratios until the 1990s. In 1992 the debt ratio in

[41] Ivanyna et al. (2015).

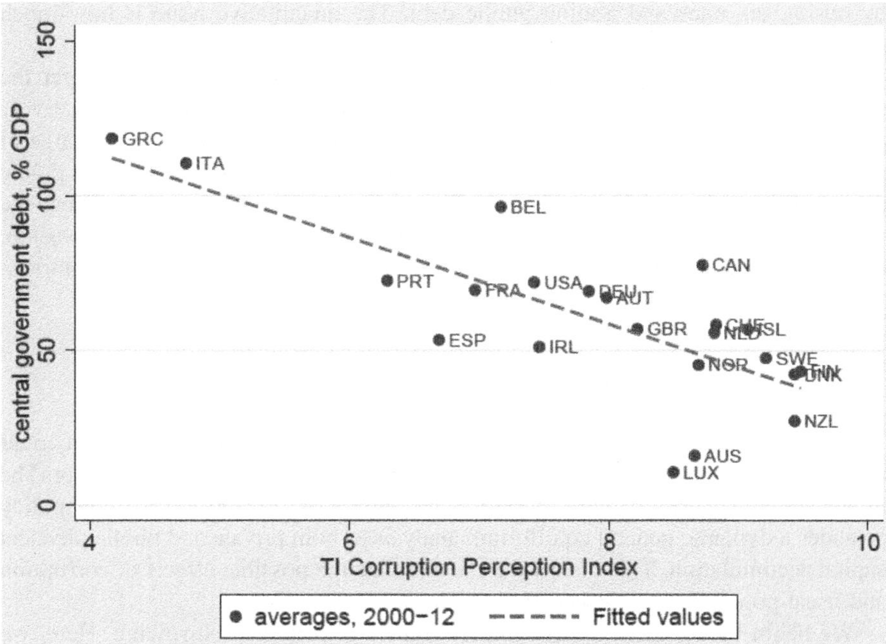

Fig. 1.3 Central government debt vs. corruption in OECD countries, 2000–2012. *Note Y-axis*: central government debt, % GDP; datasource - IMF FAD database. *X-axis*: Transparency International (TI) Corruption Perception Index, 1 – largest possible corruption, 10 – smallest possible corruption. Slope coefficient of the trend line is −20.6 (statistically significant at less than 1% level). Included are OECD member countries with high income status in 2000–2012, except Japan

Turkey was less than 30 percent, by 2002 it was almost 80 percent. Some of the fundamental sources of Turkey's government deficits included inefficient state-owned industries and a lack of official checks against corruption.

Recent research has established a strong cross-country connection between corruption and debt, even across developed economies.[42] This connection can be seen in Fig. 1.3 which plots central government debt ratios against the corruption index from the World Governance Indicators for OECD countries. The positive trend line is statistically significant at the 3 percent level.

In Chap. 7, we extend our initial analysis of the connection between corruption and taxes from Chap. 6 in the attempt to explain the correlation in Fig. 1.3. We first specify a model without corruption where the fundamentals of the economy cause the optimal debt level to be zero. Next, we introduce a theory of both corruption and tax evasion, two illegal activities connected by a "culture of corruption" effect. The opportunity for corruption creates an incentive for public officials to enlarge budgets

[42]Kaufman (2010), Grechyna (2010, 2012), Cooray and Schneider (2013) and Achury et al. (2015).

by raising tax rates and issuing public debt. The quantitative issue is how much public debt can be generated from the corruption mechanism alone.

We calibrate institutional safeguards against corruption in order to target the range of tax evasion estimated across developed countries. Even the relatively modest implied differences in institutional safeguards needed to target the range of tax evasion in developed countries are shown to generate a wide variation in public debt to private capital ratios, ranging from zero to over 100 percent. Thus, the variation in corruption, that is consistent with observed variation in tax evasion, has the potential to generate significant differences in debt policy across countries.

1.6 Economic Growth

The results from Chap. 5 and 6 suggest that corruption reduces the funds that could have been used for public investment, raises tax rates, and increases public debt. The model used in these chapters to assess the impact of corruption on fiscal policy provides a dynamic general equilibrium analysis of both private and public physical capital accumulation. This means we can simulate the possible effects of corruption and fiscal policy on production and growth.

We begin by constructing a scenario with no government borrowing. Here, we find that the negative effects of introducing corruption are relatively small. With much higher tax rates and substantial government corruption, one might expect a large decline in output. However, remember that tax evasion is also higher. The untaxed income increases the funds available for private investment, helping to mediate the negative effects of higher tax rates on private capital accumulation. In addition, the higher tax rate actually increases the funding for public investment, despite tax evasion. The extra funds serve to mediate the rise in the fraction of the budget that is diverted for private use. Thus neither private capital nor public capital falls dramatically. The relatively modest effect of corruption on output may help explain why it has been difficult to undercover a robust negative correlation between corruption and economic growth in cross-country data.[43]

Next, we consider what happens when we allow corruption and borrowing to interact. We have seen in the data that there is a positive association between corruption and public debt. Whether public debt has an *important* negative effect on output is in some doubt because detecting an output effect has proved elusive in previous empirical work. Reinhart and Rogoff (2009, 2012) show that *high* levels of public debt lower economic growth. However, it has been more difficult to establish a negative connection across *all* debt levels.[44]

Our simulations suggest that the rise in debt associated with corruption does have an important negative impact on production. A higher average debt level reduces the average value of both private and public capital. The crowding out of private capital

[43]Svensson (2005).

[44]See, for example, Kumar and Woo (2010).

results from private saving being diverted to purchases of government debt. The crowding out of public capital results from budget pressures associated with debt and interest repayment.

Based on our results we revisited the corruption-debt-output connection empirically. We regress growth in GDP per capita on initial GDP per capita, public debt as a fraction of GDP, a control-of-corruption measure, and an interactive term that is the product of debt and corruption controls. The regression shows a negative and statistically significant effect of debt on growth. Increasing controls on corruption has a positive and statistically significant effect on growth. Moreover, the interaction term involving corruption and debt also has a positive and statistically significant effect on growth. A given level of debt has a smaller negative effect on growth the stronger are the controls on corruption. This supports the idea that it's the combination of debt and corruption that is most detrimental to growth because this interaction causes more of the borrowed funds to be diverted from public investment.

1.7 Modeling the Culture of Corruption

In this section we take an initial look at the simplest way to simultaneously model both the guilt associated with illegal activity and the role played by culture. We follow the approach sketched here in Chaps. 6 and 7, where culture is introduced into a complete growth model.

When representing individual preferences using a utility function, there are the usual expressions capturing the satisfaction or utility received from consuming goods and services. Added to these expressions, is now a new term capturing the disutility caused by guilt from illegal activity. Furthermore, the disutility is decreasing in the average corruption among public officials as a group.

The illegal activity of private households is tax evasion, denoted by v—the fraction of their income that is not reported for tax purposes. The illegal activity of public officials is denoted by u—the fraction of the public investment budget that is diverted for private use. The disutility associated with these illegal activities is given by $\frac{\phi}{2\overline{u}^{\chi}} v^2$ and $\frac{\phi}{2\overline{u}^{\chi}} u^2$, where

ϕ and χ are nonnegative preference parameters and $\overline{u}$ is the *average* rate of corruption among public officials.

Higher values of ϕ imply a stronger distaste for illegal activity. The disutility of illegal activity is also affected by the average level of corruption among government officials. The greater is the average level of corruption the less guilt an individual experiences from their own illegal activity. We refer to this as the "culture of corruption" effect. The strength of the culture of corruption effect is determined by χ. In applying the model to develop a quantitative theory, the parameter values are set or calibrated to match certain stylized facts, such as estimates of the rates of tax evasion and corruption. The quadratic form of the disutility term reflects our assumption that the marginal loss in utility is increasing in illegal activity.

There will also be income losses associated with tax evasion and corruption. The extent of these losses is determined by the effectiveness of institutions that are designed to detect illegal activity. The parameter θ^{τ}, that lies between zero and one, denotes the fraction of unreported income that the household can recover for private use. The parameter captures the traditional monetary deterrent to tax evasion. The more difficult it is to hide income from the government, the less of it can be recovered and used, thus lowering the benefit of evasion. For example, the government could lower access to productive public services for firms in the underground economy that are trying to avoid taxes. As the government clamps down on the untaxed sector by making it more difficult for those firms to use productive public services, θ^{τ} falls and the income earned in the underground economy falls as well.

Some studies introduce a causal mechanism running from corruption to tax evasion that works through θ^{τ}.[45] If government officials are corrupt, then it is less costly to avoid detection of tax evasion because the officials are more likely to look the other way or require smaller bribes. To focus on a complimentary mechanism, the influence of the cultural effect established by the corrupt behavior of government officials, we assume that θ^{τ} is exogenous throughout.

In similar fashion, θ^{g} is a parameter, with a value between zero and one, reflecting the fraction of diverted public funds that the official can recover for private use. The parameter captures the effect of institutional safeguards that make it difficult to steal public funds and then use them openly without detection, working like the standard monetary deterrent to illegal activity. If $\theta^{g} = 1$, then either the safeguards against corruption are nonexistent or the corruption is actually legal rent seeking.

These simple elements allow us to model both the psychological and economic determinants of tax evasion and corruption in a tractable way. Tractability is imperative because our objective is not to explain illegal activity per se. Rather, we want to study how tax evasion and corruption affect fiscal policy and economic growth in a formal macroeconomic model that allows us to identify and quantify causal mechanisms.

1.8 The Big Three: Growth Slowdown, Wage Inequality, and Fiscal Crisis

The developed world faces three major economic problems that are interconnected and all affected by corruption and rent seeking. The economic problems of the twenty-first century are a fiscal crisis associated with mounting explicit and implicit debt obligations, slowing real economic growth, and rising wage inequality.

Over the last 40 years developed countries have both rapidly expanded pay-as-you-go (PAYG) social transfer programs, where current workers finance the benefits of current retirees, and accumulated large amounts of public debt. The average debt to GDP ratio of OECD countries exceeds 100 percent, a historically unprecedented

[45]See, for example, the recent papers by Alm et al. (2016) and Litina and Palivos (2016).

value during a period with no major wars. The official debt numbers, what is known now as *explicit debt*, are actually relatively small when compared to the *implicit debt* associated with the developed world's PAYG transfer programs to retired households.

Populations in developed countries continue to age, with increasing fractions of the population reaching retirement over the course of the twenty-first century. In addition, the costs of providing medical insurance to these households, and to younger poor households who receive medical insurance as a welfare transfer, has risen faster than wages since WWII. The social transfer programs associated with current policy carry an implicit obligation to payout benefits far into the future to all the workers who have paid, and will continue to pay, taxes under the PAYG financing scheme.

U.S. policies are shifting heavy fiscal burdens to repay debt and finance retirement programs onto future generations. They also have hurt future generations indirectly by contributing to a slowdown in economic growth. Part of the decline in the economic growth rate is due to a decline in domestic saving rates. Domestic investment rates have also declined over this period, but not as sharply as national saving because of the influx of foreign saving. Most of the foreign funding has come from Japan and China. However, Japan has its own fiscal crisis and China is seeking to reduce national saving in order to expand domestic consumption. Thus, whether the supply of foreign funding will continue is in serious question. The growing scarcity of international funds will also be affected by the fact that many developed countries will be simultaneously seeking foreign financing for their expanding public debt.

The crowding out of private investment is not the only growth-reducing consequence of the fiscal crisis. The government has been forced to neglect public investment. Public infrastructure has depreciated to an embarrassing state in many rich countries. In addition, the fraction of federal funding for the basic research that lays the foundation for technological progress has also been squeezed by rising transfer spending and debt service. The same fiscal policies that are raising the net tax rates for future generations are also reducing their ability to pay.

As discussed in previous sections, the rise in government borrowing is partly explained by corruption. However, why are the majority of households in developed countries not more concerned about the rise in public debt and the delay in responding to the, by now, obvious reality that the social transfer programs are not sustainable into the future? The broad middle class seems increasingly willing to allow intergenerational borrowing—i.e. to allow the government leeway in violating one of the principles of good governance.

A household favors "intergenerational borrowing" when it desires to increase current spending by borrowing and then leave the debt for their children to pay. The desire to increase current household spending, beyond the lifetime means of the current generation, is the result of three related phenomenon. First, after more than a century of steady growth, real income for the middle class has become stagnant since the 1970s. There have been no real income gains for the middle class for over 40 years. Second, the importance of advanced education has risen dramatically over that time period, i.e. there has been a rising wage premium to achieving a college degree—an important source of rising wage inequality. Finally, the cost of medical insurance has continued to rise in real terms. Thus, discretionary household consumption has become increasingly constrained by the lack of real income growth and the rise in the cost of important investments in health and education. Families needing to make the health and education investments that give their children a chance at success, have become increasingly willing to borrow and leave the debt for their children to repay.

One of the main points we want to stress is that the three major economic problems of the twenty-first century are closely intertwined. To improve the prospects for the future requires that all three be simultaneously addressed. The fiscal crisis is due to aging and increasingly generous transfers to retirees. The increasingly generous transfers to retirees are promoted by a variety of interest groups representing the elderly and the medical industry. Greater transfer spending has limited the funding for government and private investment, contributing to a growth slowdown that makes it more difficult to raise taxes. Wage inequality has been rising because of an overly optimistic notion that most of the population benefits from college and the associated college prep track in high school—a notion promoted by a variety of interest groups representing universities and the highly educated elite. In fact, most students do not graduate from college and societies have made little progress in expanding the fraction of young cohorts that do graduate—a major reason for the rising skill premium. As a result, most students, who fail to complete college and receive no technical training in high school, enter the labor market with little or no productive skills—a major reason why real wages have not risen for the majority of households for decades. These poor and middle class families are struggling to get ahead and are more inclined to tolerate government debt financing.

1.9 Policy Reforms

Our ultimate goal is to sharpen and increase the discussion over the anti-growth biases in fiscal policy. In Chap. 8 we conduct a critical survey of recent ideas on how to reform government policy making. As with the rest of the book, the discussion includes governments at all levels of economic development. A common aspect of the anti-growth bias in fiscal policy is a failure of government representatives, and often the public at large, to account for future economic effects. In making current policy, there should be transparent reminders of the consequences of the policy for future generations.

At the beginning of the twenty-first century there remain countries that have failed to generate sustained economic growth, leading to massive international income disparities across the world. In many cases this is due to a rather explicit anti-growth stance on the part of the poor country's government. For both altruistic and selfish reasons, rich countries have attempted to aid poor countries in their development. A discouraging stylized fact about development in the Post WWII period is that there is no robust correlation between outside aid and a country's economic growth.[46] In Chap. 6 we use a model of cross-country income differences due to government fiscal policy to think about aid failure. In Chap. 8 we review arguments for how international organizations, such as the World Bank, might change their approach to development. In particular, we look at how to best deal with selfish anti-growth dictators in recipient countries.

At the opposite end of the development process, rich countries are currently on the verge of a major fiscal crisis. Current policies in developed countries are unsustainable because they are projected to cause massive increases in public debt that cannot realistically be financed by international lenders. We look at some of the fundamental economic drivers of the fiscal crisis that have led these countries to engage in an unprecedented redistribution of wealth from future to current generations. As stressed in the previous section, the fiscal crisis is closely connected to all the major economic issues facing rich countries—the aging of the population, the slowdown in economic growth, the rise in income inequality, and the sharp increase in the relative price of health care and higher education. Economists recommend policy reforms that address these fundamental issues and thereby indirectly address the fiscal crisis. In addition to reforming the entitlement programs, we discuss (i) increasing tax revenue using a variety of Pigovian taxes, sin taxes, and a federal sales tax, (ii) reducing government subsidies for higher education and reallocating the funds to increase programs for young children from disadvantaged families and vocational training programs in high school and (iii) increasing budgets for public infrastructure projects and basic research.

Politics and the rules of governance also play a role in the fiscal crisis. We discuss various suggestions about how countries, rich and poor alike, can reform their budget process to reduce the influence of politics and rent seeking that ignores long-run consequences. Proposed political reforms center around the following important changes.

First, and perhaps most importantly, the operations and policies of the government must be more transparent. To take action that constrains deviations from good governance, the public must first be clear about what the government is actually doing. The current bias toward intergenerational redistribution is, in part, due to a lack of transparent accounting. Budget accounting and reporting must state not only current imbalances between taxes and spending but also the future imbalances generated by current policies. It may also be a good idea to more clearly state what fraction of the budget is devoted to investment and what fraction to current consumption. In this regard, cost-benefit analysis of large government investment projects should be more common and made more public. We recommend an expanded role for the accounting offices, such as the Congressional Budget Office, that track and evaluate fiscal policy.

[46]For example, Easterly et al. (2004).

Second, there has been a steady growth in *non-discretionary* expenditures, both on the spending and tax side, that automatically grow more generous over time. These components are shielded from the annual debate over the *discretionary* components. Mandated expenditures and tax breaks now are the largest parts of budgets in most rich countries. These expenditures are heavily biased toward funding consumption and not investment. The non-discretionary components should lose their protected status and be subjected to the scrutiny of the annual budget debate.

Third, some argue that a fiscal rule is needed to restrict the temptation to allow planned expenditures to exceed planned taxes. The behavior of governments over the last 70 years has resulted in huge gaps between projected spending and projected tax revenues. The question is what type of institutional structure or rule, if any, would cause the government to become more responsible. At this point, the theoretical and practical limitations associated with fiscal rules make many pessimistic about their potential role. However, the discussion of what might be an effective fiscal rule should continue.

Finally, we consider ways to control corrupt behavior of government officials. A more transparent, simplified, and disciplined budget process, needed to control short-sighted politics generally, would go a long way to controlling corruption as well. As we have emphasized, countries that have failed to check corruption usually have problems with tax evasion. The timing of how to deal with these significant fiscal problems is crucial. We find that reducing evasion, without also addressing corruption, is a bad idea. In countries without strong safeguards against corruption, tax evasion provides a useful check against government abuses. The fact that households can avoid taxation, prevents tax rates from being raised even higher. Also, for a given tax rate, less revenue is collected and thus less is stolen by public officials. Making tax evasion harder would reduce this important check on the government and lead to higher tax rates, more corruption, and less economic growth. Corruption should be brought under control before the country worries about collecting more tax revenue and making the government larger.

1.10 Outline

One way of defining the purpose of the book is to present the main overriding issues we seek to address. We are interested in how fiscal policy contributes to answering the following questions.

Why does sustained modern economic growth fail to take-off?
Why does foreign aid to governments of developing countries fail to generate growth?
Why does long-run growth eventually slow?
Why is income inequality on the rise in developed countries?
Why have fiscal crises become commonplace, threatening the prosperity of rich countries?

Chapter 2 presents the two-period model of government investment chosen by a benevolent government in order to illustrate how fiscal policy can raise social welfare. The model is used to discuss tax versus debt financing, the allocation of investment across regions of a country, and the path of government investment over the course of development. Chapter 3 introduces selfish political motives into the two-period model, focusing on how politics distorts fiscal policy. The chapter examines the effects of the re-election motive, political polarization, rent-seeking by interest groups, and the corrupt behavior of public officials.

Chapter 4 provides a complete exposition of the overlapping-generations model, a workhorse of macroeconomics. Fiscal policy is added to the model to analyze the economic growth effects of the intergenerational redistribution caused by government debt and by pay-as-you-go social security in Chap. 5. The economic and political sources of the fiscal crisis—the huge unfunded future liabilities associated with the policies of developed countries—are discussed. Chapter 6 presents theories of endogenous fiscal policy into the overlapping-generations model. Political-economy theories are used to study the origins and effects of kleptocracies, anti-growth policies, corruption, and tax evasion. Chapter 7 extends the analysis of Chap. 6 to include debt financing, with a special emphasis on how corruption has contributed to the fiscal crisis.

Chapter 8 offers a detailed discussion of the fiscal crisis and its relationship to other important economic (aging, health care and education costs, growth slowdowns, and income inequality) and political (rent seeking, ideological polarization, and corruption) issues. Policies reforms are then offered that address not only the fiscal crisis but also its underlying economic and political determinants. Reforms of foreign aid policies are also discussed. Chapter 9 summarizes the book by providing answers to the five questions raised above and makes some broader points about societal failure. It also introduces three other potentially important economic problems of the twenty-first century: climate change, technological change in the form of labor-saving robots, and pandemics.

1.11 Exercises

Questions

1. Briefly describe the four principles of good governance.
2. Explain why the principle of efficient resource use and the principle of limiting economic disparities *may* come in conflict. Why might there be *no* conflict between these two principles?
3. Discuss the different ways that governments around the world fail to serve the national interest of their countries.

4. For each of the hypothetical events described below, inspired by real world cases, decide which of the following general governance problems is best exemplified: (i) corruption, (ii) rent seeking, (iii) legal, but selfish, policies of an autocratic government, (iv) shifting the burden of financing current government services to future generations.
   (a) a government official chooses an inflated bid from a private contractor for a bridge construction project in exchange for kickbacks
   (b) an entrepreneur who is starting a private steel producing company, threatening the revenues of the publicly run steel company, is charged with treasonous activity and thrown in jail
   (c) private developers lobby government officials to continue making low-interest government loans to help maintain a construction boom
   (d) a small group of the religious ruling elite manage one quarter of the country's income and are offered exemption from taxation or corruption charges
   (e) in a poor developing country, the government allocates vouchers to subsidize the purchase of agricultural seeds to regions on the basis of their political support
   (f) tax rates are set above revenue-maximizing levels, with collected revenues used for government patronage jobs and targeted regional transfers
   (g) representatives from a large private bank argue that removal of government regulations will increase investment and economic growth
   (h) representatives from a large university argue that increased tuition subsidies will increase human capital formation and economic growth
   (i) representatives from the medical industry argue that limiting the procedures and services that government insurance covers is unethical
   (j) the payroll tax is increased to cover shortfalls in government retirement benefits
   (k) large tax cuts are proposed to jump start a slowing economy
   (l) local electrical plants, that provide lighting to copper mines, are shut down and replaced with a large hydroelectric plant, thousands of miles away but near the country's capital, that provides similar services
   (m) politicians on a budget committee in charge of allocating funding for public investment projects approve projects near their private businesses and home districts
   (n) a leader of a small developing country has several mansions in countries across the world
   (o) the funds budgeted for construction results in a road that is half the planned length—additional funds are requested to complete the project
   (p) only 15 percent of the foreign aid earmarked for improving education in rural areas is spent on school construction in villages
   (q) a country's government banks have a policy of making "loans" to politicians, their family members, and their close political supporters, which are in fact cash transfers that are never repaid

5. Our focus is *government failure*, but perhaps the focus should be more generally placed on *societal failure*. Some argue that societal failure stems from inherent weaknesses in human nature that cause complacency, hubris, inability to deal with complexity, and a lack of orientation on the future consequences of today's actions. Why should the focus be on the government and not society as a whole?
6. Former President Suharto of Indonesian once famously dismissed the concern over his country's corruption by saying:

   > Well you come out here from Washington with these high ideas to tell us about corruption. But what you call corruption, I call family values.

   What do you think he meant by this? Why would taking family values this far be a detrimental social norm? (One way that Indonesian's family values were manifested is depicted in event (q) from Question 4 above. This practice weakened the banking sector so severely that it collapsed into a financial crisis as soon as growth in Indonesian began to slow and borrowers of actual loans started to default on their debt repayments for purely economic reasons.)

7. The historian Ramsay MacMullen (1988) argues that an important factor in the decline of Rome was an increasing corruption among the military and *decuriae* (local public officials), who began extorting the communities they were sent to serve and withholding tax collections for themselves. The following is a quote from his book:

   > So if he served in the army where everyone acted in a certain way, he would conform. Similarly, in the civil *decuriae*: they had their ways. As the unrepentant sinner said to Bishop Maximus—I draw my sense of right and wrong from my militia.

   What point is MacMullen making about the problem of corruption?

8. How is tax evasion related to government corruption?
9. How is government corruption related to government borrowing?
10. The three figures in this chapter exhibit *correlations* between two variables. Form competing explanations for each correlation where the underlying causal connection between the variables goes in opposite directions.
11. Google some data on the central government debt-to GDP ratios in OECD countries. What is the average debt ratio for the OECD countries? Which countries have the highest debt ratios?
12. Sketch out some of the different factors that have led to the growth in OECD government debt ratios.
13. Describe the Big Three economic problems facing rich countries in the 21st century. Explain why they are connected.
14. Why are high levels of public debt harmful to an economy?

References

Achury, C., Koulovatianos, C., and Tsoukalas, J., 2015, "Political Economics of External Debt Defaults," CFS Working paper Series, Goethe University.

Alm, J., and Torgler, B., 2006, "Cultural Differences and Tax Morale in the United States and Europe," *Journal of Economic Psychology*, 27, 224–246.

Alm, J., Martinez-Vaquez, J., and McClellan, C., 2016, "Corruption and Firm Tax Evasion," *Journal of Economic Behavior and Organization*, 124, 146–163.

Andreoni, J., Erard, B., and Feinstein, J., 1998, "Tax Compliance," *Journal of Economic Literature*, 36, 818–860.

Azariadis, C., and Ioannides, Y., 2015, "Thinking about Corruption in Greece," Mimeo, New York University.

Baliamoune-Lutz, and Ndikumana, L., 2008, "Corruption and Growth: Explaining the Investment Channel," Department of Economics Working Paper 2008-08, University of Massachusetts.

Barr, A., and Serra, D., 2010, "Corruption and Culture: An Experiment Analysis," 94, *Journal of Public Economics*, 862–869.

Bennett, W. and Wilezol, D., 2013, *Is College Worth It*, Nashville: Thomas Nelson.

Besley, T., 2007, *Principled Agents? The Political Economy of Good Government*, Oxford; Oxford University Press.

Binmore, K, 2007, *Playing for Real*, Oxford: Oxford University Press.

Brosio, G., and Marchese, C., 1986, *Il Potere di Spendere*, Bologna: Il Mulino.

Buehn, A., and Schneider, F., 2009, "Corruption and the Shadow Economy: A Structural Equation Model Approach," Institute for the Study of Labor Discussion Paper No. 4182.

Bueno de Mesquita, B., and Smith, A., 2011, *The Dictator's Handbook*, New York: Public Affairs.

Butler, J., Giuliano, P., and Guiso, L., 2012, "Trust and Cheating," Institute for the Study of Labor (IZA) Discussion Paper 6961.

Caplan, B., 2007, *The Myth of the Rational Voter*, Princeton: Princeton University Press.

______, 2009, "Irrational Principles," *Review of Austrian Economics*, 22, 159–167.

Cavalli-Sforza, L. and Feldman, M., 1981, *Cultural Transmission and Evolution: A Quantitative Approach*, Princeton: Princeton University Press.

Chayes, S., 2015, *Thieves of the State*, New York: Norton.

Choi, J. and Thum, M., 2005, "Corruption and the Shadow Economy," *International Economic Review*, 817–836.

Clarke, B. and N. Hardiman "Ireland: Crisis in the Banking System" in S. Konzelmann and M. Fovargue-Davies (eds.) *Banking Systems in the Crisis: The Faces of Liberal Capitalism* (Routledge, August 2012) pp 107–133

Cohen, J. and Federico, G., 2001, *The Growth of the Italian Economy 1820-1960*, Cambridge: Cambridge University Press.

Cooray, A., and Schneider, F., 2013, "How Does Corruption Affect Public Debt? An Empirical Analysis," Working Paper 1322, Johannes Kepler University of Linz.

Cost, J., 2015, *A Republic NO More*, New York: Encounter Books.

Das, S., Mourmouras, A., Rangazas, P., 2018, *Economic Growth and Development: A Dynamic Dual Economy Approach*, Switzerland: Springer.

de Wall, T, 2016, "Fighting a Culture of Corruption in Ukraine," *Carnegie Europe*, April 18.

Dreher, A., Kostogiannis, C., and McCorriston, S., 2005, "How do Institutions Affect Corruption and the Shadow Economy?" University of Exter Discussion Paper.

Erard, B. and Feinstein, J., 1994, "Honesty and Evasion in the Tax Compliance Game," *Rand Journal of Economics*, 25, 1–19.

Easterly W., Levine R., Roodman D., 2004, "Aid, Policies, and Growth," *American Economic Review*, 94(3), 774–780.

Ferguson, N., 2012, *The Great Degeneration*, New York: Penguin Books.

Fernandez, R., 2010, "Does Culture Matter?," in *Handbook of Social Economics*, ed. by J. Benhabib, A. Bisin, and M. Jackson, V1A, Chapter 11, pp. 481–510. North Holland: Elsevier.

Fischer, C., Wartick, M., and Mark, M., 1992, "Detection Probability and Taxpayer Compliance: A Review of the Literature," *Journal of Accounting Literature*, 11, 1–46.

Fisman, R., and Miguel, E., 2007, "Corruption, Norms, and Legal Enforcement: Evidence from Diplomatic Traffic Tickets," *Journal of Political Economy*, 115(6), 1020–1048.

______, 2008, *Economic Gangsters*, New Jersey: Princeton University Press.

Gatchter, S., and Schulz, J., 2016, "Intrinsic Honesty and the Prevalence of Rule Violations across Societies," *Nature*, 531, 496–499.

Glaeser, E., and Goldin, C., 2006, "Corruption and Reform: Introduction," in Glaeser, E., and Goldin, C. (editors) *Corruption and Reform: Lessons from America's History*, Chicago: University of Chicago Press.

Grechyna, D., 2012, "Public Corruption and Public Debt: Some Empirical Evidence," Mimeo, University of Auckland.

______, 2010, "Public Debt Levels and Corruption in High-Income Economies," Mimeo, Universistat Autonoma de Barcelona.

Guiso, L., Sapienza, P., and Zingales, L., 2006, "Does Culture Affect Economic Outcomes?" *Journal of Economic Perspectives*, 20, 23–48.

Haque, M.E., and Kneller, R., 2008, "Public Investment and Growth: The Role of Corruption," Centre for Growth and Business Cycle Research, Disucssion Paper Series 98, Economics, University of Manchester.

Haque, M.E., and Kneller, R., 2012, "Why Public Investment Fails to Raise Economic Growth in Some Countries: The Role of Corruption" Centre for Growth and Business Cycle Research, Disucssion Paper Series 162, Economics, University of Manchester.

Heckman, J., 2013, *Giving Kids a Fair Chance*, Cambridge, Mass.: The MIT Press

Hubbard, G. and Kane, T., 2013, *Balance: The Economics of the Great Powers*, New York: Simon and Schuster

Ivanyna, M., Mourmouras, A., and Rangazas, P., 2015, "Corruption, Public Debt, Economic Growth," Mimeo.

Johnson, S., Kaufmann, D., and Zoido-Lobaton, P., 1998, "Corruption, Public Finances, and the Unofficial Economy," World Bank Discussion Paper

Jones, C., 2015, "Bridging Corruption and Legitimacy: Amakudari," *Community: The Japan Times*, April 12.

Kaufman, D., 2010, "Can Corruption Adversely Affect Public Finance in Industrialized Countries?" *Brookings Institution Opinions* April 19.

Keefer, P., and Knack, S., 2007, "Boondoggles, Rent-Seeking, and Political Checks and Balances: Public Investments under Unaccountable Governments," *Review of Economic Statistics*, 89(3), 566–572.

Kotlikoff, L., 2003, *Generational Policy*, Cambridge, Mass: MIT Press.

Kotlikoff, L. and Burns, S., 2012, *The Clash of Generations: Saving Ourselves, Our Kids, and Our Economy*, Cambridge, Mass: MIT Press.

Kotlikoff, L. and Burns, S., 2004, *The Coming Generational Storm,* Cambridge, Mass: MIT Press.

Kumar, M., and Woo, J., 2010, "Public Debt and Growth," IMF Working Paper No. 10/174.

Lambsdorff, J., Taube, M., and Schramm, M., 2005, "Corrupt Contracting," in Lambsdorff, J., Taube, M., and Schramm, M., editors, *The New Institutional Economics of Corruption*, New York: Routledge, 1–15.

Lindbeck, J., Nyberg, S., and Weibull, J., 1999, "Social Norms and Economic Incentives in the Welfare State," *Quarterly Journal of Economics*, 114, 1–35.

Litina, A. and Palivos, T., 2016, "Corruption, Tax Evasion, and Social Values, *Journal of Economic Behavior and Organization*, (forthcoming).

Lyons, J., and Luhnow, D., 2016, "Brazil's Giant Problem," *Wall Street Journal.*

MacMullen, R., 1988, *Corruption and the Decline of Rome*, New Haven: Yale University Press.

Mourmouras, A., and Rangazas, P., 2009, "Fiscal Policy and Economic Development," *Macroeconomic Dynamics*, 13, 450–476.

Mulligan, C., Gill, R., and Sala-i-Martin, X., 2004, "Do Democracies have Different Policies than Nondemocracies?," *Journal of Economic Perspectives*, 18, 51–74.

Mulligan, C., and Tsui, K., 2015, "Political Entry, Public Policies, and the Economy," *Research in Economics*, 69, 377–397.

Murray, C., 2008, *Real Education: Four Simple Truths for Brining America's Schools back to Reality*, New York: Three Rivers Press.
Newman, K., and Winston, H., 2016, *Reskilling America: Learning to Labor in the 21st Century*, New York: Henry Holt and Company.
Olken, B., 2007, "Monitoring Corruption: Evidence from a Field Experiment in Indonesia," *Journal of Political Economy*, 115, 200–249.
Olson, M., 1982, *The Rise and Decline of Nations: Economic Growth, Stagflation and Social Rigidities*, New Haven: Yale University Press.
Olsson, I., 2014, "Trajectory of Corruption in Turkey's EU Venture," in B. Temel (editor) *The Great Catalyst: European Union Project and Lessons from Greece and Turkey*, Plymouth, UK: Lexington Books.
Orviska, M., and Hudson, J., 2002, "Tax Evasion, Civic Duty, and Law Abiding Citizens," *Journal of Political Economy*, 19, 83–102.
Padro i Miquel, G., 2007, "The Control of Politicians in Divided Societies: The Politics of Fear," *Review of Economic Studies*, 74, 1259–1274.
Pritchett, L., 2000, "The Tyranny of Concepts: CUDIE (Cumulated, Depreciated Investment Effort) is *Not* Capital," *Journal of Economic Growth*, 5, 361–384.
______, 1996, "Mind Your P's and Q's: The Cost of Public Investment is *Not* the Value of Public Capital," *World Bank Policy Research Working Paper* #1660.
Reeves, R., 2017, *Dream Hoarders*, Washington: Brookings Institution.
Reinhart, C., and Rogoff, K., 2009, *This Time is Different*, Princeton: Princeton University Press
______, 2012, "Public Debt Overhangs: Advanced-Economy Episodes Since 1800, *Journal of Economic Perspectives*, 26, 69–86.
Reinikka, R. and Svensson, J., 2004, "Local Capture: Evidence from a Central Government Transfer Program in Uganda," *Quarterly Journal of Economics*, 119, 679–709.
Robert, I. and Arnad, M., 2013, "Is Dishonesty Contagious," *Economic Inquiry*, 51, 722–734.
Romero, S., 2016, "Brazil's Ex-Leader, Luis Inacio Lula sa Silva, Is Held and His Home Invaded," Americas, March 4, *New York Times*.
King S, Sheffrin S., 2002, "Tax Evasion and Equity Theory: An Investigative Approach", *International Tax and Public Finance* 9(4):505–521.
Slemrod, J., 2003, "Trust in Public Finance," in S. Crossen and H.W. Sinn (eds.), *Public Finance and Public Policy in the New Century*, MIT Press, 49–88.
Schulze, G., and Frank, B., 2003, "Deterrence versus Intrinsic Motivation: Experimental Evidence on the Determinants of Corruptibility," *Economics of Governance*, 4, 143–160
Schneider, F. and Klinglmair, 2004, "The Shadow Economy and Work in the Shadow: What We (Not) Know?" IZA Discussion Paper No. 1043.
Stigler, G., and Becker, G., 1977, "De Gustibus Non Est Disputandum," *American Economic Review*, 67, 76–90.
Svensson, J., 2005, "Eight Questions about Corruption," *Journal of Economic Perspectives*, 19, 19–42.
Tanzi, V. and Davoodi, H., 1997, "Corruption, Public Investment, and Growth," *IMF Working Paper* #139.
Uslander, E., 2005, "Trust and Corruption," in Lambsdorff, J., Taube, M., and Schramm, M., editors, *The New Institutional Economics of Corruption*, New York: Routledge, 76–92.
Van der Does de Willibois, E., Halter, E., Harrison, R., Park, J., and Sharman, J., 2011, *Puppet Masters: How the Corrupt Use Legal Structures to Hide Stolen Assets and What to Do About It*, Washington: International Bank for Reconstruction and Development/World Bank.
Wallis, J., 2006, "The Concept of Systematic Corruption in American History," in Glaeser, E., and Goldin, C., (editors) *Corruption and Reform: Lessons from America's History*, Chicago: University of Chicago Press.
Woodruff, P., 1993, *Thucydides on Justice, Power, and Human Nature*, Indianapolis: Hackett Publishing Company.
Zoakos, C., 2010, "Eye-Popping Greek Corruption," *International Economy*, Spring, pp. 18–19, 64.
Zurcher, E., 2004, *Turkey: A Modern History*, London: I.B. Tauris.

2 Two-Period Model of Government Investment

This chapter presents the simplest model for studying investment. The model has two periods. The current period, denoted as period 1, and the future period, denoted as period 2. Investments are chosen and financed in period 1 and the return to investment is realized in period 2. The model has been used frequently in international macroeconomics, both as an introductory pedagogical device (e.g. Obstfeld and Rogoff 1996) and as a tool for analyzing issues on the research frontier (e.g. D'Erasmo and Mendoza 2015). Here, we use the model to examine government investment decisions. The goal of the chapter is to identify how the level and the allocation of government investment should be determined when using purely economic considerations that are in the national interest. The analysis provides the benchmark for comparison to the situation with self-interest, election politics, rent seeking, and corruption, as introduced in Chap. 3.

The four principles mentioned in Chap. 1 determine what policies are in the national interest. The first principle is that government should not be a vehicle for redistributing income to public officials or to a relatively small group of their supporters. This principle is formally represented in this chapter by assuming that the government is "benevolent"—seeking to maximize the welfare of the representative private household or the welfare of a group of different private households.

The second principle is efficiency of resource use. Maximizing social welfare requires the level and allocation of government investments to be production-efficient, so that the size of the economic pie is made as large as possible. In our setting this means investments should be made as long as their returns in future income exceed the opportunity costs of the resources used to finance them.

The third principle is that the government should limit large disparities in consumption and equalize opportunities for economic success. This principle applies when there are households with different initial conditions. The utilitarian social welfare function used in chapter weighs each of the country's households equally. This social welfare function implies that some redistribution of resources maximizes total welfare because of the diminishing marginal value of individual household consumption.

M. Ivanyna et al., *The Macroeconomics of Corruption*, Springer Texts in Business and Economics, https://doi.org/10.1007/978-3-030-67557-8_2

The final principle of good governance is to limit the redistribution of wealth to current generations from unborn generations, consistent with the commonly observed legal restriction that children are not obligated to repay parental debt. In accordance with the second principle of good governance, some redistribution may be called for when future generations are richer than current generations. However, the full costs of this type of redistribution should be made transparent to the current generation so that the extent of the redistribution does not become excessive.

2.1 The Life-Cycle Model of Consumption and Saving

We begin by thinking about how households make their consumption and saving decisions. To think about saving, there must be a future. A two period setting is the simplest way to introduce the future considerations that motivate saving.

Imagine a household that lives for two periods. In each period income is generated by supplying one unit of work to productive activity. The income in period 1 is denoted by y_1 and the income in period 2 by y_2. A household's lifetime satisfaction or utility is determined by consumption over the two periods of life, c_1 and c_2. For simplicity, and to allow for quantitative analysis, throughout the book we assume the *lifetime* utility function takes the form

$$U = \ln c_1 + \beta \ln c_2,$$

where $\beta < 1$ is a time discount factor that indicates the relative weight a household places on receiving utility in the future rather than today.

The *single period* utility function, ln c, has the familiar characteristic, one you may recall from introductory economics, of *diminishing marginal utility*. In other words, greater consumption increases satisfaction but at a diminishing rate. All increasing concave functions have this property because their slopes get smaller as the argument of the function increases. The natural log function we are using as our single-period utility function is simply a convenient increasing concave function.

The lifetime utility function includes the satisfaction the household expects to receive from a particular plan for both current and future consumption, combining the utility gained in each period of life. The time discount factor, β, is generally regarded to be less than one because people are impatient; they value satisfaction now over the same satisfaction experienced in the future.

The household's task is to choose a path for consumption that makes U as large as possible. The household can't just choose any consumption path because it is constrained by two considerations. First, it is limited by its income. Second, it may or may not be able to borrow and lend. Being able to borrow and lend is a crucial tool in choosing the best consumption path because, in general, households do not want their consumption to exactly match their income.

For example, suppose y_1 is very low and y_2 is very high. The household would prefer *not* to have their current consumption be very low and their future consumption be very high. This is because of the diminishing marginal utility of consuming in any one period—if consumption is constrained to exactly match income, the marginal value of consumption would be much higher in the first period than in the second period. Instead, households would prefer to *smooth* consumption over time—make consumption over time more similar than their income over time by raising c_1 above y_1 and lowering c_2 below y_2.

To manage this consumption smoothing, the household must be able to *borrow* in the first period, when income is low, and pay back the debt in the second period, when income is high. Borrowing allows the consumption path to deviate from the income path in a way that makes the household better off. In the opposite scenario, where y_1 is very high and y_2 is very low, the household wants to lower current consumption and *save* some current income, lend it, and receive repayment on the loan in the future to increase the financing of future consumption.

If the household cannot borrow and lend, then there is actually nothing to decide, it must be the case that $c_1 = y_1$ and $c_2 = y_2$. The more interesting situation allows for borrowing and lending. In this case, we assume a *complete* and *perfectly competitive credit market.* A complete credit market means there is both a financial asset and a financial liability that the household can acquire. Let the variable a_2 do "double duty" in capturing both household borrowing and lending. If a_2 is positive, it denotes an asset purchased by a household when it uses current income to save. If a_2 is negative, it denotes a liability or debt acquired by the household when it chooses to borrow. A perfectly competitive market means individual household cannot dictate the terms of the borrowing and lending agreement—the terms are instead determined by the market forces of demand and supply for credit. In particular, individual households take the market interest rate as beyond their control,

A word on a potential confusion associated with our notation. We think of the decision to borrow or lend, i.e., the choice of a_2, as taking place in period 1. So it would be perfectly reasonable to denote this choice as "a_1" instead of as a_2. The justification for using a_2 is that the repayment of the debt, or the receipt of the principle that was lent out, will occur in period 2. In addition, there will also generally be an interest payment or receipt in period 2, with the rate of interest denoted by r_2. One can go either way with the notation; the approach we have chosen is the most common convention.

With the possibility of borrowing and lending, the household's *single period budget constraints* become

$$c_1 + a_2 = y_1$$

and

$$c_2 = y_2 + (1 + r_2)a_2.$$

These budget constraints can be combined, when the household is fully free to choose the value of a_2, by solving for a_2 using the first period constraint and then substituting the solution into the second period constraint. After some algebraic rearranging, we can write the resulting equation as a *lifetime budget constraint*,

$$c_1 + \frac{c_2}{1 + r_2} = y_1 + \frac{y_2}{1 + r_2}.$$

The lifetime budget constraint, made possible by the ability to borrow and lend, says that, while consumption and income do not have to match period by period, the present value of lifetime consumption spending must equal the present value of lifetime income.

The task of the household is to choose a consumption path that makes them as happy as possible, while satisfying the lifetime budget constraint. Formally, this means choosing c_1 and c_2 to maximize U, taking as given y_1, y_2 and the perfectly competitive market interest rate, r_2. The solutions to these types of maximization problems are discussed in the Appendix. Here we simply state and discuss the optimal solutions without derivation. The household's utility maximizing demand for consumption goods and assets are

$$c_1 = \frac{1}{1 + \beta}\left(y_1 + \frac{y_2}{1 + r_2}\right)$$

$$c_2 = \frac{\beta(1 + r_2)}{1 + \beta}\left(y_1 + \frac{y_2}{1 + r_2}\right)$$

$$a_2 = y_1 - c_1 = \frac{\beta}{1 + \beta} y_1 - \frac{1}{1 + \beta} \frac{y_2}{1 + r_2}.$$

Consumption in each period is positively affected by the household's lifetime income or *wealth*. With the ability to borrow and lend, current income is not the key factor in explaining consumption—the consumption a household can afford is instead dictated by its wealth. Looking at the solution for a_2, we see that the household may save and lend ($a_2 > 0$) or may borrow ($a_2 < 0$), depending on the circumstances. Households with relatively high values of y_1 will be savers/lenders and those with relatively high values of y_2 will be borrowers. Patient households, with high values for β, will tend to lend and impatient households, with low values of β, will tend to borrow. Finally, the higher the market interest rate, r_2, the more likely the household is to save and lend current income. This last result means the "supply of market funds," provided by household saving, is an upward sloping function of the interest rate, as is typically assumed in elementary economics.

Borrowing Constraints

We have discussed the extreme situations when no credit market exists and when a full complete and perfectly competitive credit market exists. There is an important intermediate case, where the market is *incomplete*. Households are free to save but face restrictions on how much they can borrow. In the case where they cannot borrow at all, there is what is referred to as a *non-negativity constraint* on a_2, i.e. household choices must be consistent with the condition $a_2 \geq 0$.

One strategy for identifying when the non-negativity constraint is binding is to first solve the household problem with no constraints on borrowing, as we have above. Next, use the unconstrained solution for a_2 to see that the condition $a_2 \geq 0$ is equivalent to

$$y_1 \geq \frac{1}{\beta} \frac{y_2}{1 + r_2}.$$

Low values of for y_1, β, and r_2, and high values for y_2, increase the likelihood that the household would like to borrow and the condition above will *not* be satisfied. Impatient households with relatively low current income, who also face low market interest rates, will tend to be credit-constrained. In this situation, the best the household can do is choose consumption to match income in each period—just as if there is no credit market at all.

2.2 Introducing the Government

In this section we move from the discussion of an individual household to the economy as a whole. In addition, we start thinking about fiscal policy and the government's role in the economy.

The private sector is made up of households that are both consumers and producers who operate just as the household in Sect. 2.1. In the simplest two-period model, there are N of these private households but they are all *identical* and thus can be represented by a single household. The *representative household* begins period 1 with an exogenous income flow, y_1, from supplying one unit of labor to production. The household also supplies one unit of labor to production in period 2. The new twist is we now assume that the output and income in period 2 is affected by the government's provision of public capital (e.g. public education, roads, or public utilities infrastructure). Public capital per household in period 2 is denoted by g_2 (y_1 can also be viewed as a function of the available public capital, g_1, but that stock is given in the analysis). Period 2 output and income per household is determined by the following production function,

$$y_2 = A g_2^{\mu}, \tag{2.1}$$

where A is a productivity parameter, frequently referred to as total factor productivity (TFP), and $0 < \mu < 1$ gauges the impact of public capital on output.

The assumption that $\mu < 1$ captures the diminishing marginal productivity of public capital on output. The rationale for diminishing marginal productivity is that as the level of *one* productive input increases, relative to *other* inputs used in production, each additional unit of the input will not be used as intensely in producing goods. We think of y_2 as being produced using not only public capital but also using the time of a worker of given abilities (the one unit of labor supply) and, perhaps, a fixed amount other inputs such as land. The productivity of the worker increases with public capital. For example, the more public education received when young and the more roads available to move products as an adult, the more productive the worker. However, the effect of additional public capital on worker productivity diminishes as the level of capital becomes larger—additional expenditures on public education or roads have a diminishing effect.

The fact that output depends on public capital *per household*, rather than the total stock of public capital (G_2), means that there is crowding of the public capital. If the population of workers were to increase, with a fixed G_2, the productivity of an individual worker would fall. In Sect. 2.6 of this chapter, we discuss what happens if public capital is a *pure public good*, with productive services that are not affected by the population size, or an *impure public good*, with partial crowding as the population increases. The bottom line will be that the alternative assumptions about public capital primarily alter the interpretation of A.

Just as in Sect. 2.1, we assume a household's lifetime satisfaction or utility is determined by consumption over the two periods of life, c_1 and c_2, with the lifetime utility function taking the form

$$U = \ln c_1 + \beta \ln c_2, \tag{2.2}$$

where recall $\beta < 1$ is a time discount factor that measures the household's willingness to postpone receiving utility into the future.

Let's begin with the case where a credit market does *not* exist. This is a natural starting point when discussing a closed economy with identical households. If households are identical, then *all* households will want to lend or *all* households will want to borrow. There will be no possibility of credit market transactions because that requires there be a borrower *and* a lender. We initially assume that the government will finance its spending with tax rate, τ, levied on household income. With no credit market, consumption in each period is determined by the period's income and the period's income tax rate; $c_1 = (1 - \tau_1)y_1$ and $c_2 = (1 - \tau_2)y_2$.

Taxes and Government Investment

In this chapter, we assume that government policy is set by a benevolent social planner who chooses tax rates and government investment to maximize the welfare of the representative household. We also assume that public capital fully depreciates in one period, so the public investment decision in period 1 is equivalent to choosing the period 2 public capital stock.

Note that with only two periods and no debt financing of government investment, there is actually no need for period 2 taxes. With $\tau_2 = 0$, we can focus on the optimal choice of first period taxes and government investment. The first period government budget constraint is $G_2 = N\tau_1 y_1$ or $g_2 = \tau_1 y_1$, with $g_2 \equiv G_2/N$.

Using the government and private household budget constraints, the private household's welfare can be written as a function of government investment,

$$U = \ln (y_1 - g_2) + \beta \ln \left(A g_2^{\mu}\right). \tag{2.3}$$

Maximizing (2.3) with respect to g_2, yields the optimal fiscal policy set by the benevolent government,

$$g_2 = \frac{\beta\mu}{1+\beta\mu} y_1 \tag{2.4a}$$

$$\tau_1 = \frac{\beta\mu}{1+\beta\mu}. \tag{2.4b}$$

There are two reasons why government capital is valued in this setting. First, government investment is productive and thereby increases lifetime resources of the representative household. The higher the value of μ, the more productive is investment and the greater is the optimal public capital. Second, because there are no other assets available, government capital can help smooth consumption across time. This second reason explains why the time preference parameter, β, affects the optimal level of government capital in (2.4a). If households are more patient, placing a relatively large weight on future utility, then they prefer higher current period taxes and more government capital as a form of indirect saving.

Public Debt and Government Investment

Now let's introduce public debt. With public debt, the government has two ways of financing first-period investment—taxes or borrowing. The presence of public debt gives households a second asset that may help in smoothing their consumption over time in a way that better suits their preferences. Of course, for households to be interested in government debt as an asset, they have to be willing to save. So, we assume that is the case. If the representative household wants to borrow, they would not purchase government debt and serve as a lender to the government. However, remember from Sect. 2.1, that the government could convince households to lend by offering a sufficiently high interest rate on public debt.

Denote the total public debt issued by the government, and purchased by private households in period 1, as B_2. In period 2, the principle and interest paid to the bond holders is $(1 + r_2)B_2$, where r_2 is the interest rate on government bonds. The debt repayment obligation creates a need for the government to raise revenue in period 2, so we re-introduce the tax rate, τ_2. If we define $b_2 \equiv B_2/N$, then the two household budget constraints can be written as

$$c_1 + b_2 = (1-\tau_1)y_1 \tag{2.5a}$$

$$c_2 = (1-\tau_2)y_2 + (1+r_2)b_2, \tag{2.5b}$$

and the two government budget constraints as

$$g_2 = \tau_1 y_1 + b_2 \tag{2.6a}$$

$$(1+r_2)b_2 = \tau_2 y_2. \tag{2.6b}$$

Notice that if we combine the household and government budget constraints we can rewrite the economy's *consolidated* constraints as

$$c_1 = y_1 - g_2 \tag{2.7a}$$

$$c_2 = y_2. \tag{2.7b}$$

Surprisingly, these consolidated constraints imply that public debt neither affects the lifetime resources of the household nor the ability to alter the timing of household consumption. The optimal choice of government investment is the same as in the setting where government borrowing was prohibited.

Why does adding public debt fail to alter the government's policy and household consumption? Even if households like the idea of being able to save by purchasing government bonds, it fails to increase second period consumption opportunities because government borrowing requires that household pay higher second period taxes. The second period taxes completely offset the value of the government bonds purchased and the associated interest payments. For this reason, bonds are not a store of household wealth. Furthermore, households view period 1 taxes and period 1 bonds as equivalent means of financing government investment because both reduce first period consumption in the same way and both fail to directly increase household consumption in the second period. The result that *government bonds are not net wealth*, and *tax and bond financing are equivalent*, is a fundamental starting point in the conceptual understanding of fiscal policy (Barro 1974). However, as we shall see later in this chapter and in the next chapter, the result fails to hold for empirically important and policy relevant reasons (Kotlikoff 2003, Chap. VII).

2.3 The Small-Open Economy Model

Borrowing and lending across households is not possible when households are identical in all ways, as is the case in the representative agent model, because for a credit market to exist some households must choose to be lenders and some borrowers. In a representative agent model, either *all* households want to lend, or *all* households want to borrow. One way that the representative household could acquire assets or liabilities is to lend or borrow in an *international* market for funds. Implicit in this idea is the assumption that households in other countries have *different* income paths or time preferences.

The simplest way to introduce an international market for funds is to assume a sufficiently large number of countries are trading with each other. When many countries are engaged in trade, it may be reasonable to assume that the international market for funds is perfectly competitive at the level of an entire country. A single country is so small relative to the entire market, that it takes the international interest rate as an exogenous variable that is beyond its influence. This assumption is most accurate for smaller economies, so an open economy model with an exogenous international interest rate for funds is called the *small open economy* model.

In our model, the market for funds is one where households borrow and lend for the purpose of financing consumption. Of course markets for private consumption loans don't just appear. Consumption loan markets are limited in today's most developed economies. It takes a great deal of financial and legal institutional structure to extend, monitor, and enforce domestic, not to mention international, loan contracts for household consumption. Without the underlying financial and legal structure, the costs and risk associated with such lending would be too great for the market to exist. The laws and regulations associated with financial markets are forms of *intangible* public capital that are an important component of a country's infrastructure

In contrast, loans extended from one country's government, or group of governments, to another country's government may be feasible even when private loan markets fail to exist. Governments typically have at least some rudiments of a formal accounting and payment system that allow for funds to be transferred across borders. In addition, political or economic pressure can be used by lending governments to help enforce loan repayment. Thus, it is important to consider the situation where private households do not have access to international loan markets, and yet governments can extend loans to each other.

Private and Public Credit

Let's begin with the simplest case where *both* households and governments can borrow and lend in perfectly competitive international loan markets. We introduce the new notation a_2^* to represent the household's holdings of an international asset, $a_2^* > 0$, or an international liability, $a_2^* < 0$. We also need to adjust notation to allow for government lending as well as government borrowing. Toward this end, think of $b_2 > 0$ as government debt associated with borrowing and $b_2 < 0$ as government assets associated with lending. Furthermore, let household *saving*, s, be the accumulation of international assets and domestic government debt. Household saving could be negative, meaning that households of one country could be borrowing from other countries.

The household budget constraints can now be written as

$$c_1 + s = (1 - \tau_1)y_1 \tag{2.8a}$$

$$c_2 = (1 - \tau_2)y_2 + (1 + r^*)s, \tag{2.8b}$$

where r^* is the exogenous interest rate determined by the international market for funds. Treating r^* as an exogenous variable is where we use the assumption of a small open economy operating in a perfectly competitive international market for funds.

The government budget constraints take the same form as (2.6a and 2.6b), but now, because we allow for the possibility that the government is a net lender, we must allow for the possibility that $\tau_2 < 0$. The second period tax rate must be interpreted as a *net* tax rate, that can possibly be negative. When the government is a net lender it is able to *transfer* income to second period households, financed by interest and loan repayments from abroad, rather than tax them.

Consolidating (2.6a, 2.6b) and (2.8a, 2.8b) to form the household's *lifetime budget constraint*, gives us

$$c_1 + \frac{c_2}{1+r^*} = y_1 + \frac{y_2}{1+r*} - \left(\tau_1 y_1 + \frac{\tau_2 y_2}{1+r*}\right) = y_1 + \frac{y_2}{1+r*} - g_2. \tag{2.9}$$

As in the closed economy setting, government bonds are equivalent to first period taxes and are not net wealth. If the government borrows internationally to avoid using current taxes, domestic households will have to be taxed in the future period to repay the foreign debt and interest. Government lending requires that first period income be taxed away from households. However, the first period taxes, paid to a government for the purpose of lending them internationally, are returned with interest to the household in the form of second period transfers when the international loans are repaid.

Furthermore, the household could generate this same outcome for itself by saving and lending privately. If the government taxes more in the first period and lends the revenue, the household would simply lend less privately. The only aspect of government policy that influences the representative household's lifetime consumption possibilities is government investment, regardless of how it is financed.

The benevolent government chooses investment to maximize the lifetime wealth of the household. Maximizing the right-hand side of (2.9) by choosing g_2 generates the following *efficient* investment rule

$$\mu A g_2^{\mu-1} = 1 + r^*. \tag{2.10}$$

The efficient investment rule says that government investment should equate the marginal product of public capital to the opportunity cost of funds, as determined by the interest rate on international loan markets. Unlike (2.4a), the household preference parameter (β) that influences the optimal timing of consumption plays no role in the efficiency condition. Household can now use international consumption loans to determine the preferred time path of consumption. Government capital no longer needs to do the double duty of increasing future income and optimally smoothing consumption over time.

Given the maximum lifetime wealth that results from efficient public investment, the representative household chooses consumption across the two periods to maximize utility. Using the resulting optimal conditions for maximizing utility, the optimal consumption path satisfies

$$\frac{c_2}{c_1} = \beta(1 + r^*). \tag{2.11}$$

This expression, known as the *Euler equation*, says that consumption rises faster over the life-cycle, the higher is the interest rate. A higher interest rate raises the cost of current consumption relative to future consumption, which causes the household to choose a steeper consumption profile over time. Note that if you combine the solutions for c_1 and c_2 from Sect. 2.1, those solutions will also satisfy (2.11). The Euler equation will always hold whenever households can freely borrow and lend.

Only Public Credit

Suppose now that the market for *private* international loans does *not* exist. Governments can borrow and lend internationally, but not households. The consolidated budget constraints of the *credit-constrained* representative household are

$$c_1 = (1 - \tau_1)y_1 = y_1 - g_2 + b_2 \tag{2.12a}$$

$$c_2 = (1 - \tau_2)y_2 = y_2 - (1 + r^*)b_2. \tag{2.12b}$$

Note these budget constraints now depend on public debt because the government can do something the household cannot do—borrow. The situation differs from the closed economy case because domestic households do not have to purchase government debt, instead the debt can be sold to foreigners. So, debt financing is now possible even if domestic households are credit constrained and do not want to lend.

The government chooses g_2 and b_2 to maximize $U = \ln(y_1 - g_2 + b_2) + \beta \ln(y_2 - (1 + r^*)b_2)$, producing the following optimal conditions,

$$\mu A g_2^{\mu-1} = 1 + r^* \tag{2.13a}$$

$$\frac{c_2}{c_1} = \beta(1 + r^*). \tag{2.13b}$$

Equation (2.13a) reproduces the efficiency condition for investment given in (2.10) and Eq. (2.13b) generates the same condition for the optimal timing of household consumption over the life cycle given by (2.11). The first-best outcome, where households can also borrow and lend internationally, is reproduced because the government serves as a financial intermediary for private households. The government mimics the borrowing and lending the household prefers in order to generate the same first-best outcome that the household would have chosen if it could have directly participated in perfectly competitive international loan markets.

To understand this result in more detail, consider the perfectly closed economy we started the chapter with, where no international borrowing and lending is possible. Suppose the government, and the representative household it serves, would prefer to borrow internationally but cannot. Under this scenario, the *credit-constrained* solution for government investment in the closed economy, that satisfies (2.4a), implies $\mu A g_2^{\mu-1} > 1 + r^*$. Government *investment is inefficiently low* because the marginal product of public capital is greater than the cost of borrowing. The household does not prefer the efficient investment level because the required sacrifice of *first* period consumption would lower its welfare more than if they were able to borrow the funds in the international loan market and instead sacrifice the corresponding *second* period consumption. The credit constraint means that *both* first period consumption and government investment are too low.

If the government can borrow the required funds abroad to achieve the efficient investment level *and* raise first period consumption, the household can be made better off. Here, government bonds are not equivalent to first period taxes as a way of funding investment because, with international borrowing, the domestic household need not purchase the debt and sacrifice current consumption. Thus, issuing government debt raises the private household's lifetime wealth and welfare. The general lesson is that when private households are credit-constrained, and the government has access to an international market for credit, then government debt can be a welfare-enhancing fiscal tool.

To complete our discussion, we need to introduce an important caveat—the conclusion that government debt can be used as a welfare-enhancing fiscal tool must be interpreted carefully. We have assumed that the two periods in the model represent two periods in the life of a single household. Under this interpretation, the lifetime welfare of a credit-constrained household can unambiguously be raised by issuing public debt in international loan markets.

However, as will be discussed below, there is also a *generational* interpretation of the two-period model, with each period representing a distinct generation of the same family. In this case, the credit-constraint takes the form of a *bequest-constraint.* The bequest-constraint means that the current generation is not legally permitted to impose a debt-obligation on their children, the next generation. Positive bequests of assets are fine, but negative bequests, the bequeathing of parental debts, are not allowed. This legal restriction is reflected in the laws of most countries. The government, however, can indirectly relieve the non-negative bequest-constraint by issuing public debt on behalf of the current generation and then using taxes on future generations to force repayment (Drazen 1978). In this way, the government can circumvent the legal restriction it imposes on individual households, creating a fundamental tension in how fiscal policy affects the welfare of *different* generations.

2.4 Human Capital, Inequality, and Public Debt

In their survey of the theories of why public debt is used, Alesina and Passalacqua (2015) view the credit constraint-motivation as particularly convincing. As poorer segments of the population become more engaged in a country's politics, there is naturally more pressure to issue public debt to serve as a substitute for the inability to borrow privately. An increasing political voice for the poor offers a possible explanation for the rise in public debt observed in maturing democracies.

This explanation can be further articulated if one takes the *generational* interpretation of the two period model—with the first period representing the parent's adult lifetime and the second period the adult lifetime of their children. The utility function in our model, given by (2.2), is now interpreted as being comprised of the utility the current generation receives from its own lifetime consumption and the utility the current generation receives from the lifetime consumption of its adult children, a form of *intergenerational altruism*. The reason the generational interpretation creates a more compelling framework for analyzing public debt is that, while *life-*

cycle credit markets *may be complete*, the market for *intergenerational* credit transactions are *clearly incomplete*. Parents are allowed to lend and create an asset that could then be bequeathed to children. However, parents are not legally allowed to borrow and then leave the debt for their children to repay.

In a life-cycle credit transaction, the person who borrows is the same person who repays the debt at a later date—everything is settled within an individual's lifetime. A market for life-cycle credit transactions is close to complete in developed countries. Intergenerational credit transactions would include contracts with the parents doing the borrowing and the children repaying the debt in the future. Private intergenerational credit transactions are limited because children are not legally bound to repay the debt taken on by their parents. However, the government, by borrowing today and postponing debt repayment sufficiently far into the future, can create a credit transaction that extends across generations.

To emphasize why these considerations are important, let's go a step further. Interpret g_2 as human capital investments in children, similar to Drazen (1978), chosen by parents either directly or indirectly determined by local governments responding to household preferences in particular communities. These human capital investments include all educational investment that occur at each stage of the child's life—from pre-school investments, to primary and secondary schooling, to parental subsidy of college expenses.

We can extend the model a bit more and think of p as representing the relative price of educational inputs. Introducing the price of education inputs changes both the credit constrained choice of g_2, given by (2.4a), and the unconstrained or efficient choice of g_2 given by (2.13a). When education has a distinct relative price from other goods, these two equations take the form

"Poor" Household (Bequest-Constrained)

$$pg_2 = \frac{\beta\mu}{1+\beta\mu}y_1, \quad \text{With} \quad \mu A g_2^{\mu-1} > p(1+r^*), \tag{2.4a$'$}$$

and

"Rich" Households (Unconstrained)

$$\mu A g_2^{\mu-1} = p(1+r^*) \tag{2.13a$'$}$$

Finally, to capture what Alesina and Passalacqua (2015) have in mind, let's add some relevant heterogeneity into the mix by thinking of two household types that differ by their level of first period, or parental, income. "Poor" households have little parental income. If they cannot impose debt repayment obligations on their children (i.e. $a^* < 0$ is not allowed), their preferred investments would be represented by (2.4a′). "Rich" households, on the other hand, have high parental income. They can afford a level of g_2 that satisfies the efficiency condition in (2.13a′), even with no intergenerational credit transactions. In fact, rich parents also leave their children a positive bequest of financial assets ($a^* > 0$).

This re-interpretation and extension of the two-period model allows us to relate several important features of advanced economies that began developing over the last quarter of the 20th century. First, we have seen a rise in skill-biased technological change and a change in sectoral composition that increased the return to schooling, but at the same time created a rise in wage inequality across households with different levels of schooling (Autor 2014). Second, despite the growing return to education, there has been a slowdown in the growth of years of schooling and in economic growth (Gordon 2016; OECD 2015). Third, there has been a rise in globalization since the 1970s and expanded access to international credit (Azzimonti et al. 2014). Further, we have seen an unprecedented rise in government budget deficits and public debt (Hallerberg et al. 2009; Steuerle 2014). Finally, the relative prices of important investments in education and health have dramatically increased. In relating these five developments, we argue that the credit-constrained story for the rise in public debt can be made even more convincing.

Important Developments in Rich Countries since 1975

1. Increased return to college and increased wage inequality
2. Slowdown in the growth of schooling obtained by average worker
3. Expansion in international credit markets and a low international cost of funds
4. Rising public debt as a fraction of GDP
5. Increasing relative price of education and health care

Start with the rise in the returns to education, which in our model is captured by a rise in A and $\mu A g_2^{\mu-1}/p$, the marginal return on the current investment needed to marginally raise g_2. Rich households would have no trouble responding to the increased return by raising their preferred level of g_2 until (2.13a′) was once again satisfied—increasing investment at all stages of their child's life to ensure they can get into the best college possible or even go on to graduate school. However, poor households that are constrained by low levels of y_1 would not alter their levels of g_2. Notice that A does not enter (2.4a′).[1] Thus, a rise in A leads to a rise in wage inequality in the next generation because rich households respond to and benefit the most from a rise in A.

The wage inequality would worsen if the rising demand for educational inputs by rich households drives p up. An increase in the relative price of family investments in education and health care is the fifth important development mentioned above. A rising price of education would lower the actual investments of constrained households, as indicated by (2.4a′). Rich households increase years of schooling, although by not as much as when the relative price remains fixed, but poor

[1]The fact that A does not enter (2.4a′) can be explained by offsetting income and substitution effects that are analogous to those associated with a rise in interest rates in the standard life-cycle theory of saving. A higher value of A increases family resources that parents can access by investing less in their children. On the other hand, the opportunity cost of not investing has gone up. For more on the conflicting income and substitution effects associated with saving and investment, see Sect. 2.11 of this chapter and Chap. 4.

households reduce years of schooling for their children. This implies there may not be a strong economy-wide increase in educational attainment despite the growing return to schooling, explaining the second important development on the list.

The rising gap between the return to educational investments and the return to financial or physical assets would increase the poor household's demand for public debt to alleviate their intergenerational credit constraints. At the same time, growing access to international loan markets would lower the cost of funding the demand for public debt, the third development since 1975. Azzimonti et al. (2014) explain the rise in debt-to-GDP ratios across OECD countries as, in part, due to increasing financial liberalization across borders and lower interest rates charged to countries with high public debt.

An increase in public debt unambiguously raises the welfare of the current generation of poor households by allowing both more current consumption and more human capital investment in the next generation. However, nothing guarantees that the extra investment will raise future income enough to cover the debt costs—i.e. the consumption of the future generation could fall. Specifically, public debt raises U and c_1, but c_2 may rise or fall. Formally, this is because the optimal timing of consumption is linked to the opportunity cost of current consumption and that cost has fallen from $\mu A g_2^{\mu-1}$ to $1 + r^*$. This implies that the ratio, c_2/c_1, must fall, which includes the possibility of an *absolute* fall in c_2 (see *Problems* 13 and 14).

The possibility that the next generation from a bequest-constrained household is made worse-off by government debt is discussed in detail by Lord and Rangazas (1993). They find that deficit policies that are supported by the majority of altruistic households currently alive are likely to reduce the consumption opportunities of future generations. This is an important consideration. Most societies create laws that protect future generations from the excesses of the current generation by making it illegal for parents to shift their debt obligations to their children. If these laws are generally supported, then it should not be possible for the government to circumvent them with fiscal policy. Instead, the government should make any intergenerational redistribution clear to the public and help impose the same discipline on the country as a whole that the country's laws place on individual households.

The more households that are "poor," i.e. face constraints on intergenerational borrowing arrangements, the more relevant the model is for explaining the rise in public debt. Three factors suggest that a growing majority of households face intergenerational borrowing constraints. First, econometric studies consistently find that parent's income is positively correlated with educational attainment of children, even when measures of child ability are controlled for statistically (Heckman and Krueger 2005). If households are unconstrained, then marginal variations in parental income would *not* affect the efficient investment in education. Second, most countries have a strong "college-or-bust" mentality among the majority of households (Murray 2008; Bennett and Wilezol 2013). The real cost of college, including educating a child well enough that they can realistically enter college and complete a 4 year degree, is quite expensive. The *relative* burden of financing education has increased over time because there has been little or no increase in real income since the 1970s for the vast majority of households (Autor 2014; OECD 2015, Table 5), while the real costs of education has increased over the same period (Gordon 2016). Combine this with the rising relative price of health care and it is easy to see that both the consumption and human capital investments of the majority of households have been increasingly squeezed by economic trends. Finally, statistical studies show that educational investments, at all ages, continue to exceed the return on financial and physical assets (at least for the *average* student). Thus, it is not hard to see why the majority of households might be willing to accept the expansion in public debt—especially if the full extent of the intergenerational transfers associated with current policies is not transparent.

2.5 Public Debt Defaults

In this section we look at the possibility that the government might default on its obligations to repay bondholders. There are various forms that default may take including a suspension of interest payments or, more dramatically, a declaration that only some or none of the principle will be repaid when the bond reaches maturity. Another common, and more clandestine, method of default uses unexpected money creation to "repay" debt. Money creation tends to create inflation, so while the dollars owed the bondholder are paid, the purchasing power or *real* return to bondholders is reduced just as in the case when the default is more direct and transparent.

As public debt accumulates, lenders become increasingly concerned about a growth slow down or recession that causes a loss in tax revenue and a temptation to default. This concern can create a "crisis of confidence," where lenders sell off their government bonds, driving bond prices down and bond yields or interest rates up. Section 5.7 of Chap. 5 discusses the connection between the fiscal crisis and recessions brought on, or at least complicated, by a crisis of confidence.

Here we examine public debt default in more detail by sketching the logic from an economic model of the "crisis of confidence" developed by Calvo (1988). The formal details of model can be found in the Chapter Appendix. There are three key new components that must be added to our two-period model to address the issue of debt defaults.

First, households need an alternative way of saving so that they are not *forced* to save by purchasing government bonds. We assume there is a private *physical* asset, k, such as a house or a small business. Unlike with private financial assets (a_2), all households can simultaneously accumulate physical assets as an alternative to saving through government bonds. The private physical asset is acquired in period 1 and yields Rk units of income in period 2, so $R > 1$ can be thought of as the return from the private asset.

In equilibrium, if households are willing to hold government bonds, the bonds must pay a return equal to the private asset. Let R_b be the stated return to public debt, b_2, at the time it is purchased in period 1 and let θ be the portion of the return to public debt that is *not* repaid in period 2. The lending household's return to holding public debt is then $(1-\theta)R_b$. If both the private asset and government debt are held by households it must be that

$$(1-\theta)R_b = R. \quad \text{(asset market equilibrium condition)}$$

Note for households to buy government bonds in the first period, there cannot be an equilibrium with the expectation of *complete* default, $\theta = 1$, but *partial* default is possible in equilibrium.

Second, there must be a reason that the government may want to avoid raising taxes in the second period to repay debt, i.e. a reason that default may be a good idea. Beyond simply transferring income to the government, taxation has costs to the economy as a whole. There are various ways that taxation can create a loss of resources to the economy as the government attempts to obtain revenue from private households. These costs are known as the "excess burden" of taxation. Here we simply assume that taxes are costly to collect. The government must expend resources to collect taxes and the cost of collection increases with the level of taxation—households try harder to evade paying taxes when tax rates are high.

Third, there must also be a reason *not* to default. We assume that if a government defaults on its obligation to repay debt, it becomes even harder to collect a *given* amount of taxes. Chapter 1 presents evidence that tax evasion increases when the public is dissatisfied with its government's performance. Defaulting on public debt is certainly a source of such dissatisfaction. Thus, defaulting lowers the need to raise tax revenue but it also encourages tax evasion for any given tax rate—households feel more justified in evading taxes when the government performs poorly. If the default rate is too high, more resources will be lost to collect the smaller amount of tax revenue needed for repayment. When the government thinks about defaulting on public debt it must balance the advantage and disadvantage of its decision on the cost of taxation.

Despite the possibility of default, the government is taken to be benevolent, as we have assumed throughout this chapter. In the second period it seeks to maximize household welfare by making the two costs of tax collection as low as possible. In summary, the government attempts to minimize the costs associated with tax evasion by choosing second period taxes to balance the benefit of higher taxes, associated with reducing the cost of default, against the direct cost of raising taxes.

As shown in an Appendix, the Calvo model can generate a multiple equilibrium outcome that helps explain why the timing of a crisis of confidence is impossible to predict. This is because there are *two* possible equilibria, based on the precise nature of lenders' expectations, that *both* satisfy the asset market equilibrium condition.

If $\theta = 0$, we have the no-default outcome. However, the no-default case may not be chosen because, if the predetermined value of b_2R_b is high, the required taxes and tax collection resource costs needed to repay *all* of the government's debt obligations may be too high. The no-default case is only optimal if b_2R_b is sufficiently low—i.e. low interest rates and low debt obligations from past borrowing. If b_2R_b is sufficiently large, partial default becomes optimal, i.e. $\theta > 0$.

If households expect no default, then they will be content to hold government bonds at the relatively low interest rate, $R_b = R$. If R is low enough, the government will not default, consistent with household expectations, and we have an equilibrium where households correctly expect no default.

If households expect default, then they will still hold government debt but only at the a relatively higher interest rate on bonds that compensates them for second-period default, $R_b = \frac{R}{1-\theta}$. At this higher interest rate, the government chooses a default rate consistent with household expectations and we have a second equilibrium possibility. Note, the likelihood that the government defaults at the higher interest rate depends on how much the government borrows in period 1. A government that borrows too much in period 1, creates the possibility of future default.

Thus, we have multiple equilibrium outcomes that hinge on household expectations. Household expectations are *self-fulling*—if they expect no default, interest rates are low, and no default occurs but if they expect default, interest rates are high, and default occurs as predicted. Furthermore, a change in household expectations, specifically a "crisis of confidence," could shift the equilibrium from one with low interest rates to one with high interest rates very quickly and force the government to default.

2.6 Public Capital and Productivity

We have been assuming that public capital raises worker productivity, i.e. that $\mu > 0$. There is an empirical literature that attempts to test this assumption. The concept of public capital is quite broad and can include physical infrastructure, the stock of basic research knowledge, human capital acquired via public schooling, and even the intangible capital reflected in a country's laws and regulations—including the rules and procedures for implementing them. Empirical studies typically use national income accounting measures of public capital that are limited to physical infrastructure. Although there is some debate over the exact estimate of μ, most studies finds a positive and statistically significant effect of public infrastructure on output.

The classic empirical study of the productivity effects of public infrastructure was conducted by David Ashauer (1989). His approach allowed for a direct measure of μ, the output elasticity of public capital, which he estimated to be as high as 0.40. Subsequent research that attempted to verify his findings, using different data sets and econometric approaches, found a somewhat lower elasticity. Glomm and Ravikumar (1997) survey the empirical work in the decade following Ashauer's study and conclude that a more reasonable estimate might be 0.20. In an update of his earlier study, Ashauer (2000) found estimates close to 0.30. Several more recent studies also find estimates that cluster around 0.30 (see the survey in Bivens (2012)).

It would be useful to have estimates of the effects that extend beyond public physical infrastructure. Less tangible types of public capital may have output elasticities that differ from physical infrastructure. Ideally one would decompose public capital into its different components. For example, a recent study has estimated a parameter very similar to μ that measures the human capital elasticity of public school spending. Interestingly, Manuelli and Seshadri (2014) find a public school spending elasticity estimate of about 0.30. Their estimate is based on an assumption that public school spending has a rate of return similar to that of private physical capital, about 7 percent. Heckman and others argue that, at the levels of school spending seen in developed countries, the marginal rate of return to public school spending in the average community is much lower than 7 percent (Heckman and Krueger 2005). This is consistent with the historical analysis of Rangazas (2000, 2002) who finds a public spending elasticity of less than 0.20.

Another measurement issue in empirical studies is related to the quality of public capital and government corruption (Chakraborty and Dabla-Norris 2011). As discussed in the introduction, large portions of the funds officially budgeted for public investment are never actually invested but instead are siphoned off for consumption by public officials and private contractors. In addition, the effectiveness of the public capital that does exist is influenced by how it is maintained and operated by government bureaucrats. This issue not only applies to infrastructure, power plants, and water and sewage facilities, but also to public schools where teacher absenteeism is a problem. The inability to control for these measurement issues will create a downward bias in the estimates of output effects from public capital. After attempting to control for corruption, Bayraktar (2019) provides evidence of a positive effect of public investment on growth but one that rises with income over the early stages of development, including the possibility of a threshold effect.

2.7 Pure and Impure Public Capital

Thus far we have assumed that public capital is a private good, similar to private capital. With private capital, if one worker drives a tractor or operates a computer, then it is not possible for another worker to use the same equipment to produce output. For some types of public capital, the analogy to private capital is not accurate. If a producer is using a public road, this does not inhibit another producer from using the same road, at the same time, in any significant way.

If the transportation services provided by the road are not affected by the total number of producers using the road, then the road would be a *pure public good*—no "crowding" or reduction of services occurs as the number of producers served increases. Roads, while not pure private goods, are not pure public goods either because when the road becomes sufficiently busy with traffic, the total number of producers using the road *does reduce* the transportation services provided per producer. Roads, and many other types of public capital, are best viewed as *impure public goods* where crowding can occur.

This discussion affects the modelling of the production function that relates public capital to output. If public capital were a pure public good, then instead of writing the production function as in (2.1), we would write the production function as

$$y_2 = AG_2^{\mu} \tag{2.14}$$

where now the *total* public capital stock determines the productivity of an *individual* producer, independent of how many producers there are in the economy.

A more general way of writing the production function, that includes (2.1) and (2.14) as special cases and that introduces impure public goods, is

$$y_2 = A\left(G_2/N^{\xi}\right)^{\mu}, \tag{2.15}$$

with $0 \leq \xi \leq 1$. The parameter ξ gauges the public goods nature of public capital. If $\xi = 1$, then public capital is a private good, as in the case of private capital. If $\xi = 0$, then public capital is a pure public good. For $0 < \xi < 1$, we have an impure public good, where some crowding occurs.

Now we need to think about how taking the simple route of modeling public capital as a private good, when in fact it is more accurate to model it as a impure public good, affects the analysis. Toward this end, note that we can write (2.15) as

$$y_2 = A\left(\frac{G_2}{N^{\xi}}\frac{N}{N}\right)^{\mu} = A\left(g_2 N^{1-\xi}\right)^{\mu} \equiv \overline{A}g_2^{\mu}, \tag{2.16}$$

where $\overline{A} \equiv AN^{(1-\xi)\mu}$. The general production function in (2.16) has the same form as (2.1), but with an adjusted TFP term. This means, even if public capital is an impure public good, we can continue to model it as a private good. However, the TFP associated with a production function of the form in (2.1), i.e. expressed in terms of public capital per producer (as is done with private capital), will increase with population size. For a given ratio of public capital per producer, a larger economy will generate more output *per producer*. This is because the producers, at least to some extent, can share the total public capital, and with more producers there is a greater total public capital stock for any given value of g_2. Note that the *sharing effect*, that raises TFP, diminishes with population size because $(1 - \xi)\mu < 1$. So, for large populations, variations in population size do not affect worker productivity very much, when g_2 is held constant.

The lesson here is that we can model public capital as a private good and use (2.1), but we have to remember that the TFP associated with (2.1) is a function of population size if public capital has public good characteristics. For most of our analysis, this consideration will not be important. However, as we will see in the very next section of the chapter, there are instances where the adjusted interpretation of TFP should be kept in mind.

2.8 The Allocation of Public Capital

Now we turn to the *allocation* of public capital. This is important because, as discussed in the introduction, politics will not only affect the size of government budgets but also how a given budget is allocated across regions or neighborhoods of a country. For example, societies tend to have dramatically unequal allocations of infrastructure and educational spending across rich and poor neighborhoods. To examine the possible distortionary influence of politics, we need to start with a benchmark analysis of investment allocation based solely on economic considerations.

Suppose there are two regions P and R. Each region has a representative household with an associated initial income flow and a production function relating local public capital to future output and income. Income flows over the two periods, are y_{1P} and $y_{2P} = A_P(g_{2P})^{\mu}$, for region P, and y_{1R} and $y_{2R} = A_R(g_{2R})^{\mu}$, for region R.

To focus on allocation, we simplify the financing decision by assuming that the government does not issue debt. In period 1, the national government levies an income tax on all households equal to τ_1. The government budget constraint is

$$N_P g_{2P} + N_R g_{2R} = \tau_1 (N_P y_{1P} + N_R y_{1R}). \tag{2.17}$$

Furthermore, we assume households can borrow and lend in a perfectly competitive loan market, so public capital investment decisions are not affected by concerns over intertemporal consumption smoothing.

The household budget constraints in each region take the form,

$$c_1 + s = (1 - \tau_1)y_1 \tag{2.18a}$$

$$c_2 = y_2 + (1 + r^*)s, \tag{2.18b}$$

where we drop the regional notation when it is not necessary for clarity. Household preferences in each region take the same log form as before, see (2.2). Households choose consumption and saving to maximize utility subject to the budget constraints given by (2.18a, 2.18b). The resulting optimal consumption choices are

$$c_1 = \frac{W}{1 + \beta} \tag{2.19a}$$

$$c_2 = \frac{\beta W}{1 + \beta}, \tag{2.19b}$$

where $W \equiv (1 - \tau_1)y_1 + \frac{y_2}{1+r^*}$, lifetime after-tax *wealth*. Substituting the optimal consumption choices back into (2.2) yields a *value function* or an *indirect utility function*, giving the maximum lifetime utility associated with a particular value of wealth,

$$V(W) = (1 + \beta) \ln W. \tag{2.20}$$

We assume that the benevolent government chooses fiscal policy to maximize the sum of the utility of its citizens, a measure of aggregate welfare that weighs each individual household equally.[2] Subject to the budget constraint given in (2.17), the government then chooses the common income tax rate and public capital in each region to maximize

$$N_P V(W_P) + N_R V(W_R). \tag{2.21}$$

The government's problem generates the following rules for the optimal fiscal policy,

$$\frac{N_P y_{1P}}{W_P} + \frac{N_R y_{1R}}{W_R} = \lambda(N_P y_{1P} + N_R y_{1R}) \tag{2.22a}$$

$$\frac{1}{W_P}\frac{\mu A_P g_{2P}^{\mu-1}}{1+r^*} = \lambda \tag{2.22b}$$

$$\frac{1}{W_R}\frac{\mu A_R g_{2R}^{\mu-1}}{1+r^*} = \lambda. \tag{2.22c}$$

where λ is the Lagrange multiplier associated with the government budget constraint, which can be interpreted as the marginal value of government revenue. Equation (2.22a) says the tax rate should be chosen to equate the marginal social cost, associated with the drop in current consumption, to the marginal benefit of additional government revenue collected. Equations (2.22b) and (2.22c) say that the marginal benefit of investing in each region should be equated to the marginal cost of collecting the government revenue needed to finance the investments.

Equating (2.22b) and (2.22c) gives an allocation rule for government investment,

$$\frac{1}{W_P}\frac{\mu A_P g_{2P}^{\mu-1}}{1+r^*} = \frac{1}{W_R}\frac{\mu A_R g_{2R}^{\mu-1}}{1+r^*}, \tag{2.23}$$

i.e. the marginal *value* of investment should be equated across regions.

In general, the allocation rule does not indicate equal government investment across regions. The government should invest more in the region with low consumption and high marginal productivity of public capital. A region with lower first period income will receive higher marginal value from greater consumption associated with higher second period income. The rise in second period income will be greater the higher is the region's TFP. Remember from our discussion of impure public goods that regional TFP could differ because of differences in population size. TFP could

[2]Saez and Stantcheva (2016) develop ways to generalize the traditional utilitarian social welfare function used here in order to reflect considerations that may be important for policy formation. For example, society may want policy makers to place greater weights on households that have a greater willingness to work or that have come from disadvantaged family backgrounds.

also differ based on differences in local natural resources or other geographic characteristics such as access to the sea or to the borders of foreign countries.

The fact that (2.23) is not a pure efficiency rule that would simply determine the allocation of investment by equating the marginal product of public capital across regions, captures the possible conflict between the government efficiency principle and the principle of narrowing economic disparities. Larger investments in a poor region may be justified, even if the return on investment is relatively low, because any gain in income has a strong effect on household welfare when household wealth is low.

The possible conflict between the two principles when deciding on the allocation of investment depends on the fiscal tools available to the government. We are not allowing for any fiscal variables that *directly* address differences in first period income across the regions. Region P could be interpreted as "poor" and region R as "rich," if $y_{1P} < y_{1R}$. In principle, rich households could be targeted with higher tax rates that finance transfers of income to poor households. In this case, the investment allocation could be made strictly on efficiency grounds. However, unless the tax-transfer scheme completely equated first period incomes, then optimal government investment will be affected by income inequality. Here, public investment must again do "double duty," trying to satisfy equity and efficiency considerations.

Even if $y_{1P} = y_{1R}$, differences in regional TFP could affect lifetime income, which in turn would prevent a equalization of marginal products across regions. The only situation where (2.23) implies an investment rule that equates the marginal products across sector is where *both* first period incomes *and* TFP are equal across regions. In this special case, public capital should be equal across regions. Furthermore, because $W_P = W_R = W$, then (2.22a) gives us $\lambda = 1/W$. This implies, using (2.22b) and (2.22c), that the marginal product of public investment equals the international opportunity cost of funds. The assumptions of this special case essentially take us back to the representative agent model.

2.9 Fiscal Federalism

Fiscal federalism relates to the economics of the public sector when policies are conducted by different levels of government, i.e. national as well as regional governments, such as state and local governments. Here we study fiscal federalism by extending our analysis of the regional allocation of public capital to the situation where both national and regional governments invest.

Begin by noting that, in principle, our analysis of national governments from Sects. 2.1, 2.2, and 2.3 applies equally as well to regional governments. In particular, if the regional households, or the regional government, can borrow and lend in international credit markets, then regional investment would be efficient. The national government could also invest public capital in the region, but this would not affect the efficient level of investment. Regional governments would simply reduce their funding for investment one-for-one with the national government's investment. This would free up income, equal in value to the national governments investment, for the regional government and its households to use as they wish. Thus, national investment in a region would be equivalent to income transfers to the region. Furthermore, the income transfers would be used to finance consumption and saving in financial assets. None of the newly available income would be used for public investment.

If the national government is to have a role in determining regional investment in public capital, it must be when the regional households and governments are unable to borrow and lend in international markets. For this reason, we study the national government's allocation of public capital when regional governments and their households are credit constrained.

Tax Financing of Regional Investment

Let's start with the situation where the national government is also unable to borrow internationally. In this case, the government can still impact outcomes by redistributing income across regions in a way that raises aggregate welfare.

We first need to establish how the regional government sets its policy, taking the national policy as given. The regional government chooses a first period tax that is used to finance a local public capital investment, denoted by g_2^l, a perfect substitute for the public capital that is provided by the national government, as before, denoted by g_2. The consumption of households in the region is given by

$$c_1 = (1 - \tau_1)y_1 - g_2^l \tag{2.24a}$$

$$c_2 = y_2 = A\left(g_2^l + g_2\right)^\mu, \tag{2.24b}$$

where τ_1 is the national income tax rate.

Taking the national policy as given, the regional government chooses g_2^l to maximize the representative household's utility, $\ln c_1 + \beta \ln c_2$, subject to (2.24a, 2.24b). The resulting optimality conditions can be used to solve for regional government investment and household consumption,

$$g_2^l = \frac{\beta\mu}{1+\beta\mu}(1-\tau_1)y_1 - \frac{1}{1+\beta\mu}g_2 \tag{2.25a}$$

$$c_1 = \frac{(1-\tau_1)y_1 + g_2}{1+\beta\mu} \tag{2.25b}$$

$$c_2 = A\left(\frac{\beta\mu}{1+\beta\mu}[(1-\tau_1)y_1 + g_2]\right)^\mu. \tag{2.25c}$$

There is an important feature of these solutions. Regional households are treating g_2 as a source of disposable income; note how $(1 - \tau_1)y_1$ and g_2 appear together in (2.25b) and (2.25c). This is because of two assumptions. First, we are assuming that locally and nationally provided public capital are perfect substitutes. Second, we assume that the nationally provided public capital is not so large as to drive local public capital to zero. These two assumptions imply that national investment works like a cash transfer because a dollar of national investment will free up a dollar of local funds previously used to finance local investment. As with household income generally, the funds freed by national investment are partly consumed, as in (2.25b), and partly invested in local capital, as in (2.25c). This is why (2.25a) says that the reduction in g_2^l is not one-for-one with the rise in g_2. Despite the fact that national investment is equivalent to a cash transfer, it will raise total investment in the region to some extent.

Now let's turn to national policy. A household's maximum welfare, in either region, is found by substituting (2.25b) and (2.25c) back into the utility function to get the indirect utility or value function

$$V(\tau_1, g_2) = E + (1 + \beta\mu) \ln[(1 - \tau_1)y_1 + g_2] \tag{2.26}$$

where E is an expression involving terms that are independent of policy. Note, in particular, that the local TFP associated with public capital does not affect the marginal value of investment by the national government. This is because while a higher TFP *raises* the marginal return on investment it also *lowers* the marginal value of additional income. Under our assumption about preferences, these two effects exactly cancel. Thus, efficiency considerations related to the level of TFP and the return to investment do not enter to the government's decision making.

The national government chooses τ_1, g_{2P}, and g_{2R} to maximize the sum of household value functions,

$$N_P V_P(\tau_1, g_{2P}) + N_R V_R(\tau_1, g_{2R}), \tag{2.27}$$

subject to the government budget constraint, (2.17). The first order conditions from the national government's problem can be used to derive the following allocation rule

$$y_{1R} - \frac{N_P}{N_R}(g_{2P} - \tau_1 y_{1P}) = y_{1P} + (g_{2P} - \tau_1 y_{1P}). \tag{2.28}$$

In the absence of efficiency considerations, for the reasons stated above, the allocation rule requires an equalization of disposable income across regions.

Think of R as the rich region and P as the poor region, in the sense that $y_{1P} < y_{1R}$. To equalize disposable income, fiscal policy must create a net transfer to the household of the poor region, $(g_{2P} - \tau_1 y_{1P}) > 0$. The rich household's burden in making the transfer is $\frac{N_P}{N_R}(g_{2P} - \tau_1 y_{1P})$.

In general, there is an unintended consequence of the income transfer on investment efficiency and total output that depends on the relative size of the returns to investment in each region, $\mu A_R (g_{2R}^l)^{\mu - 1}$ and $\mu A_P (g_{2P}^l)^{\mu - 1}$. The fact that the poor region has lower income and therefore lower levels of local investment, means it is quite possible that its marginal return on investment is higher. In this case the optimal policy would not only equalize disposable income, but would also raise the economy's total output in period 2. This is an example of where the usual trade-off between equity and efficiency goals does not exist.

The effect of national policy on the investment in the poor region becomes stronger if local investment is so low that national investment drives local investment to zero. Notice from (2.25a), that there is a sufficiently large value for g_{2P} that would make g_{2P}^{l} zero. Any national investment beyond this value for g_{2P} would increase investment in the poor region one-for-one. Thus, if the goal is to raise investment and *future output*, there is a strong case for the national government focusing public investment on the poor region. However, given the social welfare function in (2.27), the best policy to raise *utility* in the poor region would be to use income transfers rather than in-kind transfers of public capital. Remember, when households are credit-constrained, both consumption and investment are too low. With income transfers, the household could optimally divide the transfers across consumption and investment, according to their time preference. This is an example of the policy tension between in-kind and cash transfers.

Bond financing of Regional Investment

Now suppose the national government can borrow on international credit markets and uses bond financing for national public investment. In period 1, government bonds, $b_2 \equiv B_2/N$, are issued to fund investment in the two regions,

$$N_P g_{2P} + N_R g_{2R} = b_2 N, \tag{2.29}$$

where $N \equiv N_p + N_R$.

In period 2, taxes must be raised to repay the debt and interest,

$$b_2 N(1 + r^*) = \tau_2(N_P y_{2P} + N_R y_{2R}). \tag{2.30}$$

The household budget constraints are then

$$c_1 = y_1 - g_2^l \tag{2.31a}$$

$$c_2 = (1 - \tau_2)y_2 = (1 - \tau_2)A\left(g_2^l + g_2\right)^{\mu}. \tag{2.31b}$$

As before, we begin by deriving local government policy to get

$$g_2^l = \frac{\beta\mu}{1 + \beta\mu} y_1 - \frac{1}{1 + \beta\mu} g_2 \tag{2.32a}$$

$$c_1 = \frac{y_1 + g_2}{1 + \beta\mu} \tag{2.32b}$$

$$c_2 = (1 - \tau_2)A\left(\frac{\beta\mu}{1 + \beta\mu}[y_1 + g_2]\right)^{\mu}. \tag{2.32c}$$

Using (2.32a, 2.32b, 2.32c), the value function for a household is now,

$$V(\tau_2, g_2) = E + (1 + \beta\mu)\ln[y_1 + g_2] + \beta \ln(1 - \tau_2).$$

Given (2.29), (2.30), and the local government response function given by (2.32a), the national government chooses τ_2, g_{2P}, and g_{2R} to maximize $N_P V_P(\tau_2, g_{2P}) + N_R V_R(\tau_2, g_{2R})$. Using the optimality conditions for the national government's problem, we derive the following equations that determine the allocation of investment.

$$\frac{\mu(1-\tau_2)\bar{y}_2}{g_{2P}^l + g_{2P}} + \frac{\mu\tau_2 y_{2P}}{y_{1P} + g_{2P}} = 1 + r^* \tag{2.33a}$$

$$\frac{\mu(1-\tau_2)\bar{y}_2}{g_{2R}^l + g_{2R}} + \frac{\mu\tau_2 y_{2R}}{y_{1R} + g_{2R}} = 1 + r^*, \tag{2.33b}$$

where $\bar{y}_2 \equiv (N_P y_{2P} + N_R y_{2R})/N$, the average income in period 2. The allocation rule is found by combining (2.33a) and (2.33b). The allocation rule is now more complicated because of the second expression found on the left-hand-side of (2.33a) and (2.33b). These *tax terms* bring in a particular efficiency consideration. They give the value of the marginal tax revenue captured by the national government due to the marginal return on public capital investment in the region. No such effect was present under first period tax financing because the first period tax base is exogenous.

To begin the interpretation of allocation rule associated with (2.33a, 2.33b), suppose the tax terms are zero. Then (2.33a, 2.33b) tells us that total investment should be equalized across regions, $g_{2P}^l + g_{2P} = g_{2R}^l + g_{2R} \equiv g$. This also would imply that $\bar{y}_2 = \bar{A}(g)^\mu$, where $\bar{A} \equiv (N_P A_P + N_R A_R)/N$, the average TFP across regions. Finally, the common investment in each sector would be privately efficient on average because the after-tax rate of return to investment would equal the opportunity cost of funds, $\mu(1-\tau_2)\bar{y}_2/g = 1 + r^*$.

Now re-introduce the tax terms. Suppose we continue to keep total investment in each region equal. From (2.32a), this would also mean that $y_{1P} + g_{2P} = y_{1R} + g_{2R}$ because $g_2^l + g_2 = \frac{\beta\mu}{1+\beta\mu}(y_1 + g_2)$ in each sector. However, the left-hand-sides of (2.33a) and (2.33b) would only be equal if second period income is equalized across sectors. This can only be true if $A_P = A_R$. Differences in TFP across sectors now create a reason to deviate from equalizing investment across regions. The presence of the tax terms mean, if the rich region has superior TFP, then total investment there must be greater there than in the poor region. The intuition for this result is that the national government collects more tax revenue by deviating from the equalization of total investment across regions and investing more in the rich region. The need to collect taxes in the future to finance debt financing creates an added incentive for the government to invest in the high TFP region.

2.10 A Note on Migration

An important extension to Sects. 2.9 and 2.10 is to allow for population migration from one region to another. For example, if economic opportunities are greater in region R than in region P, because of superior production technologies and greater local public capital provision, then households from poor regions would tend to move to rich regions.

We do observe long-term migration flows from poor to rich regions, but the pace of the migration is typically slow.[3] Urban areas tend to be richer than rural areas in developing countries. Nevertheless, history shows that it takes decades for the rural–urban migration in developing economies to be completed (even in the absence of explicit government policies that restrict migration). Evidence suggests that migration is quite costly for households in poor regions. The costs are, in part, due to incomplete markets for land and insurance that bind households to rural areas in order to protect land claims and to receive informal insurance from local social networks. Moving to the city can also be costly due to cultural and language differences, as well as incomplete social security and social safety net arrangements for new migrants. Due to the gradual and incomplete nature of internal migration across regions, it might be a reasonable approximation in the short-run to assume no migration as we have done.

However, policy with a longer term perspective must account for migration flows from poorer to richer areas. An important consideration is that migration from poor to rich areas is in the national interest of a developing economy. Workers are more productive in the rich regions because of the fundamentals that made the region rich to begin with—superior technologies or a more concentrated population that creates a larger sharing effect from public capital (see Sect. 2.6). Movement of workers away from poor regions will tend to raise national productivity and welfare, as well as equalize living standards across regions. In this sense, the national government should encourage the natural migration flow by "favoring" the rich region with its public capital allocation. When conditions in the poor region are desperate, the migration flow can become too rapid, causing a crowding of public services in rich regions. For this reason, investment in the poor region cannot be ignored. The optimal policy is a mix of public investment across regions, but one that favors the rich region on efficiency grounds (Das et al. 2018, Chap. 10; Mourmouras and Rangazas 2013).

The inclusion of migration can reverse the logic of our analysis in Sects. 2.8 and 2.9. The logic without migration says that it is in the national interest to favor the poor region because the value of nationally funded investment is higher there due to low levels of local investment. However, one way of making the poor-region households better off is to encourage migration to the richer regions by favoring

[3]See Das et al. (2018 Chaps. 7, 8, 9, and 10) for a complete discussion of the economics of internal migration across regions and sectors.

rich regions with national policy. The difference in policy recommendations is based on the precise source of differences in the return to investment in public capital.

The argument for favoring rich regions in the presence of migration predominately applies to *developing* countries. In developing countries, it is much more likely for the absence of land and insurance markets to bind workers to backward regions that have both inferior technologies and a smaller sharing effect due to less concentrated populations. In this situation $A_R > A_P$ and workers should be encourage to migrate to richer urban areas.

In *developed* countries, with complete markets and modern technologies found in all regions, the logic for favoring rich areas has much less force. Regional differences in developed economies are more likely due to under-investment in local public capital, particularly public education, in poor areas. The national government can raise national welfare by redistributing investment, or income transfers, to the poor regions of *developed countries* as indicated in Sects 2.8 and 2.9.

2.11 A Dynamic Generational Model

In this section we alter the interpretation of the investment model in a manner that will allow a more complete dynamic analysis that stretches beyond two periods. As suggested earlier, we can think of each period as representing a generation. The current generation has to choose how much to consume and how much to invest in the productivity of the next generation. For this set-up to make sense, parents must have some concern about the economic welfare of their children. Some aspect of children's economic situation must then enter the utility function of the parent. One could continue to assume the world ends after two periods, now representing two generations, but we will instead extend the future out indefinitely and allow for a truly dynamic analysis.

We take this interpretation not only to build a bridge from a simple investment model to a more complete growth model, but also to make a particular point. A major concern, addressed in some detail in Chap. 5, is that the saving and investment shares of total income are declining in the U.S. and other developed countries (Dobrescu et al. 2012; Kotlikoff 2015). As discussed in Chap. 5, one explanation for this trend is that policies have become increasingly biased toward current older generations at the expense of younger and unborn generations. This policy bias can be explained by the formation of interest groups that trade political support for government transfer payments and subsidies. In various ways, the expansion in transfers to current older generations reduces saving and investment in the future.

While politics plays an important role in explaining the decline in saving and investment shares, we also want to point out that such a decline can occur for more fundamental economic reasons. In particular, even in a world where the current generation has concern for the future generations, investment shares can fall over time in the absence of politics.

The Growth Model

Let's build a generational model from the basic elements of the closed economy, investment model discussed in Sect. 2.2. Assume that the government taxes the current generation to finance public investment that raises the productivity of the next generation. To create a generational model, we also need to change the interpretation of household preferences. We assume that the current generation gains utility from the future productivity of their children. The form of the utility function is basically the same as in earlier sections

$$U_t = \ln c_t + \beta \ln y_{t+1}, \tag{2.34}$$

but now lifetime utility is a function of parent's consumption and the adult income of their children.

The consumption of generation-t is determined by the budget constraint,

$$c_t = y_t - \tau_t y_t = y_t - g_{t+1}, \tag{2.35}$$

where the second equality comes from the assumption that the government taxes the current generation to finance investments in the future generation. Substituting (2.35) into (2.34), defines the objective function that the government maximizes when choosing its public investment. The solution for public investment from the government's maximization problem, can be used to derive the following *transition equation* for public capital,

$$g_{t+1} = \frac{\beta\mu}{1 + \beta\mu} A g_t^{\mu}. \tag{2.36}$$

First, notice how similar (2.36) is to the optimal choice of g_2 from the two-period investment model in Sect. 2.2. As before, the tax rate on current income to finance public investment is $\beta\mu/(1 + \beta\mu)$, which is also the economy's *public investment rate* out of current income. Now, however, current income is explicitly linked to past investment in *every* period, $y_t = A g_t^{\mu}$.

The basic logic for the investment rule is also essentially the same as before. The added element in (2.36) is that it makes a connection between public capital *over time*. Equation (2.36) is called a *transition equation*, in mathematics a *difference equation*, because it describes *changes* in public capital from period to period. Given some initial value for public capital, (2.36) determines the public capital in the next period. The new value of public capital then becomes the initial value, from the perspective of the next period, determining yet another value in the dynamic sequence.

The dynamic path for government capital given by (2.36) can be traced using Fig. 2.1, with g_t plotted on the horizontal axis and g_{t+1} plotted on the vertical axis. Imagine that the economy begins in period 1 with $g_t = g_1$. To find out what the capital stock will be in period 2, move vertically up to the plot of the transition equation to find g_2. In period 2, g_2 will now be the initial capital stock. To see this, move horizontally from the transition equation to the 45-degree line and then back

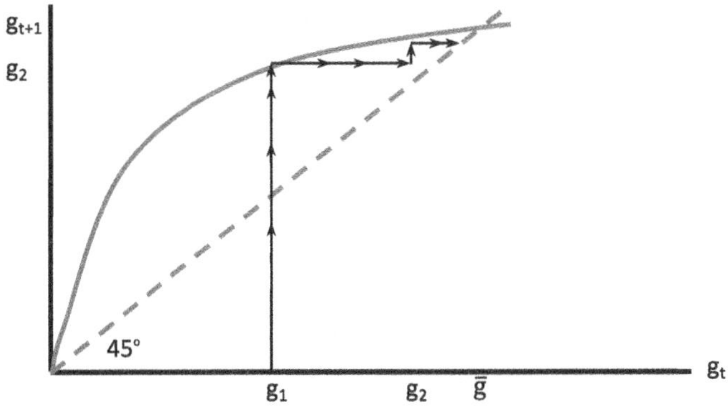

Fig. 2.1 The transition equation for government capital

down vertically to the horizontal axis. The process then repeats itself until one reaches $g_t = \overline{g}$, where the transition equation crosses the 45-degree line. At this point, the capital stock remains constant from period to period and the economy is said to have reached a *steady state* equilibrium.[4] An algebraic solution for the steady state is found by setting $g_{t+1} = g_t = \overline{g}$ in (2.36) and then solving the equation for $\overline{g} = \left(\frac{\beta\mu A}{1+\beta\mu}\right)^{\frac{1}{1-\mu}}$.

The Investment Share

In (2.36), the *fraction* of current output and income that is invested is a constant, also equal to the income tax rate. The *investment share* in the model is constant as the economy grows. To examine how investment shares may change over the course of development, we need to leave the simple log preferences in favor of a more general and flexible class of preferences represented by a *constant elasticity of substitution* (CES) utility function.

With a CES utility function it remains true that a generation-t household derives satisfaction from its own lifetime consumption, c_t, and the future lifetime income of its child, y_{t+1}. However, the CES utility function in c_t and y_{t+1} takes the form

$$U_t = \frac{\left(c_t^{1-1/\sigma} - 1\right) + \beta\left(y_{t+1}^{1-1/\sigma} - 1\right)}{(1 - 1/\sigma)}. \tag{2.37}$$

This utility function has the standard property that the marginal utility of each of its arguments is positive but diminishing. The two parameters of the function are, the now familiar, pure time discount factor (β) and a new parameter, the *intertemporal elasticity of substitution* ($\infty > \sigma > 0$). The intertemporal elasticity of substitution is a measure of the willingness to substitute current consumption for future income when the relative price of future income falls, but this won't be made clear for a while.

[4]The economy never literally reaches the steady state, although it will get arbitrarily close.

Subtracting 1 from each argument is done for a purely technical reason. It allows the logarithmic utility function, $U_t = \ln c_t + \beta \ln y_{t+1}$, to appear as a special case when $\sigma = 1$ (see the Technical Appendix and Problem 23).

Using the more general CES utility function changes the solution for optimal investment. The new solution for public investment can be used to derive the following *transition equation* for public capital,

$$g_{t+1}\left(\Gamma + g_{t+1}^{(\sigma-1)(1-\mu)}\right) = \Gamma y_t = \Gamma A g_t^{\mu}, \tag{2.38}$$

where $\Gamma \equiv (\beta\mu)^{\sigma} A^{\sigma-1}$. Just as in the more special case given by (2.36), the transition equation in (2.38) can be sketched with g_t plotted on the horizontal axis and g_{t+1} plotted on the vertical axis. The plot will look like that in Fig. 2.1. The transition equation is increasing and concave, with a unique steady state where the transition equation crosses the 45-degree line.

In general, there is not a closed form solution for g_{t+1} in (2.38). In addition to the case where $\sigma = 1$, there is a second special case where we can get an explicit closed-form solution for the transition equation. If $\sigma = (2 - \mu)/(1 - \mu) > 2$, then (2.38) becomes a quadratic equation in g_{t+1}.[5] Solving for the only positive root gives us the following transition equation,

$$g_{t+1} = \frac{\Gamma}{2}\left(\sqrt{1 + \frac{4Ag_t^{\mu}}{\Gamma}} - 1\right). \tag{2.39}$$

As mentioned, the sketch of (2.39) is of the same concave shape as displayed in Fig. 2.1. However, (2.39) has a different implication for the investment share than (2.36). Using (2.38) we can derive an expression for the economy's investment share ($\widetilde{g}_t$). Divide both sides of (2.38) by y_t and by the expression $\Gamma + g_{t+1}^{(\sigma-1)(1-\mu)}$ to find

$$\widetilde{g}_t \equiv \frac{g_{t+1}}{y_t} = \frac{\Gamma}{\left(\Gamma + g_{t+1}^{(\sigma-1)(1-\mu)}\right)}. \tag{2.40}$$

If $\sigma = 1$, the investment share is a constant throughout the entire dynamic path to the steady state. However, if $\sigma > 1$, as in (2.39), the investment share declines as government capital grows. Thus, the economy experiences an increasing consumption rate for the current generation over time—as we observe in the data for the U.S. and other developed countries.

The intuition as to why the behavior of $\widetilde{g}_t$ depends crucially on σ is as follows. As government capital grows, the return to government capital investment falls (because $\mu < 1$). The decrease in the return lowers the opportunity cost of consumption by the current generation, which creates an incentive for the current generation to consume more and investment less (a *substitution effect*). However, the lower return also

[5]Note that $\sigma = (2 - \mu)/(1 - \mu)$ is greater than 2 because it is increasing in μ, so its smallest value is when $\mu = 0$.

lowers the income of the future generation, for any level of investment, and creates an incentive for the current generation to compensate by investing more (an *income effect*). Which of these two effects dominates depends on how willingly the current generation trades off current consumption for future income. The willingness to carry out intertemporal substitution of consumption at different dates is governed by σ. The higher is σ, the more likely that the substitution effect dominates and $\widetilde{g}_t$ falls over time in a growing economy. The critical value is $\sigma = 1$, where the two effects exactly offset and $\widetilde{g}_t$ remains constant.[6]

2.12 Principles for Tax Collection

There is a large literature that extends the principles of good governance by looking at the issue of how best to collect taxes—a topic we have ignored. A fundamental issue in this literature is to find ways of minimizing the *distortionary* effects of taxation on economic behavior that lead to *excess burdens*. Excess burdens are costs that go beyond the loss in income associated with paying taxes. The excess burden of taxation includes the efficiency losses in welfare and output that occur when behaviors, such as work effort and saving choices, are altered by taxation. They also include the resource costs of collecting taxes we used in the model of Sect. 2.5. A complete discussion of *optimal taxation*, that examines the balance between equity and efficiency objectives, goes well beyond the scope of this book. A good serious introduction to this topic is Salanie (2011).

One defense of ignoring the distortionary effects of taxation is to argue that the behavior we focus on is not strongly responsive to taxation. There is certainly empirical evidence that suggests this may be a reasonable approximation with respect to labor supply and saving behavior—where the evidence for significant distortionary effects is quite inconclusive. Tax issues are raised again in the policy discussion of Chap. 8, when we discuss a variety of considerations that should influence the design of a tax system such as simplicity and transparency, sin taxes and corrective taxes that have *beneficial* effects on behavior, and tax evasion.

2.13 Conclusion

Our final section of the chapter gives a quick summary of the lessons from the two-period model of government investment. These lessons for government policy are based solely on economic logic in the absence of politics that may be in conflict with the national interest. The lessons provide a useful benchmark for comparison as we extend the analysis to include rent seeking and corruption in Chap. 3.

[6]There are other models where the investment rate in the future generation can decline as a fraction of family resources even in the case where $\sigma = 1$. See Mourmouras and Rangazas (2007) and Das et al. (2018, Chap. 4).

Basic Principles

1. Government capital is valued primarily because it raises future production and lifetime resources. When households lack access to a complete market for financial assets, government capital also provides a physical asset that can smooth consumption over time.
2. Government capital can be modeled as a private input to the production function, but if the capital is a pure or impure public good, then the associated TFP will be an increasing function of population size.
3. Public debt is equivalent to first period taxes and provides no net wealth to the nation when either (i) the economy is closed and domestic household must purchase the debt or (ii) the economy is open and private households can borrow and lend internationally. However, in an open economy where private households have no access to international credit markets, but the country's government does, public debt can be a welfare improving fiscal tool.
4. One implication of (2.3) is that financial liberalization across borders may be a reason for the rise in public debt over the last quarter of the 20th century. International lenders have been willing to purchase the public debt of developed countries, such as the United States, at low interest rates. Receiving funds from foreign sources lowers interest rates and reduces the cost of borrowing. A variety of trends in the developed world are creating incentives to allow government borrowing with little public resistance.
5. A caveat concerning (2.3) is that while debt can raise the welfare of current generations, it may nevertheless lower the welfare of future generations (even when current generations possess intergenerational altruism). Given that most societies have laws prohibiting individual households from leaving debt for their children to repay, fiscal policies should tend to exhibit the same discipline.
6. When public debt is sufficiently high, multiple financial market equilibria are possible that depend on household expectations. This creates the potential of a "crisis of confidence," where expectations dramatically switch from no-public debt default to default, causing a dramatic rise in interest rates.

Regional Issues and Inequality

1. Unless there are policy tools that can completely eliminate regional income differences, without creating distortions, the optimal allocation of government capital across regions will be determined by equity, as well as efficiency, considerations. Both equity and efficiency considerations will *tend to*, but *not necessarily*, bias government capital allocation toward poor regions. The tendency will be strongest in developed economies where TFP is similar across regions.
2. When regional governments (i) can provide the same capital inputs as national governments and (ii) have access to credit markets, there is no role for the national government in public investment. However, in *developed* economies, where regional governments are credit-constrained, the national government should

generally redistribute wealth from rich to persistently poor regions by biasing public capital allocation in that direction.
3. In *developing* economies that are undergoing major structural transformations, with gradual migration from poor to rich regions based on a superior technology in the rich region, the government should bias its funding support toward richer regions to help speed migration flows. However, poorer regions cannot be completely ignored or migration to the rich regions could become too rapid.

Identifying the Influence of Politics
While the social welfare function we assume gives equal weight to all households, the analysis does not imply equal treatment of all households under national fiscal policy. Both efficiency and equity considerations can cause different regions to be treated differently by national policy. This means that one must take care in interpreting differential treatment as stemming from a bias based on differences in political influence across regions.

A similar warning applies to explaining the observed decline in investment in future generations by current generations or the increased use of intergenerational redistribution. Political explanations based on interest groups and selfish concerns of politicians who seek re-election may not be necessary. Economic fundamentals can cause the current generation to choose a declining investment rate in future generations, or vote for the accumulation of public debt, even when they value the economic welfare of their children and there are no special-interest political motivations present.

2.14 Exercises

Questions

Questions 1–4 should be answered using the model of Sect. 2.1.

1. What is the household's lifetime budget constraint? When does it represent a meaningful constraint on household choices?
2. Which of the following are *choice variables* of the household?
   (a) y_1
   (b) y_2
   (c) c_1
   (d) c_2
   (e) a_2
   (f) r_2
3. If a household is able to borrow and lend, how does an increase in each of the following affect c_1, c_2, and a_2? Repeat the exercise when households are not able to borrow and lend.
   (a) y_1
   (b) y_2
   (c) r_2

   (d) β
4. What does it mean to be credit-constrained? What factors increase the likelihood of being credit-constrained?
5. Suppose there is a closed economy made up of identical households. Why can there be no private credit market where borrowing and lending actually takes place? What considerations determine the optimal government investment in this setting, assuming the government finances investment exclusively using first period taxes?
6. In a closed economy made up of identical households, explain the meaning of the following statements.
   (a) government debt provides no net wealth to private households
   (b) financing government investment with taxes is equivalent to using bond finance
   What considerations, not captured by the representative agent model of Sect. 2.2, might cause households to prefer bond financing over tax financing in period 1?
7. Answer the following questions, assuming there is a small-open economy where private households can borrow and lend in a perfectly competitive international credit market.
   (a) Do households prefer that the government finances public capital investment using taxes or bonds?
   (b) What is the optimal rule for government investment? What is the economic intuition behind the rule?
   (c) What is the optimal consumption path for private households? How does the international interest rate and the household's time discount factor affect the optimal path?
8. Answer the following questions, assuming there is a small-open economy where the government can borrow and lend in a perfectly competitive international credit market, but private households cannot.
   (a) Do households prefer that the government finances public capital investment using taxes or bonds?
   (b) What is the optimal rule for government investment? What is the economic intuition behind the rule?
   (c) What is the optimal consumption path for private households? How does the international interest rate and the household's time discount factor affect the optimal path?
9. When does government borrowing have the potential to raise household welfare?
10. Explain the *generational* interpretation of the two-period model. Why are private credit constraints more likely under the generational interpretation than under the *life-cycle* interpretation?
11. Under the *generational* interpretation of the two-period model, explain how the preferred investment of a "rich" household (one that makes positive bequests) is affected by the following events.
   (a) an increase in A
   (b) a decrease in r^*

(c) a proportional increase in A and p

12. Repeat *Question* 11 for the case of a "poor" household (one that is bequest-constrained).
13. Use the *generational* interpretation of the two-period model to explain why the majority of households may be in favor of government debt-financing since the 1970s.
14. *Education Policy I*
    We have seen that "poor," bequest-constrained, households prefer an inefficiently low level of educational investments. This suggests that a paternalistic government might be justified in intervening to force more education spending. Discuss the politics (by identifying winners and losers) and the overall effect on the economy of the following government interventions.
    (a) a government mandate that all children receive efficient levels of education investment (similar to an expansion of the compulsory schooling laws to insist on high school or even college graduation)
    (b) an increase in taxation across *all* households to expand education spending in "poor" communities
    (c) an increase in taxes on "rich" households to expand education spending in poor communities
15. *Education Policy II*
    In the question above, we see that there would be significant opposition to mandating higher education in "poor" communities or using economy wide taxes to finance more education spending in "poor" communities. Consider another policy approach. Suppose the government subsidizes the cost of education by lowering the price of education, i.e. by reducing the consumer price of education below the true resource cost (p), say $p' < p$. Furthermore, assume the government borrows to finance the subsidy. What is the overall effect on future output and the welfare of period 2 households?
16. *Education Policy III*
    Can students loans help overcome the bequest-constraint in a manner similar to government debt?
17. What is a public good? What is an impure public good? In Eq. (2.1) is government capital assumed to be a private or a public good? How can one generalize (2.1) to allow for the possibility that government capital is a pure or impure public good?
18. State and explain intuitively the *utilitarian social welfare function* given in (2.21).
19. Why does the rule for allocating government investment across two different regions not necessarily imply equal investment levels across regions?
20. When does regional investment by a national government have an impact on the welfare of households living under a regional government?
21. When does regional investment by a national government raise total government investment in the region? Does regional TFP affect the level of national investment in the region? Explain

22. Suppose that regional governments cannot borrow in international markets. Intuitively explain the regional investment rules of a national government with and without the ability to borrow in international markets.
23. How does internal population migration across regions affect the national government's regional investment strategy?
24. Explain the concept of a transition equation using Fig. 2.1 from 2.11.
25. Use the model from Sect. 2.11 to explain what happens to the following variables as the economy approaches the steady state from below.
    (a) government investment
    (b) worker productivity
    (c) consumption
    (d) return to government investment
    (e) growth rate of worker productivity
26. Use a transition equation to explain why a government might find it optimal to lower the rate of investment as an economy develops.
27. In the Calvo model of Sect. 2.5, why would a benevolent government default on its obligation to repay bondholders? What limits the extent of the default?
28. How can there be two possible financial market equilibria in the Calvo model? What determines which equilibrium actually occurs?
29. In the Calvo model, how does each of the following factors influence the government's decision to default on its public debt obligations?
    (a) amount of debt issued in period 1
    (b) direct cost of tax collection
    (c) impact of default on tax evasion
    (d) household expectations

Problems

Use the model of Sect. 2.1 to answer *Problems* 1–4.

1. Sketch the lifetime budget constraint with c_1 on the horizontal axis and c_2 on the vertical axis. Label each of the following features of the sketch.
    (a) x-intercept
    (b) y-intercept
    (c) slope
2. Suppose a household can borrow and lend in a perfectly competitive credit market. Assume $\beta = 0.2$ and $r_2 = 0.10$. Compute the value for the optimal choice of a_2 when
    (a) $y_1 = 10$ and $y_2 = 0$
    (b) $y_1 = 0$ and $y_2 = 10$
    (c) $y_1 = 10$ and $y_2 = 10$
3. Assume $\beta = 0.2$, $r_2 = 0.10$, and $y_1 = y_2 = 10$. Compute U when the household cannot borrow and lend and when it can. In which case is U higher? Explain.
4. Repeat Problem 1 for a household that is free to lend but not to borrow, i.e., the choice of a_2 must satisfy the non-negativity constraint, $a_2 \geq 0$.
5. Set up and solve the optimization problem needed to derive (2.4a, 2.4b).

6. If $\mu = 1/3$, $\beta = 0.5$, $A = 6$, and $y_1 = 8$, compute the values of the following variables in the closed economy model of government investment in Sect. 2.2.
   (a) g_2
   (b) τ_1
   (c) c_1
   (d) c_2
   (e) U
7. Use the closed economy model of government investment to sketch the lifetime consumption possibilities of the representative household. Begin by noting that consumption in the two periods can be related by the following equation, $c_2 = A(y_1 - c_1)^\mu$. Continue by placing current consumption on the horizontal-axis and future consumption on the vertical-axis. What is the horizontal intercept? The vertical intercept? If you know calculus, what is the slope? If you don't know calculus, you should plot a few points by using the parameter assumptions from *Problem* 6.
8. Derive the lifetime budget constraint, given by (2.9), of a household trading in a perfectly competitive open economy.
9. Derive (2.10, 2.11) and (2.13a, 2.13b). Be sure to state the underlying assumptions made in the two different cases.
10. Place g_2 on the horizontal axis and then separately plot the left-hand-side and the right-hand-side of (2.10) as functions of g_2. Use the diagram to locate the productively efficient level of g_2. Use the figure to determine what happens to the productively efficient g_2 when there is an increase in A. Repeat for an increase in r^*.
11. Derive the adjusted first order conditions that replace (2.13a, 2.13b) when the government faces a binding borrowing constraint. Let s^g denote government saving that could finance loans to the international credit market, if positive. The borrowing constraint means $s^g \geq 0$.
12. *Preferences in Two Dimensions*
    A common way of sketching preferences involves the concept of an *indifference curve*. In our model an indifference curve associated with the household's lifetime utility function gives *all combinations* of c_1 and c_2 that generate a *given level* of satisfaction. For a given level of satisfaction or utility, $\overline{U}$, the combinations of c_1 and c_2 that are used to construct an indifference curve are defined by the condition, $\overline{U} = \ln c_1 + \beta \ln c_2 = \ln\left(c_1 c_2^\beta\right)$. Recall that the natural exponential function is the inverse of the natural log function, $e^{\ln x} = x$. If we take the exponential of both sides of the condition defining an indifference curve, we get $e^{\overline{U}} = c_1 c_2^\beta$ or $c_1 = e^{\overline{U}}/c_2^\beta$. The last expression gives the value of c_1 that generates the same satisfaction level $\overline{U}$ for different possible values of c_2, forming consumption pairs that the household is indifferent to because they all yield the same utility.
    Assume $\beta = 0.50$ and consider 5 different values of c_2: 1, 4, 9, 16, 25.
    (a) If $\overline{U} = 1$, what are the values for c_1 that correspond to each of the 5 values of c_2?

(b) If $\overline{U} = 2$, what are the values for c_1 that correspond to each of the 5 values of c_2?
(c) Use the five c_1–c_2 pairs to sketch the two indifference curves from (a) and (b) on a diagram with c_1 on the horizontal axis and c_2 on the vertical axis.
(d) Why are the indifference curves downward sloping? Give an economic interpretation of the slope. Why do you think the slope becomes flatter as you move along the horizontal axis by considering higher values of c_1?

Sketches of indifference curves are important in the analysis of *Problems* 13 and 14.

13. *Credit-Constrained Investment in Pictures* (An extension of *Problem* 7)
Let's sketch the solution associated with maximizing (2.3), assuming it is consistent with a closed credit-constrained economy (i.e. g_2 is less than the efficient level). Our sketch will display the consumption possibilities over the two periods. Plot c_1 on the horizontal axis and c_2 on the vertical axis. Note that the consumption possibility frontier (*CPF*) is generated by choosing different values of g_2 that serve to generate different values for c_1 and c_2.
(a) State the maximum possible values of c_1 and c_2 in general form (variables not numbers). Label them on the sketch.
(b) Show $dc_2/dc_1 = -\mu A g_2^{\mu-1}$ and $d^2c_2/dc_1^2 = \mu(\mu-1)Ag_2^{\mu-2}$. Use these results to determine the shape of the sketch. If you don't know calculus, use your numerical plot from Problem 7 to guide the sketch of the curve's shape.
(c) Display the consumption solution associated with (2.4a, 2.4b) by depicting a tangency between the *CPF* and the indifference curve corresponding to the maximum value of (2.3). Note: the indifference curve generated by the log utility function will have the standard convex shape, so just assume that to be true. What is the value of c_1 at the point of tangency? The value of c_2? Again in general form.

14. *A Portrait of Investment with International Borrowing*
Following up on *Problem* 13, suppose now that the country can borrow abroad at the international interest rate, r^*.
(a) Label the credit-constrained solution from *Problem* 13 on the *CPF* with the letter *A*. Is the absolute value of the slope of the *CPF* at *A* greater than, equal to, or less than $1 + r^*$?
(b) Starting at point *A*, in which direction must you move along the *CPF* to reach the point associated with a productively efficient level of investment? Go in this direction, choose a point associated with efficient investment, and label the point *B*.
(c) We know that *B* does *not* represent an optimal consumption combination. Why?
(d) The economy can achieve the efficient investment level and at the same time increase the value of c_1 by borrowing internationally. Draw a tangent line with the slope $-(1 + r^*)$ through the point *B*. The economy can increase c_1 by moving along this tangent line, away from point *B* in the south easterly

direction. Sketch a tangency between an indifference curve and this tangent line at a point labelled C, where c_1 is greater than its value at point A but c_2 is less than its value at point A.

(e) If the model represents a single generation that lives for two periods, is the representative household better off at C than at A? What welfare implication do you draw if we interpret the model as representing two distinct generations that live for one period?

15. Explicitly incorporate a price, p, for investment goods and derive (2.4a′)
16. If $\mu = 1/3, p = 1, A = 6$, and $r^* = 0.10$, find the productively efficient value of g_2. What is the preferred value of g_2 for a bequest-constrained household, if $\beta = 0.5$ and $y_1 = 8$? Suppose that rich and poor households live in distinct communities and the level of g_2 is determined at the community level to match the household preferences. If rich households plan to make positive bequests and poor households are bequest-constrained, what is the resulting income gap for the children from rich and poor communities when they become adult workers?
17. Repeat *Problem* 16 in the following two new scenarios: (a) the value of A rises to 12 and (b) the value of A rises to 12 *and* the value of p rises to 1.5.
18. Suppose that, in contrast to the assumption of *Problem* 16, the value of g_2 is determined at the national level and is common across all households. Further assume that when g_2 is determined at the national level that it reflects the preferences of rich households and is productively efficient. Using the parameter assumptions of *Problem* 16, compute the utility of a poor household when g_2 is determined at the community level and when it is determined at the national level. Assume the common level of g_2 is paid for by a first-period tax that is also equal for all households. Explain your results.
19. We know that "rich" households will invest the efficient amount in education, call it g_2^{eff}, creating an efficient level of future income, y_2^{eff}. Think of the efficient investment as a reduction in their current income. The remaining income that can be used for consumption and bequest saving is $y_1 - g_2^{eff}$.
    (a) Reinterpret the saving theory from Sect. 2.1 to write down an expression for the optimal bequest saving of a "rich" household in an open economy.
    (b) Suppose the government reduces a "rich" household's income by one unit and transfers it to a poor household. Write an expression for how much bequest saving would fall and how much education investment would rise (assume $p = 1$). Use these expressions to write an expression for the *total* change in future (period 2) income, summing changes across both households, caused by the transfer.
    (c) Why does your final expression in (b) NOT guarantee that total future income will rise? What could the government do to be sure that future income rises?
20. Suppose the governments in two locations (countries, cities, regions) provide the same value of g_2. The two locations, A and B, are otherwise identical except

the population size in location B is twice that of location A. If $\xi = \mu = 1/3$, what is the ratio of y_2 in location B relative to location A?

21. Use the Lagrangian method for constrained optimization to derive (2.22a, 2.22b, 2.22c) and (2.23).
22. In the model used to allocate public capital across regions or communities, assume $N_P = N_R$. From (2.17), we then have $g_{2P} + g_{2R} = \tau_1 y_1$, where $y_1 \equiv (y_{1P} + y_{2R})/2$. This implies $g_{2R} = \tau_1 y_1 - g_{2P}$. Now sketch both sides of the equality in (2.23) as functions ofg_{2P}, i.e. plot the left and right hand sides of (2.23) with g_{2P} on the horizontal axis. Locate the welfare maximizing value of g_{2P} using the diagram. Use the diagram to show what happens to the optimal g_{2P} if each of the following increase:
    (a) A_R,
    (b) A_P,
    (c) r^*.

    What happens if y_{1P} decreases and y_{1R} increases, leaving the value of y_1 unchanged?
23. Derive the behavior of a local regional government operating in a federal system as given by (2.25a, 2.25b, 2.25c) and (2.26).
24. In a federal system, total investment in a particular region is $g_2^l + g_2$. Use (2.25a) to derive an equation for total investment in the region. If $\beta = 0.5$ and $\mu = 0.4$, compute the effect of an increase in g_2 on total investment, i.e. compute $d(g_2^l + g_2)/dg_2$. For what values of g_2 is your computation valid? What is the value of $d(g_2^l + g_2)/dg_2$ when g_2 become sufficiently high to render your first computation invalid?
25. Show that the general *CES* utility function, given in (2.34), includes the log utility function as a special case.
26. Maximize (2.34) with respect to g_2 and derive the transition equation given in (2.36).
27. Use (2.38) to derive the two explicit transition equation given by (2.36) and (2.39). Use calculus to show that these two transition equations are concave functions.
28. Let's study the dynamic transition of the model using (2.36) from Sect. 2.11, while making the following parameter assumptions:$A = 1$ and $\beta = \mu = 0.5$.
    (a) What is the steady state value for g?
    (b) Trace the transition path out for five periods if the initial public capital stock is 0.01. Do the same if the initial public capital stock is 0.08.
29. Let's study the dynamic transition of the model using (2.39) from Sect. 2.11, while making the following parameter assumptions: $\sigma = 3, A = 1$ and $\beta = \mu = 0.5$. Compared to *Problem* 28, we are now focusing on a situation where σ differs from 1; in this case, a value greater than 1.
    (a) What is the value for Γ?
    (b) Trace the transition path out for five periods if the initial public capital stock is 0.01.

(c) Based on your transition path calculations, what would be a good approximate value for the study state g?

30. Use (2.40) to compute the investment rates associated with the transition path you calculated in *Problem* 29.

The next three *Problems* are based on the explicit Calvo model presented in the chapter Appendix.

31. In the Calvo model derive the optimal value of each of the following when the default rate is positive.
    (a) $\tau_2 y_2$
    (b) x
    (c) θ
32. *Equilibrium interest and default rates in the Calvo model*
    (a) Show that $\frac{x^*}{b_2 R} \geq 1$ if there is a default equilibrium.
    (b) In the default-equilibrium, show $\frac{x^*}{b_2 R_2} = (1 - \xi)\frac{R}{R_b} + \xi < 1$ and confirm that $\theta^* = 1 - \frac{R}{R_b}$ by using the formula for the optimal θ. If $R = 1.05$ and the default rate is 0.20, what is the equilibrium interest rate when households expect default?
33. Carefully show that household consumption is lower in the equilibrium with default than in the equilibrium without default.

Appendix

Calvo Model of Public Debt Default

Three new elements are needed to model public debt default in the two-period model. First, households need an alternative way of saving so that they are not *forced* to save by purchasing government bonds. We assume there is a private *physical* asset, k, such as a house or a small business. Unlike the private financial assets from the main text (a_2), all households can simultaneously accumulate physical assets as an alternative to saving using government bonds. The private asset is acquired in period 1 and yields Rk units of income in period 2, so $R > 1$ can be thought of as the return on the private asset.

In equilibrium, if households are willing to hold public debt, debt must pay a return equal to the private asset. Let R_b be the stated return to public debt, b_2, at the time it is purchased in period 1 and θ be the portion of the return to public debt that is *not* repaid in period 2. The return to holding public debt is then $(1 - \theta)R_b$ and if both the private asset and government debt are held by households then

$$(1 - \theta)R_b = R. \quad \text{(asset market equilibrium condition)}$$

Note for households to buy government bonds in the first period, there cannot be an equilibrium with the expectation of *complete* default, $\theta = 1$. It is also important to note that we are assuming households correctly anticipate the government's second period behavior, but when the government actually makes its default choice, the government *does not* take into account how it affects household expectations and the value of R_b at which it can issue debt to the market (households in the bond market are smarter than the government, at least in the Calvo model).

Second, there must be a reason that the government may want to avoid raising taxes in the second period to repay debt, i.e. a reason that default may be a good idea. There are various ways that taxation can create a loss of resources to the economy as the government attempts to obtain revenue from private households, collectively known as the "excess burden" of taxation. Here we simply assume that taxes are costly to collect.

Households generate second period income from work, y_2, and from the two assets discussed above. Government tax revenue comes from taxing labor income only, $\tau_2 y_2$. The government must expend resources to collect taxes and the cost of collection increases with the level of taxation. The per household resource cost of raising taxes is $\frac{\chi}{2}(\tau_2 y_2)^2$, where $\chi > 0$. As tax rates rise, households increase their effort to evade taxation, raising the cost to the government of tracking income and enforcing tax laws. Revenue collected from taxation, net of collection costs, is $x \equiv \tau_2 y_2 - \frac{\chi}{2}(\tau_2 y_2)^2$.

Third, there must also be a reason *not* to default. We assume that if a government defaults on its obligation to repay debt, it becomes harder to collect taxes at *any* given tax rate. Chap. 1 presents evidence that tax evasion increases when the public is dissatisfied with its government's performance. Let $\xi\theta b_2 R_b$ be the extra per-household resource cost to the government when it chooses to default on some of its public debt obligation. Assume $0 < \xi < 1$, so the government losses a portion of the revenue that it gains in defaulting because collecting taxes becomes more costly as tax evasion intensifies. Thus, the total resource cost of collecting taxes when the government defaults is $\frac{\chi}{2}(\tau_2 y_2)^2 + \xi\theta b_2 R_b$.

The government budget constraint for period 2, per household, is now defined as

$$x = (1 - \theta)b_2 R_b + \xi\theta b_2 R_b, \quad \text{(government budget constraint)}$$

net taxes are used to repay a portion of the government's debt and to cover the extra resource cost associated with defaulting. The household's second period budget constraint, determining how second period taxation and public debt default affects consumption and welfare, is

$$c_2 = y_2 + Rk + [(1 - \theta)b_2 R_b - \tau_2 y_2]. \quad \text{(household budget constraint)}$$

Second period consumption is financed by work, private asset ownership, and the government debt that is repaid, net of the taxes owed. The squared-brackets contain the variables that the government can affect in period 2, θ and τ_2 (remember the government acts as if the bonds and interest rate at which bonds are sold to the market in period 1 are given, i.e. $b_2 R_b$ is predetermined before its period 2 behavior).

The government is benevolent, as we have assumed throughout this chapter. In the second period, the government seeks to maximize household welfare by maximizing the expression in the square brackets, the return to government debt net of second period taxes paid.

If $\theta = 0$, we have the no-default outcome. In this case, from the government budget constraint, we have $x = b_2R_b = b_2R$, and the expression in the bracket is $-\frac{\chi}{2}(\tau_2y_2)^2$. Here, the government minimizes taxes so that x just covers the cost of debt repayment. However, the no-default case might not be chosen by the government because, if the predetermined value of b_2R_b is high, the required taxes and tax collection costs needed to repay *all* of its debt obligations may be too high. We will see that the no-default case is only optimal if b_2R_b is sufficiently low—i.e. low interest rates and low debt obligations from past borrowing.

If b_2R_b is sufficiently large, partial default is preferred, i.e. $\theta > 0$. To find the exact extent of government default, we first solve the second period government budget constraint for θ in terms of other fiscal variables,

$$\theta = \frac{b_2R_b - x}{(1-\xi)b_2R_b}.$$

Substituting the solution for θ into the expression surrounded by square-brackets in the household budget constraint gives us

$$(1-\theta)b_2R_b - \tau_2y_2 = \frac{\xi\tau_2y_2 - \frac{\chi}{2}(\tau_2y_2)^2}{1-\xi} - \frac{\xi}{1-\xi}b_2R_b.$$

Given its past borrowing decisions, the benevolent government needs is choose τ_2 to make the expression above as large as possible and thereby maximize the value of c_2. Again assuming that the government takes b_2R_b as given, the problem boils down to maximizing

$$\xi\tau_2y_2 - \frac{\chi}{2}(\tau_2y_2)^2.$$

In words, the government is choosing second period taxes to balance the *benefit* of higher taxes, associated with reducing the default rate and the associated cost (the value $\xi\tau_2y_2$ captures how much the extra costs of tax collection *fall* as the default rate falls with higher taxes), against the direct *cost* of raising taxes (a higher value of $\frac{\chi}{2}(\tau_2y_2)^2$).

The optimal solution is

$$\tau_2y_2 = \frac{\xi}{\chi}, \quad x^* \equiv \frac{\xi}{\chi}\left(1-\frac{\xi}{2}\right), \quad \theta^* = \frac{b_2R_b - x^*}{(1-\xi)b_2R_b} = \frac{1}{1-\xi}\left(1-\frac{x^*}{b_2R_b}\right).$$

The higher the added cost of defaulting (ξ), relative to the direct cost of raising taxes (χ), the higher the optimal tax rate. Note that once b_2R_b is sufficiently high to make θ^* positive, higher values of b_2R_b will raise the optimal default rate towards 1 (remember it can't be 1 in equilibrium or no household would hold government debt).

We have two possible equilibrium outcomes depending on household expectations. If households expect no default, then they will be content to hold government bonds at the relatively low interest rate, $R_b = R$. If at $R_b = R$, $\theta^* \leq 0$, the government will not default, consistent with household expectations. If households expect default, then they may still hold government debt but only at a relatively higher interest rate on bonds that compensates them for second period default, $R_b = \frac{R}{1-\theta^*}$. This presents a second possible equilibrium with a higher interest rate and $\theta^* > 0$.

Note, the more the government borrows in period 1, the greater is the chance that θ^* is positive, for any given interest rate. Thus, first period government borrowing creates the possibility of future default and the possibility of multiple equilibrium outcomes that hinge on household expectations. Which of the two equilibria prevails cannot be predicted. Furthermore, a change in household expectations, specifically a "crisis of confidence," could quickly shift the equilibrium from one with low interest rates to one with high interest rates, forcing the government to default.

Another important feature of this model can be seen by using the asset market equilibrium condition to write the second period government budget constraint as

$$x = (1 - \theta)b_2R_b + \xi\theta b_2R_b = b_2R + \xi b_2[R_b - R] \geq b_2R.$$

Net taxes must be higher in the case with default, which means that households have lower consumption and are worse off in the default-high interest rate equilibrium because of the added resource cost of tax collection. This inferior outcome can occur because the government fails to fully recognize that defaulting is anticipated by the market, raising both R_b and taxes.

References

Alesina, A., and Passalacqua, A., 2015, "The Political Economy of Government Debt," in Taylor, J., and Uhlig, H. (editors), *Handbook of Macroeconomics*, Amsterdam: North Holland.

Ashauer, D., 1989, "Is Public Expenditure Productive?" *Journal of Monetary Economics*, 23, 177-200.

______, 2000, "Public Capital and Economic Growth: Issues of Quantity, Finance, and Efficiency," *Economic Development and Cultural Change*, 48, 391-406.

Autor, D., 2014, "Skills, Education, and the Rise in Earnings Inequality of the other 99 Percent," *Science*, 344, 843-851.

Azzimonti, M., de Francisco, E., and Quadrini, V., 2014, "Financial Globalization and the Raising of Public Debt," *American Economic Review*, 104, 2267-2302.

Barro, R., 1974, "Are Government Bonds Net Wealth?," *Journal of Political Economy*, 82(7), 1095-1118.

Bayraktar, N., 2019, "Effectiveness of Public Investment on Growth in Sub-Saharan Africa," *Eurasian Economic Review*, 9, 421-458.

Bennett, W., and Wilezol, D., 2013, *Is College Worth It*?, Nashville Tennesse: Thomas Nelson.

Bivens, J., 2012, "Public Investment: The Next "New Thing" for Powering Economic Growth," *EPI Briefing Paper #338*, Washington: Economic Policy Institute

Calvo, G., 1988, "Servicing the Public Debt: The Role of Expectations," *American Economic Review*, 78, 647-661.

Chakraborty, S., and Dabla-Norris, E., 2011, "The Quality of Public Investment," *B.E. Journal; of Macroeconomics*, 11, 1-29.
Das, S., Mourmouras, A., Rangazas, P., 2018, *Economic Growth and Development: A Dynamic Dual Economy Approach*, Cham: Springer.
D'Erasmo, P., and Mendoza, E., 2015, "Distributional Incentives in an Equilibirum Model of Domestic Sovereign Debt Default," *Journal of the European Economic Association*, (forthcoming).
Dobrescu, L., Kotlikoff, L., and Motta, A., 2012. "Why aren't Developed Countries Saving?," *European Economic Review*, 56(6), 1261-1275.
Drazen, A., 1978, "Government Debt, Human Capital, and Bequests in a Life-Cycle Model," *Journal of Political Economy*, 86, 505-516.
Glomm, G. and Ravikumar, B., 1997, "Productive Government Expenditures and Long-run Growth," *Journal of Economic Dynamics and Control, 21*, 183-204.
Gordan, R., 2016, *The Rise and Fall of American Growth: The U.S. Standard of Living since the Civil War*, Princeton: Princeton University Press.
Hallerberg, M., Strauch, R., and von Hagen, J., 2009, *Fiscal Governance in Europe*, Cambridge: Cambridge University Press.
Heckman, J. and Krueger, A., 2005, *Inequality in America: What Role for Human Capital Policies*, Cambridge, Mass: MIT Press
Kotlikoff, L., 2003, *Generational Policy*, Cambridge, Mass: MIT Press.
Kotlikoff, L., 2015, "America's Fiscal Insolvency and its Generational Consequences," Testimony to the Senate Budget Committee, February 25, 2015.
Lord, W., and Rangazas, P., 1993, "Altruism, Deficit Policies, and the Wealth of Future Generations," *Economic Inquiry*, 31, 609-630.:
Manuelli R. and Seshadri A., 2014, "Human Capital and the Wealth of Nations," *American Economic Review*, 104 (9):2736–2762.
Mourmouras A and Rangazas, P., 2007, "Foreign Aid Policies and the Sources of Poverty: A Quantitative Framework, " *IMF Staff Papers*, 54, 59-90.
Mourmouras, A. Rangazas, P., 2013, "Efficient Urban Bias," *Journal of Economic Geography* 13 (3), 451–471.
Murray, C., 2008, *Real Education*, New York: Three Rivers Press.
Obstfeld, M., and Rogoff, K., 1996, *Foundations of International Macroeconomics*, Cambridge, Mass: MIT Press.
OECD, 2015, *The Future of Productivity*, Paris: OECD Publishing.
Rangazas, P. 2000, "Schooling and Economic Growth: A King-Rebelo Eexperiment with Human Capital," *Journal of Monetary Economics*, 46, 397-416.
Rangazas, P., 2002, "The Quanity and Quality of Schooling and U.S. Labor Productivity Growth (1870-2000)," Review of Economic Dynamics, 54, 932-964.
Saez, E., and Stantcheva S., 2016, "Generalized Social Marginal Welfare Weights for Optimal Tax Theory," *American Economic Review*, 106, 24-45.
Salanie, B., 2011, *The Economics of Taxation*, Cambridge, Mass: MIT Press.
Steurle, C., 2014, *Dead Men Ruling*, New York: Century Foundation Press.

3 Politics and Corruption in the Two-Period Model

Chapter 2 tells us that benevolent national policy makers, motivated to maximize aggregate welfare, make efficient investments in public capital and favor poor regions in the allocation of that capital in order to increase economic growth and equalize regional income. In contrast to this optimistic view of government policy, the evidence from Chap. 1 indicates there are autocratic regimes that are far from benevolent. Many countries have failed to experience sustained modern growth and their living standards have diverged from, rather than converged to, those of rich countries. Empirical evidence indicates that income convergence across regions within a given country was characteristic of the twentieth century (Barro and Sala-i-Martin 1991, 1992). However, the rate of convergence was quite slow over the first 75 years of the century. Over the last 40 years, incomes have ceased to converge and may have actually diverged. (Arcalean et al. 2012; Ganong and Shoag 2013; Sacchi and Salotti 2011). The situation has been complicated by a slowdown in aggregate productivity growth that has reduced private and government resources that could be used to deal with persistent inequality.

These observations from the second half of the 20th century dramatically contradict the theory of policy making from Chap. 2. Policy makers have generally failed to make the investments that lay the foundation for robust growth—such as schooling, health services, communication infrastructure, and roads—especially in poorer countries and regions. Real-world policy is evidently not completely driven by equity and efficiency considerations that maximize aggregate welfare.

In addition to the disappointing record on growth and income convergence, we have seen government debt and intergenerational redistribution associated with transfers to retired households grow unchecked since the last quarter of the twentieth century. These policy trends threaten economic growth in richer countries. Chapter 2 identified economic fundamentals that can cause an increase in consumption by current generations at the expense of future generations. However, it is unclear that these fundamentals can fully explain the extent and the timing of the intergenerational redistribution associated with government fiscal policy around the developed world.

M. Ivanyna et al., *The Macroeconomics of Corruption*, Springer Texts in Business and Economics, https://doi.org/10.1007/978-3-030-67557-8_3

In the attempt to better explain economic policies, this chapter introduces selfish motives on the part of policy makers. While they may have one eye on the national interest, as in Chap. 2, the other eye is fixed on individual gains such as being re-elected or increasing personal income. Our main purpose is to highlight the ways that politics and selfish motives distort fiscal policy and lower national welfare.

We begin by explicitly modeling policymakers who may be selfish and short-sighted in designing tax and investment policies. We also consider legal political transactions where support for re-election is traded for special treatment under the nation's fiscal policy. This approach is based on Grossman and Helpman (1994) who first formalized the idea that special interest groups can exert political pressure via contributions to electoral campaigns, creating equilibria in which general public welfare is reduced relative to the first best optimum. As in Chap. 2, our application focuses on the possible distortions to the level of taxation and the allocation of government investment across regions of the country.

We present the argument of Tabellini and Alesina (1990) that political polarization creates a bias toward deficit financing. There is a belief that political parties have become more strongly aligned with specific groups, causing them to become more divided about the composition of government spending. For example, there is debate over whether spending should be focused on transfers to the poor and lower-middle class or on "tax expenditures" and write-offs that reduce the tax burdens of corporations in the hopes of encouraging private investment. Polarization means that policies will be quite different depending on which party is in power. In a highly polarized environment, uncertainty over the winner of future elections lowers the expected cost to the current ruling party of accumulating debt obligations that serve to constrain future levels of discretionary spending aimed at specific groups.

We examine how rent seeking by interest groups affects investment levels. The fundamental problem of interest group politics, known as the *common pool problem*, is that the revenue used to finance policies targeted to *specific groups* comes from a *general* tax fund. As a result each group pushing for government benefits only pays a relatively small fraction of the tax expense. To study the effects of interest group politics, we use a set-up similar to Tornell and Lane (1999), where there are groups of households—such as provincial governments and local communities, unions, industry and consumer advocates— that have political connections with central government officials. Using their connections, the groups compete for public transfers and subsidies. Within this framework, we can think about how the expansion in the number of interest groups, a natural occurrence in maturing democracies (Olson 1982), affects the level of taxation and government investment.

Finally, we turn to illegal political corruption. Public officials are modelled as having selfish interests that extend beyond seeking political support and re-election. Public officials have control over the funds budgeted for public investment and we assume they can seize some of the funds for themselves. The public officials then consider the fiscal policy that is in their interest when they have this opportunity to divert public funds for personal use. We show that larger government budgets increase the rate of corruption, if unchecked by strengthened institutional safeguards. Furthermore, the theft of funds is only the direct effect of corruption. Corruption also influences the design of fiscal policy itself. The opportunity for corruption creates incentives for policy makers to raise taxes and expand budgets in a way that undermines economic growth.

3.1 Fiscal Policy with Policy Makers

Let's revisit the analysis of Sects. 2.1 and 2.2, but this time with explicit policy makers. As before there are N private households that live for two periods. The private household/producer has exogenous first period income y_1. Second period income and output is positively affected by public capital per person in the economy, $y_2 = Ag_2^{\mu}$. Unlike Chap. 2, we now explicitly acknowledge that there are also $N^g = \varepsilon N$ identical public officials that determine fiscal policy, where ε is an exogenous parameter determining the size of public sector employment relative to the private workforce. In addition to income taxes (τ_1, τ_2) and public capital purchases (g_2), the officials choose their own salaries and perquisites, which we refer to as government consumption (c_1^g, c_2^g). Note that while the government officials do not produce goods, they do consume the public services (roads, public utilities, etc.) and dilute the public capital for private producers. So, we define public capital per household as $g_2 \equiv G_2/(1 + \varepsilon)N$.

The government budget constraints, expressed per unit of private producers/households, for the two periods are

$$\tau_1 y_1 = \varepsilon c_1^g + (1 + \varepsilon) g_2 \tag{3.1a}$$

$$\tau_2 y_2 = \varepsilon c_2^g. \tag{3.1b}$$

The budget constraints of private households are as they were in Chap. 2,

$$c_1 = (1 - \tau_1) y_1 \tag{3.2a}$$

$$c_2 = (1 - \tau_2) y_2. \tag{3.2b}$$

Subject to (3.1) and (3.2), the public officials choose $\tau_1, \tau_2, g_2, c_1^g, c_2^g$ to maximize their preferences

$$\ln c_1^g + \beta^g \ln c_2^g + \gamma(\ln c_1 + \beta \ln c_2). \tag{3.3}$$

The preferences include the utility received directly from the official's own consumption and the altruistic satisfaction received indirectly from the utility of the private households that they serve. The altruistic parameter γ measures the relative weight officials place on the welfare of private citizens. We have also allowed the public official's time discount parameter to possibly differ from those of private households. For example, if public officials are both selfish and more short-sighted than private households, then we have $\gamma < 1$ and $\beta^g < \beta$.

Using the four budget constraints to eliminate τ_1, τ_2, c_1, c_2, the officials problem can be reduced to the maximizing (3.3) by choosing g_2, c_1^g, c_2^g. The three resulting optimal conditions are

$$\frac{1}{c_1^g} = \frac{\gamma\varepsilon}{y_1 - (1+\varepsilon)g_2 - \varepsilon c_1^g} \tag{3.4a}$$

$$\frac{\beta^g}{c_2^g} = \frac{\beta\gamma\varepsilon}{Ag_2^\mu - \varepsilon c_2^g} \tag{3.4b}$$

$$\frac{\beta\mu Ag_2^{\mu-1}}{Ag_2^\mu - \varepsilon c_2^g} = \frac{1+\varepsilon}{y_1 - (1+\varepsilon)g_2 - \varepsilon c_1^g} \tag{3.4c}$$

Equations (3.4a) and (3.4b) equate the marginal benefit of public sector consumption to the marginal cost of forgone private sector consumption weighed by the public official's altruism toward private households. Equation (3.4c) equates the marginal benefit of greater second period consumption resulting from greater future period public capital to the marginal cost of forgone first period consumption needed to finance the investment.

Solving (3.4a), (3.4b), (3.4c) for the three government purchases gives us the following expression for government investment

$$g_2 = \left[\frac{\widetilde{\beta}\mu}{1+\widetilde{\beta}\mu}\right]\frac{y_1}{1+\varepsilon} \tag{3.5}$$

where $\widetilde{\beta} \equiv \beta\left[\frac{(\beta^g/\beta)+\gamma}{1+\gamma}\right]$. Note that if government officials are not selfish and have the same time preference as private households, then $\widetilde{\beta} = \beta$. If, in addition, fiscal policy can be determined without the need for hired public officials, $\varepsilon = 0$, then we get the same expression for g_2 found in Chap. 2 (see (Eq. 2.4a) from Chap. 2). The extensions in this chapter allow us to explain differences in g_2 across countries based on differences in the "quality" of government. Governments that are inefficiently large (high ε) and staffed with selfish and short-sighted officials (low γ and β^g) will have low levels of public capital and worker productivity.

The quality of government for the purpose of generating growth does not necessarily match up with the strength of a country's democratic institutions. One can imagine the following connection of the model's parameters with different hypothetical political regimes.

	Democracy	Pro-Consumption Autocracy	Pro-Growth Autocracy
ε	Low	High	Low
γ	High	Low	Low
β^g	Equal to β	Less than β	Greater than β

A democracy may do a good job of minimizing patronage jobs and representing household preferences, but those preferences may not generate high growth if households are impatient. The "Growth Miracle" countries of the second half of the twentieth century were famously dictatorships that imposed high taxes and public investment rates on poor private households in order to generate high growth. Dictatorships, however, are risky for growth because the dictators may ignore the population's preferences for the purpose of generating high consumption for themselves and their supporters, who often comprise a bloated government bureaucracy.

As might be anticipated from our Chap. 2 analysis, if the government can borrow in international credit market, one can show that public capital investment will satisfy an adjusted efficiency condition (see *Problem* 3)

$$\frac{\mu A g_2^{\mu-1}}{1+\varepsilon} = 1 + r^*. \tag{3.6}$$

The "adjustment" is that the cost or price of providing public capital to a country's producers depends on the relative size of the public sector that also uses the country's infrastructure. So, relatively large governments continue to result in lower public capital per worker and lower worker productivity when borrowing is possible. However, the preferences of public officials no longer matter. If government officials are selfish and short-sighted officials (low γ and β^g), it no longer reduces public investment. Policy makers choose the (adjusted) efficient level of investment to maximize the country's resources and then use taxes and debt to generate the desired *level* and *timing* of government consumption. This is an added benefit to having access to international capital markets that did not exist under the assumptions of Chap. 2.

3.2 The Politics of Investment Allocation

In Sect. 2.8 of Chap. 2, a benevolent national government chooses the allocation on public capital investment across two regions of the country. There we saw, in the special case where all exogenous characteristics of the regions are identical, that the national government will allocate public capital equally across regions in a manner that obtained productive efficiency; the marginal product of capital is equated to the international opportunity costs of funds. We assume this same special case here so that we can clearly see how politics distort the first-best outcome.

Start with the fiscal policy-maker from Chap. 2, who can be thought of as the chairman for the committee charged with the budgeting and allocation of public investment projects. Suppose now that this public official is interested in being re-elected to his current position as a representative from region R. As in Chap. 2, assume the basic sentiment of the official is to serve the national interest. Following this sentiment, and being even-handed as the chairmen of the investment committee, gives the official some reasonable probability of being re-elected.

However, the probability of being re-elected increases if he shows favoritism to region R. A local politician from the region, in return for seeing more investment projects come his way, would campaign on behalf of the national representative to boost his chances of re-election. We assume that the campaigning involves the use of the local politician's time, c_R. The utility value to the national official, associated with the increased probability of being re-elected, is an increasing function of campaign time, $\psi N_R \ln(1 + c_R)$. The satisfaction of representing a region is proportional to the region's population size, a measure of its importance. The parameter $\psi > 0$ confounds both the satisfaction associated with re-election and the effectiveness of local campaigning in raising the probability of re-election.

Campaigning is a costly activity. The forgone leisure time used in campaigning is valued by the local official. The utility loss from forgone leisure is given by $\xi \ln(1 + c_R)$, where $\xi > 0$ is a preference parameter measuring the value of forgone leisure time.

The preferred policy of the national official, in the absence of campaigning by the local official from his region, is to choose the efficient investment allocation that is in the national interest. The common efficient level of investment satisfies the condition $\mu A g_2^{\mu-1} = 1 + r^*$, which implies, $g_2 = (\mu A/(1 + r^*))^{\frac{1}{1-\mu}}$. The efficient level of investment maximizes household wealth, net of the required first period tax. The maximum wealth associated with the *efficient* investment policy is, $\widehat{W} = y_1 + \frac{A g_2^{\mu}}{1+r*} - g_2 = y_1 + \left(\frac{A g_2^{\mu-1}}{1+r*} - 1\right) g_2 = y_1 + \left(\frac{1}{\mu} - 1\right) g_2$. The maximum household utility is then, $\widehat{V} = (1 + \beta) \ln \widehat{W}$, and aggregate welfare is $N\widehat{V}$.

The general expression for aggregate welfare, under *any arbitrary* fiscal policy, is $N_P V_P + N_R V_R$, where

$$V_P = (1 + \beta) \ln\left((1 - \tau_1) y_1 + \frac{A(g_{2P})^{\mu}}{1 + r^*}\right)$$

and

$$V_R = (1 + \beta) \ln\left((1 - \tau_1) y_1 + \frac{A(g_{2R})^{\mu}}{1 + r^*}\right).$$

If policy is to deviate from the efficient one, the new policy must provide at least the same satisfaction to the national official as following the efficient investment plan that maximizes aggregate welfare. One could use a bargaining framework to determine how the gains from political trading are split, but this would add little additional insight. Instead, we simply assume that the national official must be indifferent to the proposed policy deals. For the national policy to favor region R, the local official's campaigning must generate sufficient value from the increased chance of re-election to compensate for the loss in aggregate welfare. This requirement can written as

$$\psi N_R \ln(1 + c_R) + N_P V_P + N_R V_R = N\widehat{V}. \tag{3.7}$$

Condition (3.7) implicitly defines the required local campaigning as a function of national fiscal policy,

$$\ln\left(1+c_R\right)=\left(1/\psi N_R\right)\left(N\widehat{V}-N_P V_P-N_R V_R\right). \tag{3.8}$$

The local official lobbies for the fiscal policy that maximizes the welfare of the R region household, taking into account the utility loss from the required campaigning and the national government budget constraint, $N_P g_{2P} + N_R g_{2R} = \tau_1(N_P y_{1P} + N_R y_{1R})$. The local official's objective function is $V_R - \xi \ln\left(1 + c_R\right)$. Substituting (3.8) into the objective function and ignoring terms the local official cannot influence, we get

$$\left(1+\frac{\xi}{\psi}\right)\ln\left((1-\tau_1)y_1+\frac{Ag_{2R}^{\mu}}{1+r^*}\right)+\frac{\xi}{\psi} \\ \times\frac{N_P}{N_R}\ln\left((1-\tau_1)y_1+\frac{A}{1+r^*}\left(\frac{\tau_1 y_1 N-g_{2R}N_R}{N_P}\right)^{\mu}\right). \tag{3.9}$$

The local official maximizes (3.9), which takes into account the required campaigning needed to obtain deviations in policy that favor region R, by choosing τ_1 and g_{2R}.

The first order condition for g_{2R} can be used to derive the following allocation rule for public capital,

$$\frac{W_R}{W_P}\left(\frac{g_{2R}}{g_{2P}}\right)^{1-\mu}=1+\frac{\psi}{\xi}>1. \tag{3.10}$$

If $g_{2P} = g_{2R}$, the left-hand-side of (3.10) is exactly one. For the ratio to exceed one, it must be the case that $g_{2R} > g_{2P}$. Politics and lobbying from the representative's region biases the allocation toward region R. The size of bias is increasing in the value of being re-elected and the effectiveness of campaigning (ψ), and is decreasing in the value of forgone leisure time spent campaigning (ξ).

Using (3.10) and the first order condition for τ_1, the conclusion can be sharpened to show

$$\frac{\mu A}{1+r^*}g_{2P}^{\mu-1}>1>\frac{\mu A}{1+r^*}g_{2R}^{\mu-1}. \tag{3.11}$$

The investment in region P is inefficiently low and the investment in region R is inefficiently high. This outcome is expected if one thinks of tax revenue as given, but is not obvious here because tax revenue is endogenous. The government could raise taxes and have inefficiently high investment in both regions or lower taxes and have inefficiently low investment in both regions.

In the U.S., state representatives and senators work hard to position themselves on committees that can direct infrastructure projects back to their home districts. Some of the favorite committees include the Senate Military Construction Committee, Senate Defense Appropriation Committees, Senate Energy and Water Appropriations Committee, Transportation and Infrastructure Committee, and various committees that disperse funds for interstate highway construction. The public capital projects generated from these committees are not well-designed or coordinated by a coherent national policy. The projects do offer a political prize to those who serve on the committees. The committees consistently lobby for increased budgets, with the vast majority of spending going to states of the committee members (Grossman 1994; Cost 2015, Chap. 10).

Some claim that criticizing the misallocation of investment caused by the re-election motive is naïve and overly simplistic. It is argued that offering local projects, on a purely political basis, in exchange for votes is an essential part of the process of passing broader policies that are in the national interest (Evans 2004; Frisch and Kelly 2011). More colorfully put, "pork barrel politics greases the wheel" and gets things done. The premise is that the incentives for politicians to vote for legislation in the national interest are weak because the policy benefits are diluted across the general public rather than concentrated on their particular supporters and voters. From this perspective, efforts to expose and eliminate pork barrel projects are misplaced because trading these projects for important votes is a necessary feature of a well-functioning democracy.

We disagree with this line of argument. Not only is pork barrel politics inefficient, it also creates a moral hazard problem that could make it more costly to pass important legislation. With pork barrel politics, politicians are encouraged to strategically oppose legislation that they actually favor in the attempt to receive payment for their vote. Policies in the national interest should naturally attract a majority of favorable votes, without the need for pork barrel trading. Good policies that fail to receive majority support have likely not been sufficiently defended and marketed to politicians and voters. Chapter 8 discusses ways to improve support for policies that raise social welfare without the need to buy votes with inefficient investment projects.

The model can also be interpreted as representing a state (governor) or national (president) politician that is elected by households in both regions. One region may have the political influence and organization to be effective campaigners for the state or national politician, while the other region may not. Think of the R region as being made up of "rich" households and the P region, "poor" households. Households in the R region can use their campaign support to distort the investment budget in their favor. For example, richer households push for college subsidies, lowering the funds available for pre-school and vocational programs that may yield high returns for the children of poor households.

Election politics, and other types of lobbying and rent seeking, inflict costs on the nation's economy. To place greater weight on the benevolent policy considerations from Chap. 2, societies should search for political institutions that limit the degree to which political ambition and rent seeking distort fiscal policy. For example, one extreme possibility might be to turn fiscal policy over to professional bureaucrats led by an appointed finance minister, in the same way that countries have allowed monetary policy to be conducted by an independent central bank. Chapter 8 will discuss political reforms in depth.

3.3 Fiscal Federalism with Politics

This section uses the general framework developed in the previous section to analyze regional income convergence. The goal of the previous section was to show how politics can distort the fiscal policy of a benevolent policy maker who was interested in maximizing aggregate welfare. Here we examine the limits of national policy in assisting development in the poor region of a country when the central government is dominated by concerns for the rich region. In this situation the only way the poor region can exert influence on national policy is to support the incumbent administration against challengers in upcoming national elections. In this situation, politically motivated exchanges *could* raise aggregate welfare.

Our motivation is provided by the persistence of poor, backward regions in generally fast-growing middle- and high-income countries, as discussed in the Chapter's introduction. The absence of income convergence suggests that real world fiscal policy can differ dramatically from the Chap. 2 principle of reallocating capital and income toward poor regions. Extending the fiscal federalism model with political self-interest reveals some of the limits of national fiscal policy in promoting growth in poor regions and helps explain the disappointing convergence record.

We assume that the national government is fundamentally aligned with the more powerful rich region: a starting point that is consistent with the lack of income convergence. For the incumbent administration of the national government to shift attention to the poor region requires the delivery of votes in the next national election (in exchange for a larger allocation of public investment).

Corruption makes an appearance at the local level of government as one factor that limits development in the poor region. We define corruption as the diversion of funds for the personal use of regional officials connected to the investment projects. Tanzi (2000) has argued that institutional checks are stronger at the central government level and that corruption is more prominent at the regional/local level. While this idea remains controversial, it is important to understand the incentives and effects of national fiscal transfers when local corruption is a concern.

Extending the Fiscal Federalism Model

Chapter 2 established that if the regional households, or the regional government, can borrow and lend in international credit markets, then regional government investment would be efficient. In this situation, the national government could also invest public capital in the region, but this would not affect the efficient level of investment. Regional governments would simply reduce their funding for investment one-for-one with any increase in the national government's investment. This would free up income, equal in value to the national governments investment, for the regional government and its households to use as they wish. Thus, national investment in a region would be equivalent to income transfers to the region. Furthermore, the income transfers would be used to finance consumption and saving in private financial assets. None of the newly available income would be used for public investment. Neither aggregate economic growth nor future regional income inequality would be affected by national policy.

If the national government is to have a role in determining regional investment in public capital, it must be in the situation where the regional households and governments are unable to borrow and lend in international markets. For this reason, we study the national government's allocation of public capital when regional governments and their households are credit constrained.

We begin by developing a theory of the local official's behavior in the poor region. The objective function of the local official takes the form

$$\ln \left(u\left(g_{2P}^{l}+g_{2P}\right)\right)-\xi \ln \left(1+c_{p}\right)+\gamma V_{P}. \tag{3.12}$$

The local official has the opportunity and willingness to engage in corruption. The official values funds that are diverted from investment projects for personal consumption, whether the funds are collected from local households (g_{2P}^{l}) or the central government (g_{2P}). The fraction of funds, u, that are diverted for personal use is a choice variable.

As in the previous section, the second term of the objective function reflects the lost time and utility associated with campaigning. In this application, the campaigning is for re-election of the central government administration, or the nation's "president," who then exerts pressure on the budgeting and allocation of public capital.

The last term in the objective function is the satisfaction the local official receives from the utility of the local households, which includes the local officials themselves. This term captures the utility from income generated by legal means. We are assuming that the local officials do not value legal and illegal income equally; the two sources of income are not perfect substitutes because of the guilt or risk associated with illegal income flows and because of possible altruism toward local households.

The utility of the local private households is related to policy variables by computing the household's value function, defined as

$$\begin{aligned} V_{P}\left(u, g_{2P}^{l}; \tau_{1}, g_{2P}\right) = {} & \ln \left(\left(1-\tau_{1}\right) y_{1P}-g_{2P}^{l}\right) \\ & +\beta \ln \left[A_{P}\left(\left(1-u\right)\left(g_{2P}^{l}+g_{2P}\right)\right)^{\mu}\right]. \end{aligned} \tag{3.13}$$

The value function gives the maximum utility of a private household given the fiscal policy set at the local and national levels.

No Political Influence

Suppose $\psi=0$. Without an ability to influence national policy, the local official would choose u and g_{2P}^{l} to maximize (3.12) subject to (3.13), *taking the central government's fiscal policy as given*. When ψ is positive, the local official can influence national policy (g_{2P}) by offering campaign support (c_P). In this case, the calculation we are about to do can be thought of as an intermediate step in a sequential solution to the complete problem facing the local official. In other words, the choice of u and g_{2P}^{l} must satisfy optimal conditions of the same form even when g_{2P} andc_P are also chosen. The optimal choices of local corruption and total investment in the poor region are given by

$$(1-u)\left(g_{2P}^{l}+g_{2P}\right)=\frac{\beta\mu}{1+\beta\mu}\frac{\gamma\beta\mu}{1+\gamma\beta\mu}[(1-\tau_1)y_{1P}+g_{2P}] \tag{3.14a}$$

$$u=\frac{1}{1+\gamma\beta\mu}. \tag{3.14b}$$

Investment is a fraction of the resources that are available to the local region. The marginal rate of investment is relatively low in the poor region because of the "corruption tax," $u = 1/(1 + \gamma\beta\mu)$. The investment fraction is increasing in the relative weight placed on the utility of poor-region households. If γ is low, much of the funding available to the poor region will be diverted as illegal income for private consumption by the local officials and the effect on investment will be weak. Despite the possibly high returns on investment in the poor region, local corruption can cause investment to be low. Controlling corruption in the poor region is clearly important for development.

Under our assumptions, with no political influence coming out of the poor region, $g_{2P} = 0$. Region P is underdeveloped because of low initial income and saving, corruption, and neglect from an unsympathetic national government. In this setting one can give a positive spin to politics. The central government would ignore the poor region without the possibility of political trades. However, as will be demonstrated below, much of the funding pried from the national government in political deals is consumed by corrupt local officials.

Let's begin by taking a closer look at the situation without politics, where the poor region is ignored. With no assistance from the central government, investment in the poor region is

$$(1-u)g_{2P}^{l}=(1-u)\frac{\beta\mu}{1+\beta\mu}(1-\tau_1)y_{1P}.$$

If we assume that the more developed rich region has successfully ridded itself of corruption problems, investment there will be chosen to maximize the welfare of its representative citizen, taking as given the investment support from the central government. Formally, their officials choose local investment to maximize

$$\ln\left((1-\tau_1)y_{1R}-g_{2R}^{l}\right)+\beta\ln\left(A_R\left(g_{2R}^{l}+g_{2R}\right)^{\mu}\right),$$

yielding total investment in the rich region of

$$g_{2R}^{l}+g_{2R}+\frac{\beta\mu}{1+\beta\mu}((1-\tau_1)y_{1R}+g_{2R}).$$

Given that the central government is only supporting the rich region, all of the national income tax is going to finance g_{2R}, so that $g_{2R}=\tau_1\left(y_{1R}+\frac{N_P}{N_R}y_{1P}\right)$.

Substituting the central government budget constraint into the expression for optimal investment in the rich region and dividing that expression by local investment in the poor region we have the following investment ratio,

$$\frac{g_{2R}^l + g_{2R}}{(1-u)g_{2P}^l} = \frac{(y_{1R}/y_{1P}) + \tau_1(N_P/N_R)}{(1-u)(1-\tau_1)}.$$

The investment gap between regions is increasing in the initial difference in income, the national income tax, the corruption in the poor region, and the relative size of the population in the poor region. In the absence of politics, there are several reasons for the relatively low income and lack of convergence of the poor region.

Equilibrium with Political Influence

Now suppose that ψ is positive, the poor region's official has the ability to influence voting and the votes are important for the re-election of the central official. We assume that the poor region's official offers policy proposals that keep the central official indifferent about moving away from his preferred policy by compensating the central official with political support. The compensating political support can be determined by equating the utility of the central official under the preferred policy, with no political support from the poor region, to the utility of the central official under any arbitrary policy chosen by the poor region's official. Proceeding as in the previous section, the required political campaigning from the poor region in order to convince the central official to choose a g_{2R} that deviates from his preferred policy is

$$c_P = \left(\frac{(1-\tau_1)y_{1R} + g_{2R}^0}{(1-\tau_1)y_{1R} + g_{2R}}\right)^{\frac{1+\beta\mu}{\psi n_P}} - 1, \tag{3.15}$$

where g_{2R}^0 denotes the preferred policy choice of the central official and n_P is the relative population size of the poor region. Policies that are proposed with smaller investments made in the rich region require increased campaigning to deliver added political support from the poor region that adequately compensates the central official. The more effective the campaigning and the greater the relative population of the poor region (ψn_P), the less campaigning is needed to derive the required votes.

The poor region official now selects τ_1 and g_{2P}, as well as u and g_{2P}^l, to maximize (3.12) subject to (3.13), (3.15), and the national government budget constraint. The resulting political equilibrium is given by

$$u = \frac{1}{1+\gamma\beta\mu} \tag{3.16a}$$

$$(1-\tau_1)y_{1P} + g_{2P} = \frac{\gamma(1+\beta\mu)}{1+\gamma(1+\beta\mu) + \frac{\xi(1+\beta\mu)}{\psi n_P}} R_P \tag{3.16b}$$

$$
\begin{aligned}
(1-u)\left(g^{l}_{2P}+g_{2P}\right) &= \frac{\beta\mu}{1+\beta\mu}\frac{\gamma\beta\mu}{1+\gamma\beta\mu}[(1-\tau_1)y_{1P}+g_{2P}] \\
&= \frac{\beta\mu}{1+\beta\mu}\frac{\gamma\beta\mu}{1+\gamma\beta\mu}\frac{\gamma(1+\beta\mu)}{1+\gamma(1+\beta\mu)+\frac{\xi(1+\beta\mu)}{\psi n_P}}R_P, \qquad (3.16c)
\end{aligned}
$$

where $R_P \equiv y_{1P} + \frac{y_{1R}}{n_P}$ denotes the aggregate first period income of the economy per household in the poor region. The corruption tax is repeated in (3.16a). The difference between (3.16) and (3.14) is now the resources available to the poor region are a function of its political influence. With politics, the disposable income available to the poor region (3.16b) and the total investment in the poor region (3.16c) are now functions of the aggregate income of the economy.

The cost of political influence ($\xi/\psi n_P$) and the local official's altruism (γ) determine the share of aggregate resources flowing to the poor region and the portion that is ultimately invested. A lower cost of political influence raises the poor region's share. As before, the share to poor households naturally increases with the local official's altruism, or aversion toward illegal income. The investment share of the poor region's resources is increasing in $\beta\mu$. A greater weight placed on future generations and greater productivity of investment both raise investment.

Italy in the twentieth century gives a clear example of what the model is attempting to capture. Emmott (2012, Chap. 5) provides a description of Italy as a country with backward regions that have persistently failed to converge to rich regions. In 1951, GDP per capita in the southern regions of Italy was about half of that found in the rest of the country. After 50 years, the weak convergence of this poor region had only moved their relative GDP per capita to 58 percent at the end of the twentieth century. While most of national funding flows to the rich regions that dominate national politics, the southern regions have received some infrastructure funding from the national government. However, the regional political support for national politicians that was exchanged for these projects has been generated largely by corrupt local officials and criminal groups. Government spending in the South has been woefully ineffective at delivering productive services for the general population. Even when political support directs national funding toward poor regions it often does not raise welfare for the majority of households because of the corruption tax.

A Note on Decentralization

Let's now think about what it means for the government to be centralized or decentralized in this setting. The extent to which the government is centralized in our model is measured by the national tax rate, τ_1. The higher the value of τ_1, the greater the national government expenditures and the lower the local government expenditures. The composition of expenditures by level of government is a common measure of the degree of government centralization. However, the equilibrium of the model is not sensitive to the value of τ_1. Instead, the equilibrium is determined by aggregate resources, political influence, and altruism.

To make this point concrete, we can write net national expenditures sent to the poor region as

$$n_P(g_{2P} - \tau_1 y_{1P}) = \frac{[1 + \gamma(1 + \beta\mu)]y_{1R} - \frac{\xi(1+\beta\mu)}{\psi}y_{1P}}{1 + \gamma(1 + \beta\mu) + \frac{\xi(1+\beta\mu)}{\psi}}.$$

The net transfer is independent of the 'size' of the central government and is instead determined by (i) the difference in *before-tax* income across regions and (ii) the cost of providing political support to the central government. Suppose that τ_1 falls, perhaps associated with a 'trend toward decentralization.' The fall in the national tax implies a decline in *total* national expenditures, but the *net* expenditure remains the same. Thus, the central government has become more progressive. So, the central government is smaller but is more progressive and nothing changes.

This 'irrelevance result' seems inconsistent with the raw data documenting recent co-trends of decentralization and greater regional inequality. However, the irrelevance result does hold up against the econometric evidence that attempts to estimate the *conditional* correlations between decentralization and regional inequality, *holding other things constant*. For richer countries, the econometric estimates suggest either no relationship or a negative relationship between decentralization and regional inequality (e.g. Rodriguez-Pose and Ezcurra 2010; Sacchi and Salotti 2011). It is only for lower- and middle-income countries that decentralization has a positive conditional correlation with regional inequality.

One way of explaining the positive correlation in developing countries is based on internal migration from the poor region to the rich region. Development is typically associated with urbanization, as the economy goes through the structural transformation away from traditional agriculture and toward industry. While our model does not explicitly incorporate migration, one can see that it might play an important role. Urbanization would cause *n*, the relative size of the poor region, to fall. Other things being constant, this would weaken the political influence of the poor region. Weaker political influence lowers the poor region's share of aggregate resources and lowers total investment there (see (3.16b) and (3.16c)). Lower investment in the poor region would lead to increased regional inequality. Thus, it may be weakened political power, and not decentralization per se, that is linked to the increase in regional inequality. For this reason, the positive correlation between decentralization and inequality in developing countries may be spurious. Internal migration may be causing an increase in income inequality, while a different set of factors may be resulting in the decentralization of government.

3.4 Foreign Funding and Regional Inequality

The previous two sections offer some potential reasons for the slow, and now stalled, regional convergence witnessed for more than a century in many countries of the world. Regional income convergence within many countries of the world has been disappointing. The lack of convergence has motivated richer countries and international institutions to provide external funding for backward regions. However, the efficacy of this funding will be influenced by the same features identified in Sect. 3.3 that have prevented more rapid convergence.

National policy is naturally biased toward richer and more politically influential regions. A backward region's share of national transfers is based on its relative political influence. The costlier it is for this region's officials to deliver votes to the central government, the lower the region's share of national resources. This causes the fraction of any outside funds coming into the country, regardless of how they are earmarked, that are invested in the poor region to be low. In part, this is due to an inverse relationship between central funding and outside funding of investment in the backward region, similar to the inverse relationship between regional and national investment within the country. Finally, corruption is negatively correlated with the state of development. The more backward regions of a country will have relatively high corruption. Corruption taxes all sources of funding for investment—local, national, and international—making it difficult to generate growth.

Foreign Funding for the Poor Region

The persistence of backward regions in countries such as Italy has become a major policy concern. The acceleration of regional economic and financial integration in the 1980s and 1990s helped raise the level of transfers to backward regions. Countries with backward regions received additional 'structural' or 'cohesion' funding from supranational entities to help them develop poor areas as a quid pro quo for the country agreeing to reduce barriers to trade and international capital flows. Mourmouras and Rangazas (2016) further extend the model developed in Sect. 3.3 to examine the effects of foreign transfers motivated by the development of poor regions. Below is a summary of their conclusions.

Foreign funding increases the country's resources, R_p. From (3.16c), we see that a one unit increase in R_p gives rise to much less than a one unit increase in regional investment. The funds are partly transferred to rich households, as g_{2P} is reduced, partly 'taxed' by local corruption, and partly converted to local household consumption as g^l_{2P} is reduced.

The fact that so much of the funding is redirected away from investment in the poor regions, makes one wonder whether stricter conditions could realistically be imposed that would raise the portion of outside funds that are invested. It would be relatively difficult to monitor and control the local politician's behavior, but perhaps it may be possible to do so at the central level.

The outside donors could require that g_{2P}remain fixed as a *condition* for the funding. This condition would keep central officials indifferent about the inflow of funds and clearly make local officials and local households better off, so the added condition would be accepted if not welcomed.

The Structural Funds provided by the EU actually impose an even stronger condition on the recipient country. Structural Funds require a *co-financing condition* where the central government *increases* funding to the poor region. For a given inflow of funds to the poor region, the EU pays a fraction and the recipient country's central government pays the remainder. In political equilibrium, the cost imposed on the central government must be compensated for by increased political support from the poor region. Thus, the cost of the co-financing condition is actually borne by the local official of the poor region. However, it is not clear if the policy will make the local official better off, and thus it is not clear if the country would be anxious to receive the outside aid under these terms. Mourmouras and Rangazas show that there exists some positive inflow of funds from outside the country that will keep the central government indifferent and make the local official better off. They also show that the co-financing condition will generate the same increase in local investment as under the weaker condition requiring that g_{2P} is kept constant. However, the outside authority is able to achieve this outcome at a lower financial cost because the recipient country's central government will absorb part of the cost (in exchange for compensating increase in political support from the poor region).

Supranational alliances of foreign countries can potentially promote development in backward regions. Tough conditions are needed to prevent central government offsets to outside investment funding targeted to the poor region. This provides a justification for the co-financing conditions associated with EU Structural Funds. In our model, co-financing conditions improve the welfare of households in the backward region, have a neutral effect on central government officials, and lower the welfare of local officials in the poor region and households in the rich region.

Focusing on Corruption

To address the problem of local corruption, a major impediment to growth in backward regions, we need to think more deeply about the possible determinants of corruption. In the model of Sect. 3.3, the corruption tax is solely a function of preference parameters of local officials. In Sect. 3.7, we introduce a more elaborate model of corruption that identifies other determinants that could be impacted by policy. It is a simplified version of the model that provides the foundation for the complete macroeconomic analysis of corruption in Chaps. 6 and 7.

3.5 Political Polarization

We now present an argument that helps explain the rise in public debt witnessed over the last quarter of the twentieth century. The idea is that political polarization can create a tendency to rely on debt financing (Tabellini and Alesina 1990; Drazen 2000, pp. 301–306). In the United States, for example, it is commonly believed that politics has become more polarized, partly due to configuring more homogenous districts from which political representatives are selected (Bueno de MesQuita and Smith 2011, p. 267). Based on the model of this section, the rise in polarization can cause a rise in public debt. We extend the model to include debt and public investment to think about how polarization affects investment efficiency and to consider the consequences of some fiscal rules designed to control debt policy.

Polarization and Deficit Bias

Consider two regions or political parties, denoted by P and R, that could lead the national government. Households differ only in terms of the regions they are from or the political parties they are aligned with. The population of households is evenly split across the two regions or political parties. The income of all households is the exogenous value y in each period. For simplicity, we also assume that the income tax is predetermined at the rate τ in each period. The economy is small and open to international borrowing and lending at the exogenously determined world interest, r^*.

In the first period, the government makes potentially different transfers to the two household types, z_1^P and z_1^R. The government can augment the financing of the transfers by issuing government debt in the international bond market. The per capita government budget constraint in the first period is

$$\mathrm{T}_1 \equiv \tau y + b_2 = \frac{z_1^P}{2} + \frac{z_1^R}{2}.$$

The debt issued in the first period is repaid in the second period, and thus reduces the revenue available to make second period transfers. In the second period, the per capita budget constraint is

$$\mathrm{T}_2 \equiv \tau y - (1 + \mathrm{r}^*) b_2 = \frac{z_2^P}{2} + \frac{z_2^R}{2}.$$

The utility flow to the government led by representatives from region/party j in period i is

$$\gamma^j \ln\left((1-\tau)\mathrm{y} + \mathrm{z}_i^R\right) + \left(1-\gamma^j\right) \ln\left((1-\tau)\mathrm{y} + \mathrm{z}_i^P\right),$$

where the preference parameter γ^j is the relative weight, bound between zero and one, that the government led by type j places on the utility of the R-household type. We assume that all governments discount future utility by the time discount factor, β.

The government in power in the current period forms an expectation of being re-elected in the second period. The current government may or may not be choosing the transfer allocation in the next period. The expected lifetime utility function of a type-j government is

$$\begin{aligned} &\gamma^j \ln\left((1-\tau)\mathrm{y} + \mathrm{z}_1^R\right) + \left(1-\gamma^j\right) \ln\left((1-\tau)\mathrm{y} + \mathrm{z}_1^P\right) \\ &+ \beta E\left\{\gamma^j \ln\left((1-\tau)\mathrm{y} + \mathrm{z}_2^R\right) + \left(1-\gamma^j\right) \ln\left((1-\tau)\mathrm{y} + \mathrm{z}_2^P\right)\right\}, \end{aligned}$$

where the expectation is taken over the uncertain transfers in period 2, which depend on which party is in office at that date.

First, suppose that the government is always even-handed, regardless of region or party. In this case we have $\gamma^j = ½$. An even-handed government chooses equal transfers across households, $z_i^R = z_i^P = \mathrm{T}_i$, in each period, eliminating any uncertainty. The even-handed government would choose debt to satisfy the condition

$$\frac{1}{y+b_2} = \frac{\beta(1+\mathrm{r}^*)}{y-(1+\mathrm{r}^*)b_2}.$$

If $\beta(1 + \mathrm{r}^*) = 1$, an assumption we make to establish a clear baseline, the even-handed government chooses not to issue debt.

Now suppose that there is extreme polarization, so that $\gamma^R = 1$ and $\gamma^P = 0$. The optimal transfer allocation of a type-R government is $z_i^R = 2\mathrm{T}_i$ and $z_i^P = 0$ and for a type-P government it is just the opposite. Assume the type-R government is currently in power, but that there is only a 50 percent probability that they will stay in power. Using the optimal within period transfer allocations and the government budget constraints, the objective function of the type-R government is

$$\ln(y+\tau y+2b_2) + \frac{\beta}{2}\ln(y+\tau y-2b_2(1+\mathrm{r}^*)).$$

The optimal condition for public debt is

$$\frac{1}{y(1+\tau)+2b_2} = \frac{1}{2}\frac{1}{y(1+\tau)-2(1+\mathrm{r}^*)b_2}.$$

With polarization, the politically optimal debt level must be strictly positive to equate the marginal benefit to the, now lower, marginal cost of debt. The marginal cost of debt is lower because uncertainty about re-election serves to lower the effective discount factor on future utility of the current ruling party and its supporters. There is only a 50 percent probability that the R-government and its supporters will receive transfers and suffer a drop in future consumption because of the debt re-payment. This creates a bias toward issuing debt relative to the situation with an even-handed government.

Public Investment

Now let's reintroduce public investment, as in previous sections. First period worker productivity and income is exogenous and denoted by y_1. Let g_2 represent government investment in public capital during the first period. Public capital is a determinant of productivity and income in period 2, $y_2 = Ag_2^{\mu}$.

The government continues to make potentially different transfers to the two household types, z_1^P and z_1^R. As before, the government can augment the financing of the transfers by issuing government debt in the international bond market. Now the government must also choose the level of g_2. The per capita government budget constraints in the first and second periods are

$$\mathrm{T}_1 \equiv \tau y_1 + b_2 - g_2 = \frac{z_1^P}{2} + \frac{z_1^R}{2}.$$

$$T_2 \equiv \tau y_2 - (1 + r^*)b_2 = \frac{z_2^P}{2} + \frac{z_2^R}{2}.$$

Begin with the scenario where the government is always even-handed, regardless of region or party. In this case we have $\gamma^j = ½$ and the even-handed government chooses equal transfers across households, $z_i^R = z_i^P = T_i$, in each period, eliminating any uncertainty associated with the party in power in period 2. The even-handed government's choices of debt and investment generate the first best outcome characterized by the familiar optimality conditions,

$$\mu A g_2^{\mu-1} = 1 + r^*$$

$$\frac{c_2}{c_1} = \beta(1 + r^*).$$

Now return to the situation of extreme polarization with $\gamma^R = 1$ and $\gamma^P = 0$. The optimal transfer allocation of a type-R government is $z_i^R = 2T_i$ and $z_i^P = 0$ and for a type-P government it is just the opposite. Assume the type-R government is currently in power, but that there is only a 50 percent probability that they will stay in power. Using the optimal within-period transfer allocations and the government budget constraints, the objective function of the type-R government is

$$\ln(y_1 + \tau y_1 + 2(b_2 - g_2)) + \frac{\beta}{2}\{\ln(y_2 + \tau y_2 - 2b_2(1 + r^*)) + \ln(y_2(1 - \tau))\}.$$

Compared to our previous analysis, there is an additional term in the second period because y_2 is now endogenous.

The resulting first order conditions are

$$\frac{2}{y_1(1+\tau) + 2(b_2 - g_2)} = \beta \frac{1 + r^*}{y_2(1+\tau) - 2(1 + r^*)b_2}$$

$$\frac{2}{y_1(1+\tau) + 2(b_2 - g_2)} = \frac{\beta}{2}\left\{\frac{1+\tau}{y_2(1+\tau) - 2(1 + r^*)b_2} + \frac{1}{y_2}\right\}\mu A g_2^{\mu-1}.$$

Combing these conditions, yields the following expression that reveals how polarization alters public investment,

$$\frac{\mu A g_2^{\mu-1}}{1 + r^*} = \frac{1}{1 + \frac{z_2^R}{2y_2}}$$

As long as there are positive second period transfers to type-R households, in the event that the type-R government is re-elected, the return on government investment must be *less than* the opportunity cost of funds. Government investment is too large in the presence of political polarization.

The intuition for the result is that polarization causes government investment to have an asymmetric benefit over debt reduction in raising the expected welfare of type-R households. Public investment raises private income in *both* future states of nature, regardless of the party in power. Reducing debt only benefits the type-R household if the type-R government is re-elected and $z_2^R > 0$. The value of deficit reduction will be less than the value of greater investment because investment provides some insurance against the potentially low consumption associated with the "bad" state of nature, where the type-R government is thrown out and no net transfers are received by type-R households.[1] In a polarized political environment there will be a push for investment spending as well as more borrowing.

Fiscal Rules

An important concern motivating this book is the appearance of persistently high government budget deficits that have caused public debt to GDP ratios to continually rise in most developed countries since the 1980s. The fiscal situation among the OECD countries has led to calls for fiscal rules that would limit government's ability to use debt financing. The fact that political polarization, which by all counts has been on the rise for some time, can generate a deficit bias provides a possible rationale for fiscal rules. We have also seen that political polarization can cause inefficiently high investment in public capital. The predicted positive connection between polarization and investment received some indirect evidence in the aftermath of the highly polarized U.S. presidential election of 2016. New public infrastructure legislation was the one area of common ground that Republicans and Democrats were universally eager to agree on.

Would prohibiting debt financing improve policy outcomes in our model of extreme political polarization? First, note that ex ante welfare of the current generation is reduced by constraining the decision to borrow—which is one important reason why fiscal rules are opposed. The less obvious issue is how a constraint on borrowing would affect public investment and growth. This issue matters for the welfare of future generations whose productivity is impacted by public capital.

We can examine effects on public investment by looking at a constrained solution where the type-R government must choose non-positive values of b_2; i.e. the government is allowed to lend in international credit markets but not borrow. Re-doing the optimal choice of fiscal policy, assuming a binding constraint on government debt, gives the following optimal conditions for debt and public investment

$$\frac{2}{y_1(1+\tau) - 2g_2} > \beta \frac{1+r^*}{y_2(1+\tau)}$$

[1]This result is in contrast to Peletier et al. (1999) who find that polarization does not alter the efficient investment choice. They assume that public investment does not increase private income, only the resources available to the government. The Appendix to this chapter explains the difference in results in more detail.

$$\frac{2}{y_1(1+\tau)-2g_2}=\frac{\beta}{2}\left\{\frac{1+\tau}{y_2(1+\tau)}+\frac{1-\tau}{(1-\tau)y_2}\right\}\mu A g_2^{\mu-1}$$

$$=\frac{\beta}{y_2}\mu A g_2^{\mu-1}$$

Combing the conditions, yields the following inequalities

$$\mu A g_2^{\mu-1}>\frac{1+r^*}{1+\tau}$$

The restriction on borrowing leads to inefficient public investment. So, it is not necessarily an improvement over the unconstrained case.[2]

Another fiscal rule, that has received attention in the face of rising public debt, restricts government borrowing only to the financing of public investment—the so-called "golden rule of public investment." We can examine this fiscal rule by requiring $b_2 = g_2$. Under the golden rule, public investment does not restrict period 1 transfers because it is fully bond-financed. So, the type-R government chooses the level of investment that maximizes the expected value of the future utility of the type-R households. This is equivalent to choosing investment to maximize

$$\ln\{y_2(1+\tau)-2(1+r^*)g_2\}+\mu\ln g_2.$$

The resulting condition for optimal public investment is

$$\frac{\mu A g_2^{\mu-1}}{1+r^*}=\frac{1+\mu}{1+\tau}.$$

Again the investment condition is consistent with both under and over investment, depending on the size of the exogenous tax rate. In low-tax economies the golden rule leads to inefficiently low investment and the opposite is true in high-tax economies. A low tax rate reduces the benefit of public investment in generating transfers in the good state of nature relative to the borrowing costs that squeeze the budget and reduce transfers.

The theoretical case for rules is not strong—they reduce ex ante utility of the current generation and do not generally lead to productively efficient levels of public investment. There are also many practical problems. Proposals built on strong rules that would likely alter policy outcomes, such as balanced budget amendments to the U.S. constitutions, are typically viewed by politicians as being overly restrictive and thus lack the support needed to pass the legislation. Weaker rules increase the likelihood that politicians will find ways to circumvent

[2]Despite the difference in the unconstrained case, the result that a borrowing constraint leads to inefficiently low public investment is consistent with Peletier et al. (1999).

restrictions. There is also the problem that what is actually needed are limits on the government's ability to conduct short-sighted redistribution of income across generations—which, as we will see more explicitly in Chap. 5, can be done without a rise in government borrowing. Analysis of the effectiveness of fiscal rules, by those familiar with budget politics, generally end with pessimistic conclusions (see for example Hallerberg et al. (2009) and Penner (2014)). In Chap. 8 we discuss alternative ways of restricting fiscal policy.

3.6 Interest Groups and Rent Seeking

Now let's think about interest groups and the common pool problem. Suppose that there are m groups of households. Each group is represented by a single household-type. For simplicity only, we assume there are an equal number of households in each group (M), so that the total population of households is $N = mM$ or $N/M = m$. While the households representing the different groups differ politically and compete with each other over government transfers (z), they are identical in terms of preferences, productivity, and the ability to generate transfers through rent seeking activity such as lobbying the government.

Each household lives for two periods and is endowed with one unit of time each period. The productivity of household time (y) is determined by public investments carried out by the central government (roads, communications infrastructure, public schooling, and public health provisions). Productivity in the current period (y_1) is given (based on past investments), but future productivity (y_2) is determined by current period investment decisions made by the central government (g_2). We continue to assume $y_2 = Ag_2^{\mu}$, with $0 < \mu < 1$. In each period, households choose how much time to devote toward productive activity (h) and how much to devote toward procuring government transfers (1-h), which we call "rent-seeking." Activities that generate government transfers are lobbying, legal actions, unproductive government employment, and efforts to obtain national funds for unproductive local projects. Time devoted to work generates net income equal to $(1 - \tau)yh$, where τ is the income tax rate.

We assume the technology for generating transfers is $z = \varphi_0(1 - h)^{\varphi}y$, where the parameters satisfy $0 < \varphi_0$ and $0 < \varphi < 1$. There is diminishing marginal productivity associated with devoting time to rent-seeking. Individual productivity is equally effective in work and in rent-seeking. We make this assumption because we know of no evidence, casual or otherwise, suggesting that education and skill affects the

[3]Easterly (2001) argues that increased education will not lead to increased production when the incentives are not right. "One clue as to why education is worth little more than hula hoops to a society that wants to grow comes from what educated people are doing with their skills. In an economy with extensive government intervention, the activity with the highest returns to skills might be lobbying the government for favors. In an economy with many government interventions, skilled people opt for activities that redistribute income rather than activities that create growth" (p. 82).

productivity of work differently from the productivity of rent-seeking.[3] Even when interpreting rent-seeking as unproductive public employment, education "credentials" could increase the size of the transfer in the form of a high government "wage."

The economy is small and open, with private and public access to international loan markets at the perfectly competitive interest rate r^*. The period budget constraint of the household is given by $c = (1 - \tau)yh + z$. Household preferences are given by $\ln c_1 + \beta \ln c_2$, where $\beta > 0$ is the household's constant time discount factor. Households also take account of the government budget constraint in period i,

$$(1 + r^*)Nb_i + Ng_{i+1} + M\sum_{j=1}^{m} z_{ij} = Nb_{i+1} + \tau_i My_i \sum_{j=1}^{m} h_{ij}, \tag{3.17}$$

where b_{i+1} and g_{i+1} represents public debt and public investment per household, and z_{ij} is the household transfer to group j. While groups individually vie for group specific transfers, we assume that all groups can agree and coordinate on public investment that benefits *all* households. For simplicity, we assume $b_1 = 0$ and, because of the two-period framework, $b_3 = g_3 = 0$.

Cooperative Solution

If groups coordinate, perhaps through the leadership of a strong central government, then each group understands that there is no way to obtain positive net transfers at the expense of the other groups. In other words, it is understood that transfers per group will equal taxes per group. This recognition removes all incentives to divert resources to competitive rent-seeking, making it optimal to set $h = 1$.

The central government then chooses g_2 to maximize the representative household's utility. The result is the productively efficient government investment, $g_2 = (\mu A/(1 + r^*))^{\frac{1}{1-\mu}}$.

Non-cooperative Solution

If the groups do not coordinate their decisions, then each chooses rent-seeking taking the others' behavior as given. Households act under the belief that some of the tax burden of raising their transfers can be passed off to other groups. This is known as the *common pool problem* because spending on each interest group is funded from a common pool of tax revenue. Under our assumptions, the central government and the different interest groups play a *non-cooperative* Nash game, where all actions are taken simultaneously (see A.7 of the Appendix).

[4]A household from group j has after-tax income $(1 - \tau_i)y_i h_{ij}$. The effect of an increase in h_{ij} is $y_i\left[1 - \tau_i - \frac{d\tau_i}{dh_{ij}} h_{ij}\right]$. Differentiating the budget constraint with respect to h_{ij}, gives $\frac{d\tau_i}{dh_{ij}} h_{ij} = -\frac{\tau_i}{m}$. Substituting into the expression for the change in disposable income gives $y_i\left[1 - \tau_i + \frac{\tau_i}{m}\right]$, where we have used the fact that $h_i = h_{ij}$ under our symmetry assumption. The variable y_i does not appear in (3.18) because it appears on both sides and can be cancelled.

We treat each group symmetrically, so the first order conditions for the common choice of h in each period i is

$$1-\tau_i\left(1-\frac{1}{m}\right)=\varphi_0\varphi(1-h_i)^{\varphi-1}\left(1-\frac{1}{m}\right). \tag{3.18}$$

The left-hand-side is the marginal benefit of allocating time to production, the after-tax increase in output.[4] This expression is adjusted for the fact that when a group increases its productive work, the tax base increases and tax rates can be lowered. However, the lower taxes are spread across the entire economy so that the individual group only enjoys $1/m$ of the tax saving. The right-hand side is the opportunity cost of allocating time to productive activity; the forgone net transfers that would result from further rent-seeking. Marginal increments in rent-seeking yield a positive net transfer because each group views the tax-price of a dollar of transfers as $1/m$. Again, this is because the tax increase needed to raise transfers to just *one* group will be spread over m groups via a higher income tax rate.

In general equilibrium, one must account for the effect of all household decisions, and public investment, on the economy's income tax rate. Since all households are identical, the government budget constraints can be written as

$$\tau_1=\frac{g_2-b_2+\varphi_0(1-h_1)^{\varphi}}{y_1h_1}. \tag{3.19a}$$

$$\tau_2=\frac{(1+\mathrm{r}^*)b_2+\varphi_0(1-h_2)^{\varphi}}{y_2h_2} \tag{3.19b}$$

Note that, in the end, taxes must cover transfers to each household, so that no households actually gains from rent seeking. The two period budget constraints of the government and the representative household are

$$\tau_1y_1h_1+\frac{\tau_2y_2h_2}{1+r^*}=g_2+z_1+\frac{z_2}{1+r^*} \tag{3.20a}$$

$$c_1+\frac{c_2}{1+r^*}=y_1h_1+\frac{y_2h_2}{1+r^*}-g_2 \tag{3.20b}$$

In period 1, the central government's choice of g_2 is $g_2=\left(\frac{\mu Ah_2}{1+r^*}\right)^{\frac{1}{1-\mu}}$. Note that rent-seeking reduces investment by lowering time devoted to productive activity and thereby lowering the return to investment.

Substituting public investment and (3.19b) into (3.18), dated for period 2, gives the equation that determined period 2 rent seeking,

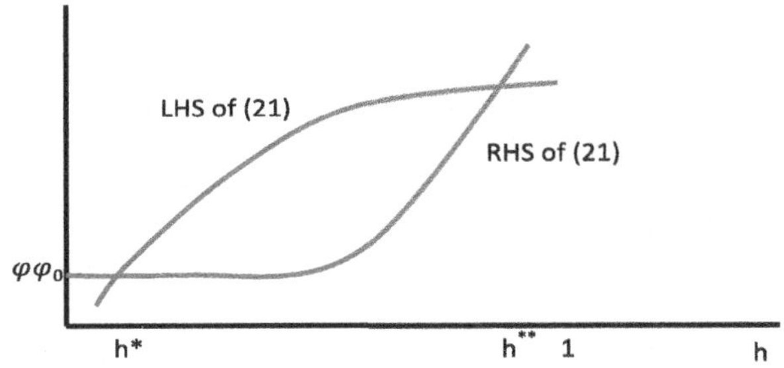

Fig. 3.1 Rent seeking Equilibria

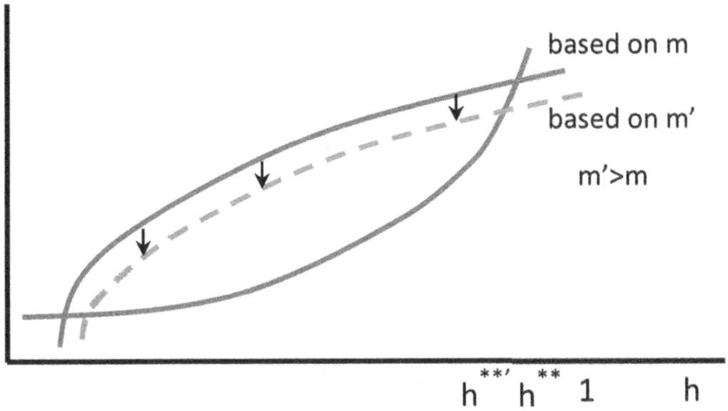

Fig. 3.2 An Increase in the Number of Interest Groups

$$\frac{1}{1-\frac{1}{m}} - \frac{(1+r^*)b_2 + \varphi_0(1-h_2)^{\varphi}}{(Ah_2)^{\frac{1}{1-\mu}}\left(\frac{\mu}{1+r^*}\right)^{\frac{\mu}{1-\mu}}} = \frac{\varphi\varphi_0}{(1-h_2)^{1-\varphi}}. \tag{3.21}$$

The left-hand side now accounts for the fact that the tax rate is decreasing in the common value of h chosen by all groups (both because transfers fall and the tax base rises with h), causing the tax rate to fall with h.

Sketching (3.21) reveals that there are two possible equilibrium outcomes as depicted in Fig. 3.1. Rent-seeking unambiguously lowers income and welfare, so the **equilibrium with higher h Pareto dominates the *equilibrium with lower h. The * economy with low levels of h has a high tax rate. In fact the tax rate is so high that the economy is on the wrong side of the Laffer Curve—an increase in tax rates will reduce tax revenue. The Pareto inferior equilibrium also violates the second order condition associated with optimal rule given by (3.18). An increase in productive activity, away from the value satisfying (3.18), generates a marginal benefit that exceeds the marginal cost, suggesting that the choice of h does not maximize the welfare of an individual interest group. For these reasons, we ignore the *equilibrium and focus on an economy in the **equilibrium.

An increase in the number of interest groups (m) will decrease the left-hand side and cause a downward shift as exhibited in Fig. 3.2. An increase in the number of groups implies the cost of demanding additional transfers by any one group is less expensive (because their tax share is smaller). The lower relative cost of rent seeking results in less productive work, more rent seeking, more transfers, and higher tax rates. As indicated above, greater rent seeking also causes a decrease in public investment. Thus, the rise in m predicted by Olson (1982) raises taxes, reduces investment, and lowers welfare.

Also note that greater public debt causes a similar downward shift in the left-hand-side because it creates an exogenous increase in tax rates. Figure 3.2. applies to this case as well. Thus, a higher debt burden also increases rent seeking and lowers investment. The factors leading to increased government borrowing that were discussed in Chap. 2 can indirectly lead to increased rent seeking and lower investment.

Foreign Aid

Mourmouras and Rangazas (2009) use the rent-seeking model to consider the effects of loans to the poor country extended by international lenders. They consider *conditional* loans that are perfectly enforceable, a strong assumption. The first condition, motivated by the "golden rule," is that the loan must be used exclusively for investment. This condition keeps the funds out of the "common pool" of resources that interest groups compete over for transfers.

However, even under the assumption of perfect enforcement of the golden rule condition, good outcomes are not guaranteed. The obligation to pay off debt creates a need for additional tax revenue. If the economy starts in the **equilibrium, the additional revenue needed to pay off debt requires an increase in tax rates. The higher tax rates discourage work and gives rise to additional rent seeking.[5] Furthermore, if the period 2 work level is held constant, the public investment may not generate enough additional earnings to both pay the debt and increase consumption (since the initial level of rent-seeking may lower the return to investment below $1 + r$). Finally, since productive work declines further when taxes rise to repay debt, there is a greater likelihood that future income will not rise enough to cover the debt obligations and the poor country may end up being worse off.

An apparently favorable event such as providing investment loans to a credit-constrained country can make it worse off. Excessive rent-seeking lowers the return to investment other things constant. While $\mu A g_2^{\mu-1}$ might be relatively high, a lack of productive work can make $\mu A g_2^{\mu-1} h_2$ quite low. For this reason, the central

[5]Higher taxes would also hit the wages paid to those in unproductive government employment. However, interest groups would work to protect their after-tax wages by lobbying for higher before-tax wages, so that their net transfer from the government remains the same. Thus, taxes will primarily lower the reward to productive work.

government of the poor country may actually be reluctant to consider international borrowing. The reluctance is stronger if the government realizes that the higher taxes needed to repay the loans will generate further attempts to avoid taxes by allocating even more labor away from productive work and toward rent-seeking. Pressuring the country to accept loans may lead to poor outcomes in this situation.

We now consider conditions that could reasonably be imposed by the donors that would lead to more work in the second period, and thereby guarantee welfare improvements. One set of conditions that works is the following:

(a) every dollar loaned must be invested (the golden rule)
(b) second period tax rates must remain fixed (at pre-loan levels, $\overline{\tau}_2$)
(c) loan repayment must be financed by cuts in transfer spending.

Mourmouras and Rangazas show that these conditions are sufficient to increase h_2.

A strategy of extending the conditions of development loans to aspects of domestic fiscal policy can only be implemented successfully if it is supported by the central government of the poor country. The idea is to strategically strengthen the ability of the central government to impose spending cuts that are in the national interest. Acting alone, the government may not be politically capable of making such cuts. However, the donor's conditionality may be used to "steel" the backs of the Finance Minister and his staff to insist on needed cuts. Krueger (1990) argues that, among government officials, finance ministers in developing countries are the most likely to be focused on the national interest.

"Spending ministers will tend to become advocates of programs and policies falling within their domain. By contrast, finance ministries tend to be public interest agencies to a greater degree (p. 18). Typically, each spending ministry will want to increase spending, believing it in the social interest that those activities within its particular domain are the most important. The finance ministry, by contrast, will be more concerned about raising revenue, and is therefore less likely to represent special interest (p. 19–20)."

In practice, rather than imposing across-the-board cuts in government consumption and transfers, the Finance Minister would likely "negotiate" cuts with the donors in the areas where spending was believed to be particularly unproductive. Behind the scenes, it would be very much the case that the Finance Minister "owns" the policy agreements with the donor community.[6]

[6]In stressing the importance of cutting government consumption to repay loans, we do not deny that in many poor countries the allocation of government consumption is inefficient. Productive bureaucrats are paid too little and unproductive ones are paid too much. We feel the level of government consumption is a bigger problem in many countries and an easier problem to address. Although difficult to implement, the best policy would be to cut government consumption overall and reallocate spending to productive government employees.

3.7 Determinants of Corruption

Let's now think about the causes of corruption in more detail. Suppose that there is only one region in the country. Public officials are some fraction of the total number of private households, εN, where $0 < \varepsilon < 1$. The public officials only serve the government in period one, and then retire to the private sector in period 2. Private households work for two periods as in previous versions of the model.

The public sector investment in period 1 is completely tax-financed. All households, whether employed privately or publicly, earn the exogenous before-tax income y_1 and pay an income tax, collected at the tax rate τ_1. Public capital constructed in period 1 raises y_2, according to the production function we have used throughout the last two chapters.

The first period government budget constraint is $\tau_1 y_1 N(1+\varepsilon) = \widehat{G}_2$, where $\widehat{G}_2$ is the total amount of funds *budgeted* for public investment. Due to corruption, the amount of funds *actually invested* is less than the amount budgeted, $G_2 = (1-\overline{u})\widehat{G}_2$, where $\overline{u}$ is the average *rate of corruption*, i.e. the average fraction of the budget that is diverted for private use by the public officials. Let the value of the budget and of public capital per second period producer be denoted by $\widehat{g}_2$ and g_2.

Behavior of a Public Official

Each official is allocated an equal portion of the total investment budegt to conduct an investment project. So the budget per project is the budget per government official, $\widehat{G}_2/\varepsilon N$. The official considers the possibility of diverting public funds, earmarked to finance investment projects, for their own private use. Corruption is costly for the two reasons discussed in Chap. 1. First, resources are lost in attempting to conceal the illegal actions. The stronger are the government's detection institutions, the more resources are lost in avoiding detection. Second, households experience a loss in utility, "guilt" from violating a social norm, when diverting public funds.

The preferences of public officials are written as

$$\ln c_1^g + \beta \ln c_2^g - \frac{\phi}{2\overline{u}} u_t^2, \tag{3.22}$$

where ϕ is a nonnegative preference parameter that measures the guilt associated with corruption. Higher values of ϕ imply a stronger distaste for illegal activity. The disutility of illegal activity is also affected by the average level of corruption among government officials. The greater is the average level of corruption the less guilt an individual experiences from their own illegal activity. We refer to this as the "culture of corruption" effect.

Each public official takes the average level of corruption, the tax rate, and the total public investment budget as given when making their private choices. The public official's private choices include what fraction of their project budget to divert for their own private use. The officials maximize utility subject to their investment budget and their private lifetime budget constraint,

$$c_1^g + \frac{c_2^g}{1+r^*} = (1-\tau_1)y_1 + \theta^g u\left(\widehat{G}_{t+1}/\varepsilon N\right), \tag{3.23}$$

where θ^g is a parameter, that lies between zero and one, reflecting the fraction of diverted public funds that the official can recover for consumption. The parameter captures the effect of institutional safeguards that make it difficult to steal public funds and use them openly without detection, working like the standard monetary deterrent to illegal activity in the corruption literature.

The public official's maximization problem generates the following equation for corruption

$$u = \frac{1}{2}\left[\left(\Gamma^2 + \frac{4(1+\beta)\overline{u}}{\phi}\right)^{1/2} - \Gamma\right], \text{ where } \Gamma \equiv \frac{(1-\tau_1)y_1}{\theta^g\left(\widehat{G}_{t+1}/\varepsilon N\right)}. \tag{3.24}$$

Equilibrium Corruption

If we use the fact that $\overline{u} = u$ in equilibrium, because each public official is identical, then (3.24) simplifies to

$$u_t = \frac{1+\beta}{\phi} - \frac{(1-\tau_t)y_1}{\theta^g\left(\widehat{G}/\varepsilon N\right)} = \frac{1+\beta}{\phi} - \frac{\varepsilon}{\theta^g(1+\varepsilon)}\left(\frac{y_1}{\widehat{g}_2} - 1\right), \tag{3.25}$$

where the second equality follows from the government budget constraint.

The key intuition needed to understand (3.25) is simple. The greater is the opportunity to steal public funds, and the more value the resulting consumption generates, the more tempting it is to be corrupt. The higher is legal income, the lower is corruption. Higher income raises consumption and lowers the value of additional consumption gained by diverting public funds, an income effect that lowers the need for corruption. Holding legal income constant, corruption is higher the greater is the budget ($\widehat{g}_2$) and the easier it is to use the stolen income without detection (θ^g). This is also why corruption is decreasing in ε. The greater is the number of officials, the smaller is each official's budget and the lower is corruption.

A key feature of (3.25) is that corruption is predicted to increase as government budgets increase. This tendency can only be offset by economic growth that makes private legal income higher or by improvements in institutional quality that increase detection.

Further Issues to be Resolved

The theory underlying (3.25) provides the basis for examining some additional issues. These issues are only mentioned here, but are studied in detail in Chaps. 6 and 7.

The first issue relates to the determination of fiscal policy. The theory described here can be extended to allow the public officials to determine the level of taxes and the size of $\widehat{g}_2$. The positive effect of $\widehat{g}_2$ on corruption suggests that there is likely to be a feedback effect—a greater opportunity for corruption will cause the public officials to set larger budgets. In this way, corruption affects the determination of all aspects of fiscal policy.

We have assumed that the average level of corruption influences an individual public official's willingness to engage in corruption. As discussed in Chap. 1, the same cultural effect can apply to other illegal action, most importantly to tax evasion. The more corrupt the government is, the more willing households are to evade taxation. This provides a possible check on corruption because greater tax evasion means smaller government budgets. In Chap. 6 we will see that the presence of tax evasion allows the theory to generate realistic predictions when fiscal policy is endogenous, i.e. when public officials are allowed to choose the level of taxes and the size of investment budgets.

Finally, if there is a larger budget, we know that there will be a higher rate of corruption, other things constant. What is not clear is what happens to actual public investment. Actual public investment can be written as $g_2 = (1 - u)\widehat{g}_2$. An increase in $\widehat{g}_2$ also raises u, so the effect on g_2 is ambiguous. One needs to know how responsive the rate of corruption is to increases in the budget. To answer this question, the model must be calibrated so that quantitative results can be generated to reconcile the ambiguity.

3.8 Conclusion

Public infrastructure is critical to a country's growth. Thus, a key determinant of income gaps across countries is the gap in the quality of government across countries. Our first model of this Chapter makes clear that large governments, with selfish and short-sighted public officials, will provide inferior public infrastructure. Governance and growth are fundamentally linked via investment in public capital.

Beyond public investment, one of the primary motivations for writing this book comes from concerns about how developed countries are conducting their fiscal policy generally. The policies are simultaneously raising the tax burden on future generations, while reducing the investment in their pre-tax productivity. There are political forces associated with maturing democracies that have led societies to form this policy mix that is detrimental to economic growth and the welfare of future generations. As discussed in Chap. 2, greater political voice for broad middle class and the less wealthy segments of the population can increase government debt. This chapter identifies some additional political forces that raise transfer payments and both lower and misallocate government investment.

The growth in the number of interest groups causes a larger government primarily due to increased transfer payments targeted to specific groups. The possibility of receiving government transfers, and the higher taxes needed to fund the transfers, biases activity away from production and towards rent seeking. The higher taxes and reduced productive effort lowers the return to investment, resulting in weaker incentives to invest, both publically and privately.

The funds that are allocated for public investment are often misallocated. One form of the increase in interest groups is the increased division of a country into distinct localities that are each seeking their slice of the central government pie. In some countries, such as the U.S., this is due to redistricting that forms more pockets of relatively homogenous groups that do not represent the diversity of interests in the country as a whole (Bueno de Mesquita and Smith 2011). Representatives in charge of allocating investment budgets face strong incentives to send the projects back home, ignoring allocation rules dictated by where the economic returns to investment would be the highest. In addition, the richer and more politically influential communities will distort investment in their favor even when investment in poorer communities would increase aggregate economic growth and reduce income inequality.

For countries with particularly weak checks on corruption, much of the funding that is allocated to investment is actually never invested at all. The growth in the size and complexity of government increases the opportunity for public officials to illegally divert revenue for their own personal use. This creates a further incentive to increase revenue by borrowing. As seen in Chap. 1, corruption and public debt have a strong positive correlation, even among richer countries.

The political polarization associated with the rise in interest groups, creates yet another reason to favor deficit financing. Strongly divided parties, aligned with specific interest groups, differ dramatically over the preferred composition of government spending. Debt accumulation today serves to raise repayment obligations that constrain future discretionary spending. However, the groups represented by the current ruling party only face some *probability* of having their favorite programs constrained. If competing parties assume power, the debt repayment will largely constrain spending on *other* groups in society. For this reason, election uncertainty in a polarized political environment incentivizes borrowing.

Chapter 8 will discuss the institutional reforms needed to deal with these issues and others that seem to be a persistent problem for most developed economies.

3.9 Exercises

Questions

1. Use the model of Sect. 3.1 to explain how poor governance undermines growth.
2. There are important examples of "pro-growth" dictators. In fact, developing countries experiencing the Growth Miracles of the second half of the twentieth century were far from democratic. Use the model from Sect. 3.1 to explain how a pro-growth dictator can generate greater economic growth than a democratic state.
3. Give an intuitive explanation of why the preferences of public officials no longer matter if the country operates in a perfectly competitive open economy. Does

this mean that the quality of government no longer matters for economic growth?
4. Provide a verbal summary of the model used in Sect. 3.2. How does the re-election motive affect the regional allocation of investment?
5. The model of Sect. 3.2 makes the case against "pork barrel" spending designed to increase re-election chances. Can you think of ways that pork barrel spending may be in the national interest?
6. Use the model of Sect. 3.2 to explain how the allocation of education spending can lower economic growth and raise income inequality.
7. Section 3.3 recognizes that regions have their own governments. The regional governments provide the same services as the national government. What are the possible advantages of the national government in providing the services?
8. How does the presence of a regional government change the analysis of regional investments by a national government? What new issues arise?
9. Explain the sense in which the degree of government centralization does not affect income inequality across regions. Is this prediction consistent with the data?
10. Why does foreign aid directed to the poor regions fail to be fully effective? What can be done, in principle, to improve its effectiveness?
11. Explain why political polarization increases the use of debt financing.
12. Explain why political polarization leads to over-investment in public capital.
13. Discuss the theoretical and practical problems with fiscal rules that attempt to constrain government borrowing.
14. What is the *common pool problem* associated with government spending?
15. Explain rent seeking equilibria using Fig. 3.1. What are the costs of rent seeking on the economy?
16. How does an increase in the number of interest groups affect the economy?
17. In the presence of interest group politics, explain why greater public debt obligations increase rent seeking and lower public investment.
18. Can an investment loan to a credit-constrained economy make it worse off? Explain. What can be done, in principle, to insure that the loan makes the country better off?
19. Provide a verbal description of the microeconomic model of a public official in Sect. 3.7. How do "guilt" and "culture" affect the official's behavior?
20. Explain how an increase in each of the following affects the corrupt activity of a public official.
    (a) size of the investment budget
    (b) the official's legal income
    (c) the tax rate
21. In the presence of corruption, if the funds allocated to public investment rise, what happens to actual investment? Explain.

Problems

1. Derive Eq. (3.5) that gives public investment in the model with explicit public officials.

2. For the model in Sect. 3.1, consider a country has the following fundamental structure: $\mu = 0.40$, $\beta = 0.50$. Suppose the government of the country is characterized by the following parameters: $\varepsilon = 0.20$, $\beta^g = 0.25$, $\gamma = 0.5$. Compute the ratio of g_2 if the policy was chosen benevolently as in Chap. 2 to the g_2 actually chosen. What is the implied ratio of y_2?
3. Suppose the public officials from Sect. 3.1 operate in the open economy described in Sect. 2.2. Introduce public debt and generate the new optimal conditions for fiscal policy that replace those in (3.4). Use the new optimal conditions to derive (3.6), showing that public investment is no longer a function of the preferences of public officials.
4. Carefully explain why the local official's objective function can be written as (3.9).
5. Derive (3.10) and (3.11), the equations that show how election motives can distort investment resulting in an inefficient allocation of public capital.
6. Derive (3.14a) and (3.14b). Show that an increase in the national government's investment in the poor region raises total investment there less than one-for-one and explain why.
7. Let's calibrate the difference in investment across rich and poor regions from Sect. 3.3 when the central government favors the rich region and there is *no politics*. Suppose the initial income gap is two-fold, $y_{1R}/y_{1P} = 2$, $N_R = N_P$, and the national tax rate devoted to the central government's investment budget is 10 percent, $\tau_1 = 0.10$. As implied by the cost overruns on Italian investment projects in the second half of the twentieth century, assume $u = 0.50$ in the poor region (Tanzi and Davoodi 1997).
   (a) What is the investment gap across regions?
   (b) Assume $\mu = 0.30$. What is the gap between the marginal return to investment across regions, if $A_R/A_P = 1$? If $A_R/A_P = 2$?
   (c) Assume $\beta = 0.60$. What is the value of γ need to target $u = 0.50$?
8. What is R_p? Use the formal notation of the model to identify three reasons why an increase in R_p raises investment in the poor region less than one-for-one.
9. Based on the model from Sect. 3.3, explain how the size of the net transfer to the poor region is affected by an increase in each of the following.
   (a) τ_1
   (b) y_{1P}
   (c) y_{1R}
   (d) ξ/ψ
10. Following up on *Problem* 7, let's see what happens when there is *some political influence* by the poor region in national politics. Use the same parameter assumptions from *Problem* 7 to answer the following questions.
    (a) What share of R_p flows to the poor region if they have no political influence?
    (b) What value of ξ/ψ is required to have 40 percent of R_p flow to the poor region?

(c) Make the following assumptions about initial incomes and TFP: $y_{1P} = A_P = 1$, $y_{1R} = A_R = 2$. What is the investment level in each region, with and without politics?

11. Continuing with *Problem* 10, let's look at the *equity-growth tradeoff*. Compute I_P, I_R, $y_{2P} + y_{2R}$, and y_{2R}/y_{2P} with and without political influence from the poor region. Use the calculations to discuss the equity-growth tradeoff, if any, associated with the poor region gaining political influence.
12. In the model of political polarization, suppose the current type-R government's chances for re-election falls from ½ to ¼. What happens to first period borrowing? Explain.
13. In the model of public debt and investment from Sect. 3.5, verify that an even-handed government will choose the productively-efficient investment level.
14. Carefully derive the objective function of the type-R government, stated in Sect. 3.5, when both debt and public investment are policy choices. Starting from the first-order conditions for the optimal fiscal policy of the type-R government, show that public investment will be inefficiently large.
15. Derive the condition for optimal investment when the government is restricted by the "golden rule of public investment."
16. Use (3.21) to explain the shape and economic interpretation of the two curves displayed in Fig. 3.1.
17. Assume $\varphi_0 = 1$, $\varphi = \mu = 0.5$, $A = 4$, $r* = 1$, $b_2 = 0$, and $m = 3$. Find the equilibrium value of h_2 in the Pareto dominate equilibrium. What is the value of h_2 when $m = 6$?
18. Use Fig. 3.1 for the rent seeking model of Sect. 3.5 to argue that an increase in the country's international borrowing lowers their domestic investment.
19. Derive and explain (3.24) and (3.25).
20. Use (3.25) to explain how an increase in each of the following affects the rate of corruption.
    (a) ϕ
    (b) β
    (c) θ^g
    (d) ε
    (e) y_1
    (f) $\widehat{g}_2$

Appendix

In Sect. 3.5, we found that political polarization causes over-investment in public capital when governments are free to borrow. This result is in contrast to Peletier et al. (1999) who find that polarization does not alter the efficient investment choice. They assume that public investment does not increase private income; only the resources available to the government rise with public investment. Their assumption eliminates the insurance advantage of public investment that occurs when investment also raises *private* income regardless of which party is in power. The fact that households attach greater value to a rise in private income when no government transfers are received is what causes them to marginally favor investment over a reduction in government debt.

To see that the difference in results depends on whether public investment is assumed to affect private income, suppose that y_1 and y_2 represent income *received only by the government* to fund public spending. We now assume that every household's *private* income is *exogenous* and equal to 1 in each period. The government budget constraints become

$$\mathrm{T}_1 \equiv y_1 + b_2 - g_2 = \frac{z_1^P}{2} + \frac{z_1^R}{2}.$$

and

$$\mathrm{T}_2 \equiv y_2 - (1 + \mathrm{r}^*)b_2 = \frac{z_2^P}{2} + \frac{z_2^R}{2}.$$

As in the text, suppose that the type-R party is currently in power and that there is extreme political polarization. The government's objective function becomes

$$\ln(1 + 2(y_1 + b_2 - g_2)) + \frac{\beta}{2}\ln(1 + 2(y_2 - b_2(1 + r^*))).$$

The resulting first order conditions are

$$\frac{2}{1 + 2(y_1 + b_2 - g_2)} = \beta\frac{1 + r^*}{1 + 2(y_2 - (1 + r^*)b_2)}$$

$$\frac{2}{1 + 2(y_1 + b_2 - g_2)} = \beta\frac{\mu A g_2^{\mu-1}}{1 + 2(y_2 - (1 + r^*)b_2)}.$$

Combing the first order conditions clearly yields the efficient investment result, $\mu A g_2^{\mu-1} = 1 + r^*$, as in Peletier et al. (1999).

References

Arcalean, C., Glomm, G. and Schiopu, I., 2012, 'Growth Effects of Spatial Distribution Policies', *Journal of Economic Dynamics and Control*, **36**, 988–1008.

Barro, R., and Sala-i-Martin, X., 1991, "Convergence across States and Regions," *Brooking Papers on Economic Activity*, 107-182.

_______, 1992, Convergence, *Journal of Political Economy*, 100, 223-251.

Bueno de Mesquita, B., and Smith, A., 2011, *The Dictator's Handbook*, New York: Public Affairs.

Cost, J., 2015, *A Republic NO More*, New York: Encounter Books.

Drazen, A., 2000, *Political Economy in Macroeconomics*, Princeton University Press: Princeton, New Jersey.

Easterly, W., 2001, *The Elusive Quest for Growth*, MIT Press: Cambridge.

Emmott, B., 2012, *Good Italy, Bad Italy*, New Haven: Yale University Press.
Evans, D., 2004, *Greasing the Wheels*, Cambridge UK: Cambridge University Press.
Frisch, S., and Kelly, S., 2011, *Cheese Factories on the Moon*, Boulder: Paradigm Publishers.
Ganong, P., and Soag, D., 2013, "Why Has Regional Convergence in the U.S. Declined?," Mimeo.
Grossman, G. and Helpman, E, 1994, 'Protection for Sale', *American Economic Review*, **84**, 833–50.
Grossman, P., 1994, 'A Political Theory of Intergovernment Grants', *Public Choice*, **78**, 295– 303.
Hallerberg, M., Strauch, R., and von Hagen, J., 2009, *Fiscal Governance*, Cambridge UK: Cambridge University Press.
Krueger, A., 1990, "Government Failures in Development," *Journal of Economic Perspectives*, Summer, 9-23.
Mourmouras, A., and Rangazas, P., 2016, "Clientelistic Politics and Multi-Level Finance: Some Implications for Regional Inequality and Growth," in E. Ahmad, M. Bordignon, and G. Brosio (editors), *Multi-level Finance and the Euro Crisis*, Cheltenham, UK: Edward Elgar.
______, 2009, "Foreign Aid with Voracious Politics," *IMF Staff Papers* 56, 787-810.
Olsen, M., 1982, *The Rise and Decline of Nations:Economic Growth, Stagflation, and Social Rigidities,* New Haven: Yale University Press.
Peletier, B., Dur, R., and Swank, O., 1999, "Voting on the Budget Deficit: Comment," *American Economic Review*, 89, 1377-1382.
Penner, R., 2014, "Discussion on Federal Budegt Reform: Lessons from State and Local Governments," in J. Diamond and G. Zodrow editors, *Pathways to Fiscal Reform in the United States*, Cambridge, MA: MIT Press.
Rodriguez-Pose, A. and Ezcurra, R., 2010, 'Does Decentralization Matter for Regional Disparities?', *Journal of Economic Geography*, **10**, 619–44.
Sacchi, A. and Salotti, S., 2011, 'Income Inequality Regional Disparities and Fiscal Decentralization in Industrialized Countries', Department of Economics Working Paper 142, University Roma Tre.
Tabellini, G., and Alesina, A., 1990, "Voting on the Budget Deficit," *American Economic Review*, 80, 37-49.
Tanzi, V., 2000, 'Some Politically Incorrect Remarks on Decentralization and Public Finance', in J.-J. Dethier (ed.), *Governance, Decentralization and Reform in China, India, and Russia*, Boston, MA, Dordrecht and London: Kluwer Academic Publishers, pp. 47–63.
Tanzi, V., and Davoodi, H., 1997, "Corruption, Public Investment, and Growth," *IMF Working Paper* 139
Tornell, A., and lane, P., 1999, "The Voracity Effect," *American Economic Review*, 89, 22–46.

4 Overlapping-Generations Model of Economic Growth

This chapter introduces the one-sector neoclassical growth model with overlapping generations. The primary focus of the chapter is growth via private physical capital accumulation. We think of *private physical capital* as manmade durable inputs to the production process. For our purposes, private capital can be primarily thought of as plant and equipment that is produced in one period and then used in production in the following period.[1] To model production, we introduce *firms*, economic institutions that combine physical capital and labor to produce goods and services. In Chap. 5, we re-introduce the public capital that was the focus of Chaps. 2 and 3 and study the interaction between public and private capital accumulation, along with other effects of fiscal policy on economic growth.

The accumulation of capital must be financed or funded by household saving. We use the two-period life-cycle theory of household consumption as the basis for explaining saving behavior. At the microeconomic level, this theory is similar to that from Chaps. 2 and 3. In the life-cycle theory, households save during their working period to finance retirement consumption. However, now the economy as a whole extends beyond the two periods of a single household's life. In fact, the economy has an indefinite future as in Sect. 2.11. If each household lives for two periods, instead of a single *representative* type of household, there are *always two different generations that overlap* each period—a "young" working household and an "old" retired household.

Once the theoretical model is developed, we apply it to the real world.We show how the model can be "estimated," or more precisely *calibrated*, to make quantitative analysis possible. We then examine how well the simple model of private capital accumulation can replicate observed economic growth in the U.S. from 1870 to 2000.

---

[1] Definitions of physical capital will vary depending on the purpose at hand. In some cases physical capital is defined to include inventories, software, land, and other inputs that extend beyond plant and equipment.

M. Ivanyna et al., *The Macroeconomics of Corruption*, Springer Texts in Business and Economics, https://doi.org/10.1007/978-3-030-67557-8_4

4.1 Firms, Production, and the Demand for Capital

The first step in developing a general equilibrium model of output and income is to introduce a production technology. We assume that production takes place in "firms"— organizations that hire labor and rent capital in order to produce output. Each firm's production knowledge or "technology" is represented by a *Cobb-Douglas production function*,

$$Y_t = AK_t^{\alpha}L_t^{1-\alpha}, \tag{4.1}$$

where Y denotes output, K denotes the capital stock rented, L denotes the hours of work hired, and where A and α are technological parameters. The production function is a technological "recipe" that relates the inputs hired and used by the firm to the output that the firm is capable of producing. The parameter A is s referred to as *Total Factor Productivity* (TFP), with the same interpretation as in Chap. 2. TFP captures a wide variety of unmeasured variables that affect the productivity of labor and capital; from climate and geography that determine natural resources available and the health environment of households to laws and regulations that restrict the way that production is carried out. The parameter α is a fraction measuring the relative importance of physical capital in the production process. This interpretation of α will become more clear as the theory of the firm is developed below.

The output produced by firms is a single "all-purpose" good that can either be consumed or invested as a physical asset (somewhat like corn that can be either consumed or stored and invested as a physical asset to plant and produce more corn in the future). This abstraction avoids the complication of having two distinct sectors of production, one producing consumer goods and the other capital goods. For some purposes one may require this more elaborate two-sector model, but this is not the way to begin an analysis of a growing economy.

The Cobb-Douglas production function is a special case of what is called a "neoclassical" production function. All neoclassical production functions have three general properties: (i) positive marginal productivity, (ii) diminishing marginal productivity and (iii) constant returns to scale. Economists believe that these properties are common to most production processes.

The marginal product of an input is the increase in output that results from an increase in the use of an input. Formally, it is the *partial* derivative of the production function with respect to a particular input, holding other inputs constant (see the Technical Appendix for a discussion of partial derivatives). For a Cobb-Douglas production function, the *marginal product of labor* and the *marginal product of capital* are $(1-\alpha)AK_t^{\alpha}L_t^{-\alpha}$ and $\alpha AK_t^{\alpha-1}L_t^{1-\alpha}$. The marginal productivity of increasing the level of either input is always positive—more output results when the firm hires either more labor or more capital.

Diminishing marginal productivity means the additional output, associated with adding an additional unit of an input, decreases as more of that input is used. While output increases as the firm uses more of an input, the size of the increase gets smaller as the amount of the input used in production increases. Diminishing marginal productivity is based on the intuitive notion of "input crowding." The increasing scarcity of the input held fixed, limits the production that results from adding more of the other input. For example, if there is a given amount of capital, as more workers are hired the amount of capital that each worker can use decreases—serving to limit the rise in output. Note that the marginal product of labor expression above is decreasing in L_t, for a fixed value of K_t. The analogous observation applies to the marginal product of capital. Sketch the mathematical expression for the marginal product of labor against the level of employment to see this graphically. A similar sketch applies to the relationship between the marginal product of capital and the capital used in production.

Constant returns to scale means that if *both* inputs were increased in the same proportion, then the ability to produce output would also increase by that proportion. This property makes sense because if the firm can simply duplicate its current plant, equipment, and work force, it should be able to duplicate or double its output as well.

Finally, note that the properties we just described imply that the marginal product expressions can be simplified by combining L_t and K_t into the *capital-labor ratio*, also known as *capital intensity*, $k_t \equiv K_t/L_t$. The simplified expressions for the marginal products are, $(1 - \alpha)Ak_t^{\alpha}$ and $\alpha Ak_t^{\alpha-1}$. The marginal product of labor is increasing in capital intensity. The more capital per worker, the more productive an additional worker is. The marginal product of capital is decreasing in capital intensity. Higher capital intensity means there are fewer workers available to work with any additional capital brought to the workplace.

The fact that the marginal products of capital and labor are both functions of the capital-labor ratio, k, and not the levels of K and L, is a consequence of the constant returns to scale assumption. This property implies that the *scale* of a firm is indeterminate, i.e. the optimal size of a firm cannot be pinned down by the theory. Firms are indifferent about the level of production, but they do want to hire capital and labor in a particular ratio that depends on the relative market prices of the inputs.

From the point of view of microeconomics, the indeterminacy of firm size can be seen as a disadvantage. One is forced to simply assume that firms are of a given size and that there are enough of them competing to justify the *perfect competition* assumption that is discussed below and used throughout the book. From a macroeconomic point of view, the indeterminate size of firms can be seen as a convenient simplification. The key expressions that characterize the production side of the economy apply to both the individual firm and to the collection of firms as a whole. This is why in many macroeconomic models the distinction between the individual firms and production in the economy as a whole is not emphasized.

What makes (4.1) special in the class of neoclassical production functions is that the Cobb-Douglas functional form implies that the *shares* of national output that are paid to capital owners and workers are the *constant* output elasticity values α and $1 - \alpha$. Data shows that over the last century, income shares have in fact stayed roughly constant within and across countries. For this reason, many economists view the Cobb-Douglas functional form as a reasonable approximation to an economy's aggregate production technology. To explicitly see that (4.1) has the constant income share property, we next need to think about how capital owners and workers are paid.

We assume that markets are perfectly competitive in our production economy. As discussed in elementary economics, the notion of competitive markets applies not only to the markets for goods but also to the factor markets for labor and capital. The competitive assumption applied to the factor markets means that firms demand inputs to maximize profits taking as given the market prices of the inputs: the wage rate paid to labor (w) and rental rate on physical capital (r). No single firm is large enough to be able to influence market prices when they unilaterally change their production or input levels. The price of the economy's single output good is taken to be one. So, we can think of output and revenue as being the same. Therefore, profit can then be written as $Y_t - w_tL_t - r_tK_t$. Maximizing profits requires that firms hire capital and labor as long as the marginal benefit (marginal product) exceeds the marginal cost (factor price). Formally, the necessary conditions for profit maximization are

$$\alpha A k_t^{\alpha-1} = r_t \tag{4.2a}$$

$$(1-\alpha)Ak_t^{\alpha} = w_t. \tag{4.2b}$$

Equations (4.2a and 4.2b) say that, in order to maximize profit, the marginal product of each input must be equated to its market price, just as in the theory of competitive factor markets from intermediate microeconomics.

From the perspective of an individual firm, that takes factor prices as given, it appears that there are two independent Eqs. (4.2a) and (4.2b), to determine one unknown, k. In general, this situation leads to inconsistent solutions for k—i.e. different solutions for k from each equation. This is not the case here because of an important implication of competitive markets: economic profits are driven to zero. Competition between firms for the available resources will force factor prices to satisfy these equations, which in turn implies that economic profits are zero. Thus, (4.2a) and (4.2b) also play a role in determining the market factor prices and not only k.

To think about this last point further, first notice that we can write the production function as $Y_t = Ak_t^{\alpha}L_t$. Note that the *average product of labor* or *worker productivity* is then $y_t \equiv Y_t/L_t = Ak_t^{\alpha}$. Next, multiply each side of (4.2a) by K_t and (4.2b) by L_t to get

$$\alpha Y_t = r_t K_t \tag{4.3a}$$

$$(1-\alpha)Y_t = w_t L_t \tag{4.3b}$$

Equation (4.3a) shows that the share of output and revenue paid to owners of capital (by each firm and in the economy as a whole) is the constant, α, an interpretation that was suggested above. Moreover, if αY_t goes to capital owners as rental income, there is just enough revenue left over, $(1 - \alpha)Y_t$ to pay workers the competitive wage, implying that economic profit is zero.

The connection made in (4.3a and 4.3b) allows us to refer to α and $1 - \alpha$ as the capital and labor shares. The fact that the Cobb-Douglas technology, combined with competitive markets, implies constant factor shares is a strong prediction of the model. Remarkably, this prediction is approximately consistent with empirical evidence that shows little trend in factor shares as countries developed over the 20th century.

Our discussion suggests that the two Eqs. (4.2a) and (4.2b) are then profit-maximizing conditions that determine *two* variables: the firm's demand for capital relative to labor and, via the zero profit condition, one of the factor prices. To determine the remaining factor price, we need the final requirement of a competitive equilibrium: *market clearing*. The firm's demand for capital per worker must equal the supply of capital per worker coming from households. We will think of the rental rate on capital as the "price" that clears the capital market. With (4.2a) and (4.2b) determining the demand for capital and the competitive wage rate that generates zero profit, we then have three conditions to determine the three unknowns: r_t, w_t, and k_t.

The first step in developing the market clearing condition is to be more explicit about what we mean by the *demand* for capital in the production economy. Start by thinking of the capital-labor ratio on the left-hand side of (4.2a) as the capital-labor ratio *demanded* by firms at different market rental rates for capital. Label the firm's demand for k as k_t^d. In period t, firms will enter the capital market to rent capital that they can use in production. Solving (4.2a) for k, we can write the demand for capital in period-t as

$$k_t^d = \left[\frac{\alpha A}{r_t}\right]^{1/(1-\alpha)}. \tag{4.4}$$

Equation (4.4) indicates that as the rental rate required by the market rises, the firm's demand for capital declines. This is because, as the cost of capital rises, firms will shift towards using less capital and more labor in production.

The theory thus far gives us the firms' demand for capital intensity. Now we need to develop a theory for the supply of capital in period t. In other words, we need to discuss who owns the capital and how much capital they are willing to supply to the market. This is the focus of Sect. 4.2.

4.1.1 Capital and Labor Shares

It has amazed macroeconomists for decades that the capital and labor shares of income have exhibited no trend over the course of development. Ever since Kaldor (1957, 1961) initially documented the constancy of the factor shares, it has been consistently confirmed with new data and accepted as a stylized fact of growth. This Kaldor growth fact has been the primary reason why the Cobb-Douglas production function is used not only to exposit theory in the classroom but also as a fundamental component of economic models found on the research frontier. However, this important "growth fact" has recently been challenged.

The U.S. labor share began to show a modest decline in the 1990s and then a more dramatic fall after 2000. Over the last 20–30 years, the Bureau of Labor Statistics recorded a more than 6 percentage point decline in the labor share from 64.6 percent to 58.3 percent. A tricky feature of computing the labor share is determining how to split sole proprietors' income into wages and the return to capital. Improvements in how to make this spilt eliminates about one third of the measured decline in the labor share, but that still leaves a 4 percentage point fall from 63 to 59 percent (Elsby et al. 2013).

The recent fall in the labor share has not been restricted to the U.S.. An OECD study found a decline in the labor share occurred in 26 of 30 advanced countries between 1990 and 2009 (ILO-OECD 2015). The average fall in the labor share was also about 4 percentage points, from 66 to 62 percent.

Beyond the apparent loss of a long-established growth fact, there are concerns that the falling labor share implies a rise in income inequality. If the labor share is falling, the capital share must be rising. More of an economy's income is flowing to people who own capital. Capital ownership is heavily concentrated among the richest households, so if more income is flowing to capital owners, the rich are getting richer.

While income inequality has been on the rise recently, much of this is due to a rise in *wage* inequality. The labor compensation of CEOs and highly educated workers has dramatically increased relative to the wages of the average worker since 1980. Even a constant labor share is consistent with changes in the *distribution* of pay across workers. The fact that increasing income and wage inequality largely reflects rising education inequality is a topic that will be discussed further in Chap. 8.

There is another concern about a falling labor share for economic theory. The labor share can be written as $1-\alpha=\frac{w_tL_t}{Y_t}=\frac{w_t}{y_t}$, where $y_t \equiv Y_t/L_t$, the average product of labor or worker productivity. For the labor share to fall, wages must not be keeping up with worker productivity over time. This way of looking at the falling labor share is troubling because the neoclassical theory of the firm with a Cobb-Douglas technology suggests wages and worker productivity should move together (note that in our theory of the firm, wages are equal to the marginal product of labor, see (4.2b), which is proportional to the average product of labor). While this has been the case in the past, it seems no longer to be strictly true. Since the turn of the 21st century, wage growth has lagged growth in worker productivity.

Due to the importance of the falling labor share for economic theory and income inequality, economists have been working to figure out what could have recently changed so dramatically across so many countries to render the previously reliable Kaldor growth fact invalid. For the purpose of examining some issues it appears that a more complex production function that allows income shares to vary will be needed. An example of a production function that delivers a possible explanation for the falling labor share is provided in Sect. 9.3 of Chap. 9.

4.2 Household Saving and the Supply of Capital

In our model, households purchase capital as an asset, a type of saving used to finance retirement consumption. The capital generates funds for retirement consumption purchases when the households rent the capital to firms. So, the supply of capital referred to at the end of Sect. 4.1 results from older households attempting to generate income for retirement consumption.

To capture a retirement motive for saving in the simplest way possible, we assume households live for two periods: one when they are young and working and one when they are old and retired. This means that in any one period there are two household-types from distinct generations: a young working household and an old retired household. Macroeconomic models where different generations operate as distinct decision-makers in each period are called *overlapping-generations* models.

Including the saving behavior of households is an important extension to the Solow model of capital accumulation from undergraduate macroeconomic courses. In the Solow model saving is treated as an exogenous variable. The economy's saving rate is simply assumed to be a constant fraction of total income with no explanation provided. In contrast, we derive the saving rate. When the government is introduced in Chap. 5, the economy's saving rate will be influenced by fiscal policy.

The Supply of Labor and Capital

As just mentioned, the supply of capital that is rented to firms is owned by old retired households. They rent the capital to firms to generate income that finances their retirement consumption. Once the firms complete production using the capital, the retired households sell the capital to the young working households that are looking to save assets to finance their future retirement consumption. The sale of capital provides further resources for retirement consumption of the current old households.

Formally, the currently old households who own and supply the capital, purchased the capital as an asset during their working lives in the previous period. In period $t-1$, each young household supplied one unit of labor to firms and earned the wage, w_{t-1}. With each household supplying one unit of labor, the aggregate supply of labor in each period is then just the number of young households. In period $t-1$, the total supply of labor to all firms is the total number of young households from that generation, $L_{t-1}^s = N_{t-1}$, where N_{t-1} denotes the number of households.

The capital supplied per unit of labor results from the household's saving behavior, s_{t-1}. Young households save in period $t - 1$ by purchasing output and treating it like a physical asset that generates income during retirement by supplying or renting it to firms for use in production during period t. The firms use this physical capital to produce output and generate revenue in period t. The firms then return the capital, that has been depreciated by use in production, back to households and pay them the rental rate r_t. So, for every unit of capital that households purchase and rent to firms, they receive back in period t, $1 - \delta + r_t$, as their return to saving, where δ is the fraction of capital that depreciates from use. We somewhat loosely refer to $r_t - \delta$ as both the "rate of return to capital" and the "interest rate" on household saving.

The total supply of new capital to the market in period t is the total saving of young households in period $t-1$, $s_{t-1}N_{t-1}$. To match the demand concept in (4.4), we need an expression for the capital supplied *per worker* in period t. The supply of capital per worker in period t is $k_t^s \equiv s_{t-1}N_{t-1}/L_t^s = s_{t-1}N_{t-1}/N_t = s_{t-1}/n$, where n is the average number of children born in each young household. We treat n as an exogenous constant. The number of children each household has determines the relative population size of different generations. For example, if $n = 1$, then generations are of equal size and $N_t = N_{t-1}$. If $n > 1$, $N_t > N_{t-1}$ and there is positive population growth over time. Note that the rate of population growth is $(N_t/N_{t-1}) - 1 = n - 1$.

In summary, the factors of production supplied by the households in period t, for hire by firms, are

$$L_t^s = N_t$$

and

$$k_t^s = \frac{s_{t-1}}{n}.$$

To complete the model, we need a theory of s_t.

Household Saving

We now develop a theory of household saving. Households do not directly benefit from saving but rather use saving to create their desired lifetime consumption path. The consumption path that households prefer depends on their attitudes about consuming now rather than later in life. Household preferences are represented by a utility function. The utility function captures the household's preference for consuming at different points in their lifetime.

We assume that household preferences are represented by the time separable, log utility function we used in Chaps. 2 and 3,

$$U(c_{1t}, c_{2t+1}) = \ln c_{1t} + \beta \ln c_{2t+1}.$$

For a generation-t household, consumption in the first and second periods, c_{1t} and c_{2t+1} determine the value of lifetime utility. The utility function has the standard properties that the marginal utility of consumption in each period is positive but diminishing (try taking the first and second derivative with respect to consumption in any one period). The parameter capturing the household's preferences about the timing of consumption is the pure time discount factor (β). Typically, one assumes that $\beta < 1$ because people are generally viewed as being "impatient," i.e. they weigh utility gained from current consumption higher than utility gained from future consumption.

Households face constraints that restrict the consumption paths they can afford. In each period there is a budget constraint that must be satisfied. In the first period of life, a generation-t household has its wage (w_t) as a source of funds that can be used to purchase output for consumption (c_{1t}) or for saving (s_t). This gives the first period budget constraint, $c_{1t} + s_t = w_t$. In the second period, consumption (c_{2t+1}) is financed by the saving from the first period, $c_{2t+1} = R_t s_t$, where $R_t = 1 + r_{t+1} - \delta$ is the return from owning physical capital or what sometimes is called the "interest factor." The *two single period* budget constraints can be combined to form a *single lifetime* budget constraint that requires the present value of consumption to equal the first period wage, $c_{1t} + c_{2t+1}/R_t = w_t$.

Households maximize lifetime utility subject to the lifetime budget constraint. The solution to this problem gives us the optimal consumption and saving behavior of a household

$$c_{1t} = \frac{1}{1+\beta} w_t \tag{4.5a}$$

$$c_{2t+1} = \frac{\beta}{1+\beta} R_t w_t \tag{4.5b}$$

$$s_t = \frac{\beta}{1+\beta} w_t \tag{4.6}$$

All behavior is proportional to the household wage, via an income effect, as in Chaps. 2 and 3. Households optimally split their wage income across current consumption and saving depending on their patience, as captured by the value of the preference parameter β.

Supply of Capital per Worker

Using Eq. (4.6), dated for a generation $t-1$, and the definition of k_t^s that was introduced previously, we can now write the economy's supply of capital per worker as

$$k_t^s = \frac{\beta}{1+\beta} \frac{w_{t-1}}{n}. \tag{4.7}$$

The economy's supply of capital per worker this period is based on the saving per worker in the previous period and the growth of the economy's work force. An increase in the previous period's wage raises saving because a portion of the higher wage is consumed and a fraction is put aside to allow consumption in the future to rise as well.

The extent to which saving and capital supplied raises the capital-labor ratio in the next period, depends on the growth in the workforce. Greater fertility implies a higher rate of population growth and a faster growing workforce. As the workforce this period rises relative to the workforce in the previous period, less saving and capital will be available per worker. Thus, higher rates of population growth lower the capital-labor ratio by forcing the available capital to be spread over a larger workforce.

4.2.1 The Wage Elasticity of Work and the Interest Elasticity of Saving

It is often assumed in introductory economics courses that higher wages cause households to supply more work time and higher interest rates cause households to save more. These presumptions are not necessarily consistent with economic theory which indicates that wage and interest rate changes have *ambiguous* impacts on observed work and savings behavior. This is because of two opposing conceptual effects.

The standard claims are consistent with what economists call the *substitution effect*: when the price of a good rises, people substitute toward less expensive ways of gaining utility. A higher wage causes the opportunity cost of enjoying leisure to rise, encouraging people to work more hours and substitute more consumer goods for less leisure time. However, for people already in the work force, a higher wage also means they can afford to take some time off and enjoy more leisure—a second conceptual effect known as the *income effect*. The income effect is one important reason why hours of work generally fall as economies develop and wages rise.

The same two opposing effects influence how saving responds to interest rate changes. A higher interest rate means the cost of consuming, rather than saving, increases. This encourages households to substitute current consumption for future consumption by saving more (the substitution effect). However, for those already doing some saving, a higher interest rate increases income, allowing households to consume more today, save less, and still consume more in the future (the income effect). *Problems* 6 and 7 examine the opposing substitution and income effects of an increase in the interest rate on saving in more detail.

The theoretical ambiguities of how wage and interest rate movements affect behavior have encouraged a great of deal of empirical work that attempts to estimate which of the two opposing effects is stronger. While it is not fair to say that a consensus has been reached, many, if not most, studies find that the labor supply of full-time workers is not very responsive to changes in wages and saving is not very responsive to changes in interest rates (see, for example, the survey in Salanie (2011, Chap. 1)). In the language of economics, the wage elasticity of labor supply and interest elasticity of saving are both close to zero. For simplicity, we assume a wage elasticity of exactly zero for work because we assume that work is exogenously fixed at one full-time unit. Our assumptions about the form of the household utility function also imply that the interest elasticity of saving is zero. This is why R_t does not affect s_t in (4.6). Under our household preference assumptions, the substitution and income effects of an interest rate change *always* exactly cancel. These simplifications do not alter the insights we gain for the issues addressed in this book, but do make the exposition less complex.

4.3 Competitive Equilibrium in a Growing Economy

Before moving to the determination of the market clearing condition in the capital market, let's summarize the key actions taken in period t by each agent.

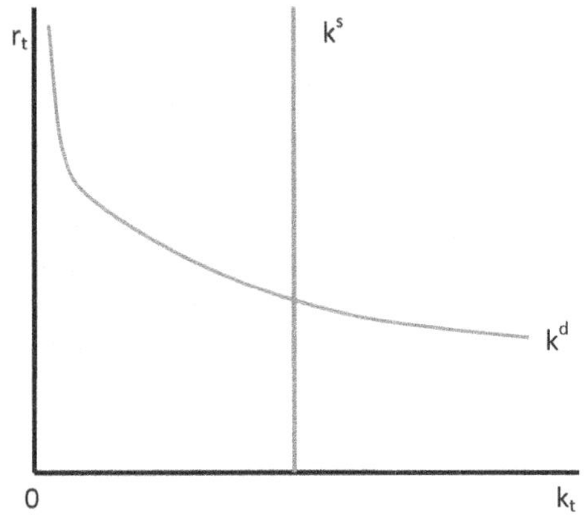

Fig. 4.1 Market clearing equilibrium in the capital market

Firms hire labor, pay each worker w_t
rent physical capital per worker, k_t^d, pay owners r_t per unit supplied

Young Households supply one unit of labor, receive w_t
purchase $s_t = nk_{t+1}^s$ units of physical capital

Old Households supply $s_{t-1} = nk_t^s$ units of physical capital, receive r_t per unit supplied

A market clearing equilibrium in the capital market requires that the firms' demand for capital per worker equals the supply of capital per worker by old households, i.e. $k_t^d = k_t^s$ for all values for t. As in other competitive markets, the market price is the mechanism for bringing the two sides of the market together. In the capital market, the market price is the rental rate on capital that is paid by those demanding capital and received by those supplying the capital. Market clearing requires finding a value of r_t that equates the demand for capital, given by (4.4), and the supply of capital, given by (4.7), in every period, as sketched in Fig. 4.1.[2]

Figure 4.1 is the standard demand-equals-supply way of thinking about how equilibrium is determined. It is analogous to the "loanable funds" market of saving and investment commonly used in introductory macroeconomics. Here, the "demand for funds" is replaced by the direct demand for physical capital to be used in production. The "supply of funds" results from household saving. The only way households can save in the model is to directly purchase physical capital and then rent it to firms to use in production. The behavior of firms and households in

[2]You can think of the value of r_t as actually determined in period $t-1$. In that period households make their saving decision based on the firms' commitments to rent capital in period t and pay the rental rate r_t. In other words, r_t is determined in period $t-1$ based on the savings behavior of households and the *planned* investment demands of firms.

demanding and supplying capital in a competitive market, determines the equilibrium return to capital and the amount of capital traded.

While intuitive, the demand-supply approach has limitations as an analytical tool. The problem is that it is a static snapshot of a dynamic economy. In general, a production economy will experience capital accumulation over time. In other words, the k_t determined in the figure will be larger than k_{t-1}. This implies that, using (4.2b), w_t will be larger than w_{t-1}. The increase in wages over time will cause the supply curve in the figure to shift to the right each period. Thus, the diagram reveals that growth in the economy is due to the effect of capital on wages. As the capital stock increases, wages increase. The increase in wages, increase saving and leads to further capital accumulation. However, there are important details of the growth process that are not revealed by this essentially static depiction.

Fortunately there is a nice way of displaying the dynamics of the economy more explicitly. One can substitute the factor price equations from (4.2a and 4.2b) into (4.7) and impose the equilibrium condition $k_t^d = k_t^s$ to get

$$k_t = \frac{\beta}{1+\beta}\frac{(1-\alpha)Ak_{t-1}^{\alpha}}{n} = \mathrm{B}k_{t-1}^{\alpha}, \tag{4.8}$$

where $\mathrm{B} \equiv \frac{\beta}{1+\beta}\frac{(1-\alpha)A}{n}$.

Mathematically, Eq. (4.8) is known as a *difference equation*, which is the discrete-time analog to the differential equation in continuous time that may be more familiar from calculus classes. The difference equation highlights the underlying dynamics of the model that is driven by changes in the capital-labor ratio over time. In economics, Eq. (4.8) is referred to as a *transition equation* because it describes how the economy evolves over time (a concept first encountered for the public capital stock in Sect. 2.11).

In words, the dynamics can be stated as follows:

Current capital → *Worker productivity* → *Wages* → *Retirement saving* → *Future capital*

The dynamic features of (4.8) can be easily sketched by plotting k_t against k_{t-1} as in Fig. 4.2.

Imagine that the economy begins at $k_{t-1} = k_1$. To find out what the capital-labor will be in period 2, move vertically up to the transition equation to find the value of k one period ahead, k_2. In period 2, k_2 will now be the initial capital-labor ratio. To trace the new starting value for k in period 2, move horizontally from the transition equation to the 45-degree line and then back down vertically to the horizontal axis. The process then repeats itself over and over until one reaches $k_t = \bar{k}$, where the transition equation crosses the 45-degree line.[3] At this point, the capital-labor ratio remains constant from period to period and the economy is said to have reached a *steady state* equilibrium. An algebraic solution for the steady state is found by setting $k_t = k_{t-1} = \bar{k}$ in (4.8) and then solving the equation for $\bar{k}$. The transition

[3]The economy never literally reaches the steady state, although it will get arbitrarily close.

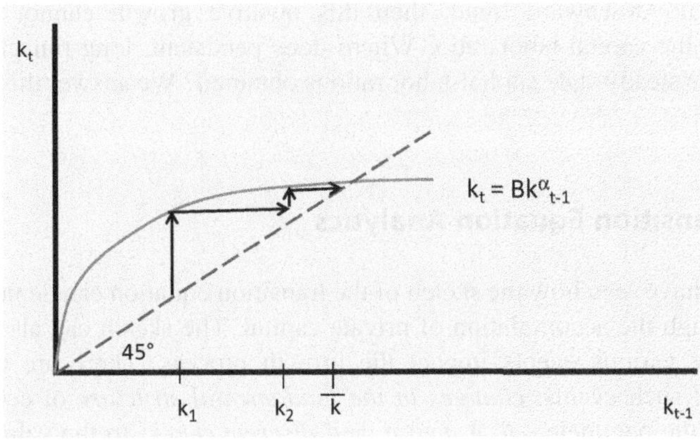

Fig. 4.2 Transitional growth

equation given by (4.8) is simple enough to allow an explicit solution for the steady state capital-labor ratio, $\bar{k} = B^{\frac{1}{1-\alpha}}$.

The transition diagram reveals an important prediction about economic growth via capital accumulation. In the early stages of growth, period to period changes in k_t are relatively large and the economy grows fast. Over time, the increases in k_t get smaller and the economy's growth rate slows down, until growth ceases altogether in the steady state. From the static demand and supply figure, we know that growth occurs due to the effect of capital accumulation on wages and saving. What the transition diagram makes clear is that the effect of capital accumulation on wages becomes weaker over time. There is a diminishing effect of k_t on w_t because $\alpha$is less than one. When an economy is undeveloped and capital is scarce, the creation of new physical capital significantly raises worker productivity and wages. However, as the economy industrializes, the impact of further capital accumulation weakens.[4]

Notice two things about the steady state. First, as k_t grows in approaching the steady state, we know from (4.2a, 4.2b) that interest rates will be falling and wages will be rising. Once the steady state is obtained, because k_t is constant, interest rates and wages must also be constant. Thus, the steady state is characterized by constant interest rates and *zero* growth in labor productivity, real wages, and consumption. In many developed countries, the *average* values of interest rates and returns to capital have been relatively constant over long-periods of time—suggesting that we might view the average position of the economy as being a steady state (with some annual business cycle fluctuations around the economy's typical or average position). However, these same economies are observed to experience *positive* growth rates in labor productivity and real wages *on average*. According to our model, if interest

[4]The weakening effect of the capital-labor ratio on wages, stems from the diminishing marginal product of capital. As capital accumulates relative to labor, the effect of further capital accumulation on output and wages gets smaller. Formally, note that the effect of an increase in k on the marginal product of labor is $(1 - \alpha)\alpha Ak^{\alpha - 1} = (1 - \alpha)\times$*marginal product of capital.*

rates show no downward trend, then this positive growth cannot come from increases in the capital-labor ratio. Where does persistent, long-run growth come from after the steady state capital-labor ratio is obtained? We answer this question in Sect. 4.4.

4.3.1 Transition Equation Analytics

Thus far we have seen how the sketch of the transition equation can depict economic growth through the accumulation of private capital. The sketch can also be used to analyze how various events impact the growth process. There are two general categories of such events: *changes in the fundamental structure* of economies, as captured by the parameters β, A, and n, and *discrete shocks* to the values of K and N due to events not captured by the gradual growth process.

Changes in the economy's structure cause shifts in the sketch of the transition equation. An increase in β raises the household saving rate. For given values of k_{t-1} and w_{t-1}, a higher saving rate out of household wages implies more capital is purchased and a higher value of k_t is supplied in the next period—an upward shift in the transition equation. Such a shift would increase growth and generate a new and higher steady state value for k.

An increase in TFP or A would have a similar effect. A higher value for A directly increases worker productivity and wages. For a given value of k_{t-1}, w_{t-1} would be higher, resulting in more saving (for the same saving rate, i.e. for the same β) and a higher value of k_t in the next period. Greater k_t implies a greater w_t, so the indirect effect on capital accumulation augments the direct effect of A on wages.

If the higher value of A is a *permanent* event, say due to a unique and lasting breakthrough idea that raises productivity such as the invention of electricity, then the transition equation would be permanently higher and the economy would eventually reach a new steady state. The event could also be a *temporary* event, unusually good weather conditions for this year's growing season. In this case the transition equation would only shift up temporarily. Any resulting increase in the economy's capital stock could not be sustained because wages and saving are unusually high during this particular period. The transition equation would shift back down and the economy would return to its original steady state position in the long-run.

Of course, shocks to A can also be *negative*. The pandemic of 2020 caused the country to restrict ways of producing and trading to stop the spread of the virus. These restrictions on face-to-face production of goods and services lowered the productivity of available capital and labor, reducing wages and shifting the transition equation down. When the health threat is over and the economy returns to normal production practices, A increases back to its original level and the economy returns to its previous steady state.

Changes in population growth also fundamentally change the structure of the economy. From looking at (4.8), an increase in n works in the opposite direction as an increase in A, shifting the transition equation downward. Faster population growth increases next period's workforce (the households using capital in the future), relative to this period's workforce (the households saving and supplying capital for the future). The relatively larger future population will dilute or spread the available capital across relatively more workers, lowering the value of k_t in the next period.

There are discrete events that can temporarily shock the value of k *directly*, for a *given economic structure*. An earthquake or other natural disasters can suddenly destroy physical capital, causing K and k to abruptly fall in value. This type of event is captured on the transition equation figure by reducing the economy's current value of k_{t-1}, moving it to the left (closer to the origin and farther from the steady state). No change in the economy's fundamentals has occurred, so the transition equation stays put. The event simply causes a movement along the existing transition equation to the left.

A sudden influx of immigrants that raises the value of N, would have a similar effect in lowering the economy's current value of k. If this was a one-time event, the economy's population growth would remain the same (so the transition equation would not shift), the value of k_{t-1} would be pushed to the left—causing the economy to continue its growth to the same steady state but from a lower initial position. This implies that an influx of workers will lower k and wages in the short-run but not in the long-run, as the capital stock, with more savers in the economy, rises to maintain the same steady state value of k as before.

4.3.2 From the Capital-Labor Ratio to Worker Productivity Growth

It is important to clearly see the connection between capital accumulation and worker productivity. Worker productivity, or more precisely *average* worker productivity, is measured by dividing the economy's workforce into the economy's total output. As discussed in Sect. 4.1, this gives us the worker productivity definition, $y_t \equiv Y_t/L_t = Ak_t^{\alpha}$. Greater capital accumulation per worker leads to greater worker productivity.

What about the effect of capital accumulation on the *growth rate* of worker productivity? The growth rate is the *percentage change* in worker productivity over time,

$$\frac{(Y_{t+1}/L_{t+1}) - (Y_t/L_t)}{(Y_t/L_t)} = \frac{(Y_{t+1}/L_{t+1})}{(Y_t/L_t)} - 1 = \frac{k_{t+1}^{\alpha}}{k_t^{\alpha}} - 1 = \left(\frac{k_{t+1}}{k_t}\right)^{\alpha} - 1.$$

Imagine an economy that is below its steady state. Capital accumulates over time *raising* the *level* of worker productivity each period. However, we also know from the transition equation diagram that changes in k from one period to the next become smaller. This means that the ratio k_{t+1}/k_t becomes smaller each period as the values of k become increasingly similar across periods, implying, from the equation above, that the *growth rate* in worker productivity *falls* over time as the economy grows. Weakening growth in capital accumulation leads to weakening growth in worker productivity. In the steady state grow ceases altogether because $k_{t+1} = k_t = \overline{k}$ and the growth rate of worker productivity is zero.

4.4 Steady State Growth—Technical Progress

The model so far predicts that growth in worker productivity and living standards will slow and eventually become zero. While there is evidence of a growth slowdown in recent decades, growth rates do not appear to be converging to zero—growth is persistent.

One explanation for persistent economic growth is ongoing technical progress—that is increasing knowledge that improves productivity. Technical progress can be thought of as improved production designs or improved factories and equipment. To grow in the steady state with the same amount of capital per worker, we have to get smarter about how we use and design the capital. There are some attempts to explicitly model the research and development process that leads to technical process, but often economists treat technical progress as an exogenous variable, as we do here.

The economic historian Joel Mokyr introduced the term *macro-inventions* to define technological breakthroughs significant enough to allow novel applications and spinoffs that impact the way we live and do business (Mokyr 1990). Jan Vijg (2011) tallied up a list of what he interpreted as macro-inventions from 10,000 BC to 2010.The list contains just over 300 inventions with a little over 100 in the last 100 years. From 1870 to 2000, a period we carefully study in Sect. 4.5, the list includes the following, among many others: electric light bulb (1875), telephone (1876), electric grid (1882), steam turbine (1884), automobile (1889), radio (1898), assembly line (1901), airplane (1903), electronic digital computer (1939), FORTRAN computer language (1957), computer mouse and graphical use interface (1964), robot (1970), microprocessor (1971), internet (1972), Cray supercomputer (1976), and horizontal fracking (2000).

Big ideas and inventions that occur sporadically are best captured by *one-time* permanent shifts in A. These ideas, however, spur on more *continual improvements and refinements* in how production occurs and the types of machines used. We need a way of capturing the ongoing "normal science" of the applications and spinoffs on the grand ideas that make workers more productive.

Think of technology as the current stock of *disembodied* blueprints for production methods and machine designs, the applications of the scientific discoveries from basic research. The state of technology in period t affects the productivity of the workforce. We assume that there is an index number, D_t, that measures the extent to which unidentified forces, such as the state of technology, influence the *effective* workforce. The effective workforce in period t is defined as $H_t = D_t L_t$, which replaces L_t as an input in the Cobb-Douglas production function. When D_t increases, it raises the effective workforce proportionately. For example, if D_t doubles, and the number of workers remains the same, the effect on production will be the same as doubling the workforce. We further assume that technical progress is such that D_t

increases from one period to the next at the constant rate, d. Thus, $H_{t+1}/H_t = n(1 + d)$, the effective workforce increases due to both population growth and technical progress.

We can model the firms as choosing H_t and paying a wage rate per unit of *effective* labor, w_t, a slight change from the previous interpretation. The total wage payment received by an actual worker will now be w_tD_t. The factor price equations given by (4.2a, 4.2b) remain the same, except we reinterpret k as the capital to *effective* labor ratio, i.e. $k = K/H$.

It is important to note that maintaining this new definition of capital intensity is harder for an economy than with the old definition. The economy must keep its capital stock growing fast enough to keep pace with not only the *number* of workers but also with their *skills*. Everything else constant, an economy would have to save at higher rate to supply its *effective* workforce with the capital it needs to maintain a given value of k.

Taking all these considerations into account, now let's think about how the equilibrium and transition equation are altered by technical progress. The firm's demand for the capital, which we can think of as a demand for the ratio of capital to effective-labor, will take the same form as (4.2a). On the household side, we need only adjust the saving function for the new concept of household wages to get $s_t = \frac{\beta}{1+\beta} w_t D_t$. The supply of capital per effective worker is defined as $k_t^s \equiv s_{t-1}N_{t-1}/D_tN_t$. Using the household saving function, the supply of capital per effective worker can be written as $k_t^s = \left[\frac{\beta}{1+\beta}\right] \frac{w_{t-1}}{n(1+d)}$. Finally, using the factor price equations, the adjusted transition equation becomes

$$k_t = \left[\frac{\beta}{1+\beta}\right] \frac{(1-\alpha)Ak_{t-1}^{\alpha}}{n(1+d)}, \tag{4.9}$$

which has the same form as (4.8), except for the presence of $1 + d$ in the denominator of the expression on the right-hand-side of the equation.

Thus, the transitional dynamics of the economy are the same as before. However, now there is an *endogenous* source of growth (increasing physical capital intensity) and an *exogenous* source of growth (technical progress). When the steady state is reached, the transitional growth from increasing physical capital intensity is over and interest rates become constant but there will continue to be positive economic growth from exogenous technical progress. Labor productivity, real wages per worker (w_tD_t), and the standard of living (measured by consumption per household), all increase at the rate $d > 0$ in the steady state.

4.4.1 Transition Equation Analytics

As is evident from (4.9) and the related discussion, the basic form and properties of the economy's transition equation are not affected by the introduction of technical change (apart from the altered interpretation of k). This means that all the results from Sect. 4.3.1, when we covered the analytics of the transition equation without technical change, continue to apply.

4.4.2 From the Capital-Labor Ratio to Worker Productivity Growth

The measure of worker productivity is changed when introducing technical progress (in fact this is the whole point of introducing it in the first place!). Output divided by the number of actual workers is now $Y_t/L_t = Ak_t^{\alpha}D_t$ (see *Problem* 16). As before, greater capital accumulation leads to greater worker productivity. However, now worker productivity also increases every period due to technical progress that raises the productivity index D_t from period to period.

What about the effect of capital accumulation on the *growth rate* of worker productivity? That story changes a bit as well. The growth rate is now

$$\frac{(Y_{t+1}/L_{t+1}) - (Y_t/L_t)}{(Y_t/L_t)} = \frac{(Y_{t+1}/L_{t+1})}{(Y_t/L_t)} - 1 = \frac{k_{t+1}^{\alpha}D_{t+1}}{k_t^{\alpha}D_t} - 1 = \left(\frac{k_{t+1}}{k_t}\right)^{\alpha}(1+d) - 1.$$

As before, imagine an economy that is below its steady state. Capital accumulates over time *raising* the *level* of worker productivity each period. However, the ratio k_{t+1}/k_t becomes smaller each period implying, from the equation above, that the *growth rate* in worker productivity *falls* over time as the economy grows. Weakening growth in capital accumulation still leads to weakening growth in worker productivity. Technical progress simply provides a constant source of growth that does *not* weaken over time. Once the economy converges to the steady state, growth from capital accumulation is exhausted but worker productivity will continue to grow at the rate d each period.

4.5 Quantitative Theory

Over the last 40 years there has been an increasing tendency for macroeconomists to *quantify* their theoretical models. Quantifying a model means determining numerical values for the model's parameters, thereby enabling the model to generate numerical predictions that can be compared to real world data. This healthy tendency to develop theories that can be quantified has greatly improved the understanding of many different phenomena and has created a progressive scientific paradigm within which to conduct macroeconomic research.

In this section, we quantify our simple growth model and compare its predictions to important qualitative patterns we commonly see in the data as economies grow. We are effectively repeating a version of the exercise conducted in the famous article by King and Rebelo (1993). They showed that the standard neoclassical model of private physical capital accumulation is not consistent with the pattern of growth rates and interest rates experienced by the U.S. as it developed.

In most cases it is not possible to use the traditional econometric approach of parameter estimation (due to a desire to limit the number of variables in the analysis, the nonlinear structure of the model, or the lack of appropriate data). Instead the model is *calibrated*. That is parameters are set so as to allow the model to *match* certain *targets*—observations or previously estimated behavioral responses.[5] Once calibrated, the model can generate predictions about the values of variables that were *not* used in the calibration. The predicted values can then be compared against data to assess the model's ability to replicate the real world. Failures to replicate important real world observations then lead to adjustments in the model, or entirely new models, that provide a better approximation. The model currently providing the best approximation should be favored to conduct *policy analysis*, where the effects of current and proposed government policies are evaluated. Continually pursuing the most accurate quantitative approximation is the best chance we have of improving our understanding of economies and policies.

Let's make these ideas more concrete by calibrating a simple neoclassical model of physical capital accumulation and then testing its predictions about economic growth. The transition Eq. (4.9) provides the basic model. The equation contains six exogenous parameters:α, β, δ, d, A, and n. To allow for endogenous growth through increasing physical capital intensity, we will have to start the economy in an initial position that is below its steady state. So, an initial value, k_1, will also have to be determined. Finally, the length of each time period in the model must be chosen. In fact, other parameter values may depend on the time-period choice.

Part of the calibration typically involves matching the steady state of the model to certain observations (for example, the interest rate or the rate of return to capital). Since all variables in the neoclassical growth model can be related back to k, we will need the steady state solution of (4.9),

$$\bar{k} = \left[\frac{\beta A}{1+\beta}\frac{1-\alpha}{n(1+d)}\right]^{\frac{1}{1-\alpha}} \tag{4.10}$$

[5]There are differences of opinion about what qualifies as an appropriate target. Some believe that calibration should *not* involve previous econometric estimation. According to this view, all parameters within a model should be set to match particular data points or statistical moments of a data set (sample means, variances, and covariances), but *not* to match econometric estimates found in the literature. Others broaden the targets to include previous statistical estimates of the model's parameters and behavioral responses, *even if the model used in the estimation is not the same as the one used in the calibration*. We are comfortable with either approach. The important point from our perspective is that all quantitative models, *however calibrated*, should be tested by comparing their predictions against observations or statistics *not* used in the calibration process. The fact that these "tests" or comparisons are not as formal and refined as traditional hypothesis testing in statistics does not particularly concern us. At this stage in the profession's understanding of macroeconomics, models that even roughly approximate reality are difficult to find. Hopefully, as our approximations become more refined, we will need to worry about more formal testing procedure.

Calibration

In our two-period life-cycle model, the first period is designated the "work-period" and the second period the "retirement –period." In this setting, it is often assumed that each period lasts 30 years. In comparison to the real world, a 30-year period makes the working life too short and the retirement period too long. The more periods we allow in the life-cycle, the more realistic the model becomes.

For example, we could instead assume that *three* twenty-year periods represent a lifetime, with two working periods (40 years) and one retirement period (20 years). However, as you add periods, the model becomes more complicated. Each additional period of life added, also adds a new generation to the economy. In a life-cycle model where each household lives for three periods, there will be a young, a middle-aged, and an old household alive in any given time period. The complication of keeping track of different generations is a clear disadvantage of using an explicit overlapping generations approach. However, advances in computing are lessening the disadvantage over time. In this book, we stick with a two-period model because it is sufficient to generate several important qualitative and quantitative implications.[6]

With the time period selected, we can begin setting other parameter values. Our application will examine the model's ability to explain growth in the U.S. from the end of the Civil War through the end of the 20th century. In applying the model, a useful way to proceed is to create a relatively simple *baseline* calibration and then do a *sensitivity analysis* by examining how results change as we deviate from the baseline calibration or model specification.

The annual rate of population growth actually fell over this historical period, from 2.3 percent in the late 19th century to about 1 percent by the end of the 20th century (Barro 1974). For the baseline calibration we set the annual rate of population growth to be one percent over all periods. Time periods in the model last 30 years, so the value for population growth in the model is the one percentage point annual rate of growth compounded for 30 years. The value of n is then chosen to satisfy the equation $n = (1.01)^{30} = 1.3478$. Sensitivity analysis reveals that our conclusions are not driven by this simplifying assumption.

The capital share of output and income has shown no systematic trend in U.S. history or across countries at different stages of development today (Gollin 2002). We set α to a commonly estimated value of 1/3.

The annual rate of depreciation on physical capital is estimated to be in a range between 5 and 10 percent (e.g. Stokey and Rebelo (1995)).[7] We set the annual rate of depreciation to 7 percent. To translate the annual depreciation rate into the depreciation rate over 30 years, think about how much capital remains each year after

[6]For a further discussion of the issues associated with quantifying overlapping generations models see Appendix B of Chap. 2 from Das et al. (2018).

[7]Estimates of the rate of depreciation in academic studies tend to be smaller than the estimates used by national income accounts, where the rate of depreciation is typically in the 10–15 percent rage. The higher the rate of depreciation, the more accurate is the simplification used in future chapters where we assume the capital stock completely depreciates after a single period of the model (associated with continual use for 30 actual years).

depreciation occurs. In any given year the physical capital stock at year's end is 93 percent of its value at the beginning of the year. If you start with one unit of capital today, then after 30 years there would be $1-\delta = (1-0.07)^{30} = 0.93^{30} = 0.1134$ units of capital. So, $\delta = 0.8866$.

Recall that we can write worker productivity or output per worker as

$$\frac{Y_t}{L_t} = \frac{Ak_t^{\alpha}D_tL_t}{L_t} = Ak_t^{\alpha}D_t. \tag{4.11}$$

So we can write the ratio of worker productivity in 1990 to worker productivity in 1870 as

$$\frac{(Y/L)_{1990}}{(Y/L)_{1870}} = \left(\frac{k_{1990}}{k_{1870}}\right)^{\alpha}\frac{D_{1990}}{D_{1870}}. \tag{4.12}$$

For the baseline case, we arbitrarily set d so that exogenous technical progress explains "half" the economy's growth (i.e. *equal* contributions from k and D in (4.12)). The annual rate of growth in labor productivity from 1870 to 1990 was about 1.6 percent (Rangazas 2002). With a growth rate of 1.6 percent per year over 120 years, labor productivity was 6.7180 times higher in 1990 than in 1870. In terms of a geometric mean of a product of two terms, half of this growth is $6.7180^{1/2} = 2.5919$. The annual rate of technical progress needed to generate this much growth is 0.7968 percent. This means that $1 + d = (1.007968)^{30} = 1.2688$, or $d = 0.2688$. As will soon become apparent, our main conclusions are not affected by the exact value of d chosen.

Finally, we set β to match the rate of return to capital. We take the rate of return to capital to be the rate of return on the Standard and Poor's 500 over the 20th century. The annual real rate of return on this portfolio of stocks averaged 7 percent over the 20th century (Kocerlakota 1996). Due the absence of any trend in the annual rate of return over the century, we assume that the U.S. economy was close to its steady state at least by the end of the 20th century. Thus, we have $1 + \overline{r} - \delta = 1.07^{30} = 7.6123$. Using (4.2a) and (4.10), we have

$$\frac{\beta}{1+\beta} = \frac{\alpha}{1-\alpha}\frac{n(1+d)}{\overline{r}} \tag{4.13}$$

Plugging the calibrated values of the other parameters into (4.13) implies $\beta = 0.1287$.

We still have to set the initial value of k_t to be consistent with the growth rate and the calibrated value of d. The idea is to set k_1 so that half of the economy's growth is explained by capital accumulation (the remaining equal contribution not explained by technical progress in (4.12)). So, choose k_1 to satisfy

$$\left(\frac{k_5}{k_1}\right)^{\alpha} = 2.5919 \tag{4.14}$$

Since both k values in (4.14) are unknown before the model simulation is run, we have to experiment with values for k_1 until we find one that satisfies (4.14).

By assuming that the economy is close to its steady state in 1990, we can get a good guess for k_1 by using (4.14) to write $k_1 = \bar{k}/17.41$. To determine the absolute values of $\bar{k}$ and k_1, we need to set a value for A. This parameter is different than the others because it only scales the level of production. There is no particular reason for us to replicate the *level* of production observed in the real world (even the real-world index numbers for GDP are arbitrary). So, we set A to be one. This implies $\bar{k} = 0.00937$ and, as an initial guess, $k_1 = 0.000538$.

To summarize, the calibrated parameters are given below.

Calibration	
n	1.3478
d	0.2688
A	1.0000
α	0.3333
β	0.1287
δ	0.8866

With the parameters calibrated, we are now almost ready to do a historical simulation. The remaining task is to set an accurate initial value of k. We need to search for a starting value that will cause half the observed growth in worker productivity to be explained via capital accumulation.

To do this, one plugs the initial guess for k_1, formed above, into (4.9) and lets the model generate the subsequent values for k_t. This guess will not generate enough growth because the economy will not reach the steady state after 4 periods (as was assumed in generating the initial guess). Lower the guess for k_1 a bit and try again. Keep tinkering with the initial value until the growth target given by (4.14) is met. Once finding the value for k_t that satisfy (4.14), you're done. Compute the predicted interest rates and labor productivity growth rates and then annualize them so they can be easily compared to the actual historical estimates. The annualized values of predicted interest rates (solid line) and growth rates (dashed line) are displayed in Fig. 4.3.

Historical Simulation

The model predicts high interest rates (14 percent) and growth rates (3 percent) for the late 19th century and then a decline in both variables over the 20th century. These predictions miss the mark for a number of reasons.

Returns to capital were probably higher in the late 19th century than during the 20th century. We do not have returns on the Standard and Poor's 500 that go back as far as 1870, but the rates of return on other assets were 2–6 percentage points higher in 1870 than in the 20th century. Wallis (2000, Fig. 4.2) reports that real interest rates on national government debt averaged about 5% in the first half of the 19th century and averaged about 2.5% during the 20th century. Barro (1974) reports that real interest rates on commercial paper were 9% from 1840 to 1880, but averaged about 3% during the 20th century. The model predicts initial interest rates out of this range, about 7 percentage points higher than in the 20th century. Also by 1900, observed

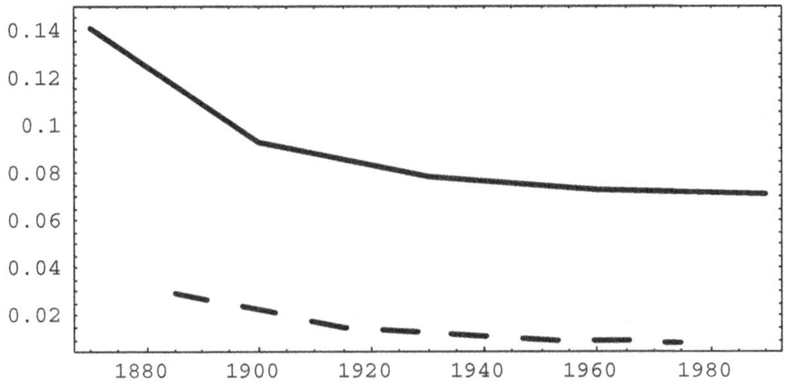

Fig. 4.3 Simulated U.S. interest rates and growth rates: 1870 to 2000. *Notes*: The solid line gives the annualized rate of return to capital and the dashed line gives the annualized growth rate of labor productivity. The annualized growth rates over 30 year periods were plotted above the midpoint of the intervals between the periods

Table 4.1 Growth rate in output per worker

1820	0.31
1840	1.82
1860	1.32
1880	1.84
1900	1.53
1920	1.40
1940	1.72
1960	2.45
1980	1.58
2000	1.62

Notes: The Table gives annual growth rates in worker productivity over two centuries of U.S. history. See Mourmouras and Rangazas (2009) for sources

interest rates showed no trend, while the model predicts a downward trend throughout the 20th century, especially in the first third of the century.

The growth rate predictions are even less accurate. Table 4.1 presents estimates of U.S. labor productivity growth rates for two centuries (Mourmouras and Rangazas 2009). Growth rates showed little trend from 1840 to 2000. In contrast, the model predicts high growth rates in the 19th century and then a steady decline.

The fundamental problem with the standard neoclassical growth model is clear. In order to satisfy (4.14), the capital-labor ratio must be set well below its steady state value in 1870. The relatively low capital-labor ratio produces relatively high returns to capital. The fact that the capital-labor ratio is well below its steady state value generates high and declining growth rates, as indicated qualitatively by the transition equation diagram in Fig. 4.2 and numerically by several of the end-of-chapter *Problems*.

The only way to make the model's predictions more accurate is to set k_1 closer to $\overline{k}$. But this means much less than half the historical growth will be explained by physical capital accumulation. More endogenous sources of growth are needed to produce a satisfactory explanation of growth in United States history.[8] One of these sources is public capital in the form of public schooling, roads, public utilities, and other aspects of government infrastructure. The next chapter extends the model to include fiscal policy.

4.6 Beyond Private Capital: Other Sources of Growth

The results of Sect. 4.5 suggest that to provide an explanation of economic growth one must go beyond the accumulation of private capital. Simply putting greater reliance on exogenous technological progress is more an admission of ignorance than a complete explanation. In addition, trendless technological progress is inconsistent with the pattern of modern growth. As emphasized by Gordon (2016), the pattern of modern growth has the appearance of a "Great Wave," with growth rates first rising, then stabilizing for many decades, before falling back down. This pattern is exhibited for the U.S. over two centuries in Table 4.2. Relying on exogenous technological change only helps make the model consistent with the middle portion of the wave pattern where growth is relatively trendless.

One way of explaining the Great Wave growth pattern is to acknowledge that growth is affected by a variety of government investments as we first discussed in Chap. 2. Tanzi and Schuknecht (2000, Tables 2.5 and 2.13) report the sum of public expenditures on education and public infrastructure as a fraction of GDP for 11 currently developed economies—Australia, Canada, France, Germany, Japan, Netherlands, Norway, Spain, Sweden, United Kingdom and the United States. They find the average government investment share rose from 2.6 percent in 1870 to 9.1 percent in 1990. The rise in the investment share helped to offset diminishing returns and maintain the economy's growth rate.

In the middle of the 20th century, the governments of advanced economies also began investing more in the funding of basic research. In the U.S. the fraction of GDP spent on government supported basic research rose and peaked at just under 2 percent in 1965 (Vijg 2011, Fig. 6.2). Basic research creates the public scientific and mathematical knowledge that often forms the basis for technological advances (Flexner 2017). For example, the theory of electromagnetism led to the introduction of the FM radio and television. The quantum theory in physics allowed the development of microprocessors, lasers, and nanotechnology. In fact it has been estimated that 30 percent of U.S. GDP is based on inventions made possible by quantum mechanics. The theory of relativity has been used to improve the accuracy of GPS tracking devices. The theory of super-conductivity allows trains to run faster and

[8] See Das et al. (2018, Chaps. 2 and 4) for an extension of the quantitative theory to include human capital accumulation through public schooling.

Table 4.2 The great wave: U.S. growth 1800–2000

Average annual growth rate in GDP per capita

1800–1840	1840–1880	1880–1920	1920–1980	1980–1990	1990–2000	2000–2010
0.58	1.44	1.78	2.18	2.28	2.16	0.62

Average annual growth rate in GDP per worker

1800–1840	1840–1880	1880–1920	1920–1980	1980–1990	1990–2000	2000–2010
1.07	1.58	1.47	1.92	1.58	1.62	

Notes: Average growth rate in GDP per capita is based on Farmer and Schelnast (2013, Table 5.1). Average growth in GDP per worker is based on Table 4.1 above brains to be scanned by MRI technologies. Government funding of basic science is one tangible factor in creating "exogenous" technological change.

In the next chapter, following the approach of Chap. 2, we will combine these government investments together under the simplifying concept of public capital. Rising rates of government investment in the early stages of economic development help explain why growth rates first rise. The fact that public capital complements private capital in production helps keep the marginal product of private capital from falling, so that growth rates and returns to private capital can remain trendless for decades. The diminishing returns to public capital investment and the leveling, and even decline, of government investment rates help to explain why growth rates eventually fall in late development.

4.7 Growth and Welfare

Comparisons of living standards over time and across countries are typically based on worker productivity or GDP per capita. However, economic welfare depends on many factors that cannot be fully traded in markets: health and longevity, home production and exchange (including a growing array of digital services provided via non-market transactions), and the quality of the environment and the sustainable use of natural resources. Personal safety and security and equality of opportunity also affect individual welfare but are missing from GDP calculations as they depend on public governance and the quality of social norms and formal and informal institutions rather than market transactions.

Recent research by Bannister et al. (2020) constructs a comprehensive measure of individual welfare by country. They find that welfare determinants, while not explicitly included in GDP measures, may be correlated with income in the sense that richer countries have more amenities and nonmarket benefits. In fact, the welfare gaps across countries are much larger than the income gaps. For example, while a U.S. household has almost 17 times higher income than a household living in Sub-Saharan Africa, the welfare gap in consumption-equivalent units is 33 when using the broadest collection of welfare determinants. Furthermore, while income gaps between advanced countries and Africa exhibit painfully slow convergence, welfare gaps have *diverged* over the last 30 years.

Capturing the multidimensional nature of individual and national welfare has long been an important objective of economic research (e.g. Tobin and Nordhaus (1972)). Recently, the United Nations adopted the Sustainable Development Goals (SDGs), which set ultimate targets (eradicate extreme poverty around the world by 2030) and contain intermediate indicators for equality, education, and gender and environmental protection. Other indicators have been developed by the OECD, the UNDP (Human Development Index) and the World Economic Forum among others. However, many approaches have been criticized for being ad-hoc and lacking theoretical foundations.

A more promising approach was presented by Jones and Klenow (2016) and extended by Bannister and Mourmouras (2017) to capture environmental and resource sustainability considerations. This approach relies on a metric called consumption-equivalent welfare, in the tradition of Lucas (1987). It is based on the economics of expected utility and combines data on consumption, leisure, inequality and mortality to calculate expected lifetime utility of different cohorts in different countries. The welfare index of country i in year t answers a simple question: what hypothetical consumption in the United States in year t, given the United States levels of *other* welfare determinants, would yield the same expected utility as the actual values of consumption, leisure, mortality and inequality in country i. The answer is expressed as a proportion of the actual consumption level in the United States. For example if the welfare determinants in country i are generally inferior to those in the United States, the computed value might be 0.5, meaning that you would have cut United States consumption in half to drive lifetime utility down to that in country i.

The calculations permit welfare analysis of a nearly thirty-year period, 1990–2017. The indices of welfare are used to compare levels of welfare across countries in 2017, as well as trends in welfare vs. income convergence over time. Welfare is found to be strongly correlated with consumption per capita but also depends significantly on mortality, inequality, leisure and non-market activities, as suggested above.

Table 4.3 presents summary statistics of levels of welfare around the world. In 2017, the last year for which Penn World Tables data on GDP (at purchasing power parity exchange rates) are available, average per capita GDP around the world was slightly over 27 percent of the U.S. level. Welfare, on the other hand, was about 23 percent. The difference is attributable to lower life expectancy, a lower consumption to income ratio, greater inequality, and lower non-market activities in the average country compared to the United States.

Table 4.3 also makes clear that the dispersion around these averages is large, over 30 percent. Looking at regional averages, advanced economies (mainly in Europe and Asia) have lower per capita GDP and welfare than the U.S., but the welfare gap is lower than the income gap, reflecting higher life expectancies and lower inequality. Developing economies on the other hand, consistently exhibit welfare gaps that are significantly greater than per capita income gaps.

They also compare the *growth rates* for income and welfare over the 1990–2017 period, presented below in Table 4.4. For the world as a whole, the population-weighted growth rate of welfare over the period is very similar to the rate of growth of (PPP adjusted) per capita income, about 4 percent per annum. This reflects the large weight in their sample of fast-growing economies (China, Indonesia), where improvements in life expectancy boosted welfare (relative to per capita income), but these gains were offset by lower consumption, lower leisure, and rising inequality during the period.

As expected, in the advanced economies of Western Europe and North America income and welfare grew more slowly than other regions (supporting the idea of convergence). Interestingly, in these advanced country regions, welfare grew by about 3 percent on average, over 1 percent per annum more than income per capita. This reflected improvements in life expectancy, as well as higher consumption and

Table 4.3 Welfare and GDP per capita around the world, 2017

	Welfare	Income	Difference	Decomposition of difference			
	(1)	(2)	Log (1)/(2)	Life exp.	C/Y	Leisure	Inequality
Average, unweighted	30.56	34.92	−0.18	−0.12	0.05	0.01	−0.02
Average, pop-weighted	22.84	27.39	−0.37	−0.13	0.17	−0.03	−0.03
Median absolute dev.	19.53	21.99	0.18	0.18	0.12	0.04	0.06
Standard deviation	31.21	34.89	0.33	0.19	0.25	0.07	0.12
Regional Averages							
United States	100.00	100.00	0.00	0.00	0.00	0.00	0.00
Advanced Economies	89.36	83.75	0.09	0.13	0.09	0.00	0.04
Emerging and Developing Europe	34.21	40.63	−0.16	−0.17	0.02	0.01	0.02
Latin America and the Caribbean	18.79	25.18	−0.29	−0.11	0.02	−0.01	−0.18
Middle East and North Africa	17.53	22.62	−0.16	−0.23	0.03	0.07	0.03
Emerging and Developing Asia	8.98	17.02	−0.59	−0.15	0.33	−0.08	−0.04
Sub-Saharan Africa	3.71	6.01	−0.33	−0.29	0.00	0.04	−0.08

Source: Authors' calculations based on WPT, IMF, World Bank and other data. The figures are average annual growth rates, and the decomposition applies to the "Difference" column. Sample size is 169 countries

leisure. Welfare would have improved even more rapidly—about 7 basis points higher per annum—had advanced economies contained inequality during the period.

Most developing country regions experienced gains in welfare that exceeded growth in income during this period. This is most evident in the countries of Central and Eastern Europe but is also true for Latin America and the Caribbean, the Middle East and North Africa and Sub-Saharan Africa. In Emerging and Developing Europe especially, welfare growth of over 4 percent per annum outstripped growth in income by 1 2/3 percent per annum, mainly because of important improvements in life expectancy and consumption, with higher leisure and lower inequality in consumption making small contributions.

Table 4.4 Growth in welfare and per capita GDP around the world, 1990–2017

	Welfare	Income	Difference	Decomposition of Difference			
	(1)	(2)	(1)–(2)	Life exp.	C/Y	Leisure	Inequality
Average, unweighted	3.45	2.64	0.82	0.85	−0.11	−0.06	0.13
Average, pop-weighted	4.07	4.07	0.00	0.81	−0.58	−0.07	−0.16
Median absolute deviation	3.35	2.53	1.02	0.84	0.28	0.11	0.17
Standard deviation	1.63	1.78	0.98	0.38	0.75	0.20	0.48
Regional Averages							
Advanced Economies	3.02	1.93	1.09	0.90	0.22	0.05	−0.08
Emerging and Developing Europe	4.16	2.50	1.66	0.92	0.68	0.03	0.03
Latin America and the Caribbean	3.96	2.75	1.21	0.82	0.14	−0.14	0.39
Middle East and North Africa	3.42	2.77	0.65	0.71	−0.07	−0.05	0.07
Emerging and Developing Asia	4.50	5.40	−0.91	0.77	−1.18	−0.10	−0.39
Sub-Saharan Africa	1.29	1.03	0.26	0.35	−0.15	−0.04	0.10

Source: Authors' calculations based on WPT, IMF, World Bank and other data. The figures are average annual growth rates, and the decomposition applies to the "Difference" column

Environmental and Sustainability (E&S) Adjustments

While revealing, calculations of welfare given above do not reflect the effect of environmental quality and resource sustainability. As is well known, market failures and externalities result in the underpricing of environmental goods and overexploitation of natural resources. The consumption-equivalent approach to measuring welfare lends itself naturally to incorporation of E&S adjustments. The authors make three adjustments to baseline calculations given above to include health effects of air pollution, the impact of climate change on GDP over time, and the sustainability in countries' use of natural resources. Accounting for E&S adjustments further widen the welfare gaps across rich and poor countries.

The first adjustment, for air pollution, captures the effect of air pollution on life expectancy by means of Disability Adjusted Life Years (DALYs) as estimated by the World Health Organization. DALYs summarize the burden of disease: one

DALY is the loss of one year of full health, including the burden of diseases (morbidity) and death (mortality). Using DALYs, adjusted life expectancy and the associated expected utility that could have been achieved without the burden of air pollution are calculated.

Except for a few advanced economies, air pollution in most countries is worse than in the United States, creating a negative contribution to the welfare index. Dramatic reductions in home air pollution in developing and emerging market countries during 1990–2017 have raised life expectancy. Improvements in air pollution have been as important as changes in leisure or inequality in some regions. However, the effect on welfare is an order of magnitude lower than the welfare effects from the general growth of life expectancy and the growth of income.

The second E&S adjustment imputes welfare losses from global CO_2 emissions. Based on evidence from historical temperature shocks, the cost of emissions are computed throughout the life of a representative household in each country. The welfare costs of CO_2 emissions are calculated under a business-as-usual (BAU) assumption, which assumes that global emissions remain at the current (2017) level. Under BAU, emissions lead to higher temperatures and lower output and consumption. The measured effects are country-specific because the negative effects from rising temperatures and changing precipitation have an empirical relationship with a country's GDP. Across the globe, climate change lowers welfare relative to the United States. In doing their calculations, the authors consider the uncertainty associated with climate projections. For example, some climate models predict that the earth will be much warmer in 2050 than the business as usual (BAU) baseline. Households have risk averse preferences and the uncertain nature of climate change adds a quantitatively important dimension to expected utility and welfare calculations. Uncertainty over climate change is rising over time, exerting a larger negative effect on welfare through this mechanism. A major motivation for policies seeking to limit global warming is to provide insurance against potentially bad outcomes that raise uncertainty and lower welfare.

The third adjustment considers the sustainability of consumption over time. A country's consumption is deemed unsustainable if its national wealth (the sum of produced, natural and human capital) decreases over time. To implement the sustainability calculation, the concept of *adjusted (or genuine) net saving* (ANS) is used, which adjusts a country's Net National Saving as it appears in the standard national income and product accounts for depletion of natural capital and additions to human capital stocks. When a country's ANS is negative, the economy is depleting its natural resources and running down its comprehensive wealth. Again, uncertainty about the country incidence and extent of resource sustainability is shown to be quantitatively important. Accounting for sustainability lowers welfare relative to the United States in the Middle East and Africa.

4.8 Exercises

Questions

1. Define the following concepts and give an example of each.
   (a) *technology*
   (b) *capital*
   (c) *physical capital*
   (d) *human capital*
2. Explain the meaning of (4.2a) and (4.2b). What variables are determined by these two equations?
3. Let's relate the discussion of the firm to something you know well. Think of the physical capital stock as fixed, as in the short-run model of the competitive firm from introductory and intermediate microeconomics. Sketch the marginal product of labor as a function of the employment level of a firm. Next, add the competitive market wage rate to the diagram. Finally, locate the firm's profit-maximizing employment level. How does the profit-maximizing demand for labor change if there an increase in the firm's capital stock? An increase in A? An increase in the market wage? In forming your answer, only think about how an *individual* firm's demand for labor would change.
4. Write out the average and marginal products of labor in terms of the capital-labor ratio. What is the conceptual difference between the two notions of productivity?
5. When assuming the Cobb-Douglas production function what are the capital and labor shares? Is the model's treatment of income shares consistent with empirical evidence? Explain.
6. Explain the differences between *rental rate*, *rate of return on capital*, and *interest rate*.
7. Explain how each of the following affects current consumption, future consumption, and saving: (a) wages, (b) return to capital, and (c) the preference parameter β.
8. What is the interest elasticity of saving in the model of the household? Is this consistent with the empirical evidence? Explain.
9. How is the transition equation related to the capital market equilibrium?
10. Explain why an increase in this period's capital stock causes an increase in next period's capital stock. Why does the linkage become weaker as the economy accumulates more capital?
11. As the economy moves toward the steady state from below what happens to its growth? What happens to the growth rate if it heads to the steady state from above?
12. What happens to each of the following variables as an economy approaches its steady state from below?
    (a) worker productivity
    (b) the growth rate of worker productivity
    (c) wages
    (d) interest rates or the rate of return to capital

13. Explain the effect of each of the following events on the transition equation.
    (a) an increase in total factor productivity
    (b) an increase in the economy's saving rate
    (c) an increase in the economy's population growth rate
    (d) a permanent one-time jump in the economy's population size
    (e) a natural disaster that destroys part of the economy's capital stock
14. Suppose that economy A and economy B have identical structures (production technologies, preferences, and population growth rates), but economy A has a higher capital-labor ratio. Which country is "richer"? Which country grows faster? Your answer explains what is known as *conditional convergence.* Show, by example, that if two countries do *not* have identical structures that *absolute* or *unconditional convergence* is not guaranteed.
15. Why is it clear that the model must include technological progress in order to match empirical data?
16. Let the annualized value of d be defined as d^a. Assume that $d^a = 0.01$.
    (a) What is d if each period in the model last 30 years? (Hint: recall how r_t and r_t^a are related from Problem 3)
    (b) What is the annualized growth rate of worker productivity, Y_t/L_t, in the steady state? In thinking about this question it may help to refer to the results of *Problem* 16.
    (c) What can you say about the annualized growth rate in worker productivity as the economy approaches the steady state from below?
17. Explain what it means to calibrate a model. Briefly describe the calibration of the model of physical capital accumulation in Sect. 4.4. Mention the basis on which each parameter was set. How was the initial value of k determined?
18. Discuss the design and the results of the calibration experiment when the model of physical capital accumulation was used to historically replicate growth in the U.S. from 1870 to 1990.
19. What are some important sources of growth, other than private capital and exogenous technological change, not captured in the model of this chapter?
20. From 1870 to 1990, average years of schooling of an American worker increased from about 7 to 14. If the return to a year of schooling is a 10 percent gain in worker productivity, what was the total increase in worker productivity due to schooling over this historical period?
21. U.S. economic growth has been referred to as a "Great Wave." What does this mean? How can one explain this pattern of economic growth?

Problems

1. Show that (4.1) exhibits the neoclassical properties of diminishing marginal productivity and constant returns to scale.
2. Derive Eqs. (4.2a, 4.2b) and (4.3a, 4.3b). How are they related?
3. The time periods of the model are rather abstract, representing an entire working life, say 30 years. We interpret r_t as the compounded rental rate earned over the

30 year period. We can think of an *annualized* rental rate, r_t^a, by introducing the definition, $1 + r_t = \left(1 + r_t^a\right)^{30}$.
Suppose that the annualized return to capital is 7.4% or $r_t^a = 0.074$. Assuming that $A = 1$, and $\alpha = 1/3$, find the numerical values for the following variables that are consistent with a perfectly competitive equilibrium given this particular value for r_t^a
(a) r_t
(b) k_t
(c) w_t
(d) economic profit
Assuming the same value for r_t^a, redo the calculations if $A = 30$. Intuitively explain the effect on (b)-(d) of assuming the higher value for A.
4. What is total income in the model with capital and production? Show that the value of output is equal to the value of income.
5. Derive the optimal life-cycle behavior given by (4.5a, 4.5b) and (4.6).
6. Sketch the lifetime budget constraint of a households, $c_{1t} + \frac{c_{2t+1}}{R_t} = w_t$, with the two choice variables, c_{1t} plotted on the horizontal axis and c_{2t+1} on the vertical axis. What happens to the diagram if R_t increases? Conceptually decompose how the diagram is affected by an increase in R_t in terms of (a) opportunities for consumption in both periods and (b) the opportunity cost of current consumption in terms of forgone future consumption. Intuitively think about how (a) and (b) affect the optimal choice of consumption in the first period—the effect of (a) is called the *income* or *wealth effect* and the effect from (b) is called the *substitution effect*. Why are the names for the effects appropriate? What must be true about these two conceptual effects of an increase in R_t to be consistent with the optimal choice of c_{1t} given in (4.5a)?
7. We can generalize household preferences by using a *Constant Elasticity of Substitution* (CES) utility function, $u_t = U(c_{1t}, c_{2t+1}) = \frac{\left(c_{1t}^{1-1/\sigma} - 1\right) + \beta\left(c_{2t+1}^{1-1/\sigma} - 1\right)}{(1-1/\sigma)}$.
The new parameter is the *intertemporal elasticity of substitution* (σ). The intertemporal elasticity of substitution is a measure of the individual's willingness to substitute current for future consumption when the relative price of future consumption falls. Subtracting 1 from each consumption term is done for purely technical reasons. It allows the commonly used logarithmic utility function, $\ln c_{1t} + \beta \ln c_{2t+1}$, to appear as a special case when $\sigma = 1$ (see the Technical Appendix section A.5).
Show if households maximize the CES lifetime utility function subject to the lifetime budget constraint, the solution gives us the following optimal consumption and saving behavior
(a) $c_{1t} = \Psi_{1t} w_t$
(b) $c_{2t+1} = \Psi_{2t} w_t$
(c) $s_t = \Psi_{1t} \beta^\sigma R_t^{\sigma-1} w_t$,
where $\Psi_{1t} \equiv \frac{1}{1+\beta^\sigma R_t^{\sigma-1}} < 1$ and $\Psi_{2t} \equiv \frac{\beta^\sigma R_t^\sigma}{1+\beta^\sigma R_t^{\sigma-1}}$.

The relative strength of the income and substitution effects identified in Problem 6 is determined by σ. The greater is the value of σ the stronger is the substitution effect and the weaker is the income effect. When $\sigma = 1$, the income and substitution effects cancel exactly and the saving rate become a constant fraction of wages.

8. Starting from the definition of k^s, derive Eq. (4.7).
9. Show that if we use the saving behavior with the CES preferences from Problem 7 that the transition equation becomes $k_t = \frac{(1-\alpha)Ak_{t-1}^{\alpha}}{n}\left[\frac{1}{1+\beta^{-\sigma}(1+r_t-\delta)^{1-\sigma}}\right]$.
10. Starting with the adjusted definition of k^s, derive the transition Eq. (4.9).
11. How do we know that the transition equation will be concave in Fig. 4.2? The concavity of the transition function establishes three crucial properties of the steady state equilibrium: (i) existence (there is a steady state), (ii) uniqueness (there is only one steady state with $k > 0$), and (iii) dynamic stability (if you start away from the steady state you will always move toward it). Use the diagram to explain this.
12. *Transition Paths I*
    Under the following parameter assumptions: $A = n = 1$, $d = 0$, $\beta = 1/2$, $\alpha = 1/3$, and an initial capital intensity of $k_0 = 0.0500$, compute the values of k_t over the next 5 periods using (4.9), which is the same as (4.8) when $d = 0$. What is the exact value of k_t in the steady state?
13. *Transition Paths II*
    Use the same assumptions as in *Problem* 12, but now let $A = 10$. Compute the values of k_t over the next 5 periods and in the steady state. Use a transition equation diagram to contrast the solution to *Problems* 12 and 13.
14. *Transition Paths III*
    Use the same assumptions as in *Problem* 13, but now let $n = 1.5$. Compute the values of k_t over the next 5 periods and in the steady state. Use a transition equation diagram to contrast the solution to *Problems* 13 and 14.
15. *Transition Paths IV*
    Use the same assumptions as in *Problem* 13, but now let $d = 0.5$. Compute the values of k_t over the next 5 periods and in the steady state. Use a transition equation diagram to contrast the solution to *Problems* 13 and 15. What is the difference between *Problems* 14 and 15?
16. In the model, adjusted for technological progress, the production function becomes $Y_t = AK_t^{\alpha}H_t^{1-\alpha}$.
    (a) If we redefine k_t as $k_t \equiv K_t/H_t$, show $Y_t = Ak_t^{\alpha}H_t$.
    (b) Show worker productivity is $Y_t/L_t = Ak_t^{\alpha}D_t$
17. Use (4.2a) and (4.10) to derive (4.13). What is the intuition explaining why an increase in A does not affect the rental rate on physical capital in the steady state?
18. The annual average growth rate of worker productivity from 1870 to 1990 has been estimated to be 1.6 percent. Given this fact compute the following.
    (a) The ratio of worker productivity in 1990 to worker productivity in 1870.

(b) If the rise in worker productivity from 1870 to 1990 is accounted for by equal contributions from physical capital accumulation and technical progress, use (4.12) to compute D_{1990}/D_{1870}.

(c) Based on your answer from (b), compute the average *annualized* value of d from 1870 to 1990.

19. Using a calculator or a computer, reproduce the values associated with the historical simulation displayed in Fig. 4.3. Note that the period growth factor, one plus the period growth rate, is $\frac{(Y/L)_{t+1}}{(Y/L)_t} = \left(\frac{k_{t+1}}{k_t}\right)^{\alpha} \frac{D_{t+1}}{D_t}$. To get the annual growth rates in the figure you must calculate *annualized* value of the period growth factor.

20. Use the results of *Problems* 7 and 9 to derive the transition for k_t when $\sigma \neq 1$. Redo the numerical exercise in *Problem* 17 when $\sigma = 0.50$. Note, using a similar approach to that described in the text, you will have to select a new initial value of k_1 to generate the required total growth by period 5. Explain the difference in the paths of k_t when $\sigma = 0.50$ and when $\sigma = 1$.

References

Bannister, G., and Mourmouras, A., 2017, "Welfare vs. Income Convergence and Environmental Externalities," *IMF Working Paper No. 17/271*, International Monetary Fund: Washington DC.

Bannister, G., Gjonbalaj, A., Ivanyna, M., and Mourmouras, A, 2020, Welfare around the World: Environmental and Sustainability Adjustments, *IMF Working Paper* (forthcoming). International Monetary Fund: Washington DC.

Barro R., 1974, "Are Government Bonds Net Wealth?," *Journal of Political Economy* 82 (6):1095–1118.

Das, S., Mourmouras, A., and Rangazas, P., 2018, *Economic Growth and Development: A Dynamic Dual Economy Approach*, Springer: New York.

Elsby, M., Hobijn, B., and Sahin, A., 2013, "The Decline of the U.S. Labor Share," *Brookings Papers on Economic Activity*, Fall, 1-63.

Farmer, K., and Schelnast, M., 2013, *Growth and International Trade: An Introduction to the Overlapping Generations Approach*, Springer-Verlag: Berlin.

Flexner, A., 2017, *The Usefulness of Useless Knowledge (with a companion essay by R. Dijgraaf)*, Princeton University Press: Princeton NJ.

Gollin D., 2002, "Getting Income Shares Right," *Journal of Political Economy* 110(2): 458-474.

Gordon, R., 2016, *The Rise and Fall of American Growth: The U.S. Standard of Living since the Civil War*, Princeton University Press: Princeton NJ.

International Labor Office (ILO) and Organization for Economic Co-operation and Development (OECD), 2015, "The Labour Share in G20 Countries," Geneva and Washington DC.

Jones, C., and Klenow, P., 2016, "Beyond GDP? Welfare across Countries and Time," *American Economic Review*, 106, 2426-2457.

Kaldor, N., 1957, "A Model of Economic Growth," *Economic Journal*, 67, 591-624.

______, 1961, "Capital Accumulation and Economic Growth," in *Theory of Capital*, edited by F. Lutz and D. Hague. St. Martin's Press: New York

King, R. and Rebelo, S., 1993, "Transitional Dynamics and Economic Growth in the Neoclassical Growth Model," *American Economic Review*, 83, 908-931.

Kocerlakota, N., 1996, "The Equity Premium: It's Still a Puzzle," *Journal of Economic Literature*, 34, 42-71.

Lucas, R., 1987, *Models of Business Cycles*, New York: Basil Blackwell.

Mourmouras A., and Rangazas P. 2009," Reconciling Kuznets and Habbakuk in a Unified Growth Model," *Journal of Economic Growth* 14(2):149–181.

Mokyr, J., 1990, *The Lever of Riches: Technological Creativity and Economic Progress*, Oxford University Press: New York.

Rangazas, P., 2002, "The Quantity and Quality of Schooling and U.S. Labor Productivity Growth (1870-2000)," *Review of Economic Dynamics* 5(4): 932–964.

Salanie, B., 2011, *The Economics of Taxation*, The MIT Press: Cambridge MA.

Stokey N, and Rebelo S., 1995, "Growth Effects of Flat-rate Taxes," *Journal of Political Economy*, 103(3):519–50.

Tanzi, V., and Schuknecht, L., 2000, *Public Spending in the 20th century*. Cambridge University Press: New York.

Tobin, J., and Nordhaus, W., 1972, "Is Growth Obsolete," in *Economic Research: Retrospect and Prospect, v. 5, Economic Growth*, National Bureau of Economic Research

Vijg, J., 2011, *The American Technological Challenge: Stagnation and Decline in the 21st Century*, Algora; New York.

Wallis J., 2000, "American Government Finance in the Long-run: 1790 to 1990," *Journal of Economic Perspectives* 14(1):61–82.

Fiscal Policy in the Overlapping-Generations Model

5

In this chapter we introduce several different features of fiscal policy into the overlapping-generations model, including taxes and transfers, government purchases of both consumption services and public capital, and government borrowing. A major objective in this chapter is to examine how fiscal policy affects private capital formation and economic growth. As suggested in Chap. 4, introducing public capital investment, first encountered in Chap. 2, is essential to build a more complete and accurate explanation of modern growth. The chapter also includes a discussion of the causes and the consequences of the fiscal crisis facing developed countries around the world. As discussed in Chaps. 2 and 3, both economic fundamentals and politics have contributed to the emergence of the fiscal crisis. The fiscal policy additions to the growth model of Chap. 4 provide the needed theoretical foundation to understand the Big Three economic problems of the 21st century that were introduced in Chap. 1 and that will be analyzed further in Chap. 8.

5.1 Introducing the Government

Now let's introduce fiscal policy and study its impact on economic growth. Similar to Chaps. 2 and 3, we consider two *sources* of government revenue: a tax on wage income (τ_t) and government debt (B_t). Government debt takes the form of one-period bonds that pay the same interest rate as private capital, a necessity if both are to be held in equilibrium. Thus, the return from holding one unit of government debt is $R_t = 1 + r_{t+1} - \delta$.

Along with the payment of principle and interest on previously issued government debt, we consider three other *uses* of funds. The first is a *net transfer,* an income payment minus any taxes collected. The net transfer is paid to old households (z_t). These transfers are similar to the social security benefits of real-world economies.

Next, there is government capital such as roads, ports, public utilities, public schools, and the stock of public knowledge (G_t). Recall from our analysis of

M. Ivanyna et al., *The Macroeconomics of Corruption*, Springer Texts in Business and Economics, https://doi.org/10.1007/978-3-030-67557-8_5

historical growth in the US, when we calibrated the *annual* depreciation rate on private capital realistically, the *period* depreciation rate in our model was close to one. For simplicity, we set $\delta = 1$ and also assume that government capital depreciates completely after one period. This means that choosing next period's public capital stock is the same as choosing government investment in the current period.

Finally, there are the wages paid to government officials (w_tD_t). The government work force is a fraction (ε) of the private work force of young households that are employed by firms. The total number of young households in period t is now $(1 + \varepsilon) N_t$. One could also assume that the government absorbs workers from the initial pool of N_t workers with no change in key results. Other than the fact that the government officials work for the government rather than for private firms, they are identical to private households, earning the same wage and possessing the same preferences.

The sources and uses of funds are summarized in the government budget constraint for period t

$$B_{t+1} + \tau_t w_t D_t(1+\varepsilon)N_t = R_{t-1}B_t + z_t(1+\varepsilon)N_{t-1} + w_t D_t \varepsilon N_t + G_{t+1}. \tag{5.1}$$

Take a moment to review what each term in the budget constraint represents. Associated with the government budget constraint for a single period are two related budget concepts the government *budget deficit* and the *primary deficit*,

$$B_{t+1} - B_t = (r_t - \delta)B_t + z_t(1+\varepsilon)N_{t-1} + w_t D_t \varepsilon N_t + G_{t+1} - \tau_t w_t D_t(1+\varepsilon)N_t.$$

$$PD_t \equiv z_t(1+\varepsilon)N_{t-1} + w_t D_t \varepsilon N_t + G_{t+1} - \tau_t w_t D_t(1+\varepsilon)N_t.$$

The budget deficit is the change in outstanding debt required in period t to reconcile the difference between all government spending, *including* interest payments on debt, and taxes collected. The *primary deficit* (*PD*) is the difference between spending, *excluding* interest payments on debt, and taxes.

Another important accounting concept is the *Government Intertemporal Budget Constraint* (GIBC). Similar to the household's lifetime budget constraint, it is a long-run constraint that combines single-period constraints to get a picture of how uses and sources of funds match up over time. The Appendix at the end of the chapter shows how combining the current and future single-period government budget constraints leads to the GIBC. The GIBC is technically more complicated than the lifetime budget constraint because the government "lives" forever and not only for two-periods, as in the case of a household. It requires the sum of the current value of outstanding debt and the present value of all non-debt related government spending to equal the present value of all taxes collected. The present value of all non-debt related government spending minus the present value of all taxes collected is the present value of primary deficits, so the GIBC can be written succinctly as

$$0 = B_t + \sum_{i=0}^{\infty} \frac{PD_{t+i}}{\prod_{j=0}^{i} R_{t-1+j}},$$

or

$$\sum_{i=0}^{\infty} \frac{-PD_{t+i}}{\prod_{j=0}^{i} R_{t-1+j}} = B_t.$$

For those not familiar with *product notation*, $\prod_{j=0}^{I} R_{t-1+j}$ is the product of $I + 1$ interest factors. For example, consider the expression, $\frac{PD_{t+1}}{R_t R_{t-1}}$. Using product notation, the denominator of this expression would be written as $\prod_{j=0}^{1} R_{t-1+j}$. It may also help to note that if the interest rate is constant over time, $\prod_{j=0}^{I} R_{t-1+j}$ would simply be R^{I+1}, the product, or compounding, of the constant R for $I + 1$ periods.

The GIBC says that the present value sum of current and future *primary surpluses* ($-PD_t$) must equal the government's initial outstanding debt obligations. In this sense the value of debt is "backed" by the present value of future budget surpluses that can be used to eventually pay off the debt. Future taxes must be raised, in excess of future non-debt expenses, to cover the government's current liability.

The GIBC has another interpretation. The future primary surpluses are needed to make *the interest payments on the outstanding debt going forward.* The present value of the future interest payments associated with rolling over and maintaining the outstanding debt level B_t is also equal to B_t itself (*Problem* 2 makes this point explicit through a numerical example). So, it is not necessary that the government ever repays its initial outstanding debt only that it collects enough in taxes to cover the ongoing interest expense associated with rolling the debt over each period.

5.1.1 The Fiscal Gap

The *fiscal gap* is a measure of the extent to which current policies, when projected into the future under reasonable assumptions about economic growth, interest rates and other economic variables, do not "add up," i.e. do not satisfy the GIBC. More specifically, the fiscal gap is defined as

$$B_t + \sum_{i=0}^{\infty} \frac{PD_{t+i}}{\prod_{j=0}^{i} R_{t-1+j}},$$

the sum of current outstanding debt and the present value of *unfunded* spending, an *implicit debt*. As we just established, this sum should be zero under sustainable fiscal policies. Many developed countries are running policies that do not come close to meeting this criterion. As will be discussed in a later section, fiscal gaps across the globe are huge. The large gaps mean that a country's debt will continue to rise over time. At some point taxes must be increased or spending must be cut. The longer countries wait to place their policies on a sustainable path, the greater the fiscal burden will be on future generations.

5.1.2 Government Capital and Private Production

As in Chaps. 2 and 3, we must model how government capital affects production. Our approach is to treat public capital as one of the variables that affects the labor productivity index, D_t.

The Cobb-Douglas production function is

$$Y_t = AK_t^{\alpha}(H_t)^{1-\alpha}, \tag{5.2}$$

where $H_t = D_tL_t = D_tN$,

Note, to reduce notation a bit, for the remainder of the chapter we assume zero population growth so that $N_{t+1} = N_t = N$. Unlike in Chap. 4, the productivity index (D) is now taken to be a function of exogenous disembodied technology (E) *and* endogenous public capital per worker ($G/((1 + \varepsilon)N)$) and is given by

$$D_t = E_t^{1-\mu}(G_t/((1+\varepsilon)N))^{\mu}, \tag{5.3}$$

where $0 < \mu < 1$ is a constant parameter, with the same interpretation as in Chaps. 2 and 3. We assume that E progresses at the exogenous rate q. In addition to this exogenous technological progress, public infrastructure raises the productivity of the private sector—roads, public education, property right protection, and the stock of public knowledge make workers and firms more productive. Because public workers also draw on the services of public capital, they contribute to the dilution of public capital across the work force, hence the division by $(1 + \varepsilon)N$.

Physical capital intensities are now defined per worker that uses the capital after adjusting for the exogenous source of productivity, E, that is after "de-trending" the growth in the capital stocks due to technical progress. We define public capital intensity as $g \equiv G/E(1 + \varepsilon)N$ and private capital intensity as $k \equiv K/EN$. The full productivity index given by (5.3) can then be written as $D_t = E_tg_t^{\mu}$.

With the new definitions, output per worker can be written as

$$Y_t/(1+\varepsilon)N = AK_t^{\alpha}\left(E_t g_t^{\mu} N\right)^{1-\alpha}/(1+\varepsilon)N = AE_t g_t^{\mu(1-\alpha)} k_t^{\alpha}/(1+\varepsilon).$$

There are five determinants of worker productivity:

A unmeasured features of an economy that do not change on a regular basis but that affect the level of productivity (natural resources, climate, reliance on markets vs a command economy approach to allocate resources, major scientific breakthroughs)

E_t state of technology or knowledge about production that evolves steadily over time (firm organization, production methods, machine design, applications of science)

g_t publicly provided capital and infrastructure (roads, public education, property right protection, funding for basic research)

k_t private physical capital (plant and equipment)

ε relative size of public sector employment that does not directly raise private production (soldiers, bureaucrats, public officials)

Firms continue to operate in perfectly competitive factor and output markets. As in Chap. 4, they rent physical capital and effective workers to produce output and maximize profits, $Y_t - w_t H_t - r_t K_t$. The profit-maximizing factor mix must satisfy

$$r_t = \alpha A\left(E_t g_t^{\mu} N\right)^{1-\alpha} K_t^{\alpha-1} = \alpha A g_t^{\mu(1-\alpha)} k_t^{\alpha-1} \tag{5.4a}$$

$$w_t = (1-\alpha) A\left(E_t g_t^{\mu} N\right)^{-\alpha} K_t^{\alpha} = (1-\alpha) g_t^{-\mu\alpha} A k_t^{\alpha}, \tag{5.4b}$$

Remember, w_t is the rental rate paid to a unit of *effective* labor. The full wage paid to an *actual* worker is $w_t D_t = (1-\alpha) A E_t g_t^{\mu(1-\alpha)} k_t^{\alpha}$. The key new feature is that public capital affects the marginal product of private inputs and factor prices.

5.1.3 Households with Taxes and Transfers

There are $(1 + \varepsilon)N$ young households in each period. The households are standard two-period life-cycle savers with the same preferences as we have assumed throughout. With fiscal policy they now face a wage tax rate (τ) when young and receive net transfers (z_{t+1}) when old. The household's lifetime budget constraint is given by

$$c_{1t} + \frac{c_{2t+1}}{R_t} = (1-\tau_t) w_t D_t + \frac{z_{t+1}}{R_t}. \tag{5.5}$$

Maximizing the log utility function from previous chapters, subject to (5.5), yields the optimal consumption and saving behavior,

$$c_{1t} = \frac{1}{1+\beta}\left((1-\tau_t)w_t D_t + \frac{z_{t+1}}{R_t}\right) \tag{5.6a}$$

$$c_{2t+1} = \beta R_t c_{1t}. \tag{5.6b}$$

$$s_t = \frac{\beta(1-\tau_t)w_t D_t}{1+\beta} - \frac{1}{1+\beta}\frac{z_{t+1}}{R_t}. \tag{5.6c}$$

Taxes reduce, and net transfers raise, lifetime wealth. Taxes reduce first period income flows used, in part, to finance saving. Future net transfers also reduce saving because they provide an alternative source of financing for retirement consumption.

5.1.4 Capital Market Equilibrium and Fiscal Policy

Households can now save by acquiring private capital or government debt—they have a portfolio choice about what assets to purchase when saving for retirement. In an environment with perfect certainty, as we assume here, in order to be willing to hold both assets households must view these assets as perfect substitutes that pay the same return. The interest rate on government debt must match the rate of return on private capital, an assumption already used in writing out the government and household budget constraints.

With two assets available to the households, the capital market equilibrium condition now requires that the sum of private capital and public debt be financed by household retirement saving,

$$K_{t+1} + B_{t+1} = (1+\varepsilon)N_t s_t. \tag{5.7}$$

5.2 The Economic Effects of Fiscal Policy—Government Purchases

To begin thinking about how fiscal policy affects economic growth, we examine the two major components of fiscal policy separately. We first focus on government purchases—both consumption purchases, such as payments to hire government officials, and investment purchases, such as public schooling and roads that raise the productivity of private sector workers. We then move to intergenerational transfers such as government debt and social security—policies that move income across generations by providing a benefit to one generation (lower taxes or greater transfers) that is financed by another generation (higher taxes or fewer transfers). Throughout the analysis, we simplify notation by assuming no technological progress or population growth: $E_t \equiv 1$, $q = 0$ and $n = 1$.

5.2.1 Government Purchases–Consumption

To separate intergenerational transfers out of the discussion, for now assume $z_t = B_t = 0$ in every period. The government then simply taxes wages to finance government purchases. The payment to government officials for their services is a type of *government consumption purchase*. To study the effects of government consumption only, also temporarily abstract from government investment by assuming $\mu = G_t = 0$ for all t. Note that with our earlier assumption about E, this implies $D_t \equiv 1$ and an actual worker's wage reverts back to $w_t = (1 - \alpha)Ak_t^{\alpha}$. The government budget constraint becomes, $\tau_t w_t(1 + \varepsilon)N = w_t\varepsilon N$, so $\tau_t = \tau = \varepsilon/(1 + \varepsilon)$. The tax rate reflects the relative size of the government employment—the government employment share.

Under these assumptions, the capital market equilibrium condition becomes

$$K_{t+1} = (1 + \varepsilon)N\frac{\beta}{1 + \beta}(1 - \tau)w_t \tag{5.8}$$

or, after substituting for τ and dividing by N,

$$k_{t+1} = \frac{\beta}{1 + \beta}(1 - \alpha)Ak_t^{\alpha}. \tag{5.9}$$

Equation (5.9) is precisely the transition equation found in an economy with no government, so the presence of a government sector that absorbs the economy's labor does not affect the capital-labor ratio or the productivity of workers in the private sector. An increase in ε does raise the wage tax, which lowers saving of private households and private capital accumulation. However, this effect is offset by the fact that the tax revenue is used to pay public sector workers who save at the same rate as private households. Overall, total saving and the private capital intensity is unaffected.

Government employment does divert labor from private sector production. Total output is $Y_t = y_t N = Ak_t^{\alpha}N$, so output per worker in the economy as a whole is $Y_t/(1 + \varepsilon)N = Ak_t^{\alpha}/(1 + \varepsilon)$. Output and income per capita falls as the government sector becomes relatively larger, as does the after-tax wage of households, $(1 - \tau) w_t = w_t/(1 + \varepsilon)$. These results depend on the government workers not being directly productive or at least their production is not measured as output. Think of soldiers that do not produce goods directly but that provide unmeasured protection services for the country. The more soldiers used to provide protection services, the fewer private goods are available per young household.

Recall from introductory economics that national income accounting attempts a crude measure of the value of untraded government services by using the wages paid to public employees. Our concept of output only includes private goods because public officials in the model do not directly provide any services. Thus, in our model the higher is ε, the lower is private output per worker (private and public). *Problem* 8 shows that the results from this section hold if instead we model the government as absorbing labor from the initial pool of N workers.

5.2.2 Government Purchases–Consumption and Investment

Now let's focus on government capital. Assume the government officials manage public capital investment projects, a form of *government investment purchases*. The government budget constraint becomes $\tau w_t D_t(1+\varepsilon)N = w_t D_t \varepsilon N + G_{t+1}$, which implies

$$g_{t+1} = \frac{\tau(1+\varepsilon)-\varepsilon}{1+\varepsilon} w_t D_t, \tag{5.10}$$

where $(\tau(1+\varepsilon)-\varepsilon)/(1+\varepsilon) = \tau - \varepsilon/(1+\varepsilon)$ can be thought of as the portion of the tax rate, net of paying government officials, that can be used to purchase goods and services needed for government investment.

The capital market equilibrium condition gives us

$$k_{t+1} = (1+\varepsilon)\frac{\beta}{1+\beta}(1-\tau)w_t D_t. \tag{5.11}$$

Equation (5.11) is a repeat of (5.8), but now D_t, a function of g_t, has been re-introduced.

Combining (5.10) and (5.11), we see that public capital is proportional to private capital,

$$g_{t+1} = \frac{\tau(1+\varepsilon)-\varepsilon}{1-\tau}\frac{1+\beta}{\beta}\frac{1}{(1+\varepsilon)^2}k_{t+1}, \tag{5.12}$$

because wages provide a common source of funding for *both* types of capital; i.e. wages determine both private saving and the government's tax base. For a given tax rate, government capital keeps pace with any growth in private capital because the higher resulting wages increase the tax base and the revenue collected to finance public investment.

We now derive a transition equation for private capital in the presence of a government. From the theory of the firm with fiscal policy we can express wages as $w_t D_t = (1-\alpha)A g_t^{\mu(1-\alpha)} k_t^{\alpha}$ and then substitute into (5.11). Next Eq. (5.12), dated for period t, allows us to use the close connection between government capital and private capital to eliminate public capital from the transition equation, expressing the equation in a more compact form as a function of private capital alone. Combining (5.11) and (5.12) mathematically gives us the following transition equation for private capital,

$$k_{t+1} = \kappa k_t^{\alpha+\mu(1-\alpha)}, \tag{5.13}$$

where $\kappa \equiv (1-\alpha)A\left[\frac{(1+\varepsilon)\beta(1-\tau)}{1+\beta}\right]^{1-\mu(1-\alpha)}\left[\frac{\tau(1+\varepsilon)-\varepsilon}{1+\varepsilon}\right]^{\mu(1-\alpha)}$. The steady state value of k_t is $\bar{k} = \kappa^{\frac{1}{1-\alpha-\mu(1-\alpha)}}$.

Note that if eliminate the need for public capital and set $\mu = g = 0$, (5.13) collapses to (5.9), the exact form of the transition equations from Chap. 4.

Government investment introduces two important differences between (5.13) and the transition equations from Chap. 4. First, the exponent on k_t has increased. The larger exponent makes the transition equation less concave and reduces the growth slowdown as capital accumulates. Recall from Sects. 4.4 and 4.5 of Chap. 4 that the sharply diminishing output growth rates and interest rates were problematic predictions of the neoclassical growth model. The fact that public capital rises with private capital reduces this problem by lessening the decline in growth rates and interest rates over the transition to the steady state and thereby providing a better fit to the historical experience of developing economies. The intuition is that as private and public capital move together, the rise in government capital raises the marginal product of private capital and reduces the force of diminishing returns associated with the rise in private capital alone.

Second, the coefficient of the transition equation, κ, is a function of the tax rate. One can show that the tax rate that maximizes the coefficient, and therefore the height of the transition equation, is $\tau* = (\mu(1-\alpha)+\varepsilon)/(1+\varepsilon)$. Tax rates above or below $\tau*$ will fail to maximize growth in private capital intensity. Tax rates that are too low fail to generate enough public capital and tax rates that are too high cost too much in reduced private saving. The tax rate $\tau*$ just balances these opposing effects to make private capital as large as possible. The connection between tax rates and the growth in the private capital stock suggests that the size of government can be too small or too big from the perspective of maximizing a country's growth rate. See *Problem* 9 for more details. *Problems* 22–24 discuss the best tax rates for achieving other objectives. In summary, the model implies that an important source of growth early in a country's development is an increase in the government's investment rate financed by a rise in taxation—see *Problem* 15 for more on this point.

5.3 The Economic Effects of Fiscal Policy—Intergenerational Transfers

Now let's shift the focus to intergenerational transfers. Government purchases play no role in the discussion, so we set $\varepsilon = \mu = 0$ and return to the situation with $D_t \equiv 1$. The government budget constraint with only taxes, transfers, and debt is

$$B_{t+1} + \tau_t w_t N = R_{t-1} B_t + z_t N. \tag{5.14}$$

The capital market equilibrium condition given by (5.7) can be used to derive the transition equation for private capital accumulation as

$$k_{t+1} = \underbrace{(1-\tau_t)w_t - \frac{(1-\tau_t)w_t + z_{t+1}/R_t}{1+\beta}}_{\text{private saving}} + \underbrace{-b_{t+1}}_{\text{public saving}}. \tag{5.15}$$

The transition equation says that private capital accumulation is the difference between *private savings*—$(1-\tau_t)w_t - \frac{(1-\tau_t)w_t + z_{t+1}/R_t}{1+\beta}$ (after tax wages minus household consumption), and *public debt*—b_{t+1}. The sum of private savings and *public savings* ($-b_{t+1}$, less borrowing is the same as more saving) is the *national savings* available to fund the private capital stock.

The transition equation cannot generally be solved explicitly for k_{t+1} because of the nonlinear effect of k_{t+1} on R_t, and possibly z_{t+1}, that occurs on the right-hand-side of (5.15). This means that, except under very special circumstances (see *Problem* 18), it will not be possible to trace out the entire transition path leading to the steady state as we have done in the past. However, we can easily do a more limited qualitative analysis of how introducing different policies impacts private capital accumulation.

To do this we use the calculus concept called the *total differential* of a function to simplify the analysis of the transition equation (see the book's Technical Appendix for a refresher of this concept). The total differential tells us how *changes* in the variables of the transition equation are related. Taking the total differential of (5.15) from an initial position with $z_{t+1} = 0$, so that a small change in R_t has no effect on the right-hand-side, gives us

$$dk_{t+1} = -w_t d\tau_t - \frac{-w_t d\tau_t + dz_{t+1}/R_t}{1+\beta} - db_{t+1}. \tag{5.16}$$

Just as (5.13) helps connect government purchases to private capital accumulation, (5.16) is the workhorse we use to think about the growth effects of intergenerational policies. The "differential" terms of the form "*dx*" should simply be thought of as "changes in the value of *x*." The changes can either be positive or negative depending on the application. The equation informs us about how policies "shift" the transition equation even in the case where we cannot explicitly derive the transition equation as in the past. Also, it is important to remember that we will think of the net transfer, z_{t+1}, as either increasing (a transfer to the old) or decreasing (a tax on the old) from the initial value of zero.

In words, (5.16) says that the change in private saving (the difference between changes in disposable income and consumption) and the change in government debt tells us the change in the national funds available for domestic investment and capital accumulation. To use (5.16), one first specifies a government policy that is defined by changes in wage taxes, net transfers to the old, and government borrowing. The policy is then plugged into (5.16) to find the impact on next period capital-labor ratio. Here are four examples.

5.3.1 Debt Policy #1

To use (5.16), we first need to set a fiscal policy by defining the associated changes in the fiscal variables under government control. Suppose the government cuts the wage tax, $d\tau_t < 0$. This results in a loss in tax revenue equal to $w_t d\tau_t < 0$. The government finances the loss in revenue by borrowing, $db_{t+1} = -w_t d\tau_t > 0$.

Suppose further that the debt issued in period t is repaid in period $t + 1$ by taxing the old in that period to cover the principle and interest, $dz_{t+1} = -R_t db_{t+1} < 0$.

Substituting these fiscal changes into (5.16), gives us

$$dk_{t+1} = -\mathrm{w}_t d\tau_t - \frac{-\mathrm{w}_t d\tau_t - db_{t+1}}{1+\beta} + \mathrm{w}_t d\tau_t$$
$$= \frac{-\mathrm{w}_t d\tau_t + \mathrm{w}_t d\tau_t}{1+\beta},$$

revealing that $dk_{t+1} = 0$. We have created a debt policy that does not impact capital accumulation or growth. The current generation receives a tax cut. However, the tax cut does not increase the household's wealth because the *same* household is responsible for repaying the debt plus interest in the next period. Wealth and household consumption do not rise, so the full tax cut is used to increase saving by purchasing the newly issued government debt. With a one-for-one rise in private saving, no "crowding out" of private capital purchases is necessary to absorb the newly issued government debt.

Thus, even in the overlapping-generations model it is possible to have debt policies with no impact, just as in Chap. 2. The key is that the households benefiting from the tax cut must be the same households that face the higher future taxes needed to repay the debt. In other words, the policy does not involve a redistribution of income across generations—no intergenerational transfer occurs. In general, this requirement is not satisfied in the overlapping-generations model because future generations can face the burden of debt repayment. Here is an example using a second debt policy.

5.3.2 Debt Policy #2

Suppose, as before, that the government cuts the wage tax and finances the loss in revenue by borrowing, $db_{t+1} = -w_t d\tau_t > 0$. Now, however, suppose the debt repayment is the responsibility not of the current generation but rather the burden is placed on some (unidentified) future generation, so $dz_{t+1} = 0$. In this case,

$$dk_{t+1} = \frac{\beta}{1+\beta}(-w_t d\tau_t) + w_t d\tau_t = \frac{w_t d\tau}{1+\beta} < 0.$$

Under Debt Policy #2, the tax cut raises the wealth and consumption of the current generation. Only a portion of the tax cut is then saved. The increase in saving is smaller than the increase on government borrowing, so household saving previously used to acquire private capital has decreased. In this case, government borrowing "crowds out" private investment and lowers economic growth. The key difference is that this second debt policy redistributes income from future generations to the current generation, causing current consumption to increase and saving to rise less than the rise in government debt.

Notice, the two policies would look identical to a "deficit hawk" that is solely focused on government debt. These examples show that government debt is not a good summary measure of the effects of fiscal policy. One has to look deeper to determine the extent to which the policy creates an intergenerational redistribution of income.

5.3.3 Government Pensions—Fully Funded

Next, think about the effects of a government-provided retirement plan. Suppose that the plan is set up in the same way as private pension plans, on a fully-funded basis. This means the worker pays income into the plan and the government saves the income on the worker's behalf by purchasing government debt. When the worker retires, there is an individual account in the worker's name that contains the debt and accumulated interest that is then used to finance the retirement benefits.

This policy is the exact opposite of Debt Policy #1. Taxes on workers are increased, $w_t d\tau_t > 0$, and used to purchase newly issued government debt that would have otherwise raised the demand for funds in financial markets, $db_{t+1} = -w_t d\tau_t < 0$. The tax revenue collected is then repaid to workers, plus interest, in the next period when they retire, $dz_{t+1} = -R_t db_{t+1} > 0$. As with Debt Policy #1, there is no effect on capital accumulation or growth.

A fully-funded pension plan is simply forced saving. It creates no intergenerational redistribution of wealth and, thus, no effect on the economy as a whole. During the first half of the 20th century, national governments around the world began setting up pension plans. The desire of the governments to assist older households, and to possibly redistribute income between rich and poor households of the same generation, caused them to deviate from the fully-funded retirement structure. To accomplish all of their objectives, governments instead set up their retirement programs on a pay-as-you-go basis.

5.3.4 Government Pensions—Pay-As-You-Go (PAYG)

Under a PAYG pension scheme, the taxes collected from current period workers are not saved by the government in individual accounts for their retirement. Instead, those taxes are used to pay benefits out to retired households in the *same* period. The tax paying workers believe that they will receive benefits when they retire in the next period, but these benefits must be funded by taxes collected from working households in the next period.

Under the PAYG scheme, taxes are collected in period t, $-w_t d\tau_t < 0$. The worker paying the taxes will receive benefits in the next period based on taxes collected from period $t + 1$ workers, $dz_{t+1} = w_{t+1} d\tau_{t+1} = w_{t+1} d\tau_t$, where the second equality holds if we think of the increase in tax rates as being equal across time. Plugging the policy into (5.16) gives

$$dk_{t+1} = -w_t d\tau_t - \frac{-w_t d\tau_t + w_{t+1} d\tau_t / R_t}{1+\beta} = -w_t d\tau_t \left(\frac{\beta}{1+\beta} + \frac{w_{t+1}/w_t R_t}{1+\beta} \right) < 0.$$

The direct effect of the tax is to lower saving. In addition, the expected future benefits raise consumption and lower saving some more. The drop in saving then lowers capital accumulation.

Note that the policy would greatly benefit the initial generation of old households that receive benefits without ever having to pay taxes. A similar benefit to older households would result every time the social security program is expanded; i.e. every time the payroll tax is raised to finance more generous benefits to current retirees. In this way, a PAYG social scheme involves an intergenerational redistribution of wealth toward older households and lowers private capital formation.

5.4 Capital Accumulation in an Open Economy

We have been working under the assumption that the economy is perfectly closed to international trade. Suppose now that private capital owners have the option of investing their capital across borders. As in Chap. 2, assume that the domestic capital owners reside in a small open economy. The perfectly competitive international rental rate on physical capital is an exogenous variable denoted by r^*. The capital owner's return to investing capital in foreign countries is then $1 - \delta + r^*$. If instead the capital is invested domestically, the return is based on the domestic marginal product of capital, $1 - \delta + \alpha A K_t^{\alpha-1} (D_t N)^{1-\alpha}$. In equilibrium these two returns must be equal. In a global economy, households will seek investments that yield the highest return on their saving. The incentive for households to chase the highest return will cause returns to equalize across countries.

To see the equilibrating process more explicitly, imagine that $\alpha A K_t^{\alpha-1} (D_t N)^{1-\alpha} > r^*$. Savings around the world would flow into the domestic economy causing K_t to increase. The increase in K_t would lower the marginal product of capital and the rental rate in the domestic economy would move down toward the going rental rate around the world. If $\alpha A K_t^{\alpha-1} (D_t N)^{1-\alpha} < r^*$, the opposite would occur. Instead of capital inflows, savings and capital would flow out of the domestic economy causing the rental rate to rise up toward r^*.

Taking the same steps followed in (5.4a) to write the domestic marginal product expression in capital intensive form, the open economy equilibrium requires that $r^* = \alpha A g_t^{\mu(1-\alpha)} k_t^{\alpha-1}$. We can then solve for the open economy domestic capital intensity as

$$k_t = \left[\frac{\alpha A g_t^{\mu(1-\alpha)}}{r^*} \right]^{\frac{1}{1-\alpha}}. \tag{5.17}$$

Notice that there are no variables related to the domestic country's national saving (such as β, wage taxes, or government borrowing). When foreign direct investment is possible, national saving does not affect capital intensity. If the fundamentals determining the return on capital are attractive (high values for A and g), foreign saving will flow into the country to build up the domestic capital stock. This suggests that a country may want to focus its policies more on the foundations of a high marginal product of capital than on increasing national saving. For example, in an open economy government borrowing to improve public infrastructure is particularly appealing because the borrowing will not drive up domestic interest rates and crowd out private investment—in fact it will unambiguously attract private capital from abroad.

The problem with this strategy is that a low saving country can become quite dependent on the conditions in international loan markets. If high saving countries begin supplying fewer funds to international markets, r^* will increase, causing a fall in the k of a low saving country. This is precisely a danger for the United States, as will be described in more detail later in the chapter. Fiscal policies in the United States have reduced national saving and increased dependence on foreign saving. As discussed later, several forces suggest that shortages of international funds will develop in the future that may significantly raise r^*.

5.4.1 Low International Interest Rates

In the open economy model, the international rate of return to capital or real interest rate, $r^* - \delta$, is exogenous. Intuitively, we can think of it as determined in a loanable funds market (similar to that found in introductory economics courses) but on a global scale not a domestic one. In a global market, the equilibrium interest rate is determined by the supply and demand for funds around the world. People often mistakenly believe the prevailing interest rates in a country are determined by the monetary policy set by that country's central bank. This may be true for the country's very short term interest rates but not necessarily for the long term interest rates that are more important for savings and investment decisions.

In the 1990s, financial markets were becoming increasingly globalized, Alan Greenspan, the chairman of the Federal Reserve (FED) in the US, saw persistently low US longer-term interest rates as a conundrum. The monetary policy of the FED had been raising short-term rates with no effect on unusually low longer-term interest rates. Ben Bernanke, who later followed Greenspan as the FED chairman, explained the conundrum based on a world saving glut. Large flows of saving from China, Japan, and Saudi Arabia were supplying funds in the US causing the long-term interest rates to be low (Bernanke 2015).

The influx of foreign saving into the US and the resulting effect of lowering long-term interest rates has many important implications for its economy. First, as indicated by Eq. (5.17) above, low interest rates mean a higher capital-labor ratio and higher real wages. The US would not be able to fund much capital formation with its paltry saving rate if its economy were closed to savings inflows from abroad.

Second, because foreign countries are using dollars obtained from selling goods to the US to buy US assets, they are not purchasing as many US goods. This causes US exports of goods to be less than US imports of goods, a trade deficit. The trade deficit is not necessary bad because the foreign purchases of US assets prevents the US capital-labor ratio from falling in line with its low national saving rate. Finally, the low interest rates have the negative consequence of providing cheap funding for *speculative*, as well as productive, investments. The housing bubble that led to the 2007 financial crisis and subsequent recession is an important example.

Why then are global interest rates so low? This was not always the case. The average global real interest rate on ten-year government debt has trended downward over the last 30 years from 6.3 percent in 1983 to approximately zero in 2012. A recent IMF study identifies the following factors that led to the decline (Furceri and Pescatori 2014). First, strong growth in emerging (middle-income) countries caused an increase in their savings rates, shifting the global supply of funds up over time. Second, the stock market is viewed as relatively more risky, largely related to the 2007 financial crisis, which caused risk-averse savers to change their portfolio mix and supply more funds to government bond markets. Third, there has been a decline in investment rates in advanced economies that have shifted the global demand for funds down. The two forces increasing the supply of funds and the one force reducing the demand for funds, caused an excess supply of funds, a savings "glut," that lowered the equilibrium value of $r^* - \delta$.

5.4.2 Open Capital Markets and Growth in Developing Countries

While capital scarcity should attract funding from abroad, the empirical evidence supporting the connection between open capital markets and economic growth is inconclusive (see, for example, Kose et al. (2009)). One reason that an open capital market might not attract foreign funding for investment in a developing country is that an unusually low capital-labor ratio does not necessarily imply an unusually high return to investment.

To see this point explicitly, note from (5.4a) and (5.17) that the marginal product of capital is not only a function of k but is also a function of A and g. If a capital scarce country also has low levels of TFP or public infrastructure, the domestic marginal product of capital could be *lower* than the equilibrium return to capital in global capital markets. To generate the high return that attracts foreign capital, a country must have policies that are conducive to high TFP and that support adequate levels of human and public capital.

The inconclusive empirical findings have inspired more thinking about why the growth effects of open capital markets have been difficult to identify. Recent research has focused on (i) new mechanisms through which growth may be indirectly promoted from openness (ii) a more detailed examination of the different forms of foreign investment and (iii) pre-conditions that a country might need in order to benefit from foreign investment (similar to the discussion in the preceding paragraph).

One type of indirect mechanism that has been considered is the connection between opening capital markets and domestic policies. In particular, some argue that the decision to open a country's capital market can act to discipline the country's monetary, fiscal, and regulatory policies to be more "pro-growth," so that the country can successfully compete for international capital. For example, Das et al. (2018, pp. 141–144) discuss this possibility using an overlapping generations growth model very similar to the one used in this chapter. A key difference is that their model includes an *endogenous* theory of fiscal policy. They show that the optimal fiscal policy changes when an economy opens its capital market. In the open economy, private capital formation is more responsive to tax rates and public capital. This creates an incentive to lower tax rates and to increase the share of a given budget that it devoted to public investment, which not only attracts foreign capital but also increases growth directly. The pro-growth policy effect makes it even more puzzling that open capital markets are not clearly associated with economic growth.

Foreign investment can be decomposed into *portfolio* investment—financial capital supplied when foreign investors purchase domestic stocks, bonds, and bank accounts, and *direct* investment—physical capital that is financed and managed by foreign multinational firms. Recent findings suggest that opening equity markets increases economic growth, while the growth effects from opening bond markets and from foreign direct investment (FDI) are less clear (see, Kose et al. (2009)).

The lack of clear growth effects from FDI is particularly puzzling. Economists have traditionally believed that FDI is more beneficial to a developing countries growth than portfolio investment for two reasons. First, in addition to augmenting the domestic capital stock, FDI may have effects on the domestic country's TFP through transfers of technology and managerial practices. Second, FDI is harder to suddenly reverse, making it less volatile than inflows of financial capital. So, why aren't there clear growth effects from FDI?

Alfaro (2016) provides a survey of the recent attempts to answer the question. In many countries FDI does not actually bring its own financing. Often foreign companies attempt to finance physical capital formation by raising the funds in the destination country—which has the potential to reduce funding for domestic firms. It also appears that for the domestic country to benefit from technological spillovers, certain preconditions must be met. The domestic economy must have threshold levels of human capital and reasonably developed financial markets for workers and domestic firms to benefit from and replicate the new production methods tied to FDI.

The main overall lesson is that a developing country can accelerate growth by opening its capital markets, but only if its domestic policies have laid the foundation for high returns to private capital—a literate and numerate workforce, reliable public infrastructure, and the beginnings of a financial sector.

5.5 The Fiscal Crisis

In Sect. 5.3, we saw that intergenerational transfers from younger and unborn households to older households, whether generated by PAYG social security or delays in paying back government debt, undermine national saving and capital accumulation. This is a major concern given that over the last 40 years developed countries have rapidly expanded PAYG social transfer programs and accumulated large amounts of public debt. Even before the COVID-19 pandemic, the average debt to GDP ratio of OECD countries exceeded 100 percent, a historically unprecedented value during a period with no major wars. The official debt numbers, what is known now as *explicit debt*, are actually relatively small when compared to the *implicit debt* associated with the developed world's PAYG transfer programs to retired households.

Developed countries continue to age, with ever greater fractions of the population reaching retirement over the course of the 21st century. In addition, the costs of providing medical insurance to these households, and to younger poor households who receive medical insurance as a welfare transfer, have risen faster than wages since WWII. The social transfer programs associated with current policy carry an implicit obligation to payout out benefits far into the future to all the workers who have paid, and will continue to pay, taxes under the PAYG financing scheme. If future taxes are insufficient to cover social transfer obligations, the programs are said to be unfunded, representing an implicit debt of the government.

Auerbach et al. (1991) developed *generational accounting*, a complete measure of the generational incidence of fiscal policy that provides an assessment of whether current fiscal policies are sustainable into the future. Section 5.6 provides a detailed discussion of this important innovation in fiscal accounting. Assuming the structure of current fiscal policy remains the same, one can forecast future government spending and compare it to future government taxes. This calculation is done for many of the developed countries of the world. In most cases, the present value calculation reveals a large gap between spending and taxes that is primarily driven by an expansion in intergenerational transfers. The *fiscal gap* adds the unfunded difference between the present value of spending and the present value of taxes to the country's current outstanding debt, forming a single measure of the government's implicit and explicit future obligations (see Sect. 5.1). In present value terms, the size of the gap between projected spending and projected taxes far exceeds the value of outstanding debt for most countries.

Consider the fiscal situation of the United States. In 2014, the fiscal gap was \$210 trillion, 16 times larger than the outstanding explicit debt (Kotlikoff 2015). To close the fiscal gap and meet its future obligations, the government would need to permanently raise all sources of federal tax revenue by about 60 percent or permanently cut all federal spending by about 40 percent. The delays in taking some combination of these actions only raises the magnitude of required fiscal reforms. Failure to take action will result in rapidly rising debt. Without fiscal reforms, the federal debt held by the public is expected to be between 200 and 300 percent of GDP toward the end of the century (Auerbach and Gale 2015; CBO 2014).[1]

U.S. policies are not only placing heavy fiscal burdens on future generations. They also have hurt future generations indirectly by contributing to a slowdown in economic growth. For three quarters of the 20th century, the average growth of worker productivity in the United States occurred at a trendless annual rate of 2.4 percent. In the last quarter of the 20th century and the early portion of the 21st century, the annual growth rate has only averaged 1.6 percent (Gordon 2016).

Part of the decline in the economic growth rate is due to a decline in the U.S. domestic saving rate. As predicted by the theory of this section, an expansion in intergenerational transfers from younger and future generations to older generations will raise the nation's consumption rate and lower its saving rate. The net national saving rate averaged about 15 percent of GDP from 1950 to 1975 (Kotlikoff 2015, Chart 2). Since then it has declined significantly. Even before the Great Recession, the net national saving rate was below 4 percent.[2]

The domestic investment rate of the U.S. has also declined over this period, but not as sharply as national saving because of the influx of foreign saving into the U.S. that has caused persistent trade deficits since 1980. Most of the foreign funding in U.S. financial markets has come from Japan and China. However, Japan has its own fiscal crisis and China is seeking to expand its domestic consumption rate. In the past decade, both countries have pulled back their lending to the U.S.. Whether the supply of foreign funding will continue to meet U.S. demand for funds is in serious question. The looming scarcity of international funds will also be affected by the fact that many other developed countries will be seeking foreign financing for their expanding public debt.

The crowding out of private investment is not the only growth-reducing consequence of the fiscal crisis. The government has been forced to neglect public investment. The public infrastructure of the United States has depreciated to an embarrassing state for such a rich country (Friedman and Mandlebaum 2012). The fraction of federal funding for the basic research that lays the foundation for technological progress was also cut over the last quarter of the 20th century (Viig 2011). The same fiscal policies that are raising the net tax rates for future generations are undermining investment and reducing future generations' ability to pay.

[1]Delays in needed reforms appear likely. Temporary improvements in government budget deficits in recent years have caused fiscal concerns to disappear from political discussions and debate (Auerbach and Gale 2015).

[2]Dobrescu et al. (2012) note that saving has fallen across the developed world. Their analysis indicates that the decline in saving is associated with societies placing an increasingly greater weight on current consumption, which is reflected in greater intergenerational transfers toward older households. The pandemic recession has caused a temporary rise in precautionary saving but it is not expected to continue once a sustained recovery is underway.

What has caused the governments of developed countries to lose their sense of fiscal responsibility?[3] The analysis from Chaps. 2 and 3 suggests that it is likely a combination of economic fundamentals and politics.

5.5.1 The Fundamentals

The most obvious fundamental that has caused the rise in intergenerational transfers is the aging of the population across the developed world. Even ignoring a rise in the political influence of the elderly, a larger fraction of retired households will cause the share of the economy's resources to be shifted in their direction. Combining an aging population with the rise in medical costs and the PAYG financing of social programs yields a recipe for growing intergenerational transfers.

Why has the public allowed the rise in public debt generally and the delay in responding to the, by now, obvious reality that the social transfer programs are not sustainable into the future? The broad middle class may be comfortable with the situation because, as we argued in Chap. 2, it is increasingly willing to burden future generations with public debt. Recall that a household is willing to allow intergenerational redistribution when it desires to increase current spending by borrowing and then leaves the debt for their children to pay.

The desire to increase current household spending beyond the lifetime means of current generations is the result of three related phenomenon. First, after more than a century of steady growth, real income for the middle class became stagnant in the 1970s. There have been no real income gains for the middle class for over 40 years. Second, the importance of advanced education has risen dramatically over time, i.e. there has been a rising wage premium associated with achieving a college degree. Finally, the cost of medical insurance has continued to rise in real terms. Discretionary household consumption has become increasingly constrained by the lack of real income growth and the rise in the cost of required investments in health and education. Families needing to make the health and education investments that give their children a chance at success have become increasingly willing to impose a debt burden on their children to do so.

The final fundamental, also discussed in Chap. 2, is the low cost of borrowing. The opening of economies in the last quarter of the 20th century increased the international flow of funds across borders. High saving rates in growing Asian economies help keep the cost of funds low for the governments of developed countries looking to borrow. While it is generally recognized that the fiscal policy of the United States is unsustainable, no fundamental policy changes have occurred to address it. The negative economic consequences of growing public debt have not yet been realized in anything close to a crisis largely because of the inflow of foreign funding. As we discussed above, there has been some crowding out of private and

[3]See Steurele (2014) for additional discussion of the politics and institutional factors behind the growing debt of the United States. Hallerberg et al. (2009) provide similar discussions for Europe.

public investments that has contributed to a slowdown in economic growth. However, the international funding provided to the United States has mediated these negative effects for the time being.

5.5.2 The Politics

The politics starts with the growth in the transfers and services that the public expects the government to provide. Mancur Olsen offers an explanation of why special interest groups tend to accumulate in stable and secure democracies (Olsen 1982). The lack of significant aggregate threats to the nation's economy and a widening of political voice as democracies strengthen embolden attempts by different domestic groups to get a larger piece of the economic pie. Politicians respond to the interest groups for political support. Driven by the perverse incentives of the common pool problem, discussed in Chap. 3, the natural political response results in more spending and a larger and more complex government where advantages and favors to special interest groups are common place but less transparent. This puts pressure on government finances, especially because expanding tax loopholes is one way of benefiting particular groups.

In most democracies, the increase in services provided by the federal government is dominated by mandatory "entitlement" programs, in particular Social Security, Medicare, and Medicaid. These programs are written into law and are largely protected from the annual discussion of the discretionary components of the budget. The programs are popular because they extend benefits to every household in the society at some point in their lifetime. For this reason, the programs have increased overtime through legislation that increases their coverage and generosity. Interest groups representing the elderly, the medical profession, drug companies, and the poor have rewarded politicians with support as a result of their attempt to protect and expand the entitlement programs.

In addition we have expanded "tax expenditures" that politicians give out in the form of tax allowances and deductions to interest groups that include homeowners, insurance providers, and rich asset holders. The increase in social spending combined with the use of tax expenditures results in a growing gap between spending and tax collection summarized by the fiscal gap.

The frustration of the middle class, stemming from the second of our economic fundamentals, likely contributed to the growth of interest groups and the increased polarization of politics. The growing polarization of politics has made it increasingly difficult to provide the political leadership needed to make hard choices for the good of the nation as a whole. As we saw in Chap. 3, increased polarization naturally carries with it a deficit bias.

In short, the country lacks both the unified leadership and the threat of an economic crisis needed to make major reforms to the institutionalized aspects of the federal budget and the political incentives that are driving the fiscal crisis. Chapter 8 discusses political and budgetary reforms that can substitute for the lack of leadership and improve the fiscal policies of developed countries.

5.6 Generational Accounting

A new accounting system for assessing the effects of fiscal policy, *generational accounting*, was developed in the early 1990s by Auerbach et al. (1991). The objective of the new system was to make the generational incidence and long-run sustainability of fiscal policy more transparent. Generational accounting is an indispensable tool for recording the extent to which fiscal policy redistributes wealth from unborn to current generations. Without it, societies cannot adequately assess whether they are satisfying the fourth principle of good governance discussed in previous chapters—limiting the fiscal burdens imposed on future generations. Generational accounting has been adopted by governments, central banks, and international organizations around the world.

The basic element of generational accounting is the computation of a *generational account* for each generation of households; those alive today, as well as unborn generations. A generational account is typically measured as the present value of the net taxes paid by the average member of a given generation over their entire life, from birth to death. This value is easiest to interpret when it is taken as a fraction of the generation's lifetime wage (the present value of the annual wages earned over the entire life-cycle of an individual). For example, under current U.S. fiscal policies, it has been estimated that the generational account of households born in the late 1990s and early 2000s is a little over 20 percent of their lifetime earnings.[4]

We can illustrate the concept of a generational account by computing it for one generation of households from our overlapping-generations model when there is PAYG social security. In practice, the generational accounting includes *all* types of government taxes and transfers for *all* generations.

The government budget constraint associated with PAYG social security is

$$\tau_t w_t N_t = z_t N_{t-1}, \tag{5.18}$$

where a payroll tax (τ_t) is levied on the wages of the current generation of workers ($w_t N_t$) in order to finance the retirement benefits of the current retirees ($z_t N_{t-1}$). The generational account for households of generation-t is defined as

$$\widehat{\tau}_t \equiv \tau_t w_t - \frac{z_{t+1}}{R_t}, \tag{5.19}$$

net lifetime taxes—the present value of the payroll taxes paid over their working life minus the benefits received in retirement. We are discounting back to the beginning of the work life rather than all the way back to birth because in our model there are no taxes or transfers received before adulthood. This means the calculation of generational accounts starts at, say, age 20. If children and teenagers do not pay much in the way of taxes and do not receive much in the way of government transfers, then whether one takes the present value relative to the beginning of life or the beginning

[4]See Kotlikoff (2003, Table 1) and Kotlikoff and Burns (2005, pp. 59–60).

of adulthood does not matter, especially if we compute the net lifetime tax *rate* as a fraction of lifetime wages. The net tax rate is less sensitive to the choice of what period you consider to be the "present" because how far you choose to discount back in the household's life would affect both the numerator and the denominator of the net tax rate calculation.

The *net lifetime tax rate* in our example is

$$\widehat{\tau}_t/w_t \equiv \tau_t - \left(\frac{z_{t+1}}{w_{t+1}}\right)\frac{1+\omega_{t+1}}{R_t}, \tag{5.20}$$

where z_{t+1}/w_{t+1} is a measure of how generous retirement benefits are relative to the taxpayer's wage of the same period and where $1 + \omega_{t+1} \equiv w_{t+1}/w_t$ is the growth factor for real wages. Using (5.18), we can rewrite (5.20) as

$$\widehat{\tau}_t/w_t \equiv \left(\frac{z_t}{w_t}\right)\frac{N_{t-1}}{N_t} - \left(\frac{z_{t+1}}{w_{t+1}}\right)\frac{1+\omega_{t+1}}{R_t}. \tag{5.21}$$

Equation (5.21) shows how demographics, economic growth, and policy affect the lifetime net tax rate of generation-t.

An increase in the generosity of the social security program over the household's lifetime would lower their net tax rate because the retirement benefits received would expand relative to the payroll tax paid while working, i.e. $z_{t+1}/w_{t+1} > z_t/w_t$. Population aging of the economy that causes an increase in the ratio of retirees to workers, N_{t-1}/N_t, raises net taxes because it raises payroll tax obligations of generation-t households during their working life. This is an important force increasing generational accounts and lifetime net tax rates as the developed world become older over this century. An increase in the growth rate of wages, ω, holding constant z_{t+1}/w_{t+1}, raises benefits received relative to taxes paid in and lowers the net tax. This is true when benefits are indexed to wage growth, i.e. real benefits rise at the rate of real wages, as they are in many countries. Finally, an increase in the interest rate raises the net tax rate because the discounting of future retirement benefits becomes more severe.

In the United States, as we have seen, the fiscal gap is huge. This implies a large burden on future generations is required to reduce the fiscal gap to zero. As a conceptual exercise, one can compute what the generational accounts must be for unborn generations to close the fiscal gap under the assumption that all unborn generations pay the same higher lifetime net tax rate. The required net tax rate for unborn generations varies with the assumptions of particular studies but is typically computed to be significantly above the lifetime net tax rates under current policy. For example, Gokhale et al. (1999) estimated that in order to restore fiscal balance, unborn generations in 1995 would need to face a lifetime net tax rate that was over 50 percent higher than that associated with fiscal policies in place at that time (this calculation used the realistic assumptions of an annual worker productivity growth rate of 1.2 percent and an annual interest rate of 3 percent). The fiscal gap in 1995 was a good deal smaller than it is today, so an update of this calculation would show an even larger required increase in the net tax rates of unborn generations.

5.7 Fiscal Crises, Financial Crises, and Recessions

Our focus has been on the long-term consequences of public debt accumulation and unfunded liabilities on economic growth. Reinhart and Rogoff (2009, 2011); Reinhart et al. (2012) have instead examined how debt accumulation leads to financial crises and potentially sharp recessions. They emphasize the sudden "crisis of confidence" that occurs when lenders become convinced that borrowers will have difficulty repaying and servicing their debt obligations. We explicitly modelled this possibility in Sect. 2.5 of Chap. 2.

A crisis of confidence causes a sell-off of debt by lenders that lowers bond prices and raises interest rates. The jump in the cost of funds reduces the incentive to finance and carry out investment projects. It also lowers the market value of existing debt holdings which can reduce household wealth and lower consumption. Finally, a decline in the value of government debt held by private banks can reduce their liquidity, making it more difficult to deal with loan defaults as the economy slips into a recession.

The repeated error of building up excessive debt during good times, as documented by Reinhart and Rogoff over the last two centuries, applies to all types of debt. However, our interest lies with the relatively recent accumulation of public debt in rich countries because this gives us an idea of what may be in store for the United States. Reinhart and Rogoff identify that when public debt to GDP ratios in rich countries exceed a threshold of around 90 percent, annual economic growth will slow by about 1 percentage point.

Their measure of public debt is called *gross* public debt which includes all public debt outstanding, including the public debt held in government accounts to fund government pensions (e.g. the social security trust fund). After 1980, there were six historical episodes in their study where rich countries have exceeded this threshold: Belgium (1982–2005), Canada (1992–1999), Greece (1993–2011), Ireland (1983–1993), Italy (1988–2011) and Japan (1995–2012). In all cases, except for Japan, real interest rates rose after the threshold was passed. The rise in real interest rates is consistent with a crisis of confidence causing a reduction in aggregate demand and a weakening of banks' liquidity that could lower real growth as described above.

The fact that Japan is an exception can be explained by a general problem with empirical studies. It is relatively easy to document the negative *correlation* between debt accumulation and economic growth but do we know the *causal* connection between the two variables? While the theory suggests the causation is going from debt to growth, there are also reasons to believe that causation could run in the opposite direction. If there is a growth slowdown, for reasons other than debt accumulation, public debt will tend to rise because of a loss in net tax revenue as income falls and because governments will carry out expansionary fiscal policy (tax cuts and spending increases) to bolster demand.

In the case of Japan, this *reverse* causation seems particularly likely. Well before its public debt build-up, Japan began experiencing a decline in both the rate of return to capital and the investment-to-GDP ratio (Fukao et al. 2015). The decline in the return to investment was due to slowdowns in both the growth of Japan's workforce and its technological progress that lowered the marginal product of capital. The accumulation of public debt began *after* a particularly sharp decline in investment in 1991 that followed a temporary recovery of investment during a short boom period in the late 1980s. After 1991, the investment rate continued its decline and the resulting growth slowdown induced an expansionary fiscal policy that caused a sharp rise in public debt. Throughout the post-1991 period, private saving rates remained very high—close to 30 percent of GDP. In fact, Japan has been able to absorb high levels of public debt and still have enough saving to be an international lender. A very high saving rate and a strong downward trend in investment demand has kept interest rates low despite the build-up of public debt, making Japan an exception.

What does this mean for the US? Contrary to the historical evidence, the US gross debt-to-GDP ratio now exceeds 100 percent with no signs of the negative threshold effect on output seen in the historical data. Unlike Japan, the US saving rate is unusually low. The fact that its cost of borrowing remains low is because the international lenders that pour their saving into US assets have not yet experienced a crisis of confidence.

However, without action, US debt ratios will continue to rise, interest payments will eat up larger shares of the budget, and social security will soon be unable to meet its pension obligations. The US is now particularly vulnerable to any event that might trigger a growth slowdown, igniting a crisis of confidence. Investment agencies, such as Moody's, expect that US debt will be downgraded sometime in the next decade (Tully 2018). Based on their studies, Reinhart and Rogoff (2011, p. 33) offer the following warning.

Perhaps soaring US debt levels will not be a drag on growth in the decades to come. However, if history is any guide, that is a risky proposition, and overreliance on US exceptionalism may only prove to be one more example of the This Time is Different Syndrome.

5.8 Ten Important Results from Economic Theory

It is a good time to take stock of what we have learned from the review of economic theory. Below are ten key findings, with the most relevant sections in parentheses.

1. An open economy allows an entire nation to finance current spending by borrowing from other countries. (2.3, 5.4)
2. If the cost of health care and education rise faster than the income of most households, the support for government debt increases. (2.4)
3. Private physical capital accumulation causes a relatively small portion of a country's economic growth. (4.4)
4. The pattern of historical growth can only be explained by technological progress along with rising rates of government investment in public infrastructure, public education, and basic research. (4.5, 5.2)

5. After a country's investment rates level off or decline, diminishing returns will dominate and growth will inevitably slow. (5.2)
6. Current US government debt is only a small portion of the unfunded liabilities associated with the nation's fiscal policy, suggesting sharp increases in future debt levels. (5.5)
7. An ongoing policy of postponing debt repayment increases consumption and crowds out private and public investment. (5.3)
8. PAYG social security raises consumption and crowds out private and public investment, slowing economic growth. (5.3)
9. The fiscal crisis is the result of a variety of factors: (i) population aging, (ii) PAYG financing of large government transfer programs, (iii) increasing relative prices of medical services, (iv) the proliferation of interest groups in a mature democracy, (v) political polarization, (vi) stagnant income growth, and (vii) low cost of foreign borrowing. (2.4, 5.5)
10. The generational accounts for future generations will rise dramatically above those of current generations. (5.6)

5.9 Exercises

Questions

1. Write down the single period government budget constraint and explain what each variable represents.
2. Define, in words, the following fiscal concepts? How does an increase in interest rates, $r_t - \delta$, affect each?
   (a) budget deficit
   (b) primary budget deficit
   (c) budget surplus
   (d) primary budget surplus
3. In words, explain the *Government Intertemporal Budget Constraint.* What is its purpose? How is it related to the *fiscal gap*?
4. Give a verbal description of how government capital is introduced into the growth model.
5. Explain how public capital affects each of the following variables.
   (a) rental rates paid to physical capital (r_t)
   (b) implicit wage or rental rates paid to a unit of human capital/effective labor supply (w_t)
   (c) wage paid to an actual working household (w_tD_t)
   (d) average product of labor in the private sector (y_t)
6. Explain how (i) the wage tax and (ii) the net transfer to old households affects
   (a) first period consumption
   (b) second period consumption
   (c) saving

7. Explain how each of the following affects output per young household in the economy.
   (a) government employment (assume no public capital)
   (b) government investment
8. Use (5.13) to explain how the addition of government investments, such as public schooling and roads, can improve the simulation results from Sect. 4.5 of Chap. 4.
9. Give an example of a policy that causes government debt to increase but does not affect economic growth. Next, discuss a policy that causes government debt to increase and results in lower economic growth. Explain the difference.
10. Explain why fully funded pension plans do not affect growth, while PAYG pension plans lower economic growth. Relate your answer to *Question* 9.
11. What are the main differences between how private capital accumulates in closed and open economies?
12. Use the profit-maximizing condition in an open economy, $r^* = \alpha A g_t^{\mu(1-\alpha)} k_t^{\alpha-1}$, to sketch the relationship between r^* and k_t. Your sketch should plot r^* and the domestic marginal product of capital on the vertical axis, and k_t on the horizontal axis. Use the sketch to explain why a country with low k_t, but also a low marginal product of capital curve, may actually lose capital, i.e. experience *capital flight*, if its capital markets are opened.
13. Describe the key features of the U.S. fiscal crisis.
14. What economic fundamentals help explain the fiscal crisis? What political factors affect the fiscal crisis?
15. The fiscal gap implies there will be greater fiscal burdens placed on future generations of workers. However, how do current fiscal policies also reduce the ability of future workers to pay for the higher taxes and absorb the lower benefits?
16. Why are international interest rates low? How does this affect the fiscal crisis?
17. What is generational accounting? What is its primary objective?
18. Write out the simple generational account for the current young generation from our model in the presence of PAYG social security. How is the generational account related to a household's lifetime net tax rate?
19. Using the simple generational account from our model with PAYG social security, intuitively discuss four factors that determine a household's lifetime net tax rate.
20. What is the fiscal gap? How is it related to the computation of generational accounts for unborn generations? Why are the generational accounts computed for unborn generations so much higher than the generational accounts associated with current fiscal policies in most countries?
21. What is a "crisis of confidence" and how is it related to the fiscal crisis? How can a crisis of confidence cause a recession?
22. What is *gross* public debt? Why is the gross public debt to GDP ratio a warning sign of economic problems?

23. In recent history when the debt to GDP ratio of rich countries exceeds 90 percent, they begin to have economic difficulties. Why might the US be an exception to this rule?

Problems

1. Assume that the current period is period 0. Suppose the interest rates over the next three periods are $r_1 - \delta = 0.20$, $r_2 - \delta = 0.15$, and $r_3 - \delta = 0.25$. Use the product notation from the definition of the GIBC to write the product of the three interest factors associated with these interest rates. What is the present value in period 0 of 100 units of tax revenue received by the government in period 3? Give an intuitive explanation of how, if the government received tax revenue equal to the present value of 100 units in period 0, they could use this revenue to free up 100 units of tax revenue in period 3.
2. Suppose the interest rate is constant over time so that $R_{t-1+j} = R$ for all j. With a constant interest rate, $\prod_{j=0}^{N} R_{t-1+j} = R^{N+1}$, as was stated in the text. This means we can write, $\sum_{i=0}^{\infty}\left(\frac{1}{\prod_{j=0}^{i} R_{t-1+j}}\right) = \sum_{i=0}^{\infty}\left(\frac{1}{R^{i+1}}\right) = \frac{1}{R}\sum_{i=0}^{\infty}\left(\frac{1}{R}\right)^i$. Now, recall from high school algebra, there is a result about the value of an infinite geometric series, just like the one above, that says, $\sum_{i-0}^{\infty} a^i = \frac{1}{1-a}$, for all values of a satisfying $0 < a < 1$.
   (a) Use the result on geometric series to show, $\frac{1}{R}\sum_{i=0}^{\infty}\left(\frac{1}{R}\right)^i = \frac{1}{r-\delta}$.
   (b) Assuming the initial stock of government debt is $B_t = 100$ and $r - \delta = 0.03$, what *constant* value of the primary surplus is needed to satisfy the GIBC?
3. How does the presence of taxes and transfers affect the sketch of the household budget constraint?
4. Write the *single, first- period* budget constraint of a generation-t working household in the presence of fiscal policy. Use the budget constraint, along with (5.6a), to derive (5.6c).
5. Solve the household maximization problem to derive (5.6a), (5.6b), and (5.6c).
6. Derive (5.15) and (5.16).
7. *Government Purchases—Employment*
   For this problem assume the following: $A = 10$, $n = 1$, $d = 0$, $N = 100$, $\beta = 1/2$, and $\alpha = 1/3$.
   (a) Compute the initial steady state values of k, y, w, and Y with no government.
   (b) Now introduce the government with a work force equal to εN, where $\varepsilon = 0.10$, but with no purchases of investment goods. Starting from the initial steady state with no government, use (5.9) to compute the transition path for k_t, y_t, w_t, τ_t, Y_t and $Y_t/(1 + \varepsilon)N$ over the next 5 periods that results from introducing the government.
   (c) Explain your answer to (b).

8. Suppose we introduce government employment in a different way. Assume the total population of all young households, regardless of where they work, is fixed in size at N. Now when public employment equal to εN is introduced, it causes private employment to shrink to $(1 - \varepsilon)N$. Assume there is no technological progress and the only government activity is taxing wages to pay government employees, i.e. $D_t \equiv 1$ and $\mu = G_t = z_t = B_t = 0$. Derive the transition equation for the capital labor-ratio and compared it to (5.9). Also write out an expression for output divided by all the workers in the economy and compare it to the comparable expression from Sect. 2.1 of this chapter. What is your conclusion about the two different ways of introducing government employment?
9. Show the tax rate that maximizes the height of the transition equation given by (5.13) is $\tau* = (\mu(1 - \alpha) + \varepsilon)/(1 + \varepsilon)$. *Hint*: it simplifies things to take the natural log of the right-hand-side of (5.13) first. Taking the natural log is a monotonic transformation, so maximize the new expression is the same as maximizing the original expression.
10. Show that (5.13) collapses to the transition Eq. (5.9), the same form as the transition equation from Chap. 4, when $n = 1$ and $\mu = 0$.
11. *Diminishing returns and the exponent on k*
We have asserted that including government capital improves the ability of the model to explain historical growth by raising the exponent on k in the transition equation. This makes sense because the higher exponent, the weaker the effect of diminishing returns from capital accumulation and the smoother the simulated paths for growth rates and interest rates.
To see this more explicitly go back to *Problem* 17 from Chap. 4 and redo the historical simulation when $\alpha = 2/3$ rather than 1/3. To do this you need to compute a new value for β that satisfies Eq. 4.13 and a new initial k that leads to an endogenous rise in worker productivity over the period of 2.59. To save some time, these values are $\beta = 0.8400$ and $k_1 = 0.0001185$. Now you can proceed just as in *Problem* 17 but with a new transition equation. Compute the associated growth rates and interest rates and compare them to the case when $\alpha = 1/3$.
12. *Transition Paths with Fiscal Policy I*
Make the following parameter assumptions: $n = 1$, $d = 0$, $\beta = 1/2$, $\alpha = 1/3$, $A = 10$, and an initial capital intensity of $k_0 = 0.0500$. Assume further that $\mu = 1/3$ and $\tau = 0.10$ (assume $\varepsilon = 0$). Using (5.13), compute the values of k_t over the next 5 periods.
13. *Transition Paths with Fiscal Policy II*
Use the same assumptions as in Problem 12, but now let $\mu = 1/3$ and $\tau = 0.20$ (assume $\varepsilon = 0$). Using (5.13), compute the values of k_t over the next 5 periods. Explain the difference between the transition paths in Problems 12 and 13.
14. *Transition Paths with Fiscal Policy II*
Use the same assumptions as in Problem 13, but consider what happens when $\mu = 1/3$ and $\tau = 0.30$ (assume $\varepsilon = 0$). Explain the difference in the three transition paths from *Problems* 12–14. *Hint*: Remember the lesson learned about tax rates in *Problem* 9 and in the text.

15. In *Problem* 11 above, we see that because the introduction of government capital raises the exponent on the current period capital stock, the transition equation sketch becomes less concave, leading to smaller predicted declines in growth rates and rates of return to capital (helping to improve the fit to US historical data). However, there remains a prediction of *at least moderately declining* worker productivity growth rates over time.
    Use a graph of the transition Eq. (5.13) to argue how the model's prediction with fiscal policy could be improved further to even possibly generate *trendless growth* rates for several periods. *Hint*: Increasing the exponent on the current capital stock makes the transition equation sketch less concave but does not create *shifts in its position from period to period.* What might cause upward shifts in the transition equation that would help maintain the predicted growth rates over successive periods? *Hint*: compare *Problems* 12 and 13.
16. Suppose the government cuts τ_t causing a loss in tax revenue, $w_t d\tau_t = -100$, and a need to increasing borrowing, $db_{t+1} = -w_t d\tau_t = 100$. The debt is repaid by taxing the old in the next period causing a reduction in their net transfers, $dz_{t+1} = -R_t db_{t+1} = R_t w_t d\tau_t = -R_t 100$. Assuming $\beta = 1/2$, what are the numerical changes in the following private sector variables?
    (a) disposable income
    (b) lifetime wealth of generation-t
    (c) consumption
    (d) private saving
    (e) capital-labor ratio
    Repeat the exercise for the case where the government postpones debt repayment into the future so that $dz_{t+1} = 0$.
17. Suppose the government raises the wage tax, τ_t, to fund a government retirement program. Assume the change in a young household's disposable income is $-w_t d\tau_t = -w_{t+1} d\tau_{t+1} = -100$. Consider two alternative uses of the tax revenue: (i) a fully-funded program where the revenue is used to purchase government debt on behalf of the worker and (ii) a PAYG program where the tax revenue immediately funds the current old household's retirement benefits. Assuming $\beta = 1/2$ and $R_t = 2$ $R_t = 2$ what are the numerical changes in the following private sector variables under each program?
    (a) lifetime wealth of generation-t
    (b) current consumption of a generation-t household
    (c) private saving of a generation-t household
    (d) capital-labor ratio
18. Here is a special case where (5.15) can be solved explicitly, as we did in Chap. 4 without the government or in (5.13) with no intergenerational policy. Assume that the only fiscal policy is PAYG social security, with an associated government budget constraint of the form $\tau w_t = z_t$. Note that we are assuming a constant payroll tax rate and a constant worker population. Remember, we have been assuming $\delta = 1$. Also assume $A = 1$, to further simplify.
    (a) Show that, under these assumptions, the transition equation given by (5.15) can be written as $k_{t+1} = \left[\frac{\alpha\beta(1-\alpha)(1-\tau)}{\alpha(1+\beta)+\tau(1-\alpha)}\right] k_t^{\alpha}$.

(b) Assuming $\alpha = 1/3$, $\beta = 1/2$, compare the steady state capital-labor ratio without social security to the steady state capital-labor ratio with $\tau = 0.15$. Are the results consistent with the analysis of PAYG social security using (5.16)?

19. In a small economy that is perfectly open to private capital flows, with $\alpha = \mu = 1/2$, determine as accurately as you can what happens to k_t and y_t if
(a) A doubles
(b) g doubles
(c) r^* doubles

20. Assume an open economy and suppose the return to owning capital in the domestic economy is taxed at the rate τ_t, so that the after-tax rental rate is $(1 - \tau_t)\alpha A K_t^{\alpha-1}(D_t N)^{1-\alpha}$. Derive an adjusted version of (5.17) that includes the taxation of income from domestic capital. How does an increase in the capital tax rate affect the capital-labor ratio?

21. Use the results from *Problem* 18 to compute 3 periods of the transition path that results from introducing social security, with $\tau = 0.15$, to an economy with no social security. Assume in the initial period, say period 0, the initial value of k_0 is the steady state without social security. Compute the lifetime net tax rates under the social security policy for the following generations: -1 (the initial old at the time the policy is introduced), 0, and 1.

Base your answers to the next three exercises on the model associated with the transition equation given by (5.13), where $y_t = A g_t^{\mu(1-\alpha)} k_t^{\alpha}$. These problems explore the tax rates that maximize steady state worker productivity and household utility, as discussed in the chapter Appendix.

22. Note that, for $E_t \equiv 1$, steady state worker productivity can be written as $\bar{y} = A\left[\frac{1+\beta}{\beta(1+\varepsilon)^2}\right]^{\mu(1-\alpha)}\left[\frac{\tau(1+\varepsilon)-\varepsilon}{1-\tau}\right]^{\mu(1-\alpha)}\bar{k}^{\alpha+\mu(1-\alpha)}$. To derive the tax rate that maximizes steady state worker productivity complete the following steps.
(i) Take the natural log of $\bar{y}$.
(ii) The expression in (i) involves the natural log of $\bar{k}$. You can write this expression in terms of the tax rate by solving for the steady state associated with the transition Eq. (5.13) and then taking the natural log.
(iii) Now the hard part. Collect terms that involve the tax rate and ignore other terms that will not be affected by the choice of the tax rate. This step is messy but you should end up concluding that maximizing worker productivity is equivalent to maximizing the expression, $\mu(1 - \alpha)\ln(\tau(1 + \varepsilon) - \varepsilon) + \alpha \ln(1 - \tau)$.
(iv) Maximize the expression from (iii) with respect to τ and solve for the tax rate.

23. Note that, for $E_t \equiv 1$, steady state utility can be written as $U = \ln((1 - \tau)\overline{w}\,\bar{g}^{\mu}) + \beta \ln(\beta R(1 - \tau)\overline{w}\,\bar{g}^{\mu}))$.
(i) Assume that $\delta = 1$, and write utility as $U = (1+\beta)\ln(1-\tau) + (1+\beta)\ln(\overline{w}\bar{g}^{\mu}) + \beta\ln\beta + \beta\ln\bar{r} = (1+\beta)\ln(1-\tau) + (1+\beta)\ln((1-\alpha)\bar{y}) + \beta\ln\beta + \beta\ln\left(\frac{\alpha\bar{y}}{\bar{k}}\right)$.

(ii) Use your analysis from Problem 22 to write out $\bar{y}$ and $\bar{k}$ in terms of the tax rate and other expressions. Collect all terms involving the tax rate and simplify. Very messy, but you should eventually conclude that maximizing utility is equivalent to maximizing the expression, $\mu(1 - \alpha)(1 + \beta)\ln(\tau(1 + \varepsilon) - \varepsilon) + (1 - \mu(1 - \alpha) + \alpha\beta)\ln(1 - \tau)$.

(iii) Maximize the expression from (ii) with respect to τ and solve for the tax rate.

24. Make the following parameter assumptions: $\varepsilon = 0$, $\beta = 1/2$, $\alpha = \mu = 1/3$. Compute the tax rates $\tau{*}{*}{*}$, $\tau{*}{*}$, and $\tau{*}$. Redo the calculations if $\varepsilon = 0.10$.

Appendix

The Government Intertemporal Budget Constraint

To begin construction of the GIBC, write the period $t + 1$ version of (5.15),

$$B_{t+2} + \tau_{t+1} w_{t+1} D_{t+1}(1+\varepsilon)N_{t+1} = R_t B_{t+1} + z_{t+1}(1+\varepsilon)N_t + w_{t+1} D_{t+1}\varepsilon N_{t+1} + G_{t+2}.$$

Next solve for B_{t+1} in (5.15) and substitute the solution into the equation above and rearrange terms to get

$$\frac{B_{t+2}}{R_t R_{t-1}} = B_t + \frac{PD_t}{R_{t-1}} + \frac{PD_{t+1}}{R_t R_{t-1}},$$

where $PD_t \equiv z_t(1 + \varepsilon)N_{t-1} + w_t D_t \varepsilon N_t + G_{t+1} - \tau_t w_t D_t(1 + \varepsilon)N_t$ is the *primary deficit (PD)*: the difference between spending, *excluding interest and debt repayments*, and taxes. We can continue this process of "solving forward" by substituting the expression above into the period $t + 2$-version of (5.15) and so on. The end result of the forward substitution, N-periods ahead, gives

$$\frac{B_{t+N}}{\prod_{i=0}^{N} R_{t-1+i}} = B_t + \sum_{i=0}^{N-1} \frac{PD_{t+i}}{\prod_{j=0}^{i} R_{t-1+j}}.$$

To continue the forward substitution out to the indefinite future, the left-hand-side of the equation above, the present value of outstanding government debt in period $t + N$, cannot "explode." In other words, government debt cannot become "too large" in present value terms. This requires that growth rate of debt be smaller than the interest rate, so that

$$\frac{B_{t+N}}{\prod_{i=0}^{N} R_{t-1+i}} \to 0, \quad \text{as} \quad N \to \infty.$$

This condition, known as the No Ponzi Game (NPG) condition, means that the government cannot continually issue new debt that is large enough to pay back *both* previously issued debt *and* the interest owed on previously issued debt. This scenario would be like the famous Ponzi schemes in finance where funds collected from new investors are used to pay off previous investors. If the government could get away with this much borrowing, it is not *constrained* at all. Note that satisfying the condition *does allow* the government to "rollover" a finite amount of debt forever, as long as it finances the interest on that debt with taxes so that the growth rate of the debt is not equal to the interest rate or greater. Using the condition that the present value of government debt goes to zero as time marches on, allows us to write the GIBC as in the text.

There is a related requirement that says for the government to remain *solvent*, the debt-to-output ratio must remain finite and not explode over time. It is possible for the government to remain solvent even if the NPG condition fails. This could happen if the growth rate of output exceeds the interest rate on government debt. There have been extended historical episodes where the growth rate of output has exceeded the real interest rate on debt. However this is normally not possible so it is also not possible for the government to indefinitely borrow ever larger amounts to pay back both past debt and interest.

Currently real interest rates are less than the growth rate of output in many countries. As mentioned in this Chapter, and as will be discussed in detail in Chap. 8, this situation will not last because there are factors that will both raise interest rates and lower output growth rates. For example, in the US, government debt is already projected to grow faster than GDP throughout the 21st century, violating the solvency condition of a stable debt-to-output ratio, even when assuming that existing interest rates and economic growth rates remain unchanged. A sharp rise in interest rates and a decrease in economic growth rates becomes more likely with the projected increase in the debt to GDP ratio.

Tax Rates

In the text, we consider the value of the wage tax rate that maximizes the height of the transition equation for the private capital-labor ratio. Maximizing the growth in private capital intensity is not necessarily a reasonable objective. Instead we might consider the tax rate that maximizes state worker productivity ($\tau{*}{*}{*}$) or steady state household utility ($\tau{*}{*}$). One can compute these tax rates as well (see *Problems* 22–24). The comparison of the three tax rates is

$$\tau{*}{*}{*} = \frac{\frac{\mu(1-\alpha)}{\mu(1-\alpha)+\alpha} + \varepsilon}{1+\varepsilon} >$$

$$\tau{*}{*} = \frac{\frac{\mu(1-\alpha)}{\mu(1-\alpha)+\alpha}\left(\frac{1+\beta}{\left(\frac{1}{\mu(1-\alpha)+\alpha}\right)+\beta}\right) + \varepsilon}{1+\varepsilon} = \frac{\mu(1-\alpha)\left(\frac{1+\beta}{1+\beta(\mu(1-\alpha)+\alpha)}\right) + \varepsilon}{1+\varepsilon} >$$

$$\tau * = \frac{\mu(1-\alpha)+\varepsilon}{1+\varepsilon},$$

because $\mu(1 - \alpha) + \alpha < 1$.

The tax rate that maximizes steady utility is perhaps the most compelling. It is higher than the tax rate that maximizes steady state capital intensity because there is a benefit to households of keeping the private capital intensity lower than the maximum. All households are savers, so a higher return to capital, other things constant, raises household welfare. The desire to keep the return to capital high creates an incentive to keep private capital intensity low. This consideration causes the policy maker to set the tax rate higher than the one that maximizes the steady state value of k.

The highest tax rate is the one that maximizes steady state worker productivity. This tax rate is higher than the rate that maximizes steady state utility because it does not account for the fact that a higher tax rate on wages lowers the after-tax wage that determines household consumption and instead only focuses on the before-tax wage associated with worker productivity.

References

Alfaro, L., 2016, "Gains from Foreign Direct Investment: Macro and Micro Approaches," *World Bank Economic Review*: *Advanced Access* 23, 2016.

Auerbach A, and Gale, D., 2015, "The Fiscal Problem: Gone Today, Here Tomorrow," University of California Berkeley, Mimeo.

Auerbach, A., Gohkale, J., and Kotlikoff, L., 1991, "Generational Accounts: A Meaningful Alternative to Deficit Accounting," in Bradford, D., editor, *Tax Policy and the Economy*, NBER 5, 55-110.

Bernanke, B., 2015, "Why are Interest Rates so Low? Part 3: The Global Savings Glut," *Brookings*, Wednesday, April 1.

Congressional Budget Office, 2014, *Budget Outlook*, Congress of the United States, Washington, DC.

Das, S., Mourmouras, A., and Rangazas, P., 2018, *Economic Growth and Development: A Dynamic Dual Economy Approach*, Cham: Springer

Dobrescu, L.I., Kotlikoff, L.J., and Motta, A, 2012. "Why aren't Developed Countries Saving?," *European Economic Review*, 56(6), 1261-1275.

Friedman, T., and Mandlebaum, M., 2012, *That Used to be Us*, New York: Picodar.

Furceri, D., and Pescatori, A., 2014, "Perspectives on Global Real Interest Rates," Chapter 3 in *World Economic Outlook: Recovery Strengthens, Remains Uneven*, IMF, Washington, DC.

Gokhale, J., Page, B., and Sturroch, J., 1999, "Generational Accounting for the United States: An Update," in Auerbach, A., Kotlikoff, L., and Leibfritz, W., *Generational Accounting around the World*, Chicago: University of Chicago Press.

Gordon, R., 2016, *The Rise and Fall of American Growth: The U.S. Standard of Living since the Civil War*, Princeton, NJ: Princeton University Press.

Hallerberg, M., Strauch, R., and von Hagen, J., 2009, *Fiscal Governance in Europe*, Cambridge: Cambridge University Press.

Kotlikoff, L., 2015, "America's Fiscal Insolvency and its Generational Consequences," Testimony to the Senate Budget Committee 25, 2015.

______, 2003, *Generational Policy*, Cambridge, Mass: MIT Press.

Kotlikoff, L., and Burns, S., 2005, *The Coming Generational Storm*, Cambridge, Mass: MIT Press.
Kose, M., Prasad, E., Rogoff, K., and Wei, S., 2009, "Financial Globalization: A Reappraisal," *IMF Staff Papers*, 56 (1), 8-62.
Fukao, K., Ikeuchi, K., Kim, YG, Kwon, HU, Makini, T, and Takizawa, M., 2015, "Lesson from Japan's Secular Stagnation," Rieti Discussion paper Series 15-E-124.
Olsen, M. 1982, *The Rise and Decline in Nations*, New Haven: Yale University Press.
Reinhart, C., Reinhart, V., and Rogoff, K., 2012, "Public Debt Overhangs: Advanced Economy Episodes Since 1800," *Journal of Economic Perspectives*, 26 (3), 69-86.
Reinhart, C., and Rogoff, K., 2011, *A Decade of Debt*, Peterson Institute for International Economics, Washington, DC.
Reinhart, C., and Rogoff, K., 2009, *This Time is Different: Eight Centuries of Financial Folly*, Princeton: Princeton University Press.
Steurele, E., 2014, *Dead Men Ruling*, New York: Century Foundation.
Tully, S., 2018, "Can America's Economy Keep Up with its Debt?", Fortune 16.
Viig, J., 2011, *The American Technological Challenge*, New York: Algora Press.

6 Politics, Corruption, and Economic Growth

Chapters 4 and 5 extended the two-period investment model to form a complete growth model. Here, we add endogenous theories of fiscal policy with selfish political motives, in the spirit of Chap. 3, to the growth model. First, we examine the consequence of a powerful kleptocracy for the economic growth of a developing country. Next, we consider a less drastic scenario, where there is interest group pressure on the government of a developing country that may bias policies against economic development. In Chap. 3, we saw how a proliferation of interest groups causes a rise in government transfers as democracies mature in the later stages of development. An important interest group during the early stages of development is comprised of large landowners. In this chapter we focus on the interaction between the political influence of landowners, the structural transformation, and the tax base that affects the growth in governments of developing countries. Finally, we examine the interplay between tax evasion and corruption by public officials and its consequences for private and public capital accumulation.

Tax evasion, a major policy issue around the world, is the newest feature of this chapter. As indicated in Chap. 1, where there is corruption there tends to be tax evasion. In developing countries, tax evasion limits growth by reducing the funding for important public infrastructure projects. In developed economies, tax evasion is one reason that expenditures exceed tax revenue, increasing the reliance on government borrowing and potentially contributing to a public debt crisis. It is becoming increasingly clear that corruption and tax evasion are related in various ways, making it difficult to talk about one without the other. To introduce the fundamentals in as simple a setting as possible, we initially abstract from government debt. The important extension to allow for government borrowing is the subject of Chap. 7.

In Sect. 6.1, we present a simple theory of taxation and public capital formation. We follow our previous approach of modeling the government as we do any other economic agent—by specifying its preferences, constraints, and objectives. There is no deep model of the politics that determine how the government is chosen or how their policies are influenced by voters and interest groups. Instead we take as given the politics of a country that determine the "reduced-form" preference parameters of

M. Ivanyna et al., *The Macroeconomics of Corruption*, Springer Texts in Business and Economics, https://doi.org/10.1007/978-3-030-67557-8_6

the government officials. The parameters dictate the government's concern with the welfare of the general population and the welfare of households that make up, or are closely connected to, the government itself. We use this model to compare the extreme cases of a well-functioning democracy, or a benevolent dictator, to a kelptocracy.

The theory can be used to quantify the role fiscal policy in determining long-run per capita income differences across countries. Think of two governments with different altruistic weights placed on the welfare of private households. The weights are calibrated by targeting the observed gap in net tax rates across countries. We find that the high net tax government has 30 percent less income than the low net tax government. We then examine how the quantitative effect of government policy in explaining income differences might be made larger.

Section 6.2 looks at the influence of interest groups on government policy in developing countries. In particular, we think about how interest groups affect the structural transformation from *traditional agriculture* to *modern manufacturing*—a common feature of the development process that is associated with the take-off to sustained economic growth. The model also offers an explanation for Wagner's Law—the tendency for the relative size of government to grow with economic development. The analysis is relevant to the early growth in the relative size of government, complementing Chap. 3's explanation for the growth in government transfer programs during the later stages of development

Sections 6.3, 6.4, and 6.5 present a dynamic quantitative theory where corruption, evasion, and fiscal policy are endogenously determined. The goal is to quantify the joint effects of corruption and evasion on fiscal policy and growth.[1] There are three main components to the theory. Evidence for these components was discussed in Chap. 1.

First, there is an interaction between corruption and evasion with causation running in both directions. We introduce a "culture of corruption" effect where the average level of government corruption affects an individual's willingness to engage in illegal behavior—in particular a households' willingness to evade taxes and an individual government official's willingness to be corrupt. Tax evasion, in turn, influences corruption by limiting the government's ability to raise funds that may be diverted for private use.

Second, we focus on the corruption associated with implementing public investment projects. Much of the previous work on corruption concentrates primarily on bribes that entrepreneurs must pay bureaucrats to avoid regulation. The corruption associated with public investment projects would seem to be at least as important for economic growth.

[1]These sections are based on Ivanyna et al. (2016). Section 6.5 focuses on the baseline case from their research. The full paper includes several extensions of the model that are not discussed here, including alternative preference specifications, an income tax rather than a wage tax, and an open economy analysis.

Third, we examine how the presence of corruption and evasion affects the determination of a country's fiscal policy. In particular we study how tax rates and public investment budgets are set when the government takes into account how its fiscal choices affect both corruption and tax evasion.

We quantify the theory by calibrating the model to match estimates of tax evasion in developing countries. We then test the model by checking its predictions across other dimensions: the size of net tax rates, the corruption associated with public investment, and the correlation between corruption and tax revenue. We find that the model's predictions are quite reasonable, but only if the culture-of-corruption effect is included. Without the cultural effect of corruption, the predicted value for net tax rates is too high, the predicted value for corruption is too low, and the correlation between corruption and tax revenue is counterfactually positive.

For an intermediate tax evasion target, we find that the presence of corruption and tax evasion increases the economy's tax rate from 19 to 35 percent, similar to the tax rate difference in Sect. 6.2 between the low and high net tax governments. While evasion helps to limit taxation, corruption creates an incentive to increase tax revenues that can be diverted for private use. Unless aversion to illegal activity is relatively low, and the response of evasion to the tax rate relatively high, the presence of corruption will dominate the restraint that evasion places on taxation and tax rates will be higher than in the baseline model. In addition to the effect on tax rates, corruption reduces the fraction of capital budgets that are actually invested. In our model only 43 percent of the capital budget is actually invested.

Surprisingly, the decrease in steady state worker productivity is only 9 percent lower compared to a baseline model without corruption and evasion. This is less than one third the worker productivity difference between the low and high tax governments using the preliminary estimates from Sect. 6.2. With much higher tax rates, and much lower public investment as a fraction of revenue collected, one might expect a larger decline in output than 9 percent. The difference is that in the corruption model, tax evasion is also high, as the model replicates the fact that 33 percent of income goes untaxed in developing countries. Unless the kleptocract from Sect. 6.2 is powerful enough to check tax evasion, some of the negative consequences of his reign on the economy as a whole will be mediated through a loss in tax revenue.

The untaxed income resulting from tax evasion increases the funds available for private investment, helping to mediate the negative effects of higher tax rates on private investment. In addition, if tax rates rise enough, total tax revenue need not fall dramatically and could even rise. The higher is tax revenue the greater are budgets for public investment. Larger investment budgets help keep public investment spending from falling dramatically despite the fact that corruption steals away a portion of the budget. These offsets keep the negative effects on growth from being large and explain why it has been difficult to establish a significant negative correlation between corruption and growth in the cross-country data.

6.1 Government: Benevolent Dictator or Kleptocrat?

We begin with the same private sector structure as the models from Chaps. 4 and 5. The overlapping-generations growth model from that chapter is briefly summarized here. Then we introduce a theory of fiscal policy formation that includes both selfish and altruistic concerns by the government.

Firms
Production takes place within standard neoclassical firms that combine physical capital and human capital to produce output from a Cobb-Douglas technology

$$Y_t = AK_t^{\alpha}(D_tN_t)^{1-\alpha}. \tag{6.1}$$

The productivity index, D, is now a function of disembodied technology, E, and government capital per adult worker, G/N, and is given by

$$D_t = E_t^{1-\mu}(G_t/N)^{\mu}, \tag{6.2}$$

where $0 < \mu < 1$ is a constant parameter. This specification captures the idea that public infrastructure raises the productivity of the private sector. We assume that E progresses at the exogenous rate q and the exogenous growth factor of the population is n.

Firms operate in perfectly competitive factor and output markets. They choose physical capital (K_t) and human capital ($H_t = D_tN_t$) to maximize profit. The profit-maximizing factor mix must satisfy

$$r_t = \alpha A g_t^{\mu(1-\alpha)} k_t^{\alpha-1} \tag{6.3a}$$

$$w_t = (1-\alpha)A g_t^{-\alpha\mu} k_t^{\alpha}, \tag{6.3b}$$

where the de-trended, for exogenous technical progress and population growth, values of public and private physical capital are defined as $g \equiv G/EN$, and $k \equiv K/EN$. The wage paid to a worker, with embodied skills indexed by D_t, is $w_tD_t = (1-\alpha)AE_tg_t^{\mu(1-\alpha)}k_t^{\alpha}$. Note also that $y_t = AE_tg_t^{\mu(1-\alpha)}k_t^{\alpha}$, where $y_t = Y_t/N$, output per worker.

Households
Households maximize the utility function $U_t = \ln c_{1t} + \beta \ln c_{2t+1}$ subject to the lifetime budget constraint, $c_{1t} + c_{2t+1}/R_t = (1-\tau_t)w_tD_t$, where $R_t \equiv 1 + (1-\tau_t)r_{t+1} - \delta$ and τ_t is the proportional net tax rate on income. For simplicity, we assume $\delta = 1$, so $R_t = (1-\tau_t)r_{t+1}$. The resulting optimal consumption and saving behavior is given by

$$c_{1t} = \frac{1}{1+\beta}(1-\tau_t)w_t D_t \tag{6.4a}$$

$$c_{2t+1} = \frac{\beta}{1+\beta}R_t(1-\tau_t)w_t D_t \tag{6.4b}$$

$$s_t = \frac{\beta}{1+\beta}(1-\tau_t)w_t D_t. \tag{6.4c}$$

Capital Market Equilibrium

The firm's demands for private physical and human capital are implicitly given by the profit maximizing conditions in (6.3a), (6.3b). The supplies of private physical and human capital from the households are made available for firms to rent in the factor markets and are given by,

$$K_{t+1} = s_t N_t \tag{6.5}$$

Using (6.4a), (6.4b), (6.4c), (6.5), and (6.6), the equilibrium transition equation for physical-capital intensity is

$$k_{t+1} = \frac{\beta}{1+\beta}\frac{(1-\tau_t)(1-\alpha)}{(1+q)n}Ag_t^{\mu(1-\alpha)}k_t^{\alpha}. \tag{6.6}$$

Government

We now introduce a "reduced-form" approach to the formation of fiscal policy. The government is run by public officials that are distinct from private households in that they derive their income from public funds and set fiscal policy with the entire future path of the economy in mind. This specification is similar to the common approach in macroeconomics of modeling the government as a benevolent social planner. Here we extend that approach by letting the degree of government altruism vary. There is no deep model of the politics that determine how the government is chosen and how their policies are influenced by voters and interest groups. Instead we take as given the politics of a country that determine the "reduced-form" preference parameters of the government. The parameters dictate the government's concern about the welfare of the general population of private households and the welfare of households that make up, or are closely connected to, the government itself. The deeper political determinants of these reduced form parameters are assumed to be given throughout the analysis. Thus, we examine how policies are formed within a given political environment.

The motivation and defense for this approach to modeling the government was discussed in Chap. 1 (Sect. 1.3). In short, we do not believe that there is a unique mapping from political institutions to the government's preferences over economic policies. Pro-growth policies may be carried out and implemented within a highly democratic political process or by a completely authoritative dictator (think of the dictators that pushed development during the Asian Tiger "Growth Miracles").

Different political institutions can give rise to similar reduced-form preferences of the policy maker. In addition, attempting to model the politics of a country is complex and requires that compromises be made in the economic modeling. Jointly modeling political and economic equilibria is particularly difficult in the economic environments that we focus on in this book—the transitional growth of overlapping generation economies.

We assume that the government officials who determine fiscal policy are some fraction, ε, of the population of private households, N_t. Government officials value their own consumption (c_t^g) as well as the welfare of the representative citizen according to a single period utility function, $\ln c_t^g + \gamma U_t$, where γ is a positive preference parameter that gauges the relative weight the government places on the welfare of private households, U_t.[2] We assume that the current government also cares about the government as an on-going institution (i.e. they care about the future operations of the government and the welfare of future government officials) and the welfare of the country's future citizens. The preferences of the government are given by[3]

$$\sum_{t=0}^{\infty} \beta^t \left(\ln c_t^g + \gamma U_t \right). \tag{6.7}$$

These complicated preferences make explicit that the government's concerns extend indefinitely into the future. This is because there is no natural time horizon for government planning. Maximizing an objective function such as (6.7) is somewhat difficult but it turns out that the solutions for the optimal fiscal policy are surprisingly simple.

The government budget constraint is

$$c_t^g \varepsilon N_t = \tau_t Y_t - G_{t+1}. \tag{6.8}$$

The left-hand side gives the government's consumption expenditures. The right-hand side is the difference between government tax revenue, net of transfers, and government expenditures on public capital. For simplicity, we assume that both private and public capital fully depreciates over what we assume to be 20–30 year-long periods of the model. So, next period's public capital stock is determined solely by this period's public investment.

To find the optimal fiscal policy, the government chooses sequences of tax rates, government consumption, and government capital to maximize the discounted utility of government officials and private households, given by (6.7), subject to a series of the budget constraints and private capital accumulation equations given

[2]Mulligan and Tsui (2015) present a theory, based on the threat of political entry, that can be viewed as making γ endogenous.

[3]For notational simplicity only, we assume the government's time discount factor is the same as that used by private households. One could allow the discount factor to differ from private households to study how the government's time preference affects policy, as we did in Chap. 3.

above.[4] In addition, the government takes into account how their policy choices affect all private sector decisions. The solution to the government's problem is[5]

$$\tau_t = \tau = \frac{1 - \alpha\beta + \beta\mu(1-\alpha)2\gamma}{1 + 2\gamma}, \tag{6.9a}$$

$$g_{t+1} = \frac{\beta\mu(1-\alpha)}{(1+q)n} A k_t^{\alpha} g_t^{\mu(1-\alpha)}, \tag{6.9b}$$

$$k_{t+1} = \frac{\beta(1-\tau)(1-\alpha)}{(1+\beta)(1+q)n} A k_t^{\alpha} g_t^{\mu(1-\alpha)}. \tag{6.9c}$$

Equation (6.9a) tells us the tax rate is constant over time. One can show that the constant tax rate τ is decreasing in γ, more concern for private households implies a lower tax rate. Equation (6.9b) gives a transition equation for the public capital stock that is analogous to that for the private capital stock. Here, the government's saving rate out of national income is a constant, $\beta\mu(1-\alpha)$. Combined with (6.9a) this tells us that a more selfish government, with a lower γ, will collect more in taxes but invest *a smaller fraction of tax revenue* in public capital—so as to maintain the *same* investment rate out of national income. Equation (6.9c) simply repeats the transition equation for private capital accumulation.

Note that, as in Chap. 5, we can use (6.9b) and (6.9c) to reduce the dynamics to that based only on the private capital-labor ratio

$$k_{t+1} = \kappa k_t^{\alpha + \mu(1-\alpha)}, \tag{6.10}$$

where $\kappa \equiv \frac{\beta(1-\alpha)A}{(1+q)n} \mu^{\mu(1-\alpha)} \left(\frac{1-\tau}{1+\beta}\right)^{1-\mu(1-\alpha)}$.

Steady State Equilibria and Income Gaps

The steady state equilibrium is characterized by the following expressions for the private and public capital intensities,

$$\overline{g} = \frac{\mu(1+\beta)}{1-\tau}\overline{k}. \tag{6.11a}$$

[4]We assume that the government can commit to its policy choices in advance. For a discussion of commitment issues in regard to the setting of fiscal policy see Ljungquist and Sargent (2004, Chap. 22).

[5]See Das et al. (2018, Appendix to Chap. 5) for a sketch of the derivation in a somewhat more complicated economy that includes the current model as a special case.

$$\bar{k} = \kappa^{\frac{1}{1-\alpha-\mu(1-\alpha)}}, \tag{6.11b}$$

which implies

$$\bar{y}_t = AE_t\Omega(1-\tau)^{\frac{\alpha}{1-\alpha-\mu(1-\alpha)}}, \tag{6.11c}$$

where $\Omega \equiv \left([\mu(1+\beta)]^{\mu(1-\alpha)} \left[\frac{\beta}{1+\beta} \frac{1-\alpha}{(1+q)n} A \right]^{\alpha+\mu(1-\alpha)} \right)^{\frac{1}{1-\alpha-\mu(1-\alpha)}}$.

Using (6.11a), (6.11b), and (6.11c), we can compute differences in worker productivity due solely to differences in fiscal policy (based on a differences in γ that work through τ). We will think of a low-tax "rich" country (*R*), with a government that behaves like a benevolent dictator, and a high-tax "poor" country (*P*), with a government that behaves like a kleptocrat. The steady state income ratio for these two countries is

$$\frac{y^R}{y^P} = \left(\frac{1-\tau^R}{1-\tau^P} \right)^{\frac{\alpha}{1-\alpha-\mu(1-\alpha)}} \tag{6.12}$$

Fiscal policy is by no means the primary reason why incomes differ across countries, as we will, in fact, see below. However, it is a reasonable candidate because there are several poor countries with unusually large governments. Table 1.1 from Chap. 1 gives examples of poor countries with levels of τ, or government purchase shares, that are about double those of the US. The average government purchase share of those countries is 0.32. The U.S. purchase share is typically between 0.15 and 0.20.

To quantify the model's predictions about income differences due to fiscal policy, we need to calibrate the model's parameters. The physical capital income share,α, is set to the standard value of 1/3. Based on the review of the empirical literature in Sect. 2.5 of Chap. 2, the output elasticity for public capital, which here is $\mu(1-\alpha)$, is set to 1/3.

Forming an extreme case from the data above, we think the rich country tax rate as 0.15 and the poor country tax rate as 0.35. The gap in the tax rates causes a gap in income of about 30 percent. While this is a significant difference in income, it does not come close to explaining the huge differences seen in Table 1.1 from Chap. 1. Das et al. (2018, Chap. 5) extend the model of fiscal policy differences to also include human capital and fertility differences. These extensions are able to generate the large income gaps observed in Table 6.1. Human capital differences not only

Table 6.1 The need for a culture-of-corruption effect

	$\chi = \varsigma = 1$	$\chi = \varsigma = 0$	$\chi = 1, \varsigma = 0$
φ	1.1	8.8	1.0
τ	0.35	0.87	0.29
u	0.57	0.39	0.68

directly affect worker productivity differences, but also indirectly create private (via saving) and public (via the tax base) physical capital differences.

One can think about how the government's role in explaining cross-country income differences might be expanded. First, the estimates of α and μ, that determine the quantitative impact of fiscal policy differences on income gaps, may be too low because they are based strictly on measures of tangible capital. As emphasized by Parente and Prescott (2000), in the case of private capital, there are substantial investments in building *intangible* capital. Private firms make investments in research and development of products and production techniques as well as in the specific human capital of their work force. The same considerations could be applied to government investment in improving laws, regulations, and the efficiency of bureaucracies. Expanded notions of capital can be used to motivate larger estimates of α and μ, and thus larger income gaps due to tax differences across countries.

Second, the effectiveness of pubic capital may differ across rich and poor countries. For example, later in this chapter, we discuss evidence suggesting that less than half of the funds in public capital budgets are actually invested. We can capture this possibility here in a simple way by writing a new embodied productivity index as $\widetilde{D}_t = E_t^{1-\mu}((1-u)G_t)^{\mu}$, where u is a parameter that takes values between zero and one, representing the fraction of the investment budget that is diverted toward public officials and private contractors. In developing countries, because of low-quality governance, the value of u may be high relative to rich countries with more checks on corruption or more experience in managing public investment projects. We can pull $1-u$ out of the expression for D and write the production function as $Y_t = \widetilde{A}K_t^{\alpha}(D_tN_t)^{1-\alpha}$, where $\widetilde{A} \equiv (1-u)^{\mu(1-\alpha)}A$. Assuming that $u = 0$ for the rich country, too optimistic as we shall see, we can rewrite (6.12) as

$$\frac{y^R}{y^P} = \left(\frac{1}{1-u}\right)^{\frac{\mu}{1-\mu}} \left(\frac{1-\tau^R}{1-\tau^P}\right)^{\frac{\alpha}{1-\alpha-\mu(1-\alpha)}}, \tag{6.12$'$}$$

So now the income gap depends on *two* aspects of fiscal policy, u and τ, the effects of which depend on the values for α and μ. The end-of-chapter *Problems* will explore these extensions further. Section 6.5 offers a much more complete analysis of corruption, including features that mediate its negative impact on economic growth.

Opening the Economy

To this point we have assumed a closed economy. If instead we assume that the economy is open to international capital flows then things are different. With k determined internationally, the government's optimal fiscal policy will also change. This is another example of how economic fundamentals affect policy determination.

In an open economy, the government will choose a more "pro-growth" fiscal policy than it did in a closed economy setting. The optimal tax rate becomes lower and a larger fraction of the government revenue is invested rather than consumed (see Das et al. (2018, Chap. 5) for the details). Thus, in addition to possible inflows of private capital, output in the country will increase due to changes in fiscal policy.

The policy differences are due to the *timing* of the impact of fiscal policy on private capital formation in open versus closed economies. In a closed economy, government policy affects private capital formation by affecting the after-tax wage of savers that fund the *next* period's private capital intensity. In an open economy, government policy affects private capital intensity by affecting the after-tax marginal product of private investments in the country—reducing it with higher tax rates and raising it with higher public capital intensity. International capital flows will anticipate and respond to these changes in private returns to investment, until the after-tax returns to investment are equalized across countries. Thus, in an open economy, government policy has a more *immediate* effect on private capital formation—this period's policy affects *this* period's capital intensity rather than this period's saving flow and *next* period's capital intensity (as in a closed economy). With discounting of the future ($\beta < 1$), the cost of high taxes and low public investment, in lowering private capital intensity, is smaller in the closed economy due to the one-period delay in their effect. In this sense, opening the economy makes private capital formation more responsive to policy changes. The government reacts to the new environment by choosing a more "pro-growth" fiscal policy stance.

Opening the economy to capital inflows can speed development. However, there may be opposition by a potentially powerful interest group. While there are clear gains in worker productivity from opening the economy, not all generations benefit. The policy affects the welfare of households by affecting factor prices. Households prefer higher current wages for themselves and higher future wages for their children. They also benefit from higher interest rates on their life-cycle saving. Opening the economy will raise wages and lower interest rates if capital flows into the economy. For *most* generations there is a net gain in utility from these factor price adjustments (the effect of higher wages is greater than the effect of lower interest rates). This is *not* true for the initial generation of young households who are alive at the time the policy is announced (or the initial old generation alive when the capital actually flows in). Their current wages are unaffected by the capital inflows (since the initial capital intensity prior to the announced policy change is fixed) and yet their interest rates on assets accumulated to finance retirement consumption are significantly lowered. The sharp drop in interest rates, with no change in current wages, causes their welfare to fall. Thus, welfare falls for the first generation and rises for all others. If this first generation of capital owners is sufficiently powerful politically, they could block attempts to open the economy.

Empirical evidence supports the theory that opening the economy to capital inflows can raise investment and economic growth. This is particularly true when the form of capital inflows is direct foreign investment (Borensztein et al. 1998; Bosworth and Collins 1999). However, for developing countries, some qualifications of this conclusion were discussed in Sect. 5.4 of Chap. 5. The growth effects of capital flows are less certain in countries with inadequate infrastructure.

Foreign Aid

As discussed in Chap. 3 the attempt to use international aid to increase growth in poor developing countries has not been generally successful. A common form of aid is *unconditional* aid that supports the budget of the poor country's government. We now think about the effects of a one-time inflow of unconditional government aid to an economy that is closed to private capital flows.

One can think of temporary unconditional aid has equivalent to a temporary jump in the value of A in the transition equation for public capital, (6.9b), but not in the other equations involving A, such as (6.1) and (6.9c). See *Problem* 4 for an explicit analysis. Unconditional aid inflows increase growth rates initially, but only by modest amounts. The modest initial increase in growth rates results from the fact that the government will save and invest a fraction of the aid causing public capital to increase as indicated in (6.9b). Greater public capital raises the marginal product of private inputs and the rental rate on human capital, which raises private saving and private physical capital accumulation in (6.9c).

After the first period, growth rates fall. The economy is unable to sustain even the modest increase in growth rates for two reasons. First, since the aid flow is only temporary, the rise in public saving cannot be sustained. Second, there are diminishing returns to public and private investment that would cause growth rates to decline back to the steady state level, even if aid inflows were permanent. In fact, growth rates eventually dip below the steady state level for several periods because the rise in the public and private capital intensity cannot be sustained and the economy must revert back to the initial steady state capital intensities. In short, unconditional aid temporarily, but not permanently, shifts the economy's transition equations upward. With no permanent structural change in the economy's dynamics, it must return to its original steady state. Consistent with the prediction of the model, the empirical analysis of Radelet et al. (2006) shows budget support raises growth rates temporarily. However, our model also suggests that there are no long-run income benefits from unconditional budget support.

6.2 Wagner's Law and Interest Groups

In Sect. 3.6 of Chap. 3, we considered the economic effects of the growth in interest groups associated with a maturing democracy. In this section we think a bit about how interest groups affect the early structural transformation from *traditional agriculture* to *modern manufacturing*—a common feature of the development process that is associated with the take-off to sustained economic growth. To do this, we obviously need to extend the one-sector model to include two sectors.

The extended model has two rather different private sector household types—workers and large landowners. The workers might farm land, but they do not own the land. The main motivation for this setup is that large landowners are viewed as having an important impact on the political economy of many developing countries. Landowners derive their income from land rents and thus seek to establish and maintain conditions where land rents are high. This motivation comes in conflict with economic progress that raises wages and the cost of labor, so large land owners tend to support policies that stifle economic growth. In this section, we focus on landowner support for fiscal policies that serve their interest.

The two sector extension also allows us to examine the connection between development and the size of government. Several studies have found a strong negative correlation between the relative size of the agricultural sector and the relative size of government, other things constant (Burgess and Stern 1993; Peltzman 1980; Stotsky and Asegedech 1997; Tanzi 1991). In fact, the studies find that the relative size of the agricultural sector is more closely correlated with the relative size of government than are other indicators of development, such as income per capita. One reason for this negative correlation is that the traditional sector generates unrecorded sales and income that are relatively difficult to tax.

The political influence of large landowners is one factor that keeps both the modern sector and the size of government small. There is a growing literature suggesting that land inequality may hamper growth. The survey by Erickson and Vollrath (2004) mentions general mechanisms for the negative effects of land inequality that work through institutions, influence over agricultural policy, credit market development, and support for public schooling. A common feature of the mechanisms is the attempt by politically powerful landowners to maintain a low-cost work force in agriculture by limiting the options of workers outside of agriculture (see Burgess and Stern (1993) for some specific examples from Latin America).

An additional way that landowners might maintain a low-cost work force is to support high tax rates on labor and capital. If incomes are easier to identify and tax in urban manufacturing, then a high tax-rate environment will favor the agricultural sector. As workers avoid high tax rates by supplying labor to agriculture, the wage rates in agriculture will be driven down to the benefit of landowners. Thus, landowner support for high tax rates will reduce the size of the modern sector, the before-tax wage rate, the tax base, and the size of government.

Households

We continue to assume that all households have the same preferences,

$$U_t = \ln c_{1t} + \beta \ln c_{2t+1}. \tag{6.13}$$

Working households supply one total unit of labor with no explicit labor/leisure choice. All working households are landless and derive their income solely from supplying labor to both the modern and traditional sectors during the first period of their lives. They can move across sectors to work without cost. They retire in the second period.

The workers only source of lifetime income is ω_t, after-tax wage income. For simplicity, we assume the government is completely unable to tax wages earned in the traditional sector. All results go through with a partial ability to tax the traditional sector. In the text we also assume the return to physical capital goes untaxed. Problem 8 extends the analysis of a wage tax to a full income tax. After-tax wage income is the sum of after-tax wages earned by workers in each sector, $\omega_t = \pi_t(1-\tau_t)w_t + (1-\pi_t)\widetilde{w}_t$, where π is the fraction of work effort supplied to the modern sector and $\widetilde{w}_t$ is the wage paid to workers in traditional agriculture.

If both sectors are to operate, workers must be indifferent about where they work. This means that after-tax wages must be equalized across sectors, $(1-\tau_t)w_t = \widetilde{w}_t$. Thus, we have a wage gap in *before-tax* wages, commonly observed in early development, resulting from taxation in the modern sector only.

Landowners have the same preferences as workers. We assume the landowners derive *first* period income from the residual income generated by traditional production, distinguished from modern sector by introducing the notation, O_t. This income may be interpreted as a combination of land rents and compensation for the landowner's work time. There is no land market and landowners pass their land holdings to their children but derive no explicit utility from doing so. Land is passed to the next generation inter vivos at the end of the first period. This timing of the land transfers allows us to bypass the effect of inheritance on the landowner's saving rate because it is not a source of retirement income (see Das et al. (2018, Chap. 8) for an analysis of how landownership affects saving rates).

The landowners lifetime income is then $O_t - \widetilde{w}_t f_t$, where f_t refers to the demand for farm labor. The production function in the traditional sector is $O_t = l_t^{\rho} f_t^{1-\rho}$, where l is land per traditional landowner. Using the first order condition for the labor demand that maximizes residual income, allows us to write landowner lifetime income as

$$\rho O_t = \frac{\rho \widetilde{w}_t f_t}{1-\rho}. \tag{6.14}$$

The associated demand for labor is,

$$f_t = \left[\frac{(1-\rho)}{(1-\tau_t)w_t}\right]^{\frac{1}{\rho}} l_t. \tag{6.15}$$

Note that, if we define the number of landowners as $\widetilde{N}_t$, then $\widetilde{N}_t f_t = (1-\pi_t)N_t$, where N continues to denote the number of young working households. So, the fraction of work effort supplied to the modern sector is $\pi_t = 1 - \frac{L}{N_t}\left[\frac{1-\rho}{(1-\tau_t)w_t}\right]^{\frac{1}{\rho}}$.

Firms

The production function in the modern sector takes the form

$$Y_t = AK_t^{\alpha}(\pi_t N_t)^{1-\alpha},$$

Where we have ignored technological progress and public infrastructure by setting $D_t \equiv 1$. For simplicity, we assume the goods produced in each sector are identical, only the production process differs—one reliant more on land and natural resources, and the other on plant and equipment (see Das et al. (2018) for two sector models where the types of goods produced in each sector differ). The standard profit-making conditions that determine factor prices are

$$w_t = (1 - \alpha)Ak_t^{\alpha}$$

$$r_t = \alpha Ak_t^{\alpha-1},$$

where $k_t = K_t/\pi_t N_t$.

Open Economy

As in Sect. 5.4 of Chap. 5 and the latter portion of Sect. 6.1, we assume that the economy is open to international capital flows. This assumption forces the domestic rate of return to capital to equal the exogenous world rental rate, $r_t = r^*$. The capital-labor ratio in the modern sector must then take a particular value, we call k^*, to equilibrate the domestic marginal product of capital to the international rental rate. This logic in turn implies that the before-tax wage in the modern sector must be fixed at particular value associated with k^* that we call w^*. In this setting the welfare of households is completely driven by the wage tax. In addition, the total capital stock of the country will vary with the size of the modern sector as defined by π_t because $K_t = k^*\pi_t N_t$. Policies that reduce labor in the modern sector will cause the economy to lose physical capital or de-industrialize.[6]

Government Policy

We take a similar approach to modeling the government to the one taken in Sect. 6.1. However, now officials only set fiscal policy during the period that they work for the government. The government officials retire in the second period just as the private agents. Government officials have preferences defined over their own lifetime consumption and the welfare of the two private-sector household types. The weight each household type receives in the setting of fiscal policy depends on their political influence.

The first period wages of government officials are financed by taxes on the wages of the private sector workers. The single period government budget constraint is $w_t^g N_t^g = \tau_t w_t \pi_t N_t$, where all government consumption is in the form of wages paid to the officials and where $N_t^g = \varepsilon N_t$ is the number of government officials. As in our previous models, the number of government officials is an exogenous fraction of the total population.

The preferences that determine government policy are given by the function, $\gamma^g V_t^g + \gamma V_t + \widetilde{\gamma}\widetilde{V}_t$, where γ^g, γ, and $\widetilde{\gamma}$ are constant preference parameters that are determined by the political power of the three agents and the V functions are the indirect utility functions of each type defined over their own consumption. We think

[6]Taxing the return to capital, in addition, to wages would not alter the results much. In an open economy, the after-tax return to capital must remain equal to the after-tax world interest rate. Thus, country specific taxes cannot alter the after-tax return. However, higher taxes on capital in a given country will reduce that country's capital-labor ratio. Thus, taxing capital in an open economy will be entirely shifted to labor by lowering before-tax wages. The primary difference between an income tax and a wage tax is that the economy reduces its capital-labor ratio as well as its total capital stock. See *Problem* 8.

of the government's preference parameters as functions of exogenous political institutions and the de facto political power of the private sector households. Countries with weaker democratic institutions, and fewer "constraints on the executive," will tend to have governments that place less weight on the welfare of the private sectors households as a whole (low values for both γ and $\widetilde{\gamma}$), or perhaps that give disproportionate influence to wealthy landowners (a high value for $\widetilde{\gamma}$ and a low value for γ).

The indirect utility functions of the three household-types can be written out as

$$V_t = E + (1+\beta)\ln(1-\tau_t) \tag{6.16a}$$

$$\widetilde{V}_t = \widetilde{E} - (1+\beta)\frac{1-\rho}{\rho}\ln(1-\tau_t) \tag{6.16b}$$

$$V_t^g = E^g + (1+\beta)(\ln\tau_t + \ln\pi_t), \tag{6.16c}$$

where the upper-case E-expressions on the right-hand-side of each equation contain exogenous constants that will not affect the policy choice. The tax rate lowers the welfare of workers by lowering the after-tax wage in the modern sector and the before-tax wage in the traditional sector. Landowners prefer a high wage tax because it lowers the cost of labor and increases total land rents. The government officials also benefit from a high tax, although they must consider that a higher tax rate lowers the tax base—i.e. the total wage bill in the modern sector.

Using (6.16a), (6.16b), and (6.16c) and the equilibrium condition for the labor share, the first order condition for the optimal tax rate is

$$\frac{\gamma^g}{\tau_t} = \frac{1}{(1-\tau_t)}\left\{\gamma^g\left(\frac{1-\pi_t}{\rho\pi_t}\right) + \gamma - \frac{1-\rho}{\rho}\widetilde{\gamma}\right\}. \tag{6.17}$$

Using (6.17) to determine the optimal tax rate is depicted graphically in Fig. 6.1.

The left-hand-side of (6.17) is the decreasing marginal benefit of taxation that stems from the marginal utility of consumption by government officials whose salaries are financed by the tax revenue. The right-hand-side of (6.17) is the increasing marginal cost of taxation, comprised of three distinct terms. The first term captures the effect of raising the tax rate on the tax base. A higher tax rate shrinks the taxable wage bill in the modern sector as workers move to the traditional sector to avoid taxation. If there was no weight placed on the welfare of private sector households ($\gamma = \widetilde{\gamma} = 0$), the government would maximize the tax revenue collected by equating the left-hand-side to the first term on the right-hand side

The second term on the right-hand-side captures the marginal cost of taxation to working households resulting from a reduction in their after-tax wage. The third term, reduces the marginal cost of taxation, because it represents the gain to landowners from the fall in traditional sector wages when the tax rate is increased. If the sum of these last two terms is positive, the optimal tax will be less than the tax rate that maximize tax revenue because of the net welfare loss that taxes inflict on the private sector. However, with sufficiently powerful landowners the net welfare effect

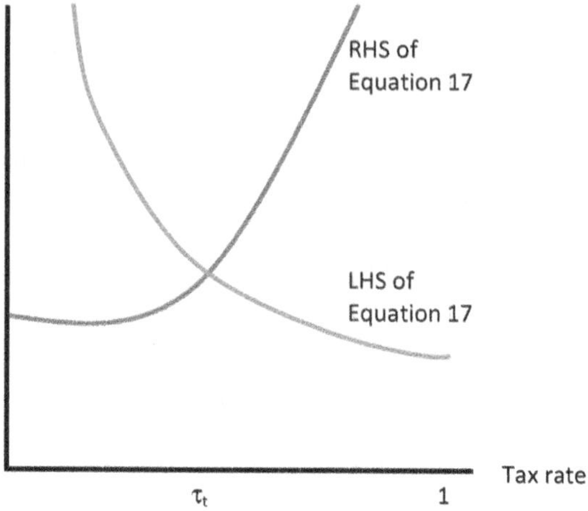

Fig. 6.1 The optimal tax

of taxation on the private sector could be positive. In this case, the tax rate would exceed the revenue maximizing level. Chapter 1 reported empirical evidence indicating that this does happen.

There are two important general points demonstrated by (6.17). First, the greater the political influence of landowners (higher $\widetilde{\gamma}$), the higher is the tax rate. A higher tax rate lowers wages, the size of the modern sector, and the economy's capital stock. Powerful landowners prevent industrialization of the economy at the expense of working households.[7]

Second, exogenous factors that cause the size of the modern sector to grow, i.e. that cause π_t to increase for a given tax rate, lower the marginal cost of taxation and cause the optimal tax rate to increase. The intuition is that the *marginal* loss in the tax base, as the tax rate rises, is smaller and less valuable, the larger is the *total* tax base. Thus, tax rates will tend to increase, other things constant, as economies grow and modernize. This result helps explain Wagner's Law, the observation that the relative size of government increases with development.[8]

The rise in the relative size of the government over the course of development is associated with constant or rising economic growth rates. On the other hand, we have seen that taxation can reduce private capital accumulation. So, what explains this apparent paradox? The answer is that the government uses some fraction of rising tax revenue to invest in public education, public health, and infrastructure, as we saw in Chap. 5 and Sect. 6.1. As the structural transformation generates a

[7]Galor et al. (2009) provide a theory and supporting evidence that larger landowners have acted to slow the accumulation of human capital for similar reasons.

[8]Our analysis ignores the growth in the size of government due to the growth in social transfers. This reason for the growth in government tends to occur in later stages of development as countries become more democratic. See Lindert (2004) for a thorough discussion of the connection between democracy and government size and Chap. 3, where we examined how a rise in interest groups increased transfer spending.

relatively larger government, there need not be a drag on growth *if* the government uses a sufficiently high fraction of the tax revenue on investment. Mourmouras and Rangazas (2009) discuss these points in more detail.

6.3 Tax Evasion

In previous sections we have given some attention to political corruption, but not tax evasion. In many countries, tax evasion is considered to be an even more important illegal activity. As indicated in Sect. 6.2, one common characteristic of developing economies is a large informal sector. The informal sector is a combination of traditional agriculture and urban production carried out by unregistered firms or by registered firms that underreport revenue for tax purposes. In developing countries, the informal sector accounts for between one third and one half of total production (LaPorta and Schleifer 2008). The average size of the informal sector, across a large number of lower and middle income countries, is between twenty and forty percent (LaPorta and Schleifer 2008; Schneider 2012). In developing countries, with limited ability to raise funds by borrowing, the lost tax revenue directly constrains important infrastructure projects, increasing the need for foreign aid.

Development does serve to shrink the informal sector for various reasons but many richer countries still possess sizeable informal sectors. The average size of the informal sector in OECD countries is estimated to be twenty percent (Schneider and Buehn 2012). In some OECD countries, the informal sector results in a significant loss in tax revenue. In Greece, the underreporting of income for tax purposes causes a loss in tax revenue of about 28 percent of total revenue (Azariadis and Ioannides 2015), an important cause of their public debt crisis.

It is generally recognized that the decision to evade taxation is influenced by more than the expected penalty associated with being detected by the authorities. The expected penalty is simply too low to explain the extent of observed compliance by tax payers. Luttmer and Singhal (2014, p. 150) mention several other potentially important determinants of tax evasion that are based on guilt and social norms.

"For example, individuals may have some intrinsic motive to pay taxes or feel guilt or shame for the failure to comply. They may comply due to reciprocal motivations: the willingness to pay taxes in exchange for benefits that the state provides to them or to others even though their pecuniary payoff would be higher if they didn't pay taxes. Individuals may be influenced by peer behavior and the possibility of social recognition or sanctions from peers. Cultural or social norms can affect the strength of these intrinsic motivation, or sensitivity to peers."

Luttmer and Singhal, as well as others mentioned in Chap. 1, provide evidence that these nonpecuniary influences are important. We take this research seriously and model nonpecuniary influences on tax evasion. In doing so, we also provide some indirect evidence for their importance. Our analysis of the interaction between corruption and tax evasion begins by creating a benchmark economy for making comparisons.

6.4 A Benchmark Economy without Corruption-Evasion

For comparative purposes, this section develops a baseline model without corruption and tax evasion. The model is a variant of the now familiar overlapping-generations framework used to study private capital accumulation in the presence of a government sector that raises taxes to finance the salaries of public officials and public investment projects.

Private Households

There are N young households in each period. The households are standard two-period life-cycle savers. They work to earn wages (w_tD_t), consume (c_{1t}), and save (s_t) in the first period to finance second period retirement-consumption (c_{2t+1}).

Household preferences are represented by the following utility function

$$\ln c_{1t} + \beta \ln c_{2t+1}, \tag{6.18}$$

where β is a parameter that gauges the relative weight placed on private future consumption. The household's lifetime budget constraint is given by

$$c_{1t} + \frac{c_{2t+1}}{R_t} = (1 - \tau_t)w_tD_t, \tag{6.19}$$

where R is the return to households saving, w is the wage rate, and τ is the tax rate on wage income.

Maximizing (6.18) subject to (6.19) yields

$$c_{1t} = \frac{(1 - \tau_t)w_tD_t}{1 + \beta} \tag{6.20a}$$

$$c_{2t+1} = \beta R_t c_{1t}. \tag{6.20b}$$

The consumption equations imply that household saving can be written as

$$s_t = \frac{\beta(1 - \tau_t)w_tD_t}{1 + \beta}. \tag{6.20c}$$

Public Officials

There is a fixed number of public officials that set and carry out fiscal policy (εN). The public officials are exogenously selected from the population of private sector households. The public officials have preferences that are identical to the private households, so the process through which they are selected is not important. The wage paid to public officials is proportional to the private sector wage, i.e. the public official's wage is ηw_t where η is an exogenous parameter. Public officials pay taxes on their wages at the same rate as private sector households and work only when young. In the benchmark economy the institutional parameters that characterize the government are then (i) the relative size of public employment (ε) and (ii) the relative pay of public officials (η).[9]

In their private lives, individual public officials take the country's fiscal policy as given when making their consumption and saving choices. The utility function of the government officials is the same form as (6.18). As a result, the private choices of the public officials are of the same form as for private households

$$c_{1t}^{g} = \frac{(1-\tau_t)\eta w_t D_t}{1+\beta} \tag{6.21a}$$

$$c_{2t+1}^{g} = \beta R_t c_{1t}^{g} \tag{6.21b}$$

$$s_t^{g} = \frac{\beta(1-\tau_t)\eta w_t D_t}{1+\beta}. \tag{6.21c}$$

At the economy-level, fiscal policy is endogenous. Collectively, the public officials vote on the current tax rate and next period's public capital (G_{t+1}) to maximize their common welfare subject to the government budget constraint, $\tau_t w_t D_t(1 + \varepsilon\eta)N = \eta w_t D_t \varepsilon N + G_{t+1}$, where we assume, as in the case of private capital, that public capital depreciates fully after one period. Solving the government budget constraint for the tax rate gives us

$$\tau_t = \frac{\eta\varepsilon}{1+\eta\varepsilon} + \frac{G_{t+1}/N}{w_t D_t}\frac{1}{1+\eta\varepsilon}. \tag{6.22}$$

Note that because we do not include government transfers in the model, τ should be interpreted as the *net* tax rate—i.e. the tax net of government transfers to private households.

Firms

Production takes place within standard neoclassical firms that combine physical capital and human capital to produce output from a Cobb-Douglas technology

$$Y_t = AK_t^{\alpha}(D_t N)^{1-\alpha}. \tag{6.23}$$

However, the productivity index (D) is a function of disembodied technology (E) *and* public capital per adult worker ($G/((1 + \varepsilon)N)$) and is given by

[9]For tractability, some features of the government must be taken as given in our analysis. However, we eventually discuss how changes in exogenous features of the government affect the results and even go as far as to indicate what may be considered the optimal levels of η and ε. In addition, note that when $\eta = 1$, the households are indifferent about working in the public or private sectors. However, this is not necessarily true after we introduce corruption and evasion. In the presence of corruption and evasion, we find that public officials are better off than private households as along as $\eta \geq 1$ (even though we assume that public officials cannot avoid taxes on their official salaries). Thus, everyone would want a government job.

$$D_t = E_t^{1-\mu}(G_t/((1+\varepsilon)N))^{\mu}, \tag{6.24}$$

where $0 < \mu < 1$ is a constant parameter. We will not focus on level differences in TFP across countries in what follows, so for simplicity we set $A = 1$. This specification captures the idea that public infrastructure raises the productivity of the private sector as in earlier chapters. We assume that E progresses at the exogenous rate q.

Firms operate in perfectly competitive factor and output markets. This implies the profit-maximizing factor mix must satisfy

$$r_t = \alpha g_t^{\mu(1-\alpha)} k_t^{\alpha-1} \tag{6.25a}$$

$$w_t = (1-\alpha) g_t^{-\alpha\mu} k_t^{\alpha}, \tag{6.25b}$$

where $g \equiv G/E(1+\varepsilon)N$ and $k \equiv K/EN$. The variables g and k are the relevant capital-labor ratios, de-trended for exogenous technological change.

Capital Market Equilibrium and Fiscal Policy

The capital stock rented to firms in period t must be accumulated as the retirement savings of the private households and government officials,

$$K_{t+1} = Ns_t + \varepsilon N s_t^g.$$

Using (6.20c), (6.21c) and (6.25a), (6.25b) gives us the transition equation for private capital intensity,

$$k_{t+1} = \frac{\beta}{1+\beta}\frac{(1+\eta\varepsilon)}{1+q}(1-\tau_t)(1-\alpha)k_t^{\alpha} g_t^{\mu(1-\alpha)}. \tag{6.26}$$

Fiscal Policy

Public officials have identical preferences and opportunities, resulting in a common preferred tax rate. In voting on fiscal policy, whether it is the entire group of officials that vote or some subset, public officials will be in complete agreement. Finding the preferred tax rate of an individual official is then sufficient to determine the country's fiscal policy.

Substituting (6.21a), (6.21b), (6.25a), (6.25b), and (6.26) into the official's utility function, gives the public official's value function in terms of fiscal variables. Writing only those components of the public official's value function that are affected by their fiscal policy choices in period t gives us

$$(1+\beta)\ln(1-\tau_t) + \beta\mu(1-\alpha)\ln g_{t+1} + \beta(\alpha-1)\ln(1-\tau_t). \tag{6.27}$$

The first expression captures the negative effect of taxation on the lifetime wages and consumption of officials. The second expression represents a positive effect from public capital accumulation. Public capital raises the marginal product of private capital causing an increase in the return on private saving that raises second period consumption for public officials. The third expression gives a negative effect of private capital accumulation on the welfare of public officials. Private capital accumulation lowers the marginal product of private capital, the rate of return on savings, and second period retirement consumption.

Maximizing (6.27) subject to government budget constraint given by (6.22) yields the optimal fiscal policy

$$g_{t+1} = \mathrm{B}\frac{(1-\alpha)k_t^{\alpha}g_t^{\mu(1-\alpha)}}{(1+\varepsilon)(1+q)} \tag{6.28a}$$

$$\tau_t = \frac{\mathrm{B}+\eta\varepsilon}{1+\eta\varepsilon}, \tag{6.28b}$$

where $0 < \mathrm{B} \equiv \frac{\beta\mu(1-\alpha)}{1+\beta\mu(1-\alpha)+\beta\alpha} < 1$. The optimal fraction of pre-tax wages invested in public capital (B) is a constant that depends positively on the productivity of public capital (μ) and the value placed on the future state of the economy (β). The optimal tax rate varies positively with the wage bill in the public sector ($\eta\varepsilon$) and the rate of investment in public capital (B).

Calibrating the Benchmark Economy

We now calibrate the steady state of the model so that we can make quantitative comparisons between the corruption and no-corruption economies. To calibrate the benchmark no-corruption model, we start with commonly used estimates for the output elasticities of private and public capital: $\alpha = 0.33$, $\mu = 0.30$.

Assuming that each period in the model last 20 years and the annualized growth in labor productivity due to exogenous technological change is 2 percent, we have, $q = (1.02)^{20} - 1 = 0.4859$. This parameter setting is motivated by the fact that the average country growth rate from 1961 to 2011, taken over a large cross-section of countries, was about 2 percent (Im and Rosenblatt 2013). In addition, the average growth rate over this period did not vary much across countries with different income levels (there has been no convergence on average). For a quick visual confirmation of this last point see Fig. 3.6 from Jones and Vollrath (2013). Overall, the data gives the appearance of countries with different steady states but common growth rates. We follow this interpretation by assuming that countries are relatively rich because of high levels of the productivity index and strong government institutions that prevent corruption.

We assume an annual time discount rate of 4 percent as is commonly used in calibration experiments (see, for example, Prescott (1986)). This implies $\beta = 0.442$, leading to an annualized rate of return on private capital of 4.2 percent.

OECD countries, although by no means completely devoid of corruption, have *relatively* low corruption and we use them to form reasonable targets for net tax rate (or the government purchase share) and the public employment share in the no-corruption case. The average for both these values in OECD countries is about 15 percent (OECD 2011). These targets lead us to set $\varepsilon = 0.15$. Finally, we assume $\eta = 1$.[10] For these parameter setting, we compute an optimal net tax rate, $\tau = 0.19$.

6.5 An Economy with Corruption and Evasion

We now introduce the possibility that households will engage in illegal activity. Each official manages a public sector investment project. They consider the possibility of diverting public funds, earmarked to finance investment projects, for their own private use. In addition, each private household now considers hiding income from the government to avoid taxation. Both activities are costly because resources are lost in attempting to conceal the illegal actions. The stronger are the government's detection institutions, the more resources are lost in avoiding detection.

The empirical literature discussed in Sect. 6.3 and Chap. 1 indicates tax evasion cannot be explained by the detection of illegal activity alone and that tax payer guilt plays role. To capture this result, we assume households experience a loss in utility, "guilt" from violating a social norm, when evading taxes. Furthermore, as the empirical evidence also suggests, the strength of the guilt associated with tax evasion varies inversely with the average level of corruption by government officials.

Similar to tax evasion, it is difficult to explain why there isn't more corruption in government, given the relatively low expected penalty (Lambsdorff et al. 2005, p. 3). As with private households that evade taxes, public officials may experience guilt associated with illegal activity. In addition, the average behavior of government officials set a social norm by which all individuals judge their own illegal actions, both tax evasion and corruption. In this sense, private households and government officials are modeled as being the same "type."

Preferences

The preferences of private households and public officials are written as

$$\ln c_{1t} + \beta \ln c_{2t+1} - \frac{\phi}{2\overline{u}_t^{\chi}} v_t^2$$

and

$$\ln c_{1t}^g + \beta \ln c_{2t+1}^g - \frac{\phi}{2\overline{u}_t^{\varsigma}} u_t^2,$$

where in this chapter ϕ, ς, and χ are nonnegative preference parameters. The illegal activity of private households is measured by v, the fraction of their income that is not reported for tax purposes. The illegal activity of public officials is measured by u,

[10] In Chap. 8 we consider reforms that increase the pay of public officials.

the fraction of the public investment budget that is diverted for private use. The last term in each expression captures the "guilt" or direct disutility of engaging in illegal activity.[11]

Higher values of ϕ imply a stronger distaste for illegal activity. The disutility of illegal activity is also affected by the average level of corruption among government officials. The greater is the average level of corruption, $\overline{u}_t$, the less guilt an individual experiences from their own illegal activity. We refer to this as the "culture of corruption" (CC) effect.

In our baseline case, we take a parsimonious approach where ς is either equal to χ(perfect symmetry of the cultural effect) or $\varsigma = 0$ (no cultural effect on corruption). Rather than consider a range of values for χ, we use the parameter simply to turn the CC effect on and off. With $\chi = 0$ there is no cultural effect (serving as a baseline comparison) and with $\chi = 1$ the average level of corruption lowers the individual's distaste for illegal conduct. Calibration exercises are used to test whether this parsimonious approach is sufficient to replicate key features of the data.

Private Households

The private household maximizes utility subject to the lifetime budget constraint

$$c_{1t} + \frac{c_{2t+1}}{R_t} = (1 - \tau_t)w_t D_t(1 - v_t) + \theta^\tau w_t D_t v_t,$$

where θ^τ is a parameter, that lies between zero and one, reflecting the fraction of unreported income that the household can recover for private use. The parameter captures the traditional monetary deterrent to tax evasion. The more difficult it is to hide income from the government, the less of it can be recovered and used, thus lowering the benefit of evasion.[12]

The maximization problem generates the following equations for tax evasion and private household saving

[11]We assume that the fraction of money stolen generates the disutility rather than absolute amount. This specification will generate fractions of income that go unreported and fraction of public budgets that are diverted for private use that are independent of the level of income. This allows us to focus on institutional determinants of corruption because increases in income alone will not alter the rate of illegal activity.

[12]One can interpret θ^τ as the fraction of the before-tax market wage that a worker can earn in the untaxed underground economy. Too see this, let the technology used in the untaxed sector be the same as in the taxed sector except that the productivity index for labor is $\theta^\tau D_t$ rather than D_t. This captures the idea that the government could lower access to productive public services for firms in the underground economy and thus lower the productivity of labor there. In this case, the profit maximizing wage offered in the untaxed sector is $\theta^\tau w_t D_t$, where we have used the fact that if the return to capital is untaxed, then the capital to effective labor ratio must be equal in each sector. As the government clamps down on the untaxed sector by making it more difficult for those firms to use productive public services, θ^τ falls and the relative wage earned in the underground economy falls as well.

$$v_t = \frac{1}{2}\left[\left(\mathrm{T}^2 + \frac{4(1+\beta)\overline{u}_t^{\chi}}{\phi}\right)^{1/2} - \mathrm{T}\right], \text{where } \mathrm{T} \equiv \frac{1-\tau_t}{\theta^{\tau} - (1-\tau_t)} \tag{6.29a}$$

$$s_t = \frac{\beta}{1+\beta}[1 - \tau_t + (\theta^{\tau} - 1 + \tau_t)v_t]w_t D_t. \tag{6.29b}$$

Evasion is increasing in τ_t and θ^{τ}.[13] Evasion is also increasing in $\overline{u}$ if $\chi \neq 0$. In fact, as $\overline{u}$ goes to zero so does v. If the government officials are not corrupt, then they will act in the private household best interests (since they have the same preferences), so there is no motivation for private household to evade taxes.[14] The term $(1 + \beta)/\phi$ is a measure of "greed" because it is a measure of the value of consumption relative to the disutility of being dishonest. Tax evasion is increasing in greed, other things constant.

Public Officials

Next, we move to the behavior of the public official. In the case of uncoordinated or decentralized corruption, each public official takes the average level of corruption, the tax rate, and the total public investment budget as given when making their private choices.[15] The public official's private choices now include what fraction of their project budget to divert for their own private use. The budget allocated to each public official is $\widehat{G}_{t+1}/\varepsilon N$, where $\widehat{G}_{t+1}$ is the amount of recorded or planned investment and not the actual investment in public infrastructure.

The officials maximize utility subject to the public budget and their private lifetime budget constraint,

$$c_{1t}^{g} + \frac{c_{2t+1}^{g}}{R_t} = \eta(1-\tau_t)w_t D_t + \theta^{g} u_t \left(\widehat{G}_{t+1}/\varepsilon N\right),$$

where θ^{g} is a parameter, that lies between zero and one, reflecting the fraction of diverted public funds that the official can recover for private use. The parameter captures the effect of institutional safeguards that make it difficult to steal public funds and use them openly without detection, working like the standard monetary deterrent to illegal activity. We assume that public officials do not have the opportunity to avoid taxation on their official salary but, of course, they pay no taxes on the income they obtain by diverting funds from public investment projects.

The maximization problem generates the following equations for corruption and the public official's private saving

[13]Schneider and Enste (2000) and Johnson, Kaufmann, and Zoido-Lobaton (1999) provide evidence that higher tax rates increase the underground economy and tax evasion.

[14]Ivanyna et al. (2016) consider alternative specifications where tax evasion occurs without corruption. These specifications do not alter the main findings.

[15]Given the range of estimates, we also adjust φ to match a low target for v of 25 and a high target of 40 percent. Using these two targets did not alter the results significantly when compared to the intermediate case reported in the text. See Ivanyna et al. (2016) for the details.

$$u_t = \frac{1}{2}\left[\left(\Gamma^2 + \frac{4(1+\beta)\overline{u}_t^c}{\phi}\right)^{1/2} - \Gamma\right], \quad \text{where } \Gamma \equiv \frac{(1-\tau_t)\eta w_t D_t}{\theta^g\left(\widehat{G}_{t+1}/\varepsilon N\right)} \tag{6.30a}$$

$$s_t^g = \frac{\beta}{1+\beta}\left[(1-\tau_t)\eta + \theta^g u_t \widehat{G}_{t+1}/w_t D_t \varepsilon N\right] w_t D_t. \tag{6.30b}$$

As with evasion, corruption is increasing in τ_t and θ^g. The larger is the budget that the official manages, relative to his official after-tax wage, the more tempting it is to be corrupt. This is also why corruption is decreasing in $\eta\varepsilon$–the larger is the official wage (increasing in η) relative to the official's budget (decreasing in the number of officials or ε), the less corruption. An increase in the official's wage raises consumption and lowers the value of additional consumption gained by diverting public funds. However, the larger is the size of the public budget, the greater is the benefit of diverting a higher fraction of it. Thus, the greater is the number of officials, the smaller is each official's budget and the lower is corruption. Note that, other things constant, tax evasion lowers corruption because it reduces the size of the official's budget. In this way evasion places a check on corruption.

The negative effect of tax evasion on corruption (u_t) occurs because the marginal value of the stolen income is smaller, the smaller is the discretionary budget relative to legal income. The underlying positive relationship between the discretionary budget and the rate of corruption implies that growth in the relative size of government, Wagner's Law, leads to more corruption unless institutions are developed that makes illegal activity more costly. Thus, in our theory, economies do not "grow out of corruption" without institutional improvement (see, also, footnote 11).

One can imagine theories where larger government budgets lead to falling corruption *rates*, as the weaker income effect of greater stolen funds lowers the marginal value of corrupt activity. However, these theories imply that larger governments *automatically* become less corrupt, without the need for institutional improvement. We find this approach less appealing because there are examples of richer countries, with relatively large government sectors, that continue to struggle with significant corruption problems.

Corruption, Evasion, and Investment for a Given Tax Rate

To build intuition about the microeconomic behavior and provide the foundation for the complete solution of the model, we first solve for the level of corruption and evasion for a given tax rate. Begin by writing out the government budget constraint to establish a connection between tax evasion, tax revenue, and the budget available for public investment,

$$\widehat{G}_{t+1} = \tau_t(w_t(1-v_t)N + \eta w_t \varepsilon N)D_t - \eta w_t \varepsilon N D_t \tag{6.31}$$

The government budget constraint implies that $\widehat{G}_{t+1}/w_t D_t \varepsilon N = \tau_t\left(\frac{(1-v_t)}{\varepsilon} + \eta\right) - \eta$. Substituting this expression into (6.30a), noting that $u_t = \overline{u}_t$ in both (6.29a) and (6.30a), and then solving for u_t in (6.30a), gives evasion and corruption with (6.32a), (6.32b) and without (6.32a′), (6.32b′) the CC effect

$$v_t = \frac{1}{2}\left[\left(\mathrm{T}^2 + \frac{4(1+\beta)\overline{u}_t^{\chi}}{\phi}\right)^{1/2} - \mathrm{T}\right], \tag{6.32a}$$

$$u_t = \frac{1}{2}\left[\left(\Gamma^2 + \frac{4(1+\beta)\overline{u}_t^{\varsigma}}{\phi}\right)^{1/2} - \Gamma\right]. \tag{6.32b}$$

$$v_t = \frac{1}{2}\left[\left(\mathrm{T}^2 + \frac{4(1+\beta)}{\phi}\right)^{1/2} - \mathrm{T}\right], \tag{6.32a′}$$

$$u_t = \frac{1}{2}\left[\left(\Gamma^2 + \frac{4(1+\beta)}{\phi}\right)^{1/2} - \Gamma\right]. \tag{6.32b′}$$

These equations allow us to solve for v and u conditional on a given value for τ. Note that for a given τ, the solutions for v and u are independent of time. So if the tax rate is stationary so are the rates of corruption and evasion (conditional on the institutional parameters η, ε, θ^{τ}, θ^{g})

Economy's Transition Equations

Next, we examine the effects of corruption and evasion on the economy's growth by examining how corruption affects public and private capital accumulation. The actual investment in public capital is the accounting measure $\widehat{G}_{t+1}$ minus the budget funds consumed by the government officials. Subtracting the portion of the capital budget that is consumed by government officials from (6.31), then dividing by E_{t+1} and N, gives us the transition equation for public capital intensity in the presence of corruption and evasion,

$$g_{t+1} = (1-u_t)(\tau_t(1-v_t+\eta\varepsilon)-\eta\varepsilon)\frac{(1-\alpha)k_t^{\alpha}g_t^{\mu(1-\alpha)}}{(1+q)(1+\varepsilon)}. \tag{6.33a}$$

The expression, $\tau_t(1 - v_t + \eta\varepsilon) - \eta\varepsilon$, is the effective tax rate on wages for the purpose of funding government investment budgets. The portion of the budget that is actually invested in public infrastructure, $1 - u_t$, is inversely related to the "corruption tax." For a given tax rate, corruption and evasion both serve to shift the transition equation for public capital downward.

The saving functions for private households and public officials, given by (6.29b) and (6.30b), can be used to derive the transition equation for private capital,

$$k_{t+1} = \frac{\beta}{1+\beta} \times \left[(1 - \tau_t + (\tau_t + \theta^\tau - 1)v_t) + \eta\varepsilon\left(1 - \tau_t + u_t\theta^g\left(\tau_t\left(\frac{1-v}{\eta\varepsilon}+1\right)-1\right)\right)\right] \times \frac{(1-\alpha)k_t^\alpha g_t^{\mu(1-\alpha)}}{1+q} \tag{6.33b}$$

The expression $1 - \tau_t + (\tau_t + \theta^\tau - 1)v_t$ can be written out as $1 - \tau_t(1 - v_t) - (1 - \theta^\tau) v_t$, where $\tau_t(1 - v_t)$ is the portion of reported income taxed away by the government and $(1 - \theta^\tau)v_t$ is the unreported income that is lost in the attempt to avoid detection. Both of these terms reduce the wage available for household saving and private capital accumulation. Public officials' saving is also lowered by the wage tax but their saving is boosted by the income stolen from their public investment budgets. The portion that these diverted funds that can be hidden from government detection helps to fund their private saving.

While corruption and evasion reduce funds available for public investment, for a given tax rate, they increase funds available for private investment. Thus, the overall effect of corruption and evasion on growth is not clear. In addition, we have not yet determined how the presence of corruption and evasion will affect the tax rate chosen by the public officials.

Corruption, Evasion, and the Tax Rate

As in the benchmark economy, because all public officials are identical, the preferred tax rate maximizes the representative public official's welfare. As in Sect. 6.4, the optimal tax rate takes in account tax rate effects on private choices, whether made by private households or public officials. Unlike Sect. 6.4, the effects on private choices now include how the tax rate alters corruption and evasion.

The representative government official's preferences, including only those terms that are influenced by the choice of the current period tax rate, can be written as

$$(1+\beta)\ln\left(1 - \tau_t + \theta^g u_t\left(\tau_t\left(\frac{1-v_t}{\eta\varepsilon}+1\right)-1\right)\right) - \frac{\phi}{2}u_t^{2-\varsigma}$$
$$+\beta\mu(1-\alpha)\ln\left((1-u_t)\left(\tau_t\left(\frac{1-v_t}{\eta\varepsilon}+1\right)-1\right)\right)$$
$$+\beta(\alpha-1)\ln\left(1 - \tau_t + (\tau_t + \theta^\tau - 1)v_t + \eta\varepsilon\left(1 - \tau_t + u_t\left(\tau_t\left(\frac{1-v_t}{\eta\varepsilon}+1\right)-1\right)\right)\right). \tag{6.34}$$

The first term gives the effect of tax rates and tax revenue on the private income and consumption of the government official. The second term is the disutility of being corrupt. The third term gives the effect of taxation working through public investment. A higher tax rate increases next period's public capital and raises the welfare of a generation-t official because it raises the marginal product and the rate of return to private capital. The last term gives the effect of taxation working through private investment. A higher tax rate lowers next period's private capital stock and raises welfare because it raises the marginal product and the rate of return to private capital.

Note that (6.32a), (6.32b) and (6.34) indicate that the optimal tax rate will be constant across time, as in the case without corruption and evasion. Our assumptions imply the rates of taxation, evasion, and corruption are independent of capital intensities, TFP (the level of A), and per capita income. It is only the quality of government institutions (captured by θ^{τ}, θ^{g}, η, and ε) that determine these key variables. Weak institutions will cause high levels of taxation and corruption resulting in low steady state capital intensities and persistently low income levels. Thus, countries will not fully develop without institutional improvements.

One can interpret the economy in Sect. 6.2 as an idealized "rich" country that has a superior steady state resulting from its institutional control over corruption (and possibly from high levels of TFP). In contrast, we now create a "poor" country with no checks on corruption or evasion. The quantitative question is how much the presence of unchecked illegal activity lowers the poor country's steady state relative to the rich country's steady state.

Calibration

It is not possible to derive an analytical expression for the optimal tax rate. We calibrate the model and attempt to find a numerical solution. As mentioned, we are interested in a poor economy without institutional checks on corruption and evasion. In our model this is captured by assuming that $\theta^{\tau} = \theta^{g} = \eta = 1$. For parameters other than ϕ we use the calibration from the no-corruption benchmark model. In our central corruption-case, we calibrate ϕ to target a value of v equal to 1/3. The target is an intermediate value for evasion based on available estimates of the relative size of the shadow economy. La Porta and Shleifer (2008, Table 1) estimate the shadow economy is between 20 and 43 percent of total GDP or total income for lower and middle income countries. Schneider (2012) estimates that the shadow economy is 26–29 percent of GDP for 116 developing economies and 33 to 38 percent for 25 transition economies.

Once the model is calibrated, we attempt to find the optimal tax rate by first substituting (6.32a), (6.32b) and (6.33a), (6.33b) into (6.34), and then by searching over a range of tax rates to find the one that maximizes (6.34). For our calibration, (6.34) is strictly concave in the tax rate. Given the optimal tax rate, the evolution of the economy is given by (6.33a) and (6.33b), the transition equations for public and private capital. Under all the calibrations we examined, the dynamic system converged monotonically to a unique steady state.[16]

Table 6.1 presents calibrations and predictions of the model with and without the CC effect. With a CC effect on both individual tax evasion and individual corruption

[16]As explained, because the rates of taxation, evasion, and corruption do not vary with capital intensities, the transition is not particularly interesting.

($\chi = \varsigma = 1$), to match the evasion target of 1/3 requires setting $\varphi = 1.1$. The implied tax rate associated with this calibration is 35 percent. Net tax rates of this magnitude are common in developing countries (see, for example, Table 1.1 from Chap. 1 or Mourmouras and Rangazas (2007)). In contrast, without a CC effect ($\chi = \varsigma = 0$), a much higher value of φ, and a much higher tax rate of 87 percent, is required to meet the target for v. With a CC effect on tax evasion only, $\chi = 1$ and $\varsigma = 0$, the tax rate is again reasonable at 29 percent.[17]

Comparing corruption across the three calibrations for the intermediate target, we see that when $\chi = \varsigma = 1$, corruption is 57 percent—more than half the investment budget is consumed by public officials. This value could be reduced by lowering θ^g, but the estimate is quite reasonable without further adjustment of parameters. Evidence from Tanzi and Davoodi (1997) suggest diverted cost overruns of almost exactly this magnitude on public investment projects in Italy. Reinikka and Svensson (2004) document that about 85 percent of funds allocated for public school projects were diverted for private use. More comprehensively, Pritchett (1996, 2000) provides evidence indicating that less than half of public investment budgets are actually invested in developing countries.

Note that without the CC effect, $\chi = \varsigma = 0$, the predicted level of corruption would be too low, less than 40 percent. Given that θ^g is set at its highest value, no adjustment can be made to improve the match by raising corruption above 40 percent. With a CC effect on tax evasion only, the corruption rate reaches 68 percent. This high value for the corruption rate could be reduced by lowering θ^g, so this prediction alone does not reject the calibration with $\chi = 1$ and $\varsigma = 0$. We need to consider the model's match to another stylized fact to determine the preferred specification. For this purpose, we focus on the relationship between government quality and tax revenue.

The empirical literature estimates an inverse correlation between corruption and tax revenue (Johnson et al. 1999; Kaufmann 2010; Tanzi and Davoodi 1997). We vary θ^g to simulate the correlation between corruption and tax revenue. We find that tax revenue clearly falls with corruption, but only if the CC effect is present. The decline in tax revenue is caused by a decline in the tax base due to a rise in evasion and a decrease in wages as capital accumulation falls with higher corruption.

This result is displayed in Fig. 6.1 where tax revenue is plotted against the range of θ^g values that generates positive corruption. One can imagine a cross-section of

[17]With no CC effect, in order to generate observed levels of tax evasion, the aversion to engage in illegal activity must be relatively high. When the aversion to engage in illegal activity is high, evasion is not very responsive to tax rate increases and the government can set high tax rates without concerns that evasion will lower the tax base. Thus, to match the observed evasion levels requires unrealistically large tax rates. When the CC effect is present, the level of tax evasion varies with corruption. The corruption-evasion interaction makes each variable more responsive to changes in parameters and helps target observed evasion levels without assuming a high degree of aversion to illegal activity. The corruption-evasion interaction and the lower aversion to illegal activity makes evasion more responsive to tax rates and causes the government to set much more reasonable tax rates.

governments with different institutional quality; the higher the value of θ^g, the lower the quality. Consistent with empirical estimates, when $\chi = \varsigma = 1$, the model predicts that worker productivity and tax revenue fall as θ^g increases. In our model, tax revenue falls when θ^g increases primarily because greater corruption causes significant increases in tax evasion. This result depends critically on the presence of the CC effect.

In contrast, when we set $\chi = \varsigma = 0$ and eliminate the CC effect, tax evasion shows little response to changes in corruption and tax rates. The relatively low responsiveness of evasion to corruption and tax rates without a CC effect causes tax revenue to increase with the level of corruption. Even in the case with a CC effect on tax evasion only, $\chi = 1$ and $\varsigma = 0$, the model is unable to generate inverse relationship between tax revenue and government quality. Thus, in terms of predictions regarding tax rates, corruption levels, and the relationship between tax revenue and government quality, the preferred calibration is clearly $\chi = \varsigma = 1$.

Corruption, Evasion, and Output

We now examine the effect of corruption on economic growth. Comparing the steady states of the rich and poor countries, we find a 9 percent decline in output from introducing unchecked corruption and evasion. With much higher tax rates and substantial government corruption, one might expect a larger decline in output than 9 percent. However, tax evasion is also high as 33 percent of income goes untaxed. The untaxed income increases the funds available for private investment, helping to mediate the negative effects of higher tax rates on private capital accumulation. In addition, much of higher tax rate actually increases the funding for public investment, despite tax evasion. The extra funds serve to offset the rise in the fraction of the budget that is diverted for private use. The share of income that is invested in public capital only falls to 2.2 percent of output from a value of 2.8 percent without corruption. Thus neither private capital nor public capital falls dramatically. The relatively modest effect of corruption on output may help explain why it has been difficult to undercover a statistically significant negative correlation in cross-country data (Svensson 2005). Another explanation is there may be a positive reverse caustion from economic growth to corruption that masks the negative effect of corruption on growth (Ivanyna et al. 2018).

6.6 Conclusion

This chapter introduced politics into the overlapping-generations model of economic growth. We showed that selfish governments without checks on corruption can easily cut per capita income to half the value found in countries with benevolent and clean governments. This estimate is only preliminary because it does not account for the corruption-tax evasion link, changes in policy motivated by corruption, and how diverted funds are used by corrupt officials. These omissions turn out to be important in assessing the impact of corruption on output. We also showed how traditional interest groups can slow the structural transformation of developing economies by promoting policies that hamper capital accumulation.

Tax evasion, an important feature of economies at all levels of development, was seriously addressed for the first time. A quantitative theoretical analysis of how corruption and tax evasion interact with each other and with the setting of fiscal policy was conducted. Our fiscal policy focus in this chapter was on the determination of the labor income tax rate and the level of public investment. Corruption tends to force the tax rate up because corrupt officials want to divert some government revenue earmarked for investment for their own private use. Evasion tends to force the tax rate down because evasion lowers the government's ability to raise revenue at higher tax rates. We find that when the model is calibrated to match typical evasion levels found in developing countries, along with other macroeconomic characteristics, the combined presence of corruption and evasion causes the net tax rate to be significantly higher than in a baseline model with no corruption and evasion. The predicted levels of corruption and the net tax rates are similar to those found in many poor developing countries.

The rise in corruption lowers the government revenue that is actually invested in public capital and the rise in the tax rate reduces private investment, causing a drop in worker productivity. However, the drop is not large, which helps explain why it has been so difficult to establish a statistically significant correlation between corruption and growth in cross-country studies. The higher tax rate increases the budget for public investment, helping to offset the diversion of public funds by public officials. The revenue stolen by public officials is partly saved and invested in private capital. Finally, the full effect of higher taxes on private household's saving is not felt because tax evasion increases. Thus, while corruption is potentially harmful to growth, it is important to account for the economy's full response including how tax policy, the officials' saving behavior, and tax evasion mediate the direct effect of corruption on growth.

In the next chapter we show that corruption may increase government borrowing. The quantitative analysis of this chapter did not allow for this possibility. The finding that corruption is not necessarily associated with a large reduction in output changes when we conduct a quantitative analysis that includes government borrowing in Chap. 7.

6.7 Exercises

Questions

1. If a kelptocracy becomes more selfish, explain what happens to each of the following.
   (a) γ
   (b) τ
   (c) $\overline{k}$
   (d) $\overline{g}$
   (e) $\overline{y}_t$
2. What is the difference between a dictatorship and a kleptocracy? Can a dictatorship have a higher value of γ than a democratic government? Explain.

3. How are τ^R and τ^P calibrated? What does the calibrated difference in tax rates imply about the difference in worker productivity across countries? Does fiscal policy explain most of the observed difference in worker productivity across rich and poor countries?
4. Why do higher values for α and μ raise the long-run impact of tax rate differences across countries on worker productivity differences across countries? How can one justify higher values for α and μ than those used in the calibration exercise from the text?
5. What is the purpose of introducing the variable u? How might u vary across rich and poor countries? What features are missing from the analysis that lessen the negative effect of corruption on output?
6. How might opening the economy create incentives for a kleptocracy to take a more pro-growth stance with its fiscal policy?
7. Does opening the economy to foreign capital flows increase growth in developing economies? Explain.
8. How are each of the three households in 6.2 affected by wage taxation?
9. Explain how powerful landowners can slow the structural transformation through their influence of tax policy.
10. Give two explanations for Wagner's Law.
11. Explain the shape of Fig. 6.1 and use it to answer *Questions* 8 and 9.
12. How does an increase the political power of the government officials in Sect. 6.2 affect tax policy? Careful—this is a bit harder than it appears.
13. Describe how fiscal policy is determined in the model of Sect. 6.4 when there is no corruption or evasion. How does the determination of fiscal policy change when corruption and tax evasion are present?
14. Explain how tax evasion changes when each of the following increase
    (a) τ_t
    (b) θ^τ
    (c) $\overline{u}_t$
    (d) ϕ
15. Assume $\varsigma = 1$ and use the expression for the equilibrium rate of corruption from *Problem* 11 to explain how u_t changes when each of the following increase
    (a) τ_t
    (b) v_t
    (c) ϕ
    (d) η
16. Explain the following statement in detail. "While corruption and evasion reduce funds available for public investment, for a given tax rate, they increase funds available for private investment. Thus, the overall effect of corruption and evasion on growth is not clear."
17. Provide evidence for the existence of a culture of corruption.
18. What is the overall effect of corruption on output? Explain why the effect is smaller than one might expect.

Problems

1. Given (6.9a), (6.9b), (6.9c) and (6.10), derive (6.11a), (6.11b), (6.11c) and (6.12).
2. Prove that τ is decreasing in γ.
3. In the following scenarios, consider the impact of fiscal policy differences on worker productivity differences across countries, using the model from Sect. 6.1. In each scenario assume that $\tau^R = 0.15$, $\tau^P = 0.35$, and $\alpha = 1/3$.
   (a) Assuming that $u = 0$, what value must μ take for fiscal policy to explain a two-fold difference in steady state worker productivity across rich and poor countries?
   (b) If $u = 0.5$ and $\mu = 1/2$, what is the difference in worker productivity across countries?
4. As suggested in Sect. 6.1, one can think of a one-time inflow of unconditional aid as equivalent to a one-time increase in the value of A in the transition Eq. (6.9b) for public capital (only). Define the new value of A in (6.9b) to be $A(1 + \Delta)$, where $\Delta > 0$. Note that the higher value of g_{t+1} will indirectly affect the transition equation for private capital accumulation. In particular, it will temporarily increase the value of the coefficient in the transition equation given by Eq. (6.10).
   (a) Derive the new temporary value for the coefficient in the transition equation for k_{t+1} when there is a one-time increase in foreign aid.
   (b) Use (6.10) to draw a transition equation explanation of the effects of foreign aid found in the text.
5. Derive the indirect utility function for each household in Sect. 6.2.
6. Show that $\frac{d\pi_t}{d\tau_t} = \frac{-1}{\rho}\frac{1-\pi_t}{1-\tau_t}$. So the *marginal* decline in the modern sector tax base is smaller the large is the tax base.
7. Derive the equation determining the optimal wage tax rate in Sect. 6.2.
8. Suppose that instead of a wage tax, the government imposes an income tax that taxes both wages and the return to capital, r_t. To keep things simple, ignore public capital and set $\mu = 0$. With an income tax, it is the *after-tax* return to capital that is equalized across countries. This means $(1 - \tau_t)r_t = (1 - \tau_t)\alpha A k_t^{\alpha-1} = r*$. Redo the analysis in Sect. 6.2 under the income tax, i.e. derive a new version of (6.17) and explain how the results change.
9. Maximize (6.27) to derive the optimal fiscal policy given by (6.28a), (6.28b).
10. Derive (6.29a) and (6.29b).
11. With $\varsigma = 1$, show how in equilibrium (6.30a) reduces to $u_t = \frac{1+\beta}{\phi} - \frac{\eta\varepsilon(1-\tau_t)}{\theta^g(\tau_t(1-\nu_t)-(1-\tau_t)\eta\varepsilon)}$.

References

Azariadis, C., and Ioannides, Y., 2015, "Thinking about Corruption in Greece," Mimeo

Borensztein, E., De Gregorio, J, Lee, J., 1998, "How does Foreign Direct Investment Affect Growth?," *Journal of International Economics*, 45, 115-135.

Bosworth, B. and Collins, S., 1999, "Capital Flows to Developing Economies: Implications for Saving and Investment," *Brooking Papers on Economic Activity 1*, 143-169.

Burgess R, Stern N., 1993, "Taxation and Development," *Journal of Economic Literature 31*(2):762-830.

Das S, Mourmouras A, Rangazas P (2018) *Economic Growth and Development: A Dual Economy Approach*. New York: Springer.

Erickson, L Vollrath D, 2004, "Dimensions of Land Inequality and Economic Development," IMF Working Paper 158. International Monetary Fund, Washington DC.

Galor, O., Moav, O., and Vollrath, D., 2009, "Inequality in Land Ownership, the Emergence of Human Capital Promoting Institutions, and the Great Divergence," *Review of Economic Studies*, 76, 143-179.

Im, F., and Rosenblatt, D., 2013, "Middle Income Traps. A Conceptual and Empirical Survey," World Bank Policy Research Paper 6594, Washington D.C.: World Bank.

Ivanyna, M., Mourmouras, A, and Rangazas, P., 2016, "The Culture of Corruption, Tax Evasion, and Economic Growth," *Economic Inquiry*, 54, 520-542.

Ivanyna, M., Mourmouras, A., and Rangazas, P., 2018, "Corruption and Economic Growth Revisited," American Economic Association Conference paper

Johnson, S. Kaufmann, D, and Zoido-Lobaton, P., 1999, "Corruption, Public Finances, and the Unofficial Economy," *World Bank Policy Research Working Paper #*2169.

______, 1998, "Regulatory Discretion and the Unofficial Economy, *American Economic Review*, 88, 387-392.

Jones, C., and Vollrath, D., 2013, *Introduction to Economic Growth*, New York: W.W.Norton & Company.

Kaufmann, D., 2010, "Can Corruption Adversely Affect Public Finance in Industrialized Countries?" *Brookings Institution Opinions*.

Lambsdorff, J., Taube, M., and Schramm, M., 2005, "Corrupt Contracting," in Lambsdorff, J., Taube, M., and Schramm, M., editors, *The New Institutional Economics of Corruption*, New York: Routledge, 1-15.

LaPorta, R., and Schleifer, A., 2008, "The Unofficial Economy and Economic Development," *Brookings Papers on Economic Activity*, Fall, 275-363.

Lindert, P., 2004, *Growing Public*, Cambridge: Cambridge University Press.

Luttmer, E., and Singhal, M., 2014, "Tax Moral," *Journal of Economic Perspectives*, 28, 149-168.

Ljungquist, L., and Sargent, T., 2004, *Recursive Macroeconomic Theory*, Cambridge: MIT Press.

Mourmouras, A., and Rangazas, P., 2009, "Fiscal Policy and Economic Development," *Macroeconomic Dynamics*, 13, 450-476.

______, 2007, "Foreign Aid Policy and Sources of Poverty: A Quantitative Framework," *IMF Staff Papers*, 54, 59-90.

Mulligan, C., and Tsui, K., 2015, "Political Entry, Public Policies, and the Economy," *Research in Economics*, 69, 377-397.

OECD, 2011, *Government at a Glance 2011*, OECD Publishing, http://dx.org/10.1787/gov_glance-2011-13-en and http://dx.org/10.1787/gov_glance-2011-27-en

Parente, S. and Prescott, E., 2000, *Barriers to Riches*, MIT Press: Cambridge.

Peltzman S, 1980, "The Growth of Government," *Journal of Law and Economics*, 23(2):209–287.

Prescott, E., 1986, "Theory Ahead of Measurement," *Quarterly Review*, Federal Reserve of Minneapolis, 10, 9-22.

Pritchett, L., 2000, "The Tyranny of Concepts: CUDIE (Cumulated, Depreciated Investment Effort) is *Not* Capital," *Journal of Economic Growth*, 5, 361-384.

______, 1996, "Mind Your P's and Q's: The Cost of Public Investment is *Not* the Value of Public Capital," *World Bank Policy Research Working Paper #*1660.

Radelet S, Clemens M Bhavnani R, 2006, "Aid and Growth: The Current Debate and some New Evidence," CGD working paper 133. Center for Global Development, Washington, DC.

Reinikka, R. and Svensson, J., 2004, "Local Capture: Evidence from a Central Government Transfer Program in Uganda," *Quarterly Journal of Economics*, 119, 679-709.

Schneider, F., 2012, "The Shadow Economy and Work in the Shadow: What We (Not) Know?" IZA Discussion Paper No. 6423.

Schneider, F., and Buehn, A., 2012, "Shadow Economies in Highly Developed OECD Countries: What are the Driving Forces," IZA DP 6891.

Schneider, F. and Enste, D., 2000, "Shadow Economies: Size, Causes, and Consequences," *Journal of Economic Literature*, 38, 77-114.

Stotsky JG, Asegedech W, 1997, "Tax effects in sub-Saharan Africa," IMF working paper 97/107. International Monetary Fund, Washington DC.

Svensson, J., 2005, "Eight Questions about Corruption," *Journal of Economic Perspectives*, 19, 19-42.

Tanzi V, 1991, *Structural Factors and Tax Revenue in Developing Countries: A Decade of Evidence,* International Monetary Fund, Washington DC.

Tanzi, V. and Davoodi, H., 1997, "Corruption, Public Investment, and Growth," *IMF Working Paper* #139.

7 Corruption and Public Debt

Chapter 5 shows how particular economic fundamentals and interest group politics are driving the formation of large fiscal gaps. Here, we stress that corruption is also an important determinant of the fiscal gap in many developed countries. We first introduce corruption and debt in the two-period model of government investment, using the generational interpretation. The model highlights the connection between corruption and government debt when the altruism toward future generations is sufficiently low. Next, we move to a more complete analysis using the overlapping-generations growth model. This section extends the quantitative theory from Chap. 6 that studied how the presence of corruption and tax evasion affects the formation of a country's fiscal policy, by including public debt as a fiscal instrument.

In our quantitative analysis, we first specify a model without corruption where the fundamentals of the economy cause the optimal debt level to be zero. Next, we introduce the theory of corruption and tax evasion from Chap. 6, where the two illegal activities are connected by a "culture of corruption" effect. The opportunity for corruption creates an incentive for public officials to enlarge budgets by raising tax rates and issuing debt. The quantitative question is how much public debt can be generated from the corruption mechanism alone.

We calibrate institutional safeguards against corruption in order to target the range of tax evasion estimated across developed countries. Even the relatively modest implied differences in institutional safeguards needed to target the range of tax evasion in developed countries are shown to generate a wide variation in public debt to private capital ratios, ranging from zero to over 100 percent. The variation in corruption that is consistent with observed variation in tax evasion has the potential to generate significant variation in debt policy across countries.

In our model the increase in public debt associated with weak institutional safeguards against corruption crowds out private and public capital and reduces output. Crowding out capital formation is just one of the costs associated with high levels of public debt. Reinhart and Rogoff (2009, 2012) provide evidence of negative growth effects from high debt levels that may result not only from crowding out, but also from inflation, higher international borrowing costs, and capital flight.

M. Ivanyna et al., *The Macroeconomics of Corruption*, Springer Texts in Business and Economics, https://doi.org/10.1007/978-3-030-67557-8_7

The common element of all the costs of debt is the reduction in domestic capital formation and growth. Gruber and Kamin (2012) provide evidence that structural deficits lead to higher interest rates in OECD, and especially in G7, countries. They also provide evidence that the higher interest rates are due to a higher real costs of domestic funds, consistent with the crowding out of private capital formation.

Unlike in Chap. 6, where government borrowing was constrained to be zero, the loss in output caused by the corruption-debt interaction is large. Without public debt, we found that introducing corruption reduced output by about 10 percent. Here the loss is three times that large.

The model exhibits interesting dynamic properties caused by the interaction between corruption and debt. de La Croix and Michel (2002) discuss situations where cycles occur in overlapping generations models, including models with public debt. Corruption offers a new reason for cycles. The dynamic equilibria in the model include periodic debt cycles, where the economy moves between periods of relatively high and relatively low levels of public debt. A high debt period is followed by a low debt period because the obligation to pay off old debt constrains the discretionary spending of the government, requiring higher tax rates and higher new borrowing to maintain the same level of discretionary spending. The higher tax rates and debt levels are too costly, in terms of reduced private capital accumulation and growth, and so discretionary spending is cut. A drop in discretionary spending reduces corruption and further reduces the incentive to issue new debt, causing debt levels to fall below those of the previous period. Thus, the model offers a fully endogenous explanation of why countries often build up public debt only to abruptly reform policies to bring debt back to more sustainable levels (Alesina and Drazen 1991; Alesina et al. 2006).

7.1 Theories of Government Debt

There is a literature that focuses on the fundamentals that determine the level of the public debt. Battaglini and Coate (2008) and Alesina and Passalaqua (2015) offer recent contributions and literature reviews. We summarize the main approaches from the literature and relate them to the approach taken in this chapter.

One explanation for government borrowing is Barro's (1979) idea of tax smoothing. He argues that, in the face of exogenous shocks to tax revenue or to the productivity of public goods, the government may want to issue debt in order to keep marginal tax rates stable. Our analysis does not contain this feature because we do not introduce exogenous shocks or the deadweight losses from marginal tax rates. Barro's focus is more on business cycle variations, our on longer term cycles. Empirical support for Barro's tax smoothing explanation is mixed (Barro 1986; Bizer and Durlauf 1990; Roubini and Sachs 1989) which provided motivation to search for alternative explanations.

A second explanation for public debt comes from a dynamic version of the common pool problem associated with government revenue (Velasco 1999, 2000; Achury et al. 2015). This explanation is closely related to the rent-seeking explanation for the expansion in government spending and public debt discussed in Chap. 3. When central government spending is influenced by fragmented interest groups, spending and deficits are biased upward. The groups see the full benefits of increased local spending but only bear a fraction of the tax costs that are spread across all households. In the model of this chapter, increased public investment increases the opportunity for corruption. Issuing public debt is a way to increase public investment budgets. Thus, corruption offers an incentive to issue debt that complements the common pool mechanism. Furthermore, in the common pool model, the accumulation of debt is only reversed if something causes the interest groups to coordinate and recognize the full cost of their spending choices. In our model there are equilibria with endogenous debt cycles where reversals in the accumulation of public debt occur automatically and repeatedly.

The possibility of endogenous debt cycles relates to a third explanation for public debt that is based on slow responses to permanent negative shocks that raise spending and lower tax revenue (Alesina and Drazen 1991). In this theory an economy is hit with a negative exogenous shock that puts it on an unstable fiscal path. Delays in responding to the resulting fiscal imbalance result from a political conflict between two groups that differ on how the government should respond. A game of attrition ensues until the weaker group concedes and fiscal reform takes place. In this theory, economies with strong executive branches or strong majorities will reform more quickly, a prediction that is consistent with the data (Alesina et al. 2006). The endogenous debt cycles of this chapters model offer a second explanation for periods of debt accumulation followed by periods of reform and fiscal consolidation.

A fourth explanation for public debt is based on political instability and strategic competition between political parties. This argument is built on the idea that debt issued today constrains the policies of future governments. In the literature, political parties are assumed to differ in their preferences for either the level or composition of public consumption (Persson and Svensson 1989) or in its composition (Tabellini and Alesina 1990). With the possibility that the other party will assume office in the future, it is optimal for the current party to constrain the choices of its rival by issuing debt. A complete exposition of this argument was presented in Chap. 3.

This strategic mechanism is not present in the model of this chapter because the current government does not account for the consequences of their choices on the policies of the next government. However, public debt does cause fiscal policies to be connected across governments because the greater the debt hangover from the previous government, the less discretionary spending on public investment, and the less corruption, by the current government. Thus, the behavior of past governments constrains the behavior of the current government even without explicit strategic intentions.

Finally, the majority of the population may want to redistribute wealth from their children and thus favor government borrowing (Cukierman and Metzler 1989). Bequest-constrained households would like to borrow and increase current spending, leaving the debt for their children to repay. This is not legally possible on an individual basis. However, the government can intermediate this generational transaction by issuing public debt or expanding PAYG social transfers. We discussed this mechanism in Chaps. 2 and 5. In this chapter, we show that sufficiently low altruism toward the next generation interactions with corruption to raise government debt.

7.2 Corruption and Altruism in the Two-Period Model

In this section we extend the analysis from Sect. 3.7 of Chap. 3 to think about how corruption might be connected to government debt. The economy is small and open, and the exogenous international interest rate is r^*. Each public official is allocated an equal portion of the total investment budget to manage an investment project. The budget per project is the budget per government official, $\widehat{G}_2/\varepsilon N$. The officials consider the possibility of diverting the tax revenue, earmarked to finance investment projects, for their own private use. The fraction of funds they divert is denoted by u. Public and private households receive the same first period income, y_1. Second period income for both household types is endogenous and is given by $y_2 = Ag_2^{\mu}$.

The preferences of public officials are written as

$$\ln c_1^g + \beta \ln c_2^g - \frac{\phi}{2\overline{u}} u^2, \tag{7.1}$$

where ϕ is a nonnegative preference parameter that measures the guilt associated with corruption. Higher values of ϕ imply a stronger distaste for illegal activity. The disutility of illegal activity is also affected by the average level of corruption among government officials, $\overline{u}$. The greater is the average level of corruption, the less guilt an individual experiences from their own illegal activity. We refer to this as the "culture of corruption" effect. Each public official takes the average level of corruption, the tax rates in each period (τ_1, τ_2), and the total public investment budget as given when making their private choices. The public official's private choices include what fraction of their project budget to divert for their own private use.

We use the generational interpretation of the two-period model and assume that the economy is bequest-constrained. Individual households, including public officials, would prefer to leave private debt to their children but face a legal restriction that prohibits it. The government, however, can issue debt (B_1) in the international credit market.

The two single-period budget constraints facing the public officials and their children are

$$c_1^g = (1 - \tau_1)y_1 + \theta^g u\left(\widehat{G}_2/\varepsilon N\right) \tag{7.2a}$$

$$c_2^g = (1 - \tau_2)y_2 \tag{7.2b}$$

where θ^g is a parameter, that lies between zero and one, reflecting the fraction of diverted public funds that the official can recover for private use. The parameter captures the effect of institutional safeguards that make it difficult to steal public funds and use them openly without detection, working like the standard monetary deterrent to illegal activity in the corruption literature. The officials maximize utility subject to their investment budget and their private lifetime budget constraint,

Formally, the officials maximize utility subject to (7.2a and 7.2b) and their public investment budget. The first order conditions for utility maximization, and the assumption that $\overline{u} = u$ in equilibrium (public officials are identical), gives the following equation for optimal corruption.

$$u = \frac{1}{\phi} - \frac{(1 - \tau_1)y_1}{\theta^g \widehat{g}} \tag{7.3}$$

where $\widehat{g} \equiv \widehat{G}_2/\varepsilon N$. The more budgeted funds ($\widehat{g}$) and the greater the fraction of those funds that can used without detection (θ^g), the higher is u. Legal after-tax income ($(1 - \tau_1)y_1$) reduces the value of stolen funds and lowers u. The disutility associated with stealing (ϕ) also lowers corruption.

Substituting (7.3) back into the official's utility function allows us to derive a value function for the official. We use the value function to determine the fiscal policy preferred by public officials. Including only those terms that can be influenced by fiscal variables, the value function can be written as

$$V^g = \ln \widehat{g} + \beta \ln (1 - \tau_2)y_2 + \frac{\phi}{2\theta^g} \frac{(1 - \tau_1)y_1}{\widehat{g}}, \tag{7.4}$$

where $y_2 = Ag_2^\mu = A\left(\frac{\widehat{G}_2(1-u)}{(1+\varepsilon)N}\right)^\mu = A\left(\widehat{g}(1 - u)\frac{\varepsilon}{1+\varepsilon}\right)^\mu$.

Fiscal Policy

The public officials jointly determine fiscal policy to maximize their common preferences, given by (7.4), subject to the government budget constraints

$$\frac{B_1}{N} + \tau_1 y_1 (1 + \varepsilon) = (y_1 + \widehat{g})\varepsilon \tag{7.5a}$$

$$\tau_2 y_2 (1 + \varepsilon) = y_2 \varepsilon + \frac{B_1}{N}(1 + r*). \tag{7.5b}$$

First, consider the optimal choice of τ_1. Intuition suggests that, because we assume households are bequest-constrained, public officials should want to make the lifetime incomes of the current generation as high as possible by setting first period taxes to zero. This intuition is *almost* correct. The first order condition for the choice of τ_1 can be written as

$$-\frac{1}{2}\frac{1}{c_1^g} + \frac{\beta(1 + \mathrm{r}*)}{c_2^g} - \frac{\beta \mu A g_2^{\mu-1}}{c_2^g} \frac{\varepsilon}{\theta^g (1 + \varepsilon)^2} \leq 0. \tag{7.6a}$$

The first two terms, of opposite sign, are related to the bequest constraint. The third term is negative and helps make the case for setting first period taxes to zero. It captures the reduction in actual investment and future income as an increase in τ_1 encourages corruption. If the first two terms net out to be negative when $\tau_1 = 0$, then the preferred policy includes no first period taxes.

The first order condition for the household's choice of saving or bequests, assuming a binding constraint, is

$$-\frac{1}{c_1^g} + \frac{\beta(1 + \mathrm{r}*)}{c_2^g} < 0. \tag{7.6b}$$

The assumption of a bequest-constraint, given by (7.6b), does not guarantee that (7.6a) is a strict inequality because the negative expression in (7.6a) is hit by ½. This happens because the marginal guilt of corruption, when the *government chooses* $\tau_1$to maximize (7.4), is smaller than the marginal guilt of an *individual public official choosing* corruption when maximizing (7.1). While an individual official takes other officials' behavior as given, the government, i.e. the collective decision of all officials coordinating on the preferred fiscal policy, takes into account how *all* households will react. If all public officials become more corrupt when after-tax legal income falls, the marginal guilt is weaker because of the cultural effect. Despite the fact that (7.6b) does not guarantee zero first period taxes, we assume that the strict inequality in (7.6a) holds, so that all changes in public investment are bond-financed.

Combining (7.5a) and (7.5b) allows us to write the after-tax income of the future generation as

$$(1 - \tau_2)y_2 = \left(\frac{1}{1 + \varepsilon}\right)[y_2 - \varepsilon(y_1 + \widehat{g})(1 + r*)]. \tag{7.7}$$

Using (7.3), we can also write

$$y_2 = Ag_2^\mu = A\left(\widehat{g}(1 - u)\frac{\varepsilon}{1 + \varepsilon}\right)^\mu = A\left(\left[\frac{(\phi - 1)}{\phi}\widehat{g} + \frac{y_1}{\theta_g}\right]\frac{\varepsilon}{1 + \varepsilon}\right)^\mu. \tag{7.8}$$

Viewing (7.8) suggests another opportunity at simplification in order to eliminate ambiguous interactions. If we set $\phi = 1$, then variation in $\widehat{g}$ does not affect g_2 and future output. This is related to the unresolved issue discussed when we introduced corruption in Chap. 3. An increase in $\widehat{g}$ also raises u, so the overall effect on g_2 is ambiguous. To resolve the ambiguity, one needs to know how responsive the rate of corruption is to increases in the budget. When $\phi = 1$, the two effects of associated with increasing $\widehat{g}$ just cancel, leaving g_2 unaffected. The defense of assuming $\phi = 1$ is that ϕ would have to differ significantly from 1 for any effect on g_2 to be large. In the quantitative theory of Sects. 7.3 and 7.4, we calibrate ϕ to match facts and let the data determine the effect of $\widehat{g}$ on g_2.

With $\tau_1 = 0$ and $\phi = 1$, choosing the optimal fiscal policy simplifies to choosing $\widehat{g}$ to maximize

$$\overline{V}^g = \ln \widehat{g} + \beta \ln [\overline{y}_2 - \varepsilon(y_1 + \widehat{g})(1 + r*)] + \frac{y_1}{2\theta^g \widehat{g}} \tag{7.9}$$

where $\overline{y}_2 \equiv A\left(\frac{\varepsilon}{1+\varepsilon}\frac{y_1}{\theta^g}\right)^\mu$. Note that while changes in $\widehat{g}$ do not affect future output, an increase θ^g lowers future output. Higher corruption diverts funds from a given investment budget and lowers future output. The first order condition for the optimal investment budget, and optimal public debt level, is

$$\frac{1}{\widehat{g}}\left(1 - \frac{1}{2}\frac{y_1}{\theta^g \widehat{g}}\right) = \frac{\beta\varepsilon(1 + r*)}{\overline{y}_2 - \varepsilon(y_1 + \widehat{g})(1 + r*)}. \tag{7.10}$$

The left-hand-side of (7.10) is the marginal benefit of choosing $\widehat{g}$. The term in the parenthesis can be written as $u + \frac{1}{2}\frac{y_1}{\theta^g \widehat{g}} > 0$. One can also verify that the marginal benefit is decreasing in $\widehat{g}$ (see *Problem* 3). The right-hand-side of (7.10) is the marginal cost of $\widehat{g}$ via the higher taxes on future generations needed to repay public debt. The marginal cost is increasing in $\widehat{g}$. The optimal choice of $\widehat{g}$ is depicted in Fig. 7.1.

Imagine now that we are looking across countries with different values for θ^g, i.e. different safeguards against corruption. An increase in θ^g increases the marginal benefit of spending because it increases the opportunity for diverting the budget to the official's private consumption. An increase in θ^g also raises the marginal cost because greater corruption lowers future output. In general, greater opportunities for corruption could raise or lower bond-financed government spending.

To explain the positive correlation between corruption and public debt, an increase in θ^g must raise the marginal benefit more than the marginal cost. This

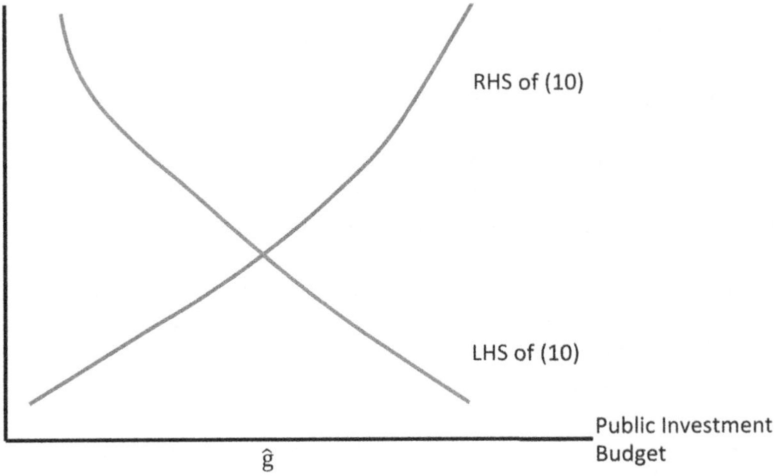

Fig. 7.1 Optimal government investment with corruption

will happen when the values of β or μ are low—i.e., when either altruism toward the future is low or government investment is not very productive. Thus, low β increases public debt directly, by increasing the likelihood of a bequest-constraint, and indirectly, by lowering the cost of spending, corruption, and higher future taxes.

In summary, we have established that corruption can *amplify* a government's tendency to use debt financing. For simplicity, our analysis assumed (i) no tax evasion, (ii) a bequest-constrained economy, and (iii) a neutral effect of the investment budget on actual investment. The assumption that the economy is bequest-constrained means there is an economic fundamental that creates a preference for borrowing over first period taxes—corruption merely raises public debt further.

The analysis of this section leaves several important questions unanswered.

1. What is the role of tax evasion in explaining the corruption-debt correlation? Will tax evasion sufficiently constrain corruption so that it causes government spending and public debt to fall or will the lost revenue from tax evasion raise government borrowing further?
2. Is corruption strong enough to raise government borrowing in the *absence* of other features that bias the government toward debt financing?
3. What is the quantitative effect of corruption on actual public investment and output?

We learned from Chap. 6 that tax evasion prevents corruption from increasing tax revenue—a more corrupt economy collects less tax revenue. In Sect. 7.4, we find this is one reason why corruption is sufficient to raise public debt, even in the absence of other features that bias the government toward borrowing. We also find that corruption significantly lowers output by raising debt and crowding out both private and public investment.

7.3 A Benchmark Economy without Corruption and Evasion

This section begins to address the unanswered questions from Sect. 7.2. We use the same approach as in Chap. 6. For comparative purposes, we first develop a baseline model without corruption and tax evasion. Section 7.4 then adds illegal activities. The model is an overlapping-generations model of private capital accumulation that is extended to include a government sector that both raises taxes and issues government debt to finance the salaries of public officials and public investment projects. In contrast to Sect. 7.2, the model economy is closed—a better assumption for addressing the public debt crisis of larger developed economies. Thus, of the possible costs of public debt mentioned in the introduction to the chapter, we include only the standard crowding-out mechanism in a perfectly domestic economy.

The Baseline Model

Production takes place within standard neoclassical firms that operate in perfectly competitive markets. The firms combine physical capital and human capital to produce output using a Cobb-Douglas technology, identical to that of Chap. 6, with $A = 1$ for simplicity. There are N young households in the private sector each period. The households are standard two-period life-cycle savers. They work to earn wages ($w_t D_t$), consume (c_{1t}), and save (s_t) in the first period to finance second period retirement-consumption (c_{2t+1}). In addition to their own consumption, households also care about the general state of the economy, which we characterize by the average level of worker productivity during both periods of their lives (y_t, y_{t+1}).

The last assumption is a form of altruism.[1] We introduce altruism so that households that become public officials have concerns about the current and future state of the economy, or equivalently the economic opportunities of future generations, and not only their own consumption.[2] This type of altruism helps to limit public debt because of concerns that government borrowing reduces private capital accumulation and economic growth.[3] When the government is able to redistribute wealth across generations, some form of concern for the future generations is crucial for choosing a sustainable fiscal policy (Kotlikoff 2003; Kotlikoff and Burns 2004, 2012; Ferguson 2012, Chapter 1). The existence of laws preventing individuals from imposing debt repayments on adult children is clear evidence that intergenerational altruism does exist.

Household preferences are represented by the following utility function

$$\ln c_{1t} + \beta \ln c_{2t+1} + \gamma\left(\ln y_t + \beta \ln y_{t+1}\right), \tag{7.11}$$

where β and γ are parameters that gauge the relative weight placed on private future consumption and the general state of the economy relative to private current consumption. The household's lifetime budget constraint is given by

---

[1]We also assumed this form of altruism as part of the sensitivity analysis of the model with no government borrowing from Chap. 6 (see Ivanyna (2016) for the details). There, introducing altruism did not affect the main results.

[2]This type of specification is based on Becker and Tomes (1976) that gave rise to a vast literature on the economics of fertility where parents choose between the quantity and quality of children (see Galor (2005) for a survey). The quality of children is measured by the children's adult wage, or the marginal product of labor, similar to our specification that uses the average product of labor of future generations. For the Cobb-Douglas production function we use, the marginal product of labor is proportional to the average product of labor and thus the two specifications are essentially equivalent. Thus, our assumption that households care about the future state of the economy is behaviorally-equivalent to an assumption of intergenerational altruism of the form, $\ln c_{1t} + \beta \ln c_{2t+1} + \beta\gamma \ln w_{t+1}$.

[3]As is well known, assuming Becker-Barro altruism, where the utility of future generations enter the utility function of the current generation, eliminates any effect on the economy from debt accumulation per se. The Ricardian Equivalence theorem that Becker-Barro altruism produces is difficult to reject in macroeconomic data, due to the absence of sufficiently powerful tests (Cardia (1997), but is clearly inconsistent with microeconomic studies that show (i) excessive sensitivity of consumption to temporary changes in income (see Johnson, Parker, and Souleles (2006) and the references therein) and (ii) consumption effects from the redistribution of resources across generations, even in households that make intergenerational transfers (Altonji et al. 1992, 1997). See also the criticisms of Becker-Barro altruism in Kotlikoff (2003, Chapter 7).

$$c_{1t} + \frac{c_{2t+1}}{R_t} = (1 - \tau_t)w_t, \quad (7.12)$$

where r is the rate of return to households saving and τ is the tax rate on wage income.

Maximizing (7.11) subject to (7.12) yields

$$c_{1t} = \frac{(1 - \tau_t)w_t D_t}{1 + \beta} \quad (7.13a)$$

$$c_{2t+1} = \beta R_t c_{1t}. \quad (7.13b)$$

The consumption equations imply that household saving can be written as

$$s_t = \frac{\beta(1 - \tau_t)w_t D_t}{1 + \beta}. \quad (7.13c)$$

As in Chap. 6, we assume that there is a fixed number of public officials that set and carry out fiscal policy (εN). The wage paid to public officials is proportional to the private sector wage, i.e. the public official's wage is $\eta w_t$where η is an exogenous parameter that determines the relative wage of public sector officials. Public officials pay taxes on their wages at the same rate as private sector households and work only when young. In the benchmark economy the institutional parameters that characterize the government are then (i) the relative size of public employment (ε) and (ii) the relative pay of public officials (η).[4]

The private choices of the public officials are of the same form as for private households

$$c_{1t}^g = \frac{(1 - \tau_t)\eta w_t D_t}{1 + \beta} \quad (7.14a)$$

$$c_{2t+1}^g = \beta R_t c_{1t}^g \quad (7.14b)$$

$$s_t^g = \frac{\beta(1 - \tau_t)\eta w_t D_t}{1 + \beta}. \quad (7.14c)$$

[4]For tractability, some features of the government must be taken as given in our analysis. However, we eventually discuss how changes in exogenous features of the government affect the results. In addition, note that when $\eta = 1$, the households are indifferent about working in the public or private sectors. However, this is not necessarily true after we introduce corruption and evasion. In the presence of corruption and evasion, we find that public officials are better off than private households as along as $\eta \geq 1$ (even though we assume that public officials cannot avoid taxes on their official salaries). Thus, everyone would want a government job.

Fiscal policy is determined by the collective actions of the public officials. The officials choose the current tax rate, next period's public capital (G_{t+1}), and now, the level of public debt (B_{t+1}). Their objective is to maximize their common preferences, which are the same as private households. The fiscal policy choices must satisfy the government budget constraint,

$\tau_t w_t D_t(1 + \varepsilon\eta)N + B_{t+1} = \eta w_t D_t \varepsilon N + G_{t+1} + B_t R_{t-1}$, where we assume, as in the case of private capital, that public capital depreciates fully after one period.

After de-trending all variables for exogenous technological progress, and using the factor price equations from profit maximization, the government budget constraint with variables expressed on a per capita basis is

$$\frac{\tau_t(1+\eta\varepsilon)(1-\alpha)k_t^\alpha g_t^{\mu(1-\alpha)}}{1+q} + b_{t+1}(1+\varepsilon) \tag{7.15}$$

$$= \eta\varepsilon\frac{(1-\alpha)k_t^\alpha g_t^{\mu(1-\alpha)}}{1+q} + g_{t+1}(1+\varepsilon) + \frac{\alpha g_t^{\mu(1-\alpha)}k_t^{\alpha-1}}{1+q}b_t(1+\varepsilon),$$

where $b \equiv B/(1 + \varepsilon)N$. The left-hand side represents the sources of funds: tax revenue and new borrowing. The right-hand-side gives the uses of funds: salaries of government officials, government investment, and interest and principle payments on past debt.

The capital market equilibrium condition requires that the sum of private capital and public debt be financed out of household retirement saving,

$$K_{t+1} + B_{t+1} = Ns_t + \varepsilon Ns_t^g. \tag{7.16}$$

De-trending (7.16), substituting (7.15) into (7.16), and collecting terms, gives us the transition equation for private physical capital in the presence of public debt

$$k_{t+1} = \frac{k_t^\alpha g_t^{\mu(1-\alpha)}}{1+q} \times \left[\frac{(1-\alpha)}{1+\beta}(\beta - \eta\varepsilon + (1+\eta\varepsilon)\tau_t) - \alpha\frac{b_t}{k_t}(1+\varepsilon) - \frac{g_{t+1}}{k_t^\alpha g_t^{\mu(1-\alpha)}}(1+\varepsilon)(1+q)\right]. \tag{7.17}$$

Negative effects on private capital accumulation, represented by the three negative terms in the square bracket, stem from the new public debt that is issued to finance marginal increases in the three categories of expenditures: the payroll of public officials, interest payments to previously issued public debt, and government investment. Higher wage taxes, on the other hand, increase private capital formation because they reduce the crowding out associated with new government borrowing more than they reduce private saving (note that τ_t enters (7.17) with a positive sign).

As in Chap. 6, we find the optimal fiscal policy by writing out the representative public official's preferences in terms of the tax rate and public investment level, which indirectly also determines public debt via (7.15). Recall that the public officials have the same preferences as private households, so in the absence of corruption and tax evasion, they will act precisely in the interest of private households. Including only those components of the public official's preferences that are affected by their fiscal policy choice gives us the following objective function to be maximized

$$(1+\beta)\ln(1-\tau_t)+\beta\mu(1-\alpha)(1+\gamma)\ln g_{t+1}+\beta(\alpha-1+\alpha\gamma)\ln k_{t+1}.$$

Substituting (7.17) into the objective function above, and then maximizing with respect to the choice of tax rates and government investment, generates the first order conditions. Solving the first order conditions, and combining with (7.15) and (7.17), generates the following solutions

$$\frac{b_{t+1}(1+\varepsilon)}{k_{t+1}}\equiv\frac{b(1+\varepsilon)}{k}=\frac{1+\beta}{\alpha(1+\gamma)-1}-1 \tag{7.18a}$$

$$\tau_t\equiv\tau=\frac{\frac{1+\beta}{1+\eta\varepsilon}\left[\frac{\alpha}{1-\alpha}\frac{b}{k}(1+\varepsilon)+\eta\varepsilon-\beta\right]+\beta[(\mu(1-\alpha)+\alpha)(1+\gamma)-1]}{1+\beta+\beta[(\mu(1-\alpha)+\alpha)(1+\gamma)-1]} \tag{7.18b}$$

$$k_{t+1}=\left(\frac{\alpha(1+\gamma)-1}{1+\beta}\right)\frac{\beta}{1+\beta}\frac{(1-\tau)(1-\alpha)(1+\eta\varepsilon)}{1+q}k_t^{\alpha}g_t^{\mu(1-\alpha)} \tag{7.18c}$$

$$g_{t+1}=\frac{\mu(1-\alpha)(1+\gamma)}{(\alpha(1+\gamma)-1)(1+\varepsilon)}k_{t+1}. \tag{7.18d}$$

An important expression in the solution is the ratio $(1+\beta)/(\alpha(1+\gamma)-1)$. The numerator $(1+\beta)$ measures the negative effect of taxation on the after-tax wage and lifetime consumption of the current generation. The denominator of the ratio $(\alpha(1+\gamma)-1)$ gives the effect of private capital accumulation on (i) the return to private capital and (ii) worker productivity in the next period. Greater private capital accumulation lowers the return to capital and the welfare of the current generations whose retirement consumption depends on income from savings $(\alpha-1)$. So, for private capital accumulation to be valued by the current generation, the altruistic benefit of higher future worker productivity in the economy $(\alpha\gamma)$ must exceed the negative effect of a lower return to savings $(\alpha(1+\gamma)-1>0)$.

In Chap. 6, without public debt or altruism, young households prefer low values of the private capital stock in the future because it raises the return on their saving. However, in that setting, the only way to lower the future capital stock is to lower saving by raising current taxes on workers. Of course, higher taxes also lower the young household's lifetime consumption, an effect that dominates the desire to lower next period capital stock (so taxation is costly). Now, policy could target lower private capital by lowering current taxes and issuing more public debt. The forces for high public debt are quite strong since it implies lower current taxes and higher future returns on private capital, both of which raise the welfare of current period households. Thus, altruism is crucial, and in fact must be quite strong, to limit government borrowing.

When altruism is strong enough to cause the current generation to value private capital accumulation, there is a benefit to current period taxes because greater tax revenue reduces public borrowing and the crowding out of private investment. The higher is the ratio $(1 + \beta)/(\alpha(1 + \gamma) - 1)$, the lower is the net benefit of taxes, the higher is public debt, and the lower is private capital accumulation. Positive levels of public debt are optimal if the ratio is sufficiently high, as indicated in (7.18a). Also note that the optimal ratio of public debt to private capital is time invariant, which implies a time invariant tax rate given in (7.18b).

In (7.18c), the transition equation for the evolution of the private capital stock simplifies to a standard concave form with capital accumulation positively affected by after-tax household wages that determine saving. However, there is a multiplicative coefficient that adjusts for the presence of public debt and the crowding out of private investment. A higher debt to capital ratio shifts the transition equation for private capital downward. Finally, (7.18d) tells us the optimal stock of public capital is proportional to the private capital stock with the factor of proportionality determined by the parameters that determine the two stocks relative importance on welfare.

Calibration

To calibrate the benchmark model, we continue to assume common values for the output elasticities of private and public capital, $\alpha = \mu = 0.30$. Assuming that each period in the model last 20 years and the annualized growth in labor productivity due to exogenous technological change is 2 percent we have $q = (1.02)^{20} - 1 = 0.4859$. We set $\varepsilon = 0.1429$ and $\beta = 0.1983$, to match reasonable values for the (i) public employment share and (ii) rate of return to capital. We also set $\eta = 1$, so that private and public workers earn the same wage.

To isolate the role played by corruption in generating public debt, we eliminate all other motives for borrowing. We consider an economy that is made up of "staunch fiscal conservatives," households whose preference is to have no government debt, in the absence of the opportunity for corruption. From (7.18a), the optimal debt ratio without corruption is zero when $1 + \beta = \alpha(1 + \gamma) - 1$. This staunch fiscal conservative condition implies $\gamma = 5.59556$.

The no debt economy generates a tax rate of 26 percent and steady state annualized marginal product of capital of 8.7 percent. This value for the marginal product is within the range of estimates for the pre-tax marginal product of capital in the rich countries (Caselli and Feyrer 2007, Table II).

7.4 An Economy with Corruption and Evasion

We now introduce the possibility that households will engage in illegal activity. Households employed in the public sector consider diverting public funds, earmarked to finance investment projects, for their own private use. Privately employed households evade taxation. The household micro-foundations for these behaviors are the same as in Chap. 6 and are summarized below.

Tax evasion and private household saving for private households are

$$v_t = \frac{1}{2}\left[\left(\mathrm{T}^2 + \frac{4(1+\beta)\bar{u}_t}{\phi}\right)^{1/2} - \mathrm{T}\right], \text{ Where } \mathrm{T} \equiv \frac{1-\tau_t}{\theta^\tau - (1-\tau_t)} \tag{7.19a}$$

$$s_t = \frac{\beta}{1+\beta}[1 - \tau_t + (\theta^\tau - 1 + \tau_t)v_t]w_t. \tag{7.19b}$$

The public official's decentralized corruption activity and private saving behavior are

$$u_t = \frac{1}{2}\left[\left(\Gamma^2 + \frac{4(1+\beta)\bar{u}_t}{\phi}\right)^{1/2} - \Gamma\right], \text{ where } \Gamma \equiv \frac{(1-\tau_t)\eta w_t}{\theta^g(G_{t+1}/\varepsilon N)} \tag{7.20a}$$

$$s_t^g = \frac{\beta}{1+\beta}\left[(1-\tau_t)\eta + \theta^g u_t \widehat{G}_{t+1}/w_t\varepsilon N\right]w_t. \tag{7.20b}$$

We use the government budget constraint to complete the link between fiscal policy and corruption. The government budget constraint can be written as $\widehat{G}_{t+1}/w_t\varepsilon N = \overline{\mathrm{B}}_t$, where $\overline{\mathrm{B}}_t \equiv \frac{\tau_t(1-v_t)}{\varepsilon} - \eta(1-\tau_t) + \frac{1+\varepsilon}{(1-\alpha)\varepsilon}\left(\frac{(1+d)b_{t+1}}{k_t^\alpha g_t^{\mu(1-\alpha)}} - \alpha\frac{b_t}{k_t}\right)$, is the *discretionary* budget, taxes net of payroll and debt repayment obligations, managed by each public official. Substituting this expression into (7.20a), noting that $u_t = \overline{u}_t$ in both (7.19a) and (7.20a), and then solving for u_t in (7.20a) allows us to write evasion and corruption as

$$v_t = \frac{1}{2}[(\mathrm{T}^2 + \frac{4(1+\beta)u_t}{\phi})^{1/2} - \mathrm{T}], \text{where } \mathrm{T} \equiv \frac{1-\tau_t}{\theta^\tau - (1-\tau_t)} \tag{7.21a}$$

$$u_t = \frac{1+\beta}{\phi} - \frac{\eta(1-\tau_t)}{\theta^g \overline{\mathrm{B}}_t}. \tag{7.21b}$$

The government budget managed by each official is increasing in newly issued debt and decreasing in previously issued debt. Everything else constant, new borrowing increases corruption, as well as tax evasion through the culture of corruption effect, and past debt obligations reduce corruption by lowering the discretionary budget, other things constant.

We need to establish new transition equations with public debt, corruption, and evasion. The capital market equilibrium condition (7.16) gives us the transition equation for private capital and the government budget constraint gives us the transition equation for public capital,

$$k_{t+1} = \frac{\beta}{1+\beta}\left[1 - \tau_t + (\tau_t + \theta^\tau - 1)v_t + \eta\varepsilon\left(1 - \tau_t + u_t\theta^g \overline{\mathrm{B}}_t\right)\right]$$
$$\times \frac{(1-\alpha)k_t^\alpha g_t^{\mu(1-\alpha)}}{1+d} - b_{t+1}(1+\varepsilon) \tag{7.22a}$$

$$g_{t+1} = \frac{\varepsilon(1-u_t)\overline{\mathrm{B}}_t}{1+\varepsilon}\frac{(1-\alpha)k_t^\alpha g_t^{\mu(1-\alpha)}}{1+q}. \tag{7.22b}$$

Similar to Chap. 6, the terms in the squared bracket of (7.22a) can be explained as follows. The expression $1 - \tau_t + (\tau_t + \theta^\tau - 1)v_t$ can be written out as $1 - \tau_t(1 - v_t) - (1 - \theta^\tau)v_t$, where $\tau_t(1 - v_t)$ is the portion of reported income taxed away by the government and $(1 - \theta^\tau)v_t$ is the unreported income that is lost in the attempt to avoid detection. Both of these terms reduce the wage available for household saving and private capital accumulation. However, unlike in Chap. 6, note that taxation also reduces the level of newly issued public debt that crowds out private capital formation. The expression $\eta\varepsilon\left(1 - \tau_t + u_t\theta^g\overline{\mathrm{B}}_t\right)$ is the income of public officials, including the stolen revenue from the public investment budget. A fraction of this income is saved and promotes private capital accumulation. Of course, as seen in (7.22b), the stolen income reduces government investment, other things constant.

As in the baseline model without corruption, to find the preferred fiscal policy, we begin by writing out the representative government official's preferences for generation-t, including only those terms that are influenced by the choice of the current period tax rate and the new debt level,

$$(1+\beta)\ln(1 - \tau_t + \theta^g u_t\bar{\mathrm{B}}_t) - \phi u_t + \beta\mu(1-\alpha)(1+\gamma)\ln g_{t+1}$$
$$+ \beta(\alpha(1+\gamma) - 1)\ln k_{t+1}. \tag{7.23}$$

Substituting (7.21) and (7.22) into (7.23), to eliminate u_t, k_{t+1}, and g_{t+1}, reduces the problem to choosing τ_t and b_{t+1} given the values of k_t, g_t, and b_t. The resulting solutions for τ_t and b_{t+1} depend on the state variables k_t, g_t, and b_t. The optimal choice for τ_t and b_{t+1}, along with transition equations for private and public capital, define a system of three difference equations in the three state variables.

An important feature of the dynamic system is the interaction between corruption and public debt. Recall that corruption is increasing in the size of the discretionary budget available for public investment (see (7.21b)). As the size of the discretionary budget increases, the marginal benefit of increasing u becomes greater—large discretionary budgets for public investment budgets create opportunities for corruption. Thus, an increase in newly issued debt to finance public investment will increase corruption. The increase in corruption will also increase tax evasion through the culture of corruption effect, thereby reducing tax revenue and further increasing government borrowing.

When the past debt and interest must be paid, the discretionary funds available for public investment are reduced. Smaller public investment budgets reduce the marginal benefit of corruption. The increase in spending obligations also increase the cost of maintaining a discretionary budget of given size because it now requires more borrowing. While there is the option to simply escalate the borrowing to pay past debt, this tends to be too costly (at least for most of our calibrations). Thus, the overhang from past debt accumulation reduces corruption, evasion, and public debt. These complimentary interactions can be strong enough to create a debt-corruption cycle; debt and corruption are relatively high one period, only to fall to lower levels the next period. From (7.21b), one can also see that the strength of the debt -corruption interaction is determined by θ^g.

Calibration and Simulation

In applying the model, our focus is on debt creation in larger developed countries. We do this for three reasons. First, we are interested in understanding the differences in debt accumulation across the developed world in recent decades. Second, developed countries have more independent central banks. Fiscal consolidations, rather than money creation and inflation, are more commonly used to reduce real debt levels in developed economies. Finally, we assume a closed economy and so do not allow for the foreign borrowing that is important for smaller and developing countries.

We calibrate the model with corruption using the same parameters as in the no-corruption economy along with the three new parameters θ^g, θ^τ, and ϕ. The calibration of the three new parameters is guided by three objectives. First, we set a target range for evasion based on estimates of tax evasion in developed countries. LaPorta and Schleifer (2008) report various measures of tax evasion suggesting that 10 to 20 percent of income goes unreported across developed countries. Second, we want to exhibit all of the different types of long-run equilibrium possibilities caused by the debt-corruption interaction. We do this by considering the entire range of values for θ^g. Finally, we want the optimal tax rates on wage income to be reasonable because they are important determinants of the levels of tax evasion that we seek to target. The marginal tax rates on wages are high in developed countries, varying from 40 to 65 percent (Prescott 2004). However, we do not include transfer payments in our model and while government investment can be interpreted broadly to include all spending related to human capital formation, we do not want spending and tax rates to be too high. We choose calibrations that generate optimal tax rates between 26 and 66 percent, but most values are between 45 and 50 percent.

Table 7.1 reports long-run equilibria for $\phi = 1.3$, $\theta^\tau = 0.7$, and a complete set of values for θ^g that range from 0 to 1. When there are two rows associated with a given value of θ^g, the long-run equilibrium is a periodic cycle. The last column gives the short-fall in the economy's worker productivity relative to the no-corruption economy. Figure 7.2 gives a diagrammatic depiction of the variety of long-run equilibria that arise as we vary θ^g in Table 7.1. The average level of debt rises with θ^g, as the checks against corruption weaken. In addition we see an interesting pattern in the dynamics. As corruption increases, we go from witnessing small periodic cycles, to unique steady states, and then back to periodic cycles. Thus, the model predicts a

Table 7.1 Equilibria with different institutional safeguards against corruption

θ^g	τ	u	v	$b(1+\varepsilon)/k$	Shortfall in y
0.00–0.39	0.26	0	0	0	
0.42	0.3	0	0	0	−7.00%
	0.45	0.38	0.1	0.11	−7.00%
0.44	0.32	0	0	0	−11.00%
	0.46	0.41	0.11	0.16	−11.00%
0.46	0.47	0.33	0.09	0.18	−19.00%
0.53	0.48	0.33	0.1	0.3	−30.00%
0.56	0.48	0.32	0.1	0.32	−33.00%
	0.48	0.34	0.11	0.34	−33.00%
0.65	0.5	0.13	0.05	0.16	−35.00%
	0.47	0.53	0.15	0.6	−35.00%
0.67	0.48	0	0	0	−33.00%
	0.46	0.6	0.16	0.6	−33.00%
1	0.66	0	0	0	−53.00%
	0.46	0.72	0.19	1.12	−58.00%

Note The computations are based on the following values for the model's parameters: $\theta^\tau = 0.7$, $\phi = 1.3$, $\eta = 1$, $\varepsilon = 0.14$, $\alpha = 0.33$, $\mu = 0.3$, $d = 0.49$, $\beta = 0.2$, $\gamma = 5.66$

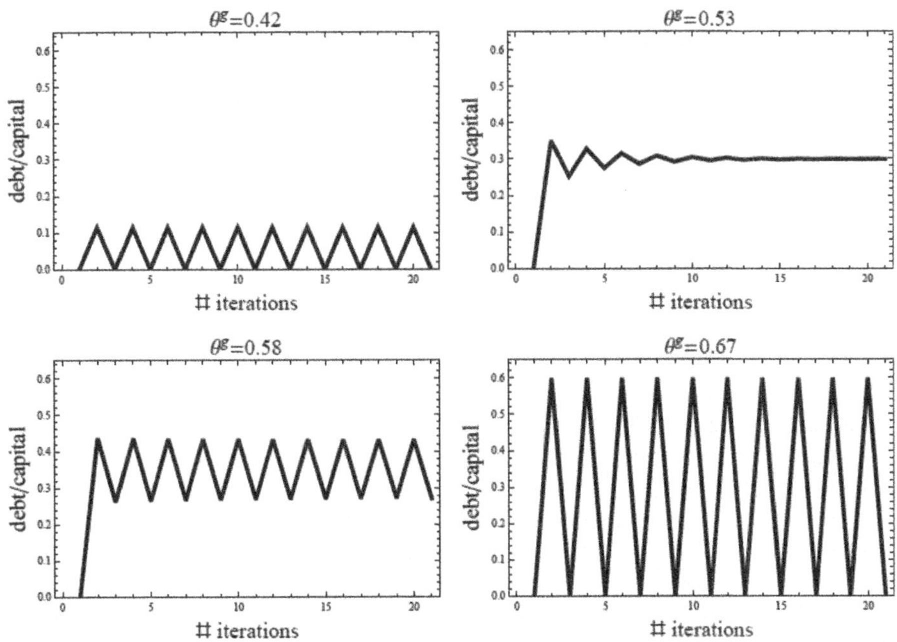

Fig. 7.2 Debt/capital dynamics for selected θ^g. Note Figures show transition paths of debt to capital ratio for different values of θ^g - institutional checks on corruption. The computations are based on the following values for the model's parameters: $\theta^\tau = 0.7$, $\phi = 1.3$, $\eta = 1$, $\varepsilon = 0.14$, $\alpha = 0.33$, $\mu = 0.3$, $d = 0.49$, $\beta = 0.2$, $\gamma = 5.66$. The initial values for state variables in all cases are $k = 0.0027$, $g = 0.0027$, $b = 0$ – as in the steady-state of the model without corruption and tax evasion

U-shaped pattern in the volatility in debt as one goes from less corrupt to more corrupt economies.

At low values of θ^g, between 0 and 0.39 in Table 7.1, there is insufficient motivation for officials to be corrupt causing corruption and debt to be zero—i.e. u is at a corner in (7.21b) thereby eliminating any incentive for borrowing. As θ^g increases, and becomes sufficiently high, corruption appears but only when the discretionary budget ($\overline{B}_t$) is sufficiently large. The discretionary budget is larger when the obligations to repay past debt are smaller. When past debt levels are zero, there is sufficient incentive to be corrupt and to borrow. However, in the period following the borrowing, the debt repayment obligations reduce $\overline{B}_t$ and lower the incentive for corruption and new borrowing. For sufficiently low values of θ^g, the reduction in $\overline{B}_t$ is enough to drive u and new borrowing back to zero. This gives rise to an equilibrium cycle defined by discontinuous jumps from an equilibrium with positive corruption and borrowing to an equilibrium with zero corruption and borrowing. This type of equilibrium cycle occurs when $\theta^g = 0.42$ in Table 7.1 and in Fig. 7.2.

At higher values of θ^g there is sufficient incentive to be corrupt even when $\overline{B}_t$ is relatively small (i.e. even when debt repayment obligations are relatively high). This creates the possibility that corruption and debt are strictly positive throughout, creating a transitional dynamic for the economy where the economy oscillates between high and low positive values of debt. The exact nature of the dynamics depends on the particular values of θ^g. For values of θ^g between 0.46 and 0.53, the oscillations dampen and converge to a unique steady state level (see Table 7.1 and Fig. 7.2 for $\theta^g = 0.53$). Near $\theta^g = 0.56$, small changes in θ^g lead to *bifurcations* or qualitative changes in the economy's dynamic behavior (Azariadis 1993, pp. 90–104; Galor 2007 p. 21 and 76). For values of θ^g between 0.56 and 0.65 the periodic cycles reappear, but with positive values of corruption, evasion, and public debt in both periods of the cycle. Finally, when θ^g exceeds 0.65, we find two periods cycles with wild swings in behavior; an absence of corruption, evasion and public debt in one period, followed by high values for each in the next.

Empirical Implications

To draw out the empirical implications of the model, we now discuss the conclusions from Table 7.1 in more detail.

Variation in institutional safeguards against corruption can generate significant variation in debt ratios.

Perhaps the most reasonable settings for θ^g are those between 0.42 and 0.65, where there are at least some temporary episodes of corruption, evasion, and public debt, and where tax rates are reasonable. Even in this limited range, the debt ratio varies between 0 and 0.60. Thus, corruption is a potentially important determinant of the observed differences in public debt across developed countries. As θ^g ranges between 0.42 and 0.65, corruption ranges from 0 to 0.55, i.e. 0 to 55 percent of funds allocated to government programs are appropriated for private use by public officials. As a point of reference for these estimates, Tanzi and Davoodi (1997) suggest that diverted funds from some public investment projects in Italy, a high corruption developed economy, were between 50 and 60 percent.

Higher debt reduces output significantly.

The differences in corruption and public debt, as θ^g ranges between 0.42 and 0.65, result in significant differences in worker productivity and private household's welfare. Average worker productivity when $\theta^g = 0.65$ is 26 percent less than when $\theta^g = 0.45$ and 34 percent less than the no corruption baseline. Average private household welfare is 38 percent less than when $\theta^g = 0.42$ and 54 percent less than in the no corruption baseline.

It should also be noted that there is little variation in tax rates as θ^g ranges between 0.45 and 0.65. The increasing magnitude of the negative effect on output as corruption increases is due to a rise in the average level of public debt that crowds out private investment. In addition, the higher debt also crowds out public investment. One way to finance interest and principle repayment on public debt is to reduce spending on public capital.

A more complete depiction of the debt dynamics leading to lower average output is given in Fig. 7.3. It shows the path of several key variables in two settings: one with weak corruption safeguards, $\theta^g = 0.62$, and one with relatively stronger safeguards, $\theta^g = 0.46$. As noted above, the first panel shows that the tax rate is similar across both institutional regimes.

The second and third panels of Fig. 7.3 show that with weaker institutional safeguards against corruption, cycles in both corruption and debt are present with large swings in both variables. However, the average corruption is similar across the regimes, while the average debt is much higher with weak institutions. This is because one way of financing the high debt repayment obligation from past governments is to issue new public debt (although significantly less than that issued in the previous period). The positive interaction between past debt and newly issued debt causes the average debt level to rise when $\theta^g = 0.62$, even though average corruption is similar across the two cases.

From panels four and five, we see that a higher average debt level reduces the average value of both private and public capital. The crowding out of private capital results from private saving being diverted to purchases of government debt. The crowding out of public capital results from budget pressures associated with debt repayment. The lower average levels of private and public capital cause a lower average value for worker productivity, as seen in panel 6 of Fig. 7.3.

There is the prevalence of two-period debt cycles.

As discussed in the introduction and literature review, it is common for countries to accumulate debt for long periods of time, often at an unsustainable pace, before abruptly carrying out reforms designed to reduce debt levels. The endogenous two-period cycles offer a possible explanation for this behavior. The accumulation of debt obligations to repay past debt directly constrains discretionary budgets. The cost of attempting to expand discretionary budgets further, by issuing even more debt, increases because of the further crowding out of private investment. Both of these considerations serve to reduce the incentive for new borrowing, corruption, evasion. Thus, there is a natural limit to debt accumulation that leads to a reversal of

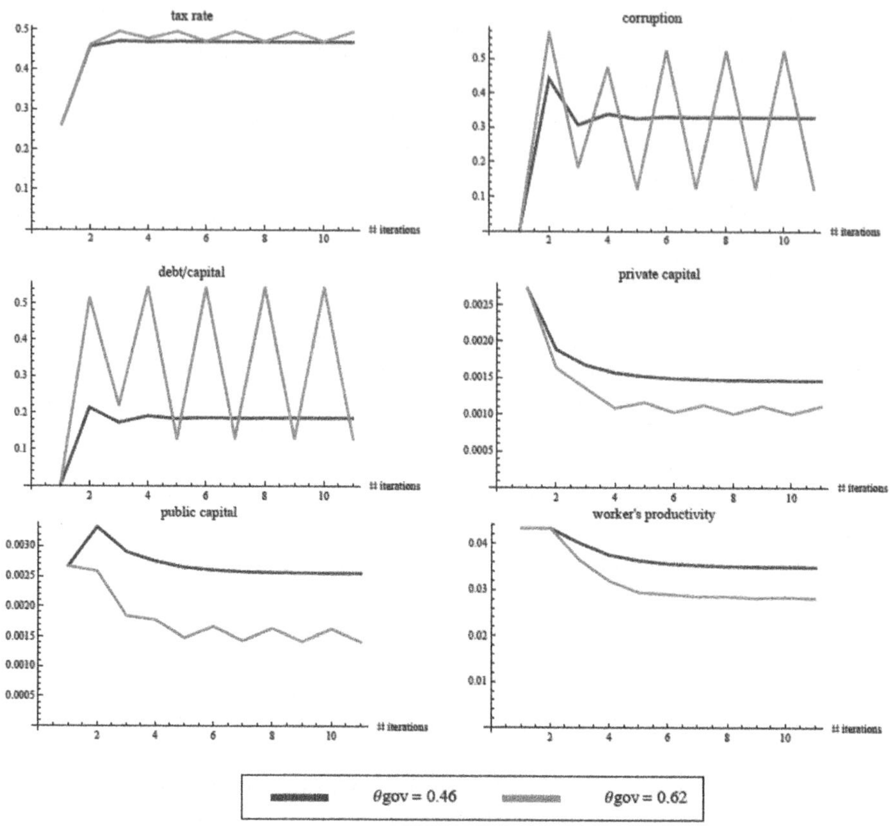

Fig. 7.3 Selected variables dynamics under different θ^g. Note The computations are based on the following values for the model's parameters: $\theta^\tau = 0.7$, $\phi = 1.3$, $\eta = 1$, $\varepsilon = 0.14$, $\alpha = 0.33$, $\mu = 0.3$, $d = 0.49$, $\beta = 0.2$, $\gamma = 5.66$. The initial values for state variables in all cases are $k = 0.0027$, $g = 0.0027$, $b = 0$ - as in the steady-state of the model without corruption and tax evasion

the government's past behavior. However, once public debt levels are reduced the incentives again swing toward encouraging more borrowing and the associated illegal activities.

An interesting observation about the debt cycles is that they do not cause output to vary. Output does not vary because when debt is high, private investment is crowded out but public investment is higher—note that public and private capital are negatively correlated in Fig. 7.3 when $\theta^g = 0.62$. The higher debt finances *both* more corruption and greater actual public sector investment. Public investment and private investment are then inversely related. Thus, debt variation within a country with given institutional safeguards is *not* associated with a variation in output.

This feature of the model has important implications for empirical work that attempts to identify a causal effect of government debt on output. Variation in debt *across countries* with different institutional safeguards against corruption is predicted to be negatively correlated with output. However, variation in debt *within a country* with fixed institutional safeguards will not be associated with output changes. Time series or panel data may have difficulty identifying a negative effect of debt, despite the fact that improved institutional safeguards reduce the average values of both corruption and debt and thereby raise output.

The model predicts a U-shaped pattern in debt volatility as the corruption level of the country increases.

This unexpected prediction offers a particularly strong test of the model that we explore in the next section.

7.5 Empirical Evidence

In this section we examine three key empirical implications of the theory: the presence of low-frequency public debt cycles, the influence of corruption on public debt, and the effect of both corruption and public debt on economic growth. As discussed, the theory has been tailored to study debt in large developed economies so we check the model's predictions for a set of large high-income countries (HIC), where the assumption that the economy is closed is likely to be the best approximation (as opposed to the reasonable modeling alternative, a small-open economy model). Given that the dividing line of when an economy is large enough for a closed economy model to be a better approximation than a small open economy model is unclear, we also include large upper-middle income countries (UMIC). This helps to increase the sample size when doing regression analysis. Resource-rich countries (RRC) are excluded. In RRC, high-level corruption will likely be focused on revenue flows from the resources themselves and not necessarily the normal fiscal budget for general infrastructure projects (Bueno de Mesquita and Smith 2012, Chapter 4). See the chapter Appendix for a list of the countries and a summary of the data.

In all of our regressions we control for the country's initial state of development by including initial real GDP per capita. Our theory focuses on institutional determinants of corruption, which may or may not be closely connected to the country's level of development. Variation in corruption, holding constant the country's state of development, captures variations in these institutional determinants. In addition, some of the UMIC may not be close to their steady state potential and including initial GDP per capita would help control for this possibility.

Public Debt Cycles

We look for the presence of low-frequency public debt cycles by netting out cycles of business cycle frequency (1–8 years) in the public debt data from 37 high HIC and 35 UMIC income countries over the 1970 to 2011 period. To eliminate the business cycle component we use the Hodrick-Prescott filter on annual debt data with a smoothing parameter of 6.25. After the business cycles are removed, the public debt trend in many of the countries contain cycles of larger amplitude and lower frequency.

To find the frequency and amplitude of these longer-run cycles we remove the linear trend from the data and then locate all local minima (troughs of the cycles) and maxima (peaks of the cycles). Removing the linear trend is appropriate because the theory of this section does not account for the rise in public debt ratios witnessed since WWII. Causes of the upward trend in debt were discussed in Chaps. 2, 3, and 5.

We find 137 local extrema in the 37 HIC from 1970 to 2011. The average time from trough to peak is 11 years. In the 35 UMIC, the number of extrema is 113 with an average time from trough to peak of 12.7 years. The average amplitude of a cycle, the change in debt from trough to peak, is 17 percentage points of GDP. It varies from 0.02 to 82 percentage points. Of the OECD countries the biggest change is 66 percentage points for Ireland from 1993 to 2005. The median change in the HIC countries is 12 percentage points, but 25 percent of the cycles have amplitudes greater than 24 percent of GDP. The amplitudes are larger in UMIC where the average amplitude is 24 percentage points and 25 percent of the cycles have amplitudes greater than 34 percent of GDP. Overall, the data reveals the presence of long-term public debt cycles of significant magnitude.

Corruption and Debt

We now move to the empirical relationship between public debt and corruption. The model produces two testable predictions about the corruption-public debt interaction. First, there should be a positive relationship between the long-term averages of corruption and debt. Second, there should be a U-shaped relationship between the amplitude of debt cycles and long-term average corruption. Empirical evidence on the first relationship is provided in Table 7.2 and evidence for the second relationship in Table 7.3.

The corruption measure is the *control of corruption* component of the Worldwide Governance Indicators formed by Daniel Kaufman of the Brookings Institution and Aart Kray and Massimo Mastruzzi of the World Bank. Their control of corruption

Table 7.2 Public debt and corruption: Empirical evidence

	(1) b/se
Control of corruption, av. 1991–2011	−23.149***
	(6.989)
Real GDP per capita, thousands USD, av. 1991–2011	2.607***
	(0.622)
Constant	41.508***
	(6.336)
N obs	49

Note: Standard errors in parentheses. * $p < 0.1$, ** $p < 0.05$, *** $p < 0.01$. Dependent variable - public debt, GDP. Sample: HIC and UMIC, non-RR, large. Large are countries with population over 1 mln on average in 1991–2011. RR – resource-rich, according to the IMF's definition. HIC – high income countries, UMIC – upper middle countries, as of 2011, World Bank classification. All variables averaged over 1990–2011. Regressions with additional controls have been tried. Results (signs and magnitudes of coefficients of interest) are qualitatively similar

Table 7.3 Public debt cycles and corruption: Empirical evidence

	(1) b/se
Control of corruption, av. 1991–2011	−12.888**
	(5.660)
Control of corruption, squared	4.948*
	(2.537)
Real GDP per capita, thousands USD, av. 1991–2011	0.177
	(0.275)
Constant	17.664***
	(2.944)
N obs	38

Note: Standard errors in parentheses. * $p < 0.1$, ** $p < 0.05$, *** $p < 0.01$. Dependent variable - public debt, GDP. Sample: HIC and UMIC, non-RR, large. Large are countries with population over 1 mln on average in 1991–2011. RR - resource-rich, according to the IMF's definition. HIC – high income countries, UMIC – upper middle countries, as of 2011, World Bank classification. All variables averaged over 1990–2011. Regressions with additional controls have been tried. Results (signs and magnitudes of coefficients of interest) are qualitatively similar

index is based on survey data from enterprises, citizens, and experts. Their measure is inversely related to the level of corruption, so the predicted relationship between the control of corruption and public debt is negative. The predicted relationship between the amplitude of public debt cycles and the control of corruption remains U-shaped.

As seen in Table 7.2, the negative relationship between the strength of controls on corruption and public debt is highly significant. Table 7.3 shows the U-shaped relationship between the size of the debt cycles and the level of corruption is also present in the data. The effect of the corruption control on debt cycles is negative and the coefficient on the control squared is positive and statistically significant at the 10 percent significance level.

To find a significant U-shaped relationship in the data is somewhat surprising, even if the theory is correct. From Table 7.1, we see that to detect a clear U-shaped relationship means there must be significant variation in θ^g in the range where θ^g is relatively high. This may not be the case in every data sample. In addition, the absence of a clear U-shaped relationship could occur because the empirical measure of corruption gives the *average* level of *actual* corruption in a country, rather than a direct indication of the fundamental institutional controls on corruption. From Table 7.1 we see that the average level of corruption does not vary much once θ^g exceeds 0.50, yet debt volatility varies dramatically as θ^g increases from 0.50 to 1.

Looking at the data more directly, we also see some evidence for the corruption-debt cycle prediction. For HIC, the mean size of the debt cycle is 21 percentage of GDP. For the 8 least corrupt countries the average is 23.7 percent, higher than the overall sample average (Switzerland-19.5, Sweden-23.7, Netherlands-33, Iceland-24.4, Denmark-24, Canada-38.7, Singapore-14.5, and New Zealand-12). Public debt in the next tier of countries, as ranked by corruption, is more stable. The stability of debt is especially true for Germany, Austria, Australia, and the UK, but is less so for the U.S. and Japan. Debt cycles then become more volatile as we move to the most corrupt countries.

Public Debt, Corruption, and Growth

Evidence for a positive association between corruption and public debt has been presented in in Table 7.2. However, we need to demonstrate a negative effect of corruption and public debt on output. A negative effect on output has proved elusive in previous empirical work. For example, see Mauro (1995) for the weak corruption-growth connection. The connection between public debt and output is also hard to detect. While it is becoming clear that high levels of public debt lowers economic growth (Reinhart and Rogoff 2009, 2012), it has been more difficult to establish a negative connection across *all* debt levels. See, for example, Kumar and Woo (2010) for the weak public debt-growth connection.

As the model suggests, it may be hard to find a negative effect of corruption and debt on output *within* a country given that corruption and debt can vary across the debt cycles with little change in output (see Table 7.1). Instead of looking at annual or 5-years averages, as is common in growth regressions, we run cross-country growth regressions over two ten year periods: 1991–2001 and 2001–2011. This approach should help capture the average level of debt across the debt cycles. The results are presented in Table 7.4. We regress growth in GDP per capita on initial GDP per capita, public debt as a fraction of GDP, the control of corruption measure, and an interactive term that is the product of debt and corruption controls.

The regression shows a negative and statistically significant effect of debt on growth. Increasing controls on corruption has a positive and statistically significant

Table 7.4 Public debt, corruption and economic growth: Empirical evidence

	(1) b/se
L10.real GDP per capita, thousands USD	−0.089***
	(0.023)
Public debt, % GDP, av. last 10 years	−0.013**
	(0.005)
Control of corruption, av. last 10 years	0.696**
	(0.317)
Control of corruption × public debt	0.011**
	(0.005)
Constant	3.902***
	(0.393)
N obs	95

Note: Standard errors in parentheses. * $p < 0{:}1$, ** $p < 0{:}05$, *** $p < 0{:}01$. Dependent variable – average GDP per capita growth in the last 10 years. Years included - 2001 and 2011 (subject to availability of data on corruption). Sample: HIC and UMIC, non-RR, large. Large are countries with population over 1 mln. RR – resource-rich, according to the IMF's definition. HIC – high income countries, UMIC – upper middle countries, as of 2011, World Bank classification. Regressions with additional controls have been tried. Results (signs and magnitudes of coefficients of interest) are similar. Fixed effect regressions bring about similar results effect on growth. Moreover, the interaction term has a positive and statistically significant effect on growth. A given level of debt has a smaller negative effect on growth the stronger are the controls on corruption. This supports the idea that it's the combination of debt and corruption that is most detrimental to growth because this combination causes more of the borrowed funds to be diverted from public investment.

7.6 Conclusion

Corruption is an important determinant of government borrowing, helping to explain differences in public debt levels across developed countries. More corrupt governments are associated with higher public debt that lowers output and welfare. The corruption-debt interaction also tends to cause periodic equilibria that exhibit cycling of debt levels. This type of equilibrium offers a possible explanation for the commonly observed pattern of debt accumulation followed by reforms that abruptly reduce debt levels. The cycling of debt can even occur when corruption levels are relatively low and thus remain relevant to developed countries with strong safeguards against corruption. Interestingly, variation in public debt across these cycles within a country, with given institutional safeguards, causes little variation in output. Thus, debt and output may be negatively correlated when looking across countries with *different* institutions but there may be little correlation within a country with *given* institutions.

7.7 Exercises

Questions

1. Read Chap. 1 and use a summary of the information there to motivate the way tax evasion and corruption are modeled.
2. Intuitively explain the three expressions that comprise the public official's objective function given by (7.4).
3. What fiscal variables does the government choose to maximize (7.4)? On what basis can first period taxes be set to zero?
4. In the two-period model of Sect. 7.2, explain how an increase in each of the following affects future worker productivity
   (a) $\widehat{g}$
   (b) y_1
   (c) θ^g
5. In (7.10), intuitively explain the marginal benefit and the marginal cost of choosing a larger government investment budget. Why does a larger investment budget imply more government debt?
6. Use Fig. 7.1 to explain how variation in θ^g affect government debt.

7. Use the model of Sect. 7.2 to explain why poor countries are more likely to depend on debt financing than rich countries. What might limit the borrowing of poor countries that is not captured by the model?
8. In Sect. 7.3, why might young households prefer low values of physical capital in the future. What does this imply about their preference for debt financing?
9. Why is the introduction of altruism about future productivity necessary once the government is allowed to borrow? How is the degree of altruism calibrated?
10. Intuitively explain the four testable predictions of the overlapping-generations model with respect to public debt and corruption.
11. Summarize the evidence supporting the predictions discussed in *Question* 10.
12. Answer each of the questions posed at the end of Sect. 7.2

Problems

1. Derive the value function of the public official given by (7.4).
2. Making use of *Problem* 1 and equation (7.2a and 7.2b), (7.3), and (7.5a and 7.5b), derive (7.6a). How does (7.6a) relate to the condition that indicates when households are bequest-constrained? If households are bequest-constrained, does it necessarily imply that first period taxes should be set to zero?
3. If $u > 0$, show the marginal benefit of $\widehat{g}$ in (7.10) is positive. Show that, as sketched in Fig. 7.1, the marginal benefit of $\widehat{g}$ is downward sloping and the marginal cost is upward sloping.
4. Use (7.15) and (7.16) to derive (7.17) and explain how each term of the transition equation affects capital accumulation.
5. Use (7.18) to explain how public debt affects private capital accumulation.
6. In Sect. 7.4, the <u>individual</u> public official's behavior, for a given fiscal policy, is modeled by maximizing

$$\ln c_{1t}^{g} + \beta \ln c_{2t+1}^{g} + \gamma(\ln y_t + \beta \ln y_{t+1}) - \frac{\phi}{2\bar{u}_t} u_t^2.$$

subject to the official's private lifetime budget constraint, $c_{1t}^{g} + \frac{c_{2t+1}^{g}}{R_t} = \eta(1 - \tau_t)w_t D_t + \theta^g u_t \left(\widehat{G}_{t+1}/\varepsilon N\right)$.

Solve this problem to derive (7.21b). Explain how each variable and parameter in (7.21b) affects the rate of corruption. (*Hint*: Naturally, start by deriving the first order conditions for consumption and corruption. Once you have the first order conditions, invoke the equilibrium condition that, since all public officials are identical, $\bar{u}_t = u_t$, <u>before</u> attempting to solve for u_t)

7. Contrast (7.18c) and (7.22a) to identify how corruption and tax evasion affect private capital accumulation.

References

Achury, C., Koulovatianos, C., and Tsoukalas, J., 2015, "Political Economics of External Debt Defaults," CFS Working paper Series, Goethe University.

Alesina, A., and Passalacqua, A., 2015, "The Political Economy of Government Debt, Taylor, J., and Uhlig, H. (editors), *Handbook of Macroeconomics*, Amsterdam: North Holland.

Alesina, A., Ardagna, S., and Trebbi, F., 2006, "Who Adjusts and When? The Political Economy of Reforms," *IMF Staff Papers*, 53, 1–29.

Alesina, A. and Drazen, A., 1991, "Why are Stabilizations Delayed?" *American Economic Review*, 81, 1170–1188.

Alesina, A., and Tabellini, G., 1990, "A Positive Theory of Fiscal Deficits and Government Debt," *Review of Economic Studies*, 57, 403–414.

Altonji, J., Hayshi, F., and Kotlikoff, L., 1992, "Is the Extended Family Altruistically Linked," *American Economic Review*, 82, 1177–98.

______, 1997, "Parental Altruism and Inter Vivos Transfers: Theory and Evidence," *Journal of Political Economy*, 105, 1121–1166.

Azariadis, C., 1993, *Intertemporal Macroeconomics*, Cambridge, Mass.: Blackwell Publishers.

Barro, R., 1979, "On the Determination of Public Debt," *Journal of Political Economy*, 87, 940–71.

Barro, R., 1986, "U.S. Deficits since World War I," *Scandinavian Journal of Economics*, 88, 195–222.

Battaglini, M., and Coate, 2008, "A Dynamic Theory of Public Spending, Taxation, and Debt," *American Economic Review*, 98, 201–236.

Becker, G. and Tomes, N., 1976, "Child Endowments and the Quantity and Quality of Children," *Journal of Political Economy*, 84, S143–S162.

Bizer, D., and Durlauf, S., 1990, "Testing the Positive Theory of Government Finance," *Journal of Monetary Economics*, 26, 123–141.

Bueno de Mesquita, B. and Smith, A., 2012, *The Dictator's Handbook*, New York: Public Affairs.

Cardia, E., 1997, "Replicating Ricardian Equivalence Tests with Simulated Time Series," *American Economic Review*, 87, 65–79.

Caselli, F. and Fyrer, J., 2007, "The Marginal Product of Capital," *Quarterly Review of Economics*, 122, 535–568.

Cukierman, A., and Metzler, A., 1989, "A Positive Theory of Government Debt and Deficits in a Neo-Ricardian Framework," *American Economic Review*, 79, 713–732.

de la Croix, D. and Michel, P, 2002, *A Theory of Economic Growth: Dynamics and Policy in Overlapping Generations,* Cambridge: Cambridge University Press.

Ferguson, N., 2012, *The Great Degeneration*, New York: Penguin Books.

Galor, O., 2005, "From Stagnation to Growth: Unified Growth Theory," in P.Aghion and S. Durlauf (eds.), *Handbook of Economic Growth*, Amsterdam: North Holland.

______, 2007, *Discrete Dynamical Systems*, New York: Springer.

Ghosh, S., and Mourmouras, I., 2004, "Endogenous Growth, Welfare, and Budgetary Regimes," *Journal of Macroeconomics*, 26, 623–635.

Gruber, J, and Kamin, S., 2012, "Fiscal Positions and Government Bond Yields in OECD Countries," *Journal of Money, Credit, and Banking*, 44, 1563–1587.

Ivanyna, M., Mourmouras, A., and Rangazas, P., 2016, "The Culture of Corruption, Evasion, and Economic Growth," *Economic Inquiry*, 54, 520–542.

Johnson, D., Parker, J., and Souleles, 2006, "Household Expenditures and Income Tax Rebates of 2001, *American Economic Review*, 96, 1589–1610.

Kotlikoff, L., 2003, *Generational Policy*, Cambridge: MIT Press.

Kotlikoff, L. and Burns, S., 2004, *The Coming Generational Storm*, Cambridge: MIT Press.

Kotlikoff, L., and Burns, S., 2012, *The Clash of Generations*, Cambridge: MIT Press.

Kumar, M., and Woo, J., 2010, "Public Debt and Growth," IMF Working Paper No. 10/174.

LaPorta, R., and Schleifer, A., 2008, "The Unofficial Economy and Economic Development," *Brookings Papers on Economic Activity*, Fall, 275–363.

Mauro, P., 1995, "Corruption and Growth," *Quarterly Journal of Economics*, 110, 681–712.
Persson, T., and Svensson, L., 1989, "Why a Stubborn Conservative Would Run a Deficit: Policy with Time-Inconsistent Preferences," *Quarterly Journal of Economics*, 104, 225–245.
Prescott, E., 2004, "Why Do Americans Work So Much More than Europeans," *Federal Reserve Bank of Minneapolis Quarterly Review*, 28, 2–13.
Reinhart, C., and Rogoff, K., 2009, *This Time is Different*, Princeton: Princeton University Press
______, 2012, "Public Debt Overhangs: Advanced-Economy Episodes Since 1800, *Journal of Economic Perspectives*, 26, 69–86.
Roubini, N., and Sachs, J., 1989, "Political and Economic Determinants of Budget Deficits in the Industrialized Democracies," *European Economic Review*, 33, 903–933.
Tanzi, V. and Davoodi, H., 1997, "Corruption, Public Investment, and Growth," *IMF Working Paper* #139.
Velasco, A., 1999, "A Model of Endogenous Fiscal Deficits and Delayed Fiscal Reforms," in Poterba, J., editor, *Fiscal Institutions and Fiscal Performance*, Chicago: University of Chicago Press, 37–58.
Velasco, A., 2000, "Debts and Deficits with Fragmented Fiscal Policymaking," *Journal of Public Economics*, 76, 105–125.

The Political Economy of Fiscal Reforms 8

In this chapter we discuss various proposals to reform government policy and process. The motivation for the reforms is resolving the fiscal crisis discussed in previous chapters. The fiscal crisis is the major issue facing the governments of developed countries during the twenty-first century. The crisis is connected with the important economic phenomena of the century, including aging of the population, slowing of long-run economic growth, and rising wage inequality. Our discussion is focused primarily on the U.S., but most of the discussion applies to the OECD countries generally.

Chapter 5 divided the root causes of the fiscal crisis into those stemming from changes in economic fundamentals and those that are directly associated with politics. This decomposition is used here as an organizing framework. We first discuss the policy changes and reforms related to the economic fundamentals that have been proposed by economists in recent years. These policy recommendations are largely based on the criteria for good governance that serves the national interest, as discussed in Chaps. 1 and 2. None of the policy recommendations have yet been passed, and in most cases have not even been proposed, by politicians. The second task of the chapter is then to explain why self-interest and politics have blocked the reforms. Beyond blocking needed reforms, interest group politics and corruption have directly contributed to the fiscal crisis.

While our main focus throughout the book has been on the twenty-first century fiscal crisis facing developed countries, we have also made points that apply to fiscal policies in developing countries. In the last section of this chapter, we summarize those points and then discuss some ideas about how foreign aid policy to developing countries could be made more effective.

M. Ivanyna et al., *The Macroeconomics of Corruption*, Springer Texts in Business and Economics, https://doi.org/10.1007/978-3-030-67557-8_8

8.1 Economic Fundamentals

The developed world faces three major long-run trends that will significantly alter the welfare of its citizens. All three trends will continue unless there are significant policy adjustments. The trends began at various times in the second half of the twentieth century, but governments have been slow to respond, which is why the related fiscal issues are rapidly approaching the "crisis" stage. The first trend is the aging of the population. For the first time in modern human history, the largest dependency group has become the old rather than young children. The second trend is a slowdown in the growth rate of worker productivity and per capita income. Over the last half century, the growth rate in developed countries has fallen by more than a full percentage point. The third trend is the rise in wage and income inequality. The decline of wage and income inequality over the middle of the twentieth century has reversed and inequality is now as high as it has ever been.

8.1.1 Aging and Rising Health Care Costs

The *demographic transition*, declining fertility and rising life expectancy, is an important stylized fact associated with growing economies. The demographic changes are both the result of, and an important cause of, economic growth.[1] As economies go through the transition, their economies naturally age. Initially, the aging means a smaller fraction of the population is made up of dependent children and a larger fraction of the population is made up of productive workers. However, as the aging continues, the fraction of the working age population begins to decrease and the fraction of older, retired households begins to rise—forming a new dependent group at the other extreme of the age distribution. Over the course of the twentieth century, the average length-of-life in the United States went from 50 to 78 years. About half of the gain in years was due to those who reached age 60 living longer. The aging is predicted to continue throughout the twenty-first century; continuing long after the Baby Boomers, those born during a uptick in fertility between 1945 and 1965, are gone. As mentioned, it is a general worldwide phenomenon; Europe, Japan, and Russia are aging even faster than the United States.[2]

Societies in the twenty-first century must adapt to having a sizeable dependent group of older households. Developed economies provide generous retirement funding in the form of income support and health insurance. Indirectly, aging of the population also causes health costs to rise because older people demand more health care than younger people. Retirement programs now make up the largest component of government spending. These economic features associated with aging have created a fiscal issue because of the PAYG financing of Social Security and Medicare (Chap. 5).

[1]Galor (2011, pp. 46–54).

[2]Kotlikoff and Burns (2012, pp. 14–15).

The U.S. Social Security program was established in 1935 and actually began as a fully funded retirement program. In the middle of the twentieth century, the twin trends of rising real wages and an increasing length of life created the potential to finance greater benefits per year over the growing length of retirement. From 1960 to 1980, the income of the young was increasingly tapped to finance more generous retirement benefits and the program morphed into a PAYG system.[3] The program was lauded for eliminating poverty rates among the elderly. Young workers did not mind because real wages were rising, making them significantly richer than their parent's generation, and they expected to receive the same generous treatment during their own retirement.

In 1965, about the time that Social Security started to grow, Medicare was established. Medicare was proposed as a logical extension to the popular Social Security program and initially the plan was for it to be fully funded.[4] As with the Social Security program, it morphed into a PAYG system to facilitate its expansion. The ability to finance retirement programs now depends crucially on the relative size of different age cohorts. Given the growing relative size of the older population, the burden on working households to finance these programs via PAYG financing will only continue to rise. In the United States, there are currently 4.8 workers to support each retiree. By the middle of this century that number will fall to 2.8.[5]

While aging is a common force driving up the size of both Social Security and Medicare, there is an additional force that has caused Medicare and Medicaid, and health expenditures in general, to rise particularly fast. Health care spending levels differ across the richer countries of the world, but all these countries have seen real health care spending rise 2–3 percentage points faster than real GDP since World War II.[6] In the United States, health care expenditures relative to GDP were 5 percent in 1960 and now are over 17 percent.[7] In addition to aging, all health economists agree that unusually rapid technological change in the medical industry is the second driver of the rising share of health expenditures. There is less agreement on why technological change in health has exceeded that in other industries and why the technological progress has caused costs to rise rather than fall.

One argument is that health care is a luxury good. As people become richer they are willing to devote ever greater shares of their budget to health services. However, health is also heavily subsidized by the government. In many countries, there is national health care provided by the government. In the United States, which relies more on the private market, there are still large government subsidies for health care.

---

[3]Lindert (2004, pp. 193–195).

[4]Cost (2015, pp. 235–237).

[5]Kotlikoff and Burns (2012, p. 20). One response to an aging population is to encourage immigration. However, many richer countries push back against more liberal immigration because people believe it lowers wages of low skilled natives and threatens "national identity." Instead some countries have tried to reverse aging by encouraging fertility through various government subsidies that support marriage and childbearing (e.g. see Emont 2020).

[6]Pauly (2014, p. 20).

[7]Sheiner (2014).

Through Medicare, health care of the old is financed by taxes on the young. The health care of the working population is subsidized by allowing employees a substantial tax break for receiving health insurance benefits rather than wages. When an employee is paid in wages, the wages are subject to taxation. If instead the labor compensation takes the form of employer-provided health insurance, the compensation is not taxed. Excluding income from taxation is called a "tax expenditure" because the government is effectively using potential tax revenue to subsidize a particular activity. Government health care policy has several negative economic consequences.

As discussed in Chap. 5, the PAYG financing of Medicare has contributed to the fall in the national saving rate, creating increased dependency on foreign funding of U.S. investment. The government subsidy of employer-provided health care is also problematic. The subsidy has been characterized as costly (in lost tax revenue) and regressive (the value of the tax exclusion rises with employee wages and tax rates).[8] It also reduces efficiency by restricting labor market mobility because job choice is linked to health care provision.[9] The matching of workers and jobs, which should be based on productivity considerations is distorted because it discourages the mobility of workers who are reluctant to give up subsidized health care as they search for different jobs or seek self-employment opportunities. The lack of mobility causes output to be lower in the long-run because workers and jobs are not as well matched and because fewer workers become self-employed entrepreneurs.

In other industries technological change tends to lower costs. Why do innovations increase the cost of health care? One reason is a system of subsidized insurance that pays for treatments regardless of effectiveness. Heavy government subsidies for health care leads to expensive technologies that do not always improve patient well-being.[10] While health expenditures as a fraction of GDP has been rising, out-of-pocket spending as a share of GDP has been falling, thereby encouraging consumption of costly treatments.[11]

Some argue that large subsidies for the medical industry are due to the government being "captured by the wealthiest seniors, doctors, hospitals, and a vast array of medical service providers, whose private interests are promoted, often instead of the public interest" (Cost 2015, p. 232). One of the important behaviors in the medical industry that is motivated by private interest is the practice of defensive medicine. More medical services, treatments, appointments, and tests are ordered to protect against law suits. While Medicare has attempted to restrict the rise in reimbursement rates for a given service, it has failed to control the quantity of services rendered. As argued by Ho (2014, p. 57), "For any service for which fixed prices exceed marginal costs, providers have the incentive to offer additional care in order to earn greater profits." Thus, government subsidies have played a role in the expansion of

[8]Gruber (2011).

[9]Kotlikoff and Burns (2012, p. 131).

[10]Ho (2014) and Skinner (2013).

[11]Sheiner (2014, Figure 4a).

expensive medical technology, treatments, and services that do not necessarily improve patient care.

Summary
The world is becoming older and the cost of caring for the elderly continues to rise faster than incomes. Aging and increasing medical costs are the primary reasons that countries face unsustainable increases in public debt and large fiscal burdens on young and future generations. Government subsidy and fee-for-service insurance reimbursement have encouraged the development of costly medical technologies and an excessive provision of health services.

8.1.2 Slowing Long-Run Economic Growth

Worker productivity growth in the U.S. began to slow in the 1970s.[12] From 1920 to 1970, the annual growth rate in worker productivity was 2.82 percent. Since 1970, the growth rate has been more than a full percentage-point lower at 1.62 percent. The OECD countries as a whole saw very high growth in worker productivity during the recovery from World War II, with an average annual growth rate of 4.3 percent from 1950 to 1972.[13] From 1972 to 1995, the growth rate naturally slowed from the high post-war recovery rate down to 2.4 percent. Since 1995, growth rates have fallen further, down to just 1.4 percent.

The robust economic growth after World War II allowed government expansion because it brought with it large increases in tax *revenues* without the need to raise tax *rates*. Even as economic growth rates began to slow, and budget deficits began to appear, it was natural for politicians and citizens to believe that the relatively high growth rates, seen for decades after WWII, would return. There was, and still is, optimism that computer-related technological advances would raise economic growth rates above those of the twentieth century, helping to rescue us from our fiscal problems.[14] However, the computer-related technological advances have been with us for some time, including the 50-year period over which economic growth rates have fallen considerably. Computer-driven technological progress has not stimulated economic growth the way earlier 20th century technological advances did.[15] To maintain the current relatively modest growth, new sources of growth will have to be quite dramatic to offset other forces that continue to put downward pressure on growth rates around the developed world. Beyond diminishing returns, there are three forces that will continue to pull growth rates down over this century unless we change our policies.

---

[12]Gordon (2016, Figure 1–2).

[13]OECD (2015, Table A1).

[14]See, for example, Brynjolfsson and McAfee (2014).

[15]See Vijg (2011) and Gordon (2016).

Reduced Saving and Investment

The first force pulling economic growth rates down is the decline in domestic saving and investment. The theory from Chap. 5 predicts intergenerational transfers from younger and future generations to older generations raise consumption and lower saving. Consistent with this prediction, the U.S. has seen a decline in its net national saving rate. The net national saving rate averaged about 15 percent of GDP from 1950 to 1975.[16] Since then it has declined significantly. Even before the Great Recession, the net national saving rate was below 4 percent. Similar trends are present in other economies, as saving has fallen across the developed world. Just as in the United States, the decline in saving is associated with societies placing increasing weight on current consumption, which is partly reflected in greater intergenerational transfers toward older households.[17]

In the U.S., domestic investment has not declined to the same extent as national saving because of an influx of foreign saving. Most of the foreign funding in U.S. financial markets has come from Japan and China. Reliance on foreign borrowing by countries such as the U.S. explains the appearance of their persistent trade deficits. From national income accounting, we know that net exports must equal the difference between national saving and domestic investment. Intuitively this just means that as trading partners purchase more U.S. assets (to fill the funding gap between national saving and domestic investment), they must necessarily purchase fewer U.S. goods.

A heavy reliance on funding from Japan and China is no longer possible. Japan is struggling with its own fiscal crisis and China is seeking to expand its domestic consumption rate. In addition, the relations between China and the U.S. have become strained. In the last decade foreign funding, and in particular funding from Japan and China, for U.S. government debt has tailed off. Thus, a continued supply of foreign funding to meet the increased borrowing of the U.S. over this century is in serious question. The scarcity of international funds will also be affected by the fact that many other developed countries will be seeking foreign financing for their expanding public debt. This all means that domestic investment is soon likely to fall more closely in line with national saving.

The rise in government funding for consumption of retired households has also been associated with a decline in *public* investment—a focus of Chaps. 2, 3, and 5. Government infrastructure investment in the U.S. measured about 3.5 percent of GDP in 1970. Today, it is about 2.5 percent and net infrastructure investment is currently only 0.5 percent. As a result of this decline, the public infrastructure of the United States has depreciated to an embarrassing state for such a rich country.[18] Public infrastructure investment has been neglected in other developed countries as well.[19]

---

16 Kotlikoff (2015, Chart 2).

17 Dobrescu et al. (2012).

18 See Friedman and Mandlebaum (2012) and Malinovskaya and Wessel (2017).

19 Aghion et al. (2013).

Another important public investment is the financing of basic research. The fraction of federal funding for the basic research, that lays the foundation for technological progress, was cut over the last quarter of the twentieth century.[20] In addition to budget pressures that are crowding out public investment, there is the concern that individual governments now face reduced incentives to invest in basic research because of the increased ease of international spillovers of knowledge.[21] If each country attempts to free ride off the basic research of other countries, technological progress across the globe will fall.

Slowdown in Human Capital Growth

The second negative force on growth is the decline in human capital accumulation. The slowdown in human capital formation has occurred along several margins—years of schooling, skill acquisition within a school-year, and pre-school investments in young children.

The average years of schooling across OECD countries increased from 10 to 12 between 1990 and 2013. It is predicted that it will take more than 50 years for the average to increase from 12 to 14.[22] The slowdown in the growth of years of education has been more dramatic in the United States, which has lost its position as the most educated country in the world. The age-cohort born in 1925 received 10.9 years of schooling, while those born 25 years later in 1950 received 13.2 years, a gain of 2.3 years. Moving forward another 25 years, saw those born in 1975 receive 13.9 years of schooling, a gain of only 0.7 years.[23]

The slowdown in the growth of years of schooling is due to the inability of rich countries to significantly raise their college enrollment rates. In the United States, the four-year college participation rate for high school graduates, age 23 and under, has shown little trend since 1970—never consistently rising above 60 percent.[24] College completion rates by age 23 have also been trendless at less than 20 percent of the age cohort.

The modest rise in years of schooling has been, in part, due to a rise in the enrollment and completion rates for older students.[25] By age 30 about 30 percent of the age-cohort obtains a 4-year degree, a little less than half of those who initially enroll. Some of the rise in years of schooling is also due to more 18 and 19 year olds enrolling into two year colleges after high school. The percent of 18–19 year olds, who have completed high school and are enrolled in some type of college has risen from 60 percent in 1990 to 66 percent in 2013.[26] The rise was almost entirely due to increased enrollment in 2-year colleges. The percentage enrolled in 4-year colleges

---

[20]Vijg (2011).

[21]OECD (2015, pp. 51–52).

[22]OECD (2014, Figure 2).

[23]Gordon (2016, p. 513) and Katz (2005, pp. 270–274).

[24]Carneiro and Heckman (2005, Figure 2.2 (a)) and Turner (2004, Figures 1.1, 1.2).

[25]Turner (2004, Figure 1.5).

[26]National Center for Education Statistics (2015).

was essentially flat at 40 percent. For 2014 and 2015, enrollments rates for 4-year colleges have continued to be flat, while enrollment rates in 2-year colleges have actually fallen.[27]

The modest rise in the years of schooling overstates the rise in human capital because all indicators suggest a decline in skills acquired by the average college student. The data we have on the quality of education is for the United States, but quality issues may be an explanation for the slowing growth in years of schooling across the OECD countries generally.

The record of college preparedness in the United States is particularly poor for such a rich and highly educated country. On the Program for International Student Assessment (PISA) test, taken by 15 year-olds across 34 OECD countries, the United States ranks 27 in math, 20 in science and 17 in reading. The relatively poor performance of the United States on the PISA test has not changed over time. Despite rising real expenditures on high school students, national test scores have also been relatively flat for the past 50 years. In fact, the test scores have recently dipped and hit lows that haven't been seen for decades.[28] Performance on measures of adult skills (basic literacy and numeracy needed for work) has also fallen off. OECD measures of basic skills peaked for cohorts born between 1978 and 1987 and have fallen since. The recent decline in scores is largest for the United States. Only about 40 percent of high school graduates are deemed prepared for success in college by their performance on the SAT and only 28 percent by their performance on the ACT. With at best a mediocre and stagnant track record in getting students ready for college, it is not surprising that enrollment and graduation rates are also relatively stagnant. Given that per pupil spending has risen over time at all levels of education, the obvious conclusion is that the marginal returns to human capital investments under current education policy are low.

Surprisingly, given the backdrop provided above, grades given in college courses are up. With no indication of an improvement in college-preparedness, the rise in grades suggests that standards and content in college are slipping and those who do graduate have less skills than in the past.[29] In 1960 about 33 percent of all grades given were As, today it is 43 percent. The rise in grades is even more dramatic at prestigious schools. In 1966, Harvard gave 22 percent As, in 2002 the percent of As was 46 percent. The rise in grades coincides with a *decline* in student study time. Students spend about 13 hours less per week studying today than in the 1960s.

The only explanation for the combination of flat college-preparedness, declining study time, and rising grades, is an elimination of course content and a lowering of standards. It is difficult to find older college professors who do not admit to eliminating content and lowering standards over their careers. In fact, it is becoming

[27]NSC Research Center (2015).

[28]See Adams (2016) and Hanushek (2005, pp. 252–259) for U.S. SAT scores and Rothwell (2016) for OECD scores of basic workforce skills.

[29]Bennet and Wilezol (2013, Chapter 4).

increasingly difficult to simply find a professor. In 1960, 75 percent of college instructors were full-time tenure track professors. Today the number is 27 percent.[30]

The labor market data for college graduates is also consistent with low or declining skills. Surveys of hiring managers have revealed that only 16 percent found college graduates well prepared with skills and knowledge needed for the job.[31] In the latter portion of the twentieth century there was a growing wage gap between college and high school graduates that suggested the market value of college students was increasing. Much of the wage gap, however, was driven by a relatively small fraction of students with *graduate* degrees. Recently, the college wage gap has flattened out. Workers with only undergraduate degrees have been struggling to find good jobs and their average real wages have been falling over the last decade.[32] It is only the very highly educated that have seen their real wages rise significantly over the past 30 to 40 years (see more on this in Sect. 8.1.3).

While real wages for most college graduates are flat or even falling, the average *rate of return* to college for those that graduate has remained high. This is because the largest cost of college for most students is the opportunity costs of not working during the college years. The opportunity cost of college has been falling because the real wages of high school graduates have been falling for some time. If the majority of children in advanced countries are not going to graduate from college, as is apparently the case, then economic growth rates cannot be improved without raising the productivity and wages of those who do *not* attend college.

There is increasing concern about educational investment in young children from low-income environments, particularly in the United States, but in other advanced countries as well.[33] Raising the productivity of workers who do not attend college is a challenging task because trends in family structure and falling real incomes for less than highly educated workers are limiting opportunities for children. On the optimistic side, there is growing evidence of high returns to early investment in children from disadvantaged family backgrounds.[34] The fact that the returns to pre-school investment in children from low income families are higher than the returns to marginal public school spending in middle and upper class neighborhoods, suggests that a reallocation of public funding could increase growth and reduce inequality.[35]

Technological Progress to the Rescue?

A decline in growth rates due to the diminishing returns associated with physical and human capital accumulation is inevitable. History shows the negative effect on growth rates can be mediated temporarily by raising investment rates, especially in

[30]Bennet and Wilezol (2013, p. 139).

[31]Bennet and Wilezol (2013, p. 146).

[32]See Abel and Deitz (2014) and Asworth and Ransom (2018).

[33]For the United States see Carneiro and Heckman (2005) and Putnam (2015). For the UK and the OECD as a group, see Besley et al. (2013) and OECD (2014, p. 45).

[34]Heckman et al. (2010).

[35]Carneiro and Heckman (2005).

human capital. However, there are ultimately growth slowdowns as investment rates level off. The prospects for sustained growth have worsened beyond this because of the reduction in investment rates, broadly defined, in favor of increased consumption.

This scenario paints a pessimistic forecast for growth in the twenty-first century. One can become even more pessimistic if there are reasons to believe that technological progress cannot continue indefinitely at the same rate we observed in the twentieth century. Charles Jones (2002) relates technological progress to the growth in researchers (scientists and engineers engaged in research and development). In the twentieth century, the growth in researchers was based on population growth and on growth in research intensity (the fraction of the available work force devoted to research). Jones points out that the only growth that is sustainable comes from population growth (as with all investment rates, the fraction of the work force devoted to research is bounded). Assuming that population growth remains similar to that of the second half of the twentieth century, long-run growth is expected to be less than ½ percent.

The issue of twenty-first century growth was made popular by an article appearing in the *Economist* (January 12, 2013), entitled "Innovation Pessimism." The article presents another reason to be pessimistic about growth. Academic research suggests that there may also be diminishing returns to research and development efforts (which Jones (2012) does not assume). Recent research by Bloom et al. (2020) finds clear diminishing returns to research effort. They conclude that larger and larger increases in research effort will be needed to maintain technological progress at its current pace. Vijg (2011) argues that the pace of technological progress will slow, and in fact has already begun to, particularly in the important areas of energy, transportation, and medicine. This pessimism is contested by those who argue that the growth impact of innovations in computing, biotechnology, and personal communications has not yet been fully realized. Brynjolfsson and McAfee (2014) claim that we are just on the cusp of a second machine-age built around the computer and the development of artificial intelligence.

Another reason to suspect a decline in technological progress in developed countries relates to immigration patterns. Developed countries tend to attract high-skilled labor from developing countries. For example, survey studies by Vivek Wadhwa (2012) have revealed the importance of immigration for innovation in the U.S. In the U.S. only 12 percent of the population is foreign born. However, this relatively small group has contributed about 25 percent of U.S. global patents. Foreigners, already in or looking to do business in the U.S., receive half of U.S. domestic patents. Immigrants are responsible for almost 30 percent of new business formation, an important determinant of job formation.

Econometric studies provide evidence consistent with the implications of Wadhwa's survey data. Hunt and Gautheir-Loiselle (2010) estimate that a 1 percentage-point increase in the immigrant share of U.S. college graduates increases patents per capita by 9–18 percent. Their estimates suggest that over the 1990s, the 1.3 percentage point increase in the immigrant share of college graduates raised patenting per capita between 12 and 21 percent. Bilgin et al. (2019) find a country's foreign student share has a robust positive association with economic growth in a cross-section of OECD countries.

As is commonly known, many high-skilled immigrants are from China and India. Wadhwa sees evidence that high-skilled immigration from Asia into the U.S. is weakening. The reason is a combination of expanding opportunities in their rapidly growing home countries and the restrictions and delays associated with the U.S. visa process. Without reform of immigration policy needed to ease entry of high-skilled labor into the U.S., there will likely be a decline in innovation and entrepreneurial activity.

To maintain growth rates similar to the twentieth century, when physical and human capital accumulation made important contributions, it won't be enough to argue that technological progress will continue, instead it will have to *accelerate*. Given what we currently know, this seems unlikely. The Congressional Budget Office (CBO) computes the estimate of the fiscal gap by assuming that twenty-first century growth rates in worker productivity and per capita income will continue to be similar to what they have been in the late 20th and early twenty-first century, about 1.5 percent. If the gloomier growth rate predictions prove to be correct, the fiscal gap is actually larger than is currently estimated.

Summary
Beginning in the 1970s, growth rates have exhibited a long-run downward trend in developing countries. Politics and economic fundamentals have created a pro-consumption bias in policy making. Intergenerational redistribution associated with fiscal policy has lowered national savings rates. The impact of lowered national saving on private investment has not yet been fully felt because of foreign funding of U.S. and European domestic investment by Japan and China, international saving flows that are not likely to maintain investment levels in the future. Government budget pressures created by the rising burden of financing consumption of the elderly have reduced spending on public infrastructure and basic research. Advances in years of schooling per worker have slowed because the fraction of the population attending and graduating from 4-year colleges has weakly increased or stalled completely. Workers who are not highly educated have seen little or no increase in their productivity and real wages for decades.

8.1.3 Rising Wage Inequality

Wage inequality has been on the rise in most developed countries over the last 40 years.[36] The United States has a particularly high degree of income inequality, but inequality is predicted to continue its rise in advanced countries generally. Trends in

[36] Cingano (2014).

inequality indicate that the average OECD country will reach the current level of income inequality in the United States by mid-century.[37]

Models of human capital often treat skilled and unskilled labor as distinct complementary inputs in production. In this case there is the possibility of *skill-biased* technological progress that raises the *relative* demand for skilled labor. Rather than technical innovations proportionally raising the productivity of human capital in general, regardless of the level of skill, there may be innovations that raise the productivity of high-human capital workers more than low-human capital workers. It is clear that more educated workers will receive higher wages than less educated workers as the education gap between workers widens. However, over the second half of the twentieth century, *both* a widening education gap *and* skill-bias technological change have increased the relative wage of the highly educated worker.

Research by Claudia Goldin and Lawrence Katz (2008) quantifies how much skill-biased technological progress raised the relative demand for high-skilled labor over the Post WWII period in the United States. They find that the *demand* for high skilled labor grew at an approximately constant rate over the period. Changes in the relative wage paid to high-skilled labor were caused by the degree to which the *supply* of skilled labor was able, or unable, to keep pace with the ongoing demand.

From 1950 to 1980 the supply of college graduates increased at about the same pace as the demand for college-educated labor, leaving the relative wage, or *skill premium*, paid to highly educated labor approximately unchanged. Think of the relative demand curve for and the relative supply curve of skilled labor shifting out by equal amounts, leaving the relative market wage paid to skilled labor unchanged (the absolute amount was rising but at the same rate as for workers with less education).

However, as we have previously discussed, the ability of a country to increase its supply of human capital is eventually subject to diminishing returns. After 1980, increases in the average years of schooling began to slow as the percentage of young workers receiving college degrees stagnated. The demand for skilled-labor began to outpace the supply of skilled labor causing the relative wage paid to highly educated workers to increase. From 1980 to 2005 the skill premium for a college graduate more than doubled. In 1980 a college graduate earned 37 percent more than a high school graduate. The skill premium rose to 87 percent by 2005 (Goldin and Katz 2008, p. 95).

Associated with the rise in income equality is the continued slow or stagnant growth in real wages and incomes for the majority of households. In the U.S., from 1980 to 2012, full-time male workers with a *graduate* degree saw their real earning rise only 1.1 percent annually. For college graduates with a bachelor's degree, the rise in real earnings was a paltry 0.5 percent. Those with some college saw no gain in real wages and those with high school degrees currently receive lower real earnings than they did in 1980. Remember only 30 percent of workers eventually complete a

[37]OECD (2014).

four-year college degree, so the vast majority of workers have not experienced a rise in real earnings since 1980.[38]

The fact that the real wages and productivity of college graduates have only weakly increased over time is not surprising. As mentioned above, instruction by full-time tenured faculty and student study time have both fallen dramatically over the same period. The human capital associated with a college degree is not what it used to be, but the skills provided to high school graduates are even a worse match for what employers are looking for.

The weak rise in wages for many college graduates is also revealed in growing wage inequality *among* college graduates. A general rise in the college premium over high school wages was an important contributor to the rise in overall wage inequality in the late twentieth century. More recently, the continued rise in wage inequality has been concentrated within the group of college-educated workers (Lemieux 2010; Autor et al. 2020). This is known as rising "residual" inequality because it cannot be explained by easily observed characteristics such as years of schooling. More than in the past, high returns to college are dependent on the major chosen and whether the student goes on to graduate school or receives on-the-job training (which can be quite extensive in many larger firms).

While real income is stagnant for the majority of households, the relative costs of health insurance and college continues to rise. Increasingly, middle class households view, not only health insurance, but also college as a necessity—a required investment if their children are to have any chance at a decent standard of living. The United States in particular has a culture that exerts strong social pressure to send children to college, a "college-for-all" mentality, with little attention paid to vocational training.[39] Despite the rising relative cost, over half of each age-cohort attends college, but only about one third complete college with a degree in hand. In addition, completion of college is taking longer, which only raises the cost further.

As discussed in Chaps. 2 and 5, discretionary household consumption has become increasingly constrained by the lack of real income growth and the rise in the cost of required investments in health and education. Families needing to make the health and education investments that they believe give their children a chance at success in today's economies, have become increasingly willing to share the financial burden with their children. This is one factor creating the popular support for increased use of public debt in many countries.[40]

And what about the majority of the nation's households that do not complete a college degree? Their opportunities to earn a decent real wage are bleak. This means their children are not likely to receive the early investments that would give them a good chance at college completion—creating a vicious cycle of relatively low

[38]Autor (2014).

[39]Bennett and Wilezol (2013), Hoffman (2011), Murray (2008), and Putnam (2015).

[40]Steuerle (2014, p. 110).

educational attainment. The problem is particularly acute in the U.S. where over 25 percent of young workers lack even basic reading and math skills.[41]

Socioeconomic status of parents is becoming an increasingly important determinant of whether a child graduates from college. Among eighth graders that receive *high* test scores, only 29 percent graduate from college if their parents are in the bottom socioeconomic quartile, while 74 percent graduate if their parents are in the top quartile. We agree with Robert Putnam (2015, p. 190) who states, "That last fact is particularly hard to square with the idea at the heart of the American Dream: equality of opportunity." James Heckman (2013, p. 3), the Nobel Prize winning economist, sums up the situation more dramatically.

> "The accident of birth is a principle source of inequality in America today. American society is dividing into skilled and unskilled, and the roots of this division lie in early childhood experiences. Kids born in disadvantaged environments are at much greater risk of being unskilled, having low lifetime earnings, and facing a range of personal and social troubles, including poor health, teen pregnancy, and crime. While we celebrate equality of opportunity, we live in a society in which birth is becoming fate."

Inequality and lack of upward mobility have become particularly problematic in the United States, but have also become a concern in many OECD countries. Growing inequality seems to be generally associated with decreasing educational opportunity for children from low-income families and the lack of skills among workers who do not graduate from a 4-year college.

Summary

Associated with the slowdown in the growth rate of average worker productivity has been a sharp rise in wage inequality. The rise in wage inequality is self-perpetuating because family background variables have become increasingly important in determining educational opportunities and achievements. Children from the majority of households have a low probability of attending and graduating from college, which many governments favor dramatically over vocational training. The importance of family background also means that wage inequality *across* households in the current generation is strongly connected with a high intergenerational wage correlation *within* families. There clearly needs to be a new strategy for increasing the skills of the majority of workers in developed countries.

8.1.4 Policies Addressing the Economic Fundamentals

Before the pandemic hit in 2020, David Wessel (2017), a fiscal policy watchdog and analyst, noted that the U.S. economy was finally recovering nicely from the Great Recession but also stated that "all is not well." Wessel believed that 2017 was a good

[41] Cingano (2014), Corak (2014), Lynch 2005, and Woessman (2015).

time to address our chronic long-term problems. Unfortunately, even before the pandemic, politicians continued to be fixated on the short-run. For example, the Tax Cuts and Jobs Act of 2017 is predicted to make government debt 20 percent higher than it would otherwise be by 2028. At this time, interest payments to service the debt will eat up 13–20 percent of government revenue, depending on how much interest rates rise, more than the budget shares of large government programs such as Medicaid or National defense (Tully 2018, b; Schwartz 2018). Covid-19 and the government's stimulus response to it have postponed any chance of long-run fiscal reforms, while at the same time making them ultimately more urgent.

This section discusses some of the policy changes needed to address the economic fundamentals driving the fiscal crisis. As we have stressed, the fiscal crisis is closely connected to the other two major economic issues of the day: slowing economic growth and rising economic inequality. It is not likely that the fiscal crisis can be permanently resolved without comprehensive policy reforms that deal with these two issues as well. While it is typically the case that policy changes are viewed in isolation, this is not necessarily sensible for both economic and political reasons. We will attempt a *comprehensive synthesis* of recent policy suggestions.

There is a political advantage to thinking about reform broadly. All realistic reforms will involve difficult give-and-take among political parties and interest groups. Thinking simultaneously across several different policy changes expands the possibility for constructive tradeoffs and compromises. In a wonderfully insightful, and even entertaining, summary of Sweden's experience with fiscal consolidation, Jens Henriksson (2007, pp. 18–19) makes this point well.

> "Presenting the consolidation measures in one package makes it clear to all interest groups that they are not the only ones being asked to make sacrifices. The idea is to signal that you are not a partisan and that budget deficits is a general problem that everyone should participate in solving.
>
> If one interest group complains, you are in trouble. But if everyone complains you are not."

In surveying policy proposals, we ignore several interesting policy suggestions in order to focus on the reforms we believe are most essential and most practical. For example, there are sound arguments for relying more on national consumption taxes than on income taxes, for eliminating Medicare and replacing it with a government-funded medical voucher program, and for converting PAYG social security to a fully funded program.[42] However, these are large and politically controversial reforms that are not likely to lead to the timely changes needed within the next decade to avert a widespread fiscal and financial crisis. The more modest reforms we stress will be difficult enough to pass.

---

[42]See, for example, Kotlikoff and Burns (2012). More recent policy reforms can be found in Riedl (2018) and Gale (2019).

Aging and Health Care Costs

Aging is changing the world as we know it and, eventually, the government will have no choice but to respond. It was right and noble for societies to provide economic support for the elderly through their governments. In 1970, real Social Security, Medicare, and Medicaid benefits per retiree were less than 40 percent of per capita income.[43] Currently, those retirement benefits have reached about 75 percent of per capita income. By the end of the twentieth century, the consumption of retirees began to exceed that of the average worker.[44] The rising consumption of the ever-larger relative population of elderly households is taking up ever-increasing chucks of the nation's income. The trend is unsustainable in an accounting sense. It also is causing national consumption rates to rise and investment rates to fall, contributing to slowing economic growth and widening income inequality. Priority number one is to cap the growth of real retirement benefits to be no faster than real income. Greater real services to the elderly can rise, but no faster than a nation's ability to pay for them.

There is concern that the Medicare and Social Security trust funds will both be exhausted within the next 10 years. At this time, benefits will have to be cut or payroll taxes will have to increase. There was a similar funding shortfall in 1982 that lead to a payroll tax increase, a gradual increase in the age for benefit eligibility, and income taxation of social security benefits.[45] The longer the country waits to bring payroll tax revenues in line with retirement benefits, the more dramatic the changes will have to be, so timing matters. From the perspective of 2015, closing the present value gap between Social Security benefits and taxes would have required a 4 percentage point increase in the current payroll tax rate from 12.4 to 16.4 percent. Each year that action is delayed, increases the required tax hike. The loss of payroll tax revenue during the pandemic will push the required tax rate calculation yet higher.

However, it would be best *not* to close the fiscal gap in the Social Security retirement program by raising the payroll tax. This solution would lower saving of working households and hurt economic growth. Instead, the adjustment should be on the benefit side. One commonly proposed solution is to further increase the ages at which one receives the minimum and maximum benefits payout.[46] This solution would increase output and saving by encouraging workers to work longer.[47] If actuaries calculate that this policy change would not close the gap between benefits and taxes, then benefits of higher income households could be cut—which would further encourage private saving among a high saving group. This combination of policy adjustments would allow both liberals and conservatives to claim victory. Liberals could argue that they saved social security, by keeping the basic structure of

[43]Kotlikoff and Burns (2012, Figure 4.2).

[44]Gokhale et al. (1996).

[45]Gokhale (2014, p. 77).

[46]Simpson-Bowles Commission (2010), Steuerle (2014), and Alm (2014).

[47]Coile and Gruber (2007), Gruber and Wise (2004) and Gustman and Steinmeier (2015).

the retirement program intact, and making it a more progressive program. Conservatives could argue that they prevented an increase in the payroll tax.

In principle, the fiscal gap in Social Security should be *relatively* simple to close, in part because it is *relatively* small—a mere 25.8 trillion.[48] In 2015, the Social Security gap was only about 12 percent of the entire fiscal gap. Much more important contributors to the overall fiscal gap are Medicare and Medicaid, government programs which are predicted to rise the fastest as a share of GDP.[49] As mentioned above, the government has no choice but to cap the budgets for the health programs so that costs grow no faster than GDP. Kotlikoff and Burns (2012) recommend that the government's health expenditures be capped at the current 10 percent of GDP by offering a basic health care insurance plan. The coverage under the basic plan would be determined by a health care panel that would revise the plan annually to make expenditures consistent with the 10 percent cap. Limiting the government's subsidy of healthcare should create incentives to limit the quantity of marginally valuable services and to make technological innovations more cost conscious.

The primary goal of the much-discussed Affordable Care Act was to increase health insurance coverage. However, certain features of the legislation attempted to control the rise in health care costs. The Act reduces the tax subsidy for employer-provided insurance somewhat by instituting an excise tax on the more expensive health plans offered to employees. It also encourages the move away from "fee-for service" insurance toward a "single fee" insurance payment to treat a given ailment and invokes penalties for bad health service such as hospital readmissions.

One new health-care proposal calls for the elimination of traditional Medicare, Medicaid, and tax subsidies for employer-provided insurance, a complete dismantling of the current broken system (Kotlikoff 2007, 2019; Kotlikoff and Burns 2012). In its place the government would provide a voucher to *everyone* for purchasing a private health insurance plan that covers approved treatments. The size of the voucher would be based on the individual's health status; people with pre-existing conditions receive larger government vouchers. Each health service covered by the plan would have a fixed treatment-budget, similar to HMO plans, thereby eliminating the problematic fee-for-service approach. Finally, the government caps the total voucher budget at some fixed fraction of GDP, a necessary feature of any plan that aims to prevent health care subsidies from increasing faster than the growth of the economy. The plan is similar to replacing the current system with Medicare Part C or Medicare Advantage and has the following advantages:

(i) provides universal health care coverage, with private insurers willing to take on less healthy patients because the size of the government payment is linked to health status

[48]Kotlikoff (2015).

[49]Auerbach et al. (2004).

(ii) eliminates tax subsidies for employer-provided health insurance and the inefficiencies associated with firms being the primary provider of worker health insurance
(iii) encourages competition among private insurers, helping to lower the price of covering the designated essential treatments or to increase additional supplementary treatments as part of the plan
(iv) fixes the total budget at some fraction of GDP, eliminating the primary driver of the fiscal gap.

Whatever the precise cost control measures, to address the fiscal crisis there must be a cap on the government budgets for providing health insurance. The capping of Medicare and Medicaid budgets puts the government in a position where it cannot provide insurance that automatically covers "the best (most expensive) available care." There will certainly be major political and legal hurdles associated with taking this position. The health economist Mark Pauly (2015, p. 36) puts the problem this way, "It is not yet acceptable for middle-class people to talk about anything but the best available care, and legal liability may prevent the emergence even of what they would accept." This is why Laurence Kotlikoff's health care plan, described above, includes malpractice reform. The government and private insurers must be able to constrain doctor and patient choices without facing law suits when expensive procedures and treatments are not covered (Kotlikoff and Burns 2012, Chapter 9). We think the middle class, having seen a decline in their ability to buy non-medical goods and services over several decades now, are ready to consider limits on what they continue to spend on health care. Even medical doctors themselves are thinking of ways of reducing the use of costly tests and treatments (Allen 2018; Gordon 2018). Better informing the public about the fiscal gap, its connection to health expenditures, and its economic consequences should also help in this regard.

Removal of Tax Expenditures

Stemming the growth in the entitlement programs is not sufficient to completely close the fiscal gap. In addition to reducing the path of future spending, more tax revenue will be needed to reduce the creation of government debt that pulls down national saving and investment. Political considerations suggest that higher taxes will almost surely be part of any grand compromise to resolve the fiscal crisis. Beyond the goal of closing the fiscal gap, extra revenue will also be needed to increase public infrastructure investment and funding for basic research—essential government investments that have been neglected. The question is how can tax revenues be increased in a way that eliminates distortions and inequities while minimizing negative growth effects?

A good place to start is to reduce "tax expenditures" – tax exemptions, deductions, credits and deferrals that lower taxes paid. The United States tax code allows for over 150 different tax expenditures. These tax expenditures are large, $1.2 trillion, larger than government spending under either Medicare and Medicaid programs or the Social Security program. In addition the vast majority of the expenditures flow to the top 40 percent of income earners.[50]

The biggest tax expenditure by far is the tax exclusion for the health insurance, provided as a form of employee compensation and totaling about $200 billion. This tax exclusion has no sound basis in economic logic. It was created during World War II when employers began competing for scarce workers by offering more attractive benefits because their potential wage offers were frozen by the wage and price controls of the period. The National War Labor Board, as a concession to business, ruled that the benefits were not wages and not subject to wage controls. To maintain consistency, the concession meant benefits should not be treated as taxable income. The health insurance tax exclusion increases the generosity of health insurance, the demand for medical services, and health care costs. As with many of the tax expenditures, it is highly regressive because high wage workers benefit the most from the reduction in their taxable income.

Other tax expenditures should also be considered for elimination or reduction. Two of the largest are the reduced tax rate on income from capital gains and the deductibility of mortgage interest on owner-occupied housing, together totaling over 150 billion in lost revenue. These tax expenditures are also regressive and they likely reduce net national saving used to fund business capital formation.

Efficiency-Promoting Taxation

As discussed by Mankiw (2009), economists are generally advocates for *Pigovian* taxes. Pigovian taxes are known as corrective taxes because they are taxes that attempt to correct inefficiencies in market resource allocation that result from decision makers not internalizing the *social* costs, or *negative externalities*, associated with their actions. As with the fiscal crisis, global warming poses a major economic threat to the world in the twenty-first century. Placing a Pigovian tax on carbon emissions would address both crises by creating a revenue source and by forcing households and firms to internalize the full costs of carbon emissions when deciding on production technologies, type of automobile, driving, and electricity use. Chapter 9 includes additional discussion of climate change and the carbon tax. A tax on gasoline also reduces negative externalities associated with congested roads such as traffic delays and accidents.

Advances in *behavioral* economics are making a case for increasing *sin* taxes. Behavioral economics identifies situations where decision making deviates from the fully rational calculus of neoclassical economics. An important source of these deviations is a lack of self-discipline. People know that they should save for retirement but have a hard time doing so, especially when retirement is far away. This is one reason why Social Security and corporate pension plans are popular institutions—they force people to do what they know they should do, but often do

---

[50]See data from the Center on Budget and Policy Priorities (2016). Eliminating tax expenditures and other simplifications of the tax code would also help to eliminate tax evasion and corruption associated with tax collection. See, for example, Awasthi and Bayraktar (2015).

not because of a lack of will. People also lack discipline in taking care of themselves. Sin taxes are consumption or sales taxes targeted on goods that make us unhealthy, such as alcohol, cigarettes, and fatty and high caloric foods. Taxing these goods raises their costs and discourages unhealthy consumption. For example, Los Angeles County is considering a tax on sugar-sweetened beverages to improve health and reduce the social costs of obesity.[51] Doctors at the Mayo clinic are pushing for higher sin taxes on alcohol and cigarettes.[52] Gruber and Mullainathan (2005) even find that higher cigarette taxes make smokers *happier* by creating incentives to reduce or eliminate the smoking habit.

The sin taxes on unhealthy behavior can also be viewed as a way of mitigating the *ex ante moral hazard* associated with the provision of health insurance. Ex ante moral hazard is what health economists call the tendency of insured individuals to engage in unhealthy behavior because they do not have to fully pay for the consequences of their actions. Ex ante moral hazard is a controversial concept but several recent studies provide empirical evidence that it does exist.[53]

If the increased revenue from reduced tax expenditures and higher Pigovian and sin taxes is not sufficient, then a general federal consumption tax, perhaps earmarked for increase public investments in infrastructure and basic research, should be considered. Many economists favor a consumption tax base over an income tax base. A complete reform of the U.S. tax code is too big a task to take on while moving quickly to avert a crisis of confidence, but the addition of a relatively small federal consumption tax may be a possible source of additional revenue needed to close the fiscal gap and avert a full-fledged financial crisis.

One of the reasons economists prefer taxing consumption rather than income is that it reduces the distortionary tax on the return to saving. Higher returns to saving have the potential to raise the rate of saving and increase economic growth. However, there is little evidence that saving rates change significantly when after-tax returns to saving increase.[54] Apart from the issue of taxing interest income, a consumption tax is superior to a *wage* tax if the goal is to lower consumption rather than saving and growth.

To see this point more clearly, let's return to the two-period life-cycle model used to examine the effects of fiscal policy on physical capital accumulation in Chap. 5. Suppose households maximize the utility function,

$$U_t = \ln c_{1t} + \beta \ln c_{2t+1},$$

subject to the two single-period household budget constraints, which now include both wage (τ^w) and consumption (τ^c) taxes,

[51]Clarke et al. (2015).

[52]Perry (2013).

[53]See Dave and Kaestner (2006), Stanciole (2008), and Dave et al. (2015).

[54]See, for example, the survey in Stupak and Marples (2016).

$$(1+\tau^c)c_{1t}+s_t=(1-\tau^w)w_t$$

and

$$(1+\tau^c)c_{2t+1}=(1+r_{t+1})s_t,\quad (1+\tau^c)c_{2t+1}=R_t s_t.$$

The consumption tax, just as with the sales tax in basic economics, drives up the price of consumption from 1 to 1 + τ^c. The variable c_{1t} represents the *actual consumption* of goods that generates utility and (1 + τ^c)c_{1t} are the *consumption expenditures*, inclusive of taxes, needed to acquire the goods.

Solving the household maximization problem allows us to derive the following first period consumption and saving functions,

$$c_{1t}=\frac{1}{1+\beta}\frac{1-\tau^w}{1+\tau^g}w_t$$

$$s_t=(1-\tau^w)w_t-(1+\tau^g)c_{1t}=\frac{\beta}{1+\beta}(1-\tau^w)w_t.$$

As before, notice that the return to saving does not affect saving behavior. This is because, with logarithmic utility, the substitution and income effects associated with a change in the return to saving exactly cancel, leaving the level of saving unaffected. In general, these two conceptual effects will not exactly cancel, but the fact that they are opposing does help explain why the estimated interest elasticity of saving is small.

Notice that the consumption tax has no effect on saving. The higher tax lowers actual consumption and raises expenditures per unit of consumption proportionally, leaving total consumption expenditures unaffected. Again, this won't necessarily be true for other utility functions but, as with interest rates effects, the opposing effects suggest that the consumption tax will not affect the saving of the young by much in either direction. The wage tax, however, reduces the income flow to savers and causes an unambiguous decline in saving. Older households are also hit by the consumption tax, but since their saving rate is zero, there is not effect on aggregate saving.

Reallocation of Human Capital Investment

To get ahead in most developed economies now requires a graduate degree. While the importance of college is increasing, the fraction of the population attending and graduating from 4-year colleges has not significantly increased for decades in the United States. This is despite the fact that the standards in college have been gradually slipping over the years and passing grades have become easier to obtain.

The average private rate of return for those graduating from college remains high, despite the rapid rise in tuition costs and fees. However, this is at least in part due to the fact that the opportunity costs of attending college, forgone wages of high school graduates, have been falling. If a high school education did more to increase productivity and wages, the average rate of return to college would fall. Zimmerman

(2014) finds private (subsidized cost to the individual) and social returns (full cost to the society) to male and poor students are high relative to similar counterparts who attend community college. As with high school education, this could reflect the poor performance and non-trivial costs of community colleges. It is also puzzling why he finds that women and students from middle class families attending 4-year colleges do *not* receive higher earnings than their counterparts that attend community colleges. It may be that high schools and community colleges are not working for males and students from poor families in particular.

In addition, focusing on the *average* rate of return from a college investment can be misleading. The rates of return vary dramatically for college graduates, with some receiving negative rates of return. Some of the variation in returns to college can be explained by a student's field of study, with STEM majors now significantly outperforming others (Carnevale et al. 2015; Lemieux 2014). It is perhaps even more important to note that the rates of return received by *marginal* students and the projected returns to *non-college students*, if they do attended college, can be low.[55] Athreya and Eberly (2013) use the fact that non-completion rates vary substantially with student preparedness and ability in order to explain why many students do not enroll despite the high college premium for college graduates on average. This means it does not make sense to try to push more students through college. In fact, consistent with the significant college dropout rates and the presence of negative returns for some graduates, many observers feel there are currently *too many* students attending college.[56]

Most students who attend colleges are looking for specific skills that make them attractive to particular employers, and not the more general knowledge and abstract analytical skills that a 4-year college experience has traditionally offered. A common frustration among college students is that they are forced to learn material that is of no practical, i.e. job-related, importance. Despite all the social pressures to become "highly educated," college is not the answer for the vast majority of the population.

To increase labor productivity growth and reduce wage inequality, human capital policy has to change dramatically. A previous section of this chapter provided evidence suggesting the *marginal* returns to investment under current education policy—where investment is predominately directed toward (4 year) college and college-prep, are low. Resources should be reallocated away from support for traditional college toward improved education for the majority of the population. State tuition subsidies and subsidized students loans are regressive policies because they largely provide aid to high ability students, who will be high wage earners as adults. These policies also drive up the pre-subsidy price of college and do not raise college attendance significantly.[57] Furthermore, the subsidies have helped finance

[55]Carneiro et al. (2011).

[56]Murray (2008), Kotlikoff and Burns (2012), and Bennett and Wilezol (2013).

[57]Gordon and Hedlund (2016) and Lucca et al. (2015).

the main factor driving up the cost of college—the constant expansion in university administration and college consumption ameneties.[58]

Much of the funding directed toward college should be invested in young children from disadvantaged families and in vocational training during high school.[59] Programs for disadvantaged children have been shown to yield average rates of return in the 6–14 percent range, higher than the returns received by many marginal college students and the returns from traditional college-prep spending in high schools of middle and high income communities.[60] Following the principles for good governance from Chap. 2, investments should be allocated toward communities and individuals where returns are high and incomes are low.

Vocational training is an integral component of human capital policy in countries such as Austria, France, Germany, and Switzerland but has been neglected and even stigmatized in others. The United States, in particular, needs a cultural shift away from the notion that college is for everyone. Students that want to learn a trade should be respected and their education should be taken seriously in high school. Social pressure to send most students through a "college-track" program leaves too many students with few skills when they enter the workforce after high school.

As with pre-school investments, vocational programs have been shown to have high returns.[61] Recent studies of students attending stand-alone vocational schools in Massachusetts found that, relative to comparable peers in traditional high schools, they not only had higher post-graduation earnings but also had higher graduation rates and similar performance on academic tests. Skills that do not require a college education are in short supply in the United States—including carpenters, electricians, technicians, welders, sales representatives, and restaurant staff.[62] These "middle-skill" jobs, which require only quality vocational training in high school (perhaps supplemented with apprenticeships), are among the fastest growing occupations.[63] They are also occupations with relatively high pay. Machine operators make $60,000 annually, technicians, drafters, and respiratory therapists

[58]See Ginsberg (2011) and Delisle (2017).

[59]Carneiro and Heckman (2005), Aghion et al. (2013), Murray (2008, pp. 147–162), Bennett and Wilezol (2013, pp. 169–172), and Bustamente et al. (2017).

[60]See Heckman et al. (2010), Heckman et al. (2013), and Garcia et al. (2020). These studies evaluate small-scale programs. The results in Walters (2015) and Attanasio et al. (2017a) indicate that large-scale pre-school programs, if properly structured, can also have lasting positive effects on cognitive and non-cognitive skills.

[61]Attanasio et al. (2017b) and Jacob (2017).

[62]Germany, in addition to having a well-respected vocational training system that serves about half of their students, performs well on basic reading and math skills of its young workforce (Lynch (2005)). See Trines (2018) for a discussion of how the German system might be used as a model for the U.S. For labor shortages in occupations not requiring a college education see Coster (2010), Duncan (2017), and Collins (2018).

[63]See Duncan (2017), Holzer and Lerman (2009), Lerman (2012), and Newman and Winston (2016).

make $70,000, and petrochemical workers make $100,000. In contrast, college graduates in liberal arts and general education make $37,000.

Short-Run Effects of Fiscal Consolidation

One of the reasons for delays in dealing with the fiscal gap is the concern that the required cuts in government spending and increases in taxes will cause large negative output effects in the short-run by reducing aggregate demand. This concern has inspired research that investigates how the loss in output from fiscal consolidation can be minimized. The research on this topic is closely related to the long tradition in economics of attempting to estimate *fiscal multipliers*—a term grounded in Keynesian economics, where exogenous changes in government spending and tax revenues were thought to have much more than one-for-one effects on output.

The best of the modern research in this area attempts to identify episodes where governments explicitly devise fiscal plans to reduce debt and then estimates the resulting output effects.[64] The identified plans can be categorized as largely tax-based (tax increases) or largely expenditure-based (spending cuts). The consensus of this research is that consolidations based largely on spending cuts tend to be associated with mild and short-lived recessions or no recessions at all. Tax-based consolidations, on the other hand, are followed by large and prolonged recessions.

The difference in the two-types of consolidation packages appears to work through very different effects on business confidence and private investment. Business confidence does not fall much after expenditure-based adjustments, promptly recovers, and then actually increases. After tax-based adjustments, business confidence instead falls for several years. As a result, spending cuts are associated with relatively small declines, or even increases, in investment—which is important in avoiding both severe recessions and negative longer run effects on economic growth.

Summary of Policy Reforms

The broad policy suggestions, that we feel should shape the debate about fiscal reforms, are listed below.

1. Increase the age at which the minimum and maximum Social Security retirement benefits are received
2. Reduce Social Security benefit levels for higher income individuals
3. Cap expenditures under Medicare and Medicaid, at the current percentage of GDP, by offering a basic plan of health care coverage that is revised annually by a health care panel
4. Increase tax revenue by eliminating tax expenditures starting with the tax exclusion for the health insurance provided as a worker benefit, the reduced tax rate on income from capital gains, and the deductibility of mortgage interest on owner-occupied housing

---

[64]Romer and Romer (2010), DeVries et al. (2011), Alesina et al. (2015, 2017) and Alesina and de Rugy (2013).

5. Increase tax revenue by increasing a variety of Pigovian taxes, sin taxes, and a federal sales tax
6. Reduce government subsidies for higher education and reallocate the funds to increase programs for young children from disadvantaged families and vocational training programs in high school
7. Increase budgets for public infrastructure projects and basic research
8. For the purpose of minimizing negative effects on output in the short-run, consolidation packages should tend to favor spending cuts over tax increases in reducing the fiscal gap
9. Ease immigrant entry, especially for the high-skilled, to increase innovation and new business formation, and to reduce the old-age dependency ratio (immigrants tend to be young).

8.2 Politics

It is clear that fiscal policy reforms are necessary because the current fiscal path will eventually lead to large shortages of government funding, resulting in a major financial crisis across the developed world. There is a fair degree of consensus among economists that the reforms suggested above are at least reasonable starting points for the policy discussion. What is much less clear is whether any of these reforms will be passed in a timely way without first addressing the ineffectiveness of our political systems. Allan Drazen (2000, p. 403), an expert on the political economy of macroeconomics, succinctly summarizes the issue this way,

> "in situations in which economic arguments clearly favor reform, one must look to political constraints to understand why reforms are not enacted or sustained, or are only enacted after long delay."

Current political systems are characterized by corruption, disproportionate influence of interest groups on policy, polarization of political philosophy among policy makers, and a bias to subsidize consumption rather than investment—all factors that many feel have become larger issues over time and that have led to the fiscal crisis to begin with. How confident can we be that the same politics will generate timely and effective reforms?

One theory is that an economic crisis is needed to generate compromise among conflicting interests that ends in meaningful reform (Drazen 2000, Chapter 10).This is a pessimistic view because one would hope that policy changes would help *avert* crises well before they happen. However, the view that crisis leads to reform may actually be *too optimistic* in practice. Consider the quote from the long-time U.S. politician, Leon Panetta, found in Wessel (2012, p. 162).

> "I used to tell students that we are either governed by leadership or crisis. And I always thought that if leadership wasn't there, then ultimately you rely on crisis to drive decisions. In the last few years, my biggest concern is that crisis does not seem to drive decisions either."

There is also no guarantee that decisions, even when made during times of crisis, are going to be good ones. A recent account of the evidence concludes that about 80 percent of fiscal attempts to reduce debt-to-GDP ratios end in failure (Alesina and de Rugy 2013). Especially in recent years, confidence in the political process is low. Fundamental changes to political systems may be needed before economic policies can be put back on the right track.

8.2.1 Corruption, Tax Evasion, and Public Debt

For several developed countries, corruption and tax evasion have played an important role in the fiscal crisis. Figure 1.3 from Chap. 1 relates corruption and public debt-to-GDP ratios for 2008. Three of the highest corruption countries in 2008, Greece, Italy, and Portugal, saw their debt-ratios rise well above the 2015 OECD average of 1.1. The 2015 ratios for Greece, Italy and Portugal were 1.9, 1.5, and 1.4. Hungary and Spain, also rated as high corruption countries in 2008, have experienced dramatic increases in their debt ratios, and are now just below and right at the OECD average respectively, 0.9 and 1.1. The Czech and Slovak Republics were high-corruption, but relatively low debt-ratio countries, in 2008. By 2015, the debt ratios in both countries almost doubled. Thus, countries with high levels of corruption, as detected by Transparency International surveys in 2008, either have high levels of public debt or have experienced large increases in public debt.

Ireland and Japan are countries with high debt ratios but are relatively clean of corruption by the standard Transparency International measures. Ireland has little in the way of petty corruption where bribes are offered to avoid laws and regulations or to obtain timely governments services. However, a survey conducted by the European Commission (2011) found that 86 percent of respondents think that corruption is a major problem in Ireland, with 84 percent noting that corruption exists in Ireland's national institutions. Niamh Hardiman (2015), in a presentation to the Joint Committee of Inquiry into the Banking Crisis, noted "Ireland ranks relatively poorly on indicators of institutional quality in the Global Competitive Index. Among the poorest ratings was the item "favouritism in decisions of government officials."

These survey findings have been confirmed by a number of tribunals that have been established over the last 30 years to investigate political corruption in Ireland (Breslin 2015). The latest was the Mahon Tribunal which uncovered financial payments and transactions made to public officials in order to influence political and policy decisions. Most importantly, corruption played a role in Ireland's housing bubble and financial crisis. The "Galway Tent" became a byword for corrupt relations between politicians, banks, and property interests. A recent review of the crisis concludes that "government priorities were more attentive to interests of the bankers, the builders, and the property developers, than they were to considerations of good governance (Clarke and Hardiman 2012, p. 39)".

In Japan, standard corruption measures fail to capture deeply institutionalized legal political corruption. The Japanese practice of *amakudari* involves systematically stockpiling assets and opportunities for the benefit of specific subgroups of public servants (Jones 2015). Part of this system involves building infrastructure of questionable utility to support quasi-public corporations charged with operating them. Japan has become a country with one of the largest collections of government-controlled physical assets. Using tax payer funds, those operating these state-connected corporations receive lucrative salaries and benefits.

It seems likely that high-level political corruption in Ireland and entrenched corruption in Japan played a role in the sharp expansion of unnecessary investment projects financed by public debt. While its corruption is missed by the Transparency International measure, Japan fits the corruption-government investment scenario described in Chap. 7.

Government corruption has clearly contributed to the accumulation of public debt in the several OECD countries, including those with the highest debt-to-GDP levels. The root cause of political corruption is a lack of transparency in government operations. Making our political systems more transparent to public scrutiny should be the number one priority of political reform.

8.2.2 Interest Groups and Public Debt

The main policy drivers of the fiscal crisis are Social Security and Medicare Programs for retirees and education subsidies for college-bound students. The policies were created with good intentions—taking care of the elderly and promoting a college education for everyone. However, they have subtle unintended consequences that slowed economic growth, raised wage inequality, and placed enormous fiscal burdens on future generations.

It is difficult to educate people on the down-side to these well-intended policies. Actually passing the legislation needed to reform the policies is partly due to a lack of information but is also due to the backing the policies receive from powerful special interest groups representing retirees, doctors, medical providers, universities, and educators. The big losers, future generations and the majority of workers who are not college educated, have almost no political representation.

Policies in the national interest of the majority of people today and in the future, currently have little chance of becoming law. Transparency about the full consequences of policies will help in this regard, but a reconsideration of campaign financing reform and rules that restrict lobbying activity is also needed. Political institutions must change to limit the disproportionate influence of well-organized and well-funded special interest groups.

8.2.3 Transparency

The power to corrupt is pervasive and goes well beyond government. It includes all major organizations: such as corporations (Stiglitz 2013), banks (Kotlikoff 2010), and even higher education (Ginsberg 2011). Unless the behavior of powerful figures in an organization is being closely watched, there is just too much temptation to behave badly and justify the bad behavior as being in the best interest of the institution. Close monitoring of official's behavior is needed to eliminate the temptation, but this first requires transparency. There must be a clear record of what the officials are doing so that they can be held accountable for their actions by interested parties.

In the case of government, transparency begins with a *complete accounting* of what fiscal policies are being carried out. For the public to understand the important implications of the policies, there also must be an *independent assessment of likely impacts*. Finally, there must be a *clear and (ever) present reporting* of the policies and their impact that politicians and general public can digest. One way of viewing an expansion in transparency is to think of it has giving increased power to relatively "non-partisan technocrats" who record and assess policy proposals on the public's behalf.

Complete Accounting

The fiscal crisis is the result of economic fundamentals that are squeezing consumption for the majority of the population and an expansion in interest groups that attempt to remedy the situation by increasing government subsidy for their individual group members. The losers in this situation are young and future generations. To quote Henriksson (2007, p. 11) again, "Remember the future has no lobbyists." The first failure of good governance around the world has been to ignore the long-run intergenerational redistribution associated with Post World War II fiscal policy of rich countries, not to mention those of many developing countries.

There was a time that economists themselves shared the blame by not supplying the essential accounting tools to the government. However, Auerbach et al. (1991) provided the needed fiscal gap and generational accounting in the late 1980s. Over the years these improved accounting tools have been increasingly used by fiscal branches of governments, international economic organizations, and think tanks. The use of fiscal gap accounting is criticized by some, who evidently would rather just close their eyes to the paths that current policy are taking us, because it requires that assumptions be made about future trends in variables such as aging, economic growth rates, and the relative price of medical services. To address concerns over the assumptions made, fiscal gap accounting computes forecasts under optimistic and pessimistic scenarios that serve to bound reality. Auerbach and Gale (2015) conduct such an exercise and show that under current policy, the U.S. debt-to-GDP would reach almost 3 (optimistic assumptions) and possibly 4.5 (pessimistic assumptions) by the end of the century. Even the most optimistic scenario is alarming.

The problem is that policy makers and the public can still dismiss or dodge these projections because computing fiscal gaps is not an institutionalized component of fiscal accounting and reporting. This is why Auerbach and Kotlikoff drafted the INFORM Act (Intergenerational Financial Obligations Reform Act) that requires the fiscal offices of the U.S. federal government(Congressional Budget Office (CBO), Government Accountability Office (GAO), and Office of Management and Budget (OMB)) to do fiscal gap and generational accounting on an annual basis. The act also requires the use of these accounting measures to evaluate major pieces of proposed legislation, if so requested by Congress. A bill called The INFORM Act was recently introduced by a bipartisan collection of senators: John Thune (R-S.D.), Tim Kaine (D-Va), Rob Portman (R-Ohio) and Chris Coons (D-Del.). Passing this bill would help discipline the political process by making it more difficult for policy makers to run from the long-run consequences of their actions.[65]

Independent Assessment of Policy Impact

Objectivity is hard to maintain. This is true even in science, let alone in highly value-laden areas such as politics. In science, we try to maintain objectivity the best we can by testing our ideas against experimental and real-world data. The importance of the ideas, and the validity and rigor of the tests, are scrutinized by anonymous expert referees in the highly competitive game of professional journal publication. It is usually the case that there is more than one referee because, after all, no one person is fully objective. If science needs careful refereeing in its pursuit of objective knowledge, then political policy-making needs it all the more.

Who are the expert referees of government policy and programs? The voting public may be the ultimate referee, but voters need lots of help in objectively evaluating the effects of the multitude of economic policies carried out by today's governments. It should not be insulting to assert that, in trying to make sense of the often subtle and nuanced effects of economic policy, the public is tempted to fall back on broad ideological reactions to simplify matters for themselves. Politicians generally support the ideological simplifications by pandering to voters to get re-elected (Caplan 2007). The politicians themselves are not trained in economics and also need technical assistance to have any chance of formulating sensible policies. Monetary policy is largely set by economists at the central banks of countries. There is no good reason by fiscal policy should be treated so asymmetrically.

The need for technical assistance in evaluating and formulating fiscal policy is why the GAO, OMB, and the CBO were created. The technical infrastructure needed to "referee" the formulation of fiscal policy is already there in most developed countries. In addition, there are many nongovernmental think-tanks and organizations, as well as academic economists, whose research is devoted to designing and assessing fiscal policy. What is now needed is a way to give the technocrats a bigger role.

In academics, the best journal referees are ones that make constructive suggestions about how submitted papers can be improved. The referees of fiscal policy should be allowed to offer the same type of feedback. Alice Rivlin, the first director of the Congressional Budget Office and the person responsible for creating its culture of fiercely objective and nonpartisan analysis, believed that initiating independent research was an important function of the organization. Of course, there have been complaints that the CBO is over stepping its bounds. These complaints

[65]See also the long-term budgeting plan proposed by Stuart Butler (2016).

should be resisted. In fact, the evaluation and feedback given from these fiscal offices needs to be given greater public visibility.[66]

Clear and (Ever) Present Reporting

One important lesson that older academics teach younger academics is that your work, no matter how good, will not speak for itself. All ideas, if they are to have impact, must be marketed. Academics market their work to other academics, who serve as their future referees at the publication stage, by doing the conference circuit. When presenting your research at conferences, one occasionally gets good "spur-of the moment" feedback from other participants. But the main objective is to sell the ideas as being important and interesting, so that others will take the work seriously enough to read and consider carefully after the talk is over. This process is somewhat distasteful to many academics, but it is a necessity, if not a duty.

If academics need to market ideas to other academics, then policy makers certainly need to market their ideas to the public. Politicians cannot be trusted to serve this role objectively. The poor performance of the budget process is direct evidence of this. The technocrats that participate in the formulation of fiscal policy need public stages where they present their work directly to the people. This should be one of their formal charges—educate the general public about fiscal policy. The fiscal gap is largely the result of an education gap. The fiscal offices of government should be expanded to help eliminate the education gap.

Congressional hearings and press briefings are good examples where instruction about fiscal policy takes place, but the audience needs to be expanded beyond the small groups participating in or watching these events. The technocrats will also need to hire effective marketers who present the research to the public. One reason that the technocrats, and many academics, are never heard is that they are not skilled in marketing. In today's world, ideas that are going to matter need slick marketing.

The annual publication of the CBO's *Long-Term Budget Outlook*, and the associated news conference, has become something of an event for the press. However, the offices associated with fiscal policy assessment should get the word out more aggressively throughout the entire year. Start by publishing research reviews, similar to those published by the Federal Reserve Banks. Federal Reserve reviews are highly visible to academics and the press, and through those channels, the articles in the reviews find their way to students and the public. These publications could include, as do the Fed reviews, ambitious analysis—including the behavioral responses to different policy proposals that determine the ultimate effects on the economy and household welfare.

A weekly PBS economic/government policy program, if done well, in the spirit of say the old *Wall Street Week* or a calmer version of the *McLauglin Group*, would be a way of reaching the public even more directly. It is critical that the public be educated, by a relatively objective source, on both the economic fundamentals at work and the fiscal crisis itself. The public has some concerns about these matters,

[66]See Joyce (2011) for a history of the CBO and a discussion of its role in policy making.

but remain largely misinformed and confused. Just as with the politicians, the public has largely ignored the debt problem because it is in their selfish interests to do so. However, if they were to fully understand the debt projections, and their likely consequences (which includes a possible financial crisis within their lifetimes), attitudes would change.

8.2.4 Budget Process and Rules

Eugene Steuerle (2014) and others have insisted that no progress on obtaining fiscal sustainability can occur until the automatic growth in many federal programs and tax expenditures is ended. Forces exogenous to the budget process, such as aging, rising health care costs, and wage increases, cause spending in Medicare, Medicaid, and Social Security programs to expand without new budget evaluation each year. Increases in home mortgages, asset values, and health insurance costs also cause lost revenue from tax deductions to automatically increase on an annual basis.

As a result of these built-in features of the budget, each year sees an increasing gap between spending and taxes that goes entirely unchecked. The growing gap due to nondiscretionary fiscal changes squeezes discretionary spending that is budgeted on an annual basis, including important public investments in education, infrastructure, and R&D. Before the more permanent fiscal reforms that need to take place can occur, the government should declare a fiscal emergency that causes the major transfer programs and tax expenditures to lose their privileged status and be brought into the annual budget debate. This may force the policy makers to think about longer-term reforms in the process.

It would also help to give the President, the elected public official who should come closest to representing the national interest, more power in the budget process. By constitutional design, the president has little actual role in the budget process. The president can veto an entire budget bill, but that is a strong and blunt instrument. Line-item vetoes have been rejected as being unconstitutional. Instead, the president is granted rescission authority, where objections can be raised about specific provisions of the budget bill. However, Congress can simply ignore the rescission requests.

Some have recommended that Congress should, at least, be required to vote on all presidential rescission requests. The main benefit of this minor enhancement of rescission authority is to involve the president in the details of the budget process by pointing out specific provisions that are not in the national interest and that merit further review and debate.

Stronger and more sweeping changes in the budget process, such as rules that require balancing the budget in some formalized manner, are tempting. However, as pointed out first in Chap. 3, it is not clear that balanced-budget rules actually work. Previous attempts at requiring budget balance have been circumvented in a variety of ways.[67] Even a perfectly enforced strict balanced budget rule would allow for substantial intergenerational redistribution, as the current PAYG Social Security program exemplifies.[68] Penner (2014, pp. 173–174), a former CBO budget director, sums up the pessimism regarding the effectiveness of new budget rules in averting a financial crisis.

> "The problem is not a lack of rules. We have plenty of rules. The problem is that Congress does not follow the rules we have."

> "It would be nice if a few extra rules could fix the federal budget process, but at this point, the problem goes far beyond anything that could be fixed by changes in rules. I do not see a complete resolution of our budget problems until we face a sovereign debt crisis similar to that now afflicting Greece."

8.2.5 Polarization

Everyone you talk to seems to bring up the increased polarization of politics in one way or another. The moderates are getting forced out of politics by extremists on both sides of the aisle. Part of the polarization arises from the frustration caused by the economic fundamentals at work in the twenty-first century that are preventing the majority of the population from getting ahead. The, at best, stagnant standard of living most households are experiencing is hard for people to understand. For those with liberal leanings it is easy to blame conservatives and for those with conservative leaning it is easy to blame liberals. There is an idea that whoever can blame the best, and the loudest, will convince the few remaining moderates to join their side and win the day. This is why educating the public about the state of the economy and what it will take to improve things is so important. The technocrats must step up to this challenge because the politicians are only adding to the confusion, as should be obvious to all the moderate voters following the 2016 presidential campaign in the United States.

There is also a purely political factor underlying the increased polarization. Every 10 years, state legislatures can redefine the political districts from which representatives to congress are elected. The tortuous geometric shape of the districts, "gerrymandering," reflects the motive to make them as homogenous as possible politically, increasing the chances that one of the parties will dominate. Instead of each district being roughly representative of the entire country's diversity, individual districts increasingly reflect the interests of only small segments of society. Redistricting has gone hand-in-hand with the rise in interest group politics.

Political scientists have an answer to gerrymandering that is consistent with our solution to improving economic policy—shift power to the technocrats and their computers.

[67] Auerbach (2012) and Penner (2014).

[68] Kotlikoff (2003).

"Many scholars of American politics have worked out lots of better ways to allocate congressional districts than the way it is done now. All methods come down to variations on a common theme: district boundaries should not be manipulated to squeeze some voters in here and others out there. Boundaries should reflect some basic principle of geometry and natural constraints of the terrain, like major rivers or mountains. As a simple principle, gerrymandering could be greatly diminished by turning redistricting over to some computer programmers and mathematical political scientists, who could design rules that are not district specific but instead apply common principles of fair representation across all districts (Bueno de Mesquita and Smith 2012, pp. 267–268)".

8.2.6 Summary

It might seem like we are recommending that fiscal policy be turned over to unelected technocrats. We are doing nothing of the kind. Let the technocrats, that society has invested its scarce resources to train, do their thing—identify costs and benefits, winners and losers of different policy options. The politicians can then debate how to weigh the winners and losers in order to come up with the final policy legislation. The role of the technocrats is to inform and discipline the debate, a role that is sorely needed and that should be enhanced. In addition, any reforms that limit the influence of special interests would help balance the political weighing of winners and losers.

8.3 Reforming Foreign Aid

The lack of a positive effect of foreign aid on the growth of developing countries has been disappointing (see Chaps. 3 and 6). What can be done to improve aid effectiveness?

8.3.1 Needed: Accountants without Borders

Countries at all stages of development need to use accounting systems and reliable information flows as a way of constraining political behavior. In order to have a chance to deal with the tendency to redistribute wealth across generations, rich countries need to institutionalize improved accounting and competing assessments of policy. The need for an improved accounting system to create government transparency is even greater in poor countries that are in the early stages of developing their government institutions. Development economists view reliable accounting as an essential step to good governance. Paul Collier (2009, p. 214), for example, makes improved government accounting one of his foundational proposals for increasing growth in poor countries,

"Public revenue will leak wherever there is a hole, so there is a large preliminary task of overhauling the practical processes by which money is spent; budgets need accountants, and lots of them. Starting from a culture in which there is no presumption of honesty, the system of financial checks needs to mirror the paranoia of the dictatorships: there needs to be so much interlocking monitoring that even if a few accountants are prepared to be corrupt, they cannot make a difference."

He argues that sound accounting is so essential to effective aid that some independent verification of a country's accounting system by the international community should be a *pre-condition* for aid support.

8.3.2 Alternative Pre-conditions for Aid

The underdevelopment of transparent accounting and evaluation systems is likely an important reason for the lack of correlation between aid and growth.[69] What should be done until a transparent accounting system is developed?

Individual countries and international institutions place or negotiate *conditions* that dictate the way that aid funds are to be used, usually with the hope of jump starting growth. However, if the use of funds cannot be tracked, then aid effectively becomes *unconditional budget support* that can be used in any way the recipient government sees fit. In many settings, this means the aid will not be used in a manner that permanently raises the standard living of the average citizen.[70]

A better substitute for the lack of transparent accounting in developing countries is to use a *selectivity rule* as a temporary or alternative *pre-condition* for aid support. A developing country should only receive international aid after it has established some track record of domestic policies that have increased growth and reduced poverty. International donors could evaluate the growth records of developing countries and deliver unconditional aid to extend domestic initiatives or policy reforms based on observed early outcomes. Explicitly using country track records should also help reduce the tendency to favor countries for geo-political purposes.

8.3.3 Multi-lateral Aid

Some interpret the historical record as evidence that donors, especially in the case of individual countries, are not actually interested in generating growth in developing countries. Rather, as suggested above, the aid is used to purchase regional influence as part of a broader geo-political strategy; such as checking a competing superpower, getting access to oil reserves and important mineral sources, making peace in the Middle East, or allowing a military base to be established.[71]

However, rich countries do not have to be sincerely altruistic to want economic growth in developing countries. Growth in poor countries that reduces world-wide

[69] Easterly et al. (2004) and Raghuram and Subramanian (2005, 2008, 2011).

[70] See Chap. 6 and Das et al. (2018, Chapter 5).

[71] Bueno de Mesquita and Smith (2012, Chapter 7).

income inequality can reduce terrorism and illegal migration flows and increase the world demand for goods. The fact that these benefits from poor-country growth are to some degree public goods to rich countries is one reason that aid should flow through international institutions such as the World Bank. Channeling aid through the World Bank should also help mediate the use of aid to advance the interests of anyone donor country.[72]

While aid flowing through the World Bank may help focus the intended purpose of aid, there still remains the necessary cooperation of the recipient countries. Much of the aid during the disappointing post-WWII period was delivered through multilateral international organizations. Even altruistic aid can be diverted away from the intended purpose in a variety of ways, which is why transparent accounting in the recipient countries and selectivity rules remain important.

8.3.4 A Knowledge Bank of Development Projects

The World Bank's most useful role in creating growth could be in providing technical assistance and policy advice to developing countries with solid pro-growth leadership. To serve this role best, the Bank should commit to becoming a "knowledge bank."[73] This means increasing its research component to conduct detailed policy evaluation, cost-benefit analysis of specific investment projects, and design of transparent accounting systems. This emphasis is analogous to giving technocrats in the accounting and evaluation offices of domestic governments a bigger role in policy determination. The Bank, and other international institutions, should focus on establishing evidence identifying growth policies and investment projects that work best and then market these ideas to developing countries that are willing to listen.

Along these lines, the United States has recently passed foreign aid legislation that attempts to improve the monitoring and evaluation of aid projects. An important feature of the legislation is to place greater reliance on government technocrats. The Government Accountability Office is to serve as an independent and objective evaluator of the aid process and project results. The goal is to determine what aid projects work and why.[74]

8.3.5 Deal with Corruption First

One aspect of technical assistance is to help developing countries establish an accounting system that can effectively track and tax income and sales. A poor country cannot fund the needed public infrastructure projects on its own without a

[72] Clemens and Kremer (2016).

[73] Clemens and Kremer (2016) and Ravallion (2016).

[74] Ingram (2016).

reliable revenue source. However, we believe that helping a developing country reduce tax evasion, without first addressing corruption, is a bad idea.[75] Technical assistance should first focus on keeping track of how the available government funds are used.

The models from Chaps. 6 and 7 include both corruption and tax evasion, so can be used to examine the interaction between the two illegal activities. Using these models, we find that only lowering tax evasion causes tax rates and tax revenue to increase, creating greater opportunities to divert public funds through corruption. The reduction in private disposable income from the higher taxes lowers private capital accumulation and the increase in corruption lowers public investment. The reduction in the private and public capital stocks causes worker productivity and the welfare of private households to fall. Improving the tax system and cracking down on tax evasion may be welfare improving but only after checks on corruption are made sufficiently strong. If diversion of public funds is made difficult, then lower evasion and higher tax revenue can raise public investment significantly.

8.4 Exercises

Questions

1. What is the *demographic transition*? How has the demographic transition contributed to the fiscal crisis?
2. Why have health care expenditures risen faster than GDP since WWII?
3. Evaluate the government subsidy of employer-provided health insurance according to the following criteria.
   (a) fairness of the tax code
   (b) labor market efficiency
   (c) output market efficiency
   Suppose the government provided a health insurance subsidy directly to households. How would it compare, according to these criteria, to subsidizing employer-provided insurance?
4. Why does theory predict that growth due to *physical* capital accumulation naturally slows down? Does the same argument apply to human capital accumulation? Explain.
5. What has happened to the national saving rate across the developed countries since WWII? Offer an explanation that applies to all developed countries.
6. What is "crowding out?" Has crowding out occurred in developed countries such as the U.S.? Does crowding out apply to public as well as private capital?
7. Provide evidence that the growth rate of human capital has slowed.
8. Offer a reason we should be optimistic that technological progress will accelerate in the twenty-first century and a reason we should be pessimistic.

[75] Ivanyna et al. (2016) simulates the effects of cracking down on tax evasion before first dealing with corruption.

9. Relate the fact that the majority of U.S. households have experienced little or no increase in their real wages since the 1970s to the rise in public debt ratios.
10. Many view the "equality of opportunity" as a defining characteristic of America. To what extent does recent American history over the last several decades live up to this ideal?
11. Explain the statement that "wage inequality across households is highly correlated with the intergenerational correlation of wages within families."
12. What is the college wage premium? How did it change from 1980 to the end of the twentieth century? Why did it change?
13. What is "residual" inequality? Offer some possible explanations for it.
14. Defend a policy reform that deals with each of the following issues related to the fiscal crisis (you can choose a different policy for each issue)
    (a) population aging
    (b) rising health care costs
    (c) insufficient tax revenue
    (d) slow growth in human capital
15. Defend a *single* fiscal reform that simultaneously addresses the fiscal crisis, the growth slowdown, and rising wage inequality.
16. How does current U.S. education policy contribute to the fiscal crisis?
17. The fiscal crisis can be dealt with by raising taxes or cutting government spending, both of which may cause a recession. Is there reason to believe that one approach is better than another in this regard? Explain.
18. Discuss how interest group politics may play a role in the increasing costs of health care.
19. Discuss how interest group politics may play a role in rising wage inequality.
20. Explain why it might be a good thing that *all* interest groups are complaining about a particular fiscal reform.
21. Give evidence or specific examples suggesting how each of the following political factors may have contributed to the rise in public debt ratios across developed countries.
    (a) corruption
    (b) transparency of government accounting
    (c) the budget process
    (d) political polarization
22. What reforms can you offer to address each of the political factors mentioned in question 21?
23. Foreign aid is generally regarded as being disappointing in its attempt to boost economic growth in developing countries. What political factors have contributed to the disappointing record?
24. Is the World Bank needed? Make an argument for and against keeping the World Bank as an international institution.
25. What reforms would improve the effectiveness of the World Bank in promoting economic development?

References

Abel, J. and Deitz, R., 2014, "Do the Benefits of College still Outweigh the Costs," *Current Issues*, New York: Federal Reserve Bank of New York.

Adams, C., 2016, "2015 SAT, ACT Suggest that Many Students are not College-Ready," *Education Week*, 35 (3), 6

Aghion, P., Besley, T., Browne, J., Caselli, F., Lambert, R., Lomax, R., Pissarides, C., Stern, N., and Van Reenen, J., 2013, *Investing for Prosperity*, Report of the LSE Growth Commission.

Alesina, A. and de Rugy, V., 2013, "Austerity: The Relative Effects of Tax Increases versus Spending Cuts," *Mercatus Research*, George Mason University.

Alesina, A., Barbiero, O., Favero, C., Giavazzi, F., and Paradisi, M., 2017, "The Effects of Fiscal Consolidations: Theory and Evidence," *NBER Working Paper #23385*.

Alesina, A., Favero, C., and Giavazzi, F., 2015, "The Output Effects of Fiscal Consolidation Plans," *Journal of International Economics*, 96, S19–S42.

Allen, M., 2018, "Unnecessary Medical Care: More Common than You Imagine," *Shots—Health News*, National Public Radio.

Alm, J., 2014, , "Discussion on Social Security's Financial Outlook and Reforms: An Independent Evaluation," in J. Diamond and G. Zodrow editors, *Pathways to Fiscal Reform in the United States*, Cambridge, MA: MIT Press.

Asworth, J. and Ransom, T., 2018, "Has the College Wage Premium Continued to Rise? Evidence from Multiple U.S. Surveys," IZA DP No.11657.

Athreya, K. and Eberly, J., 2013, "The Supply of College-Educated Workers: The Roles of College Premia, College Costs, and Risk," Working Paper 13-02, Federal Reserve Bank of Richmond.

Attanasio, O., Cattan, S., Fitzsimons, E., and Meghir, C., and Rubio-Codina, M., 2017a, "Estimating the Production Function for Human Capital: Results from a Randomized Controlled Trial in Columbia," Institute for Fiscal Studies Working Paper W17/06, London, UK.

Attanasio, O., Guarin, A., Medina, C., and Meghir, C., 2017b, "Vocational Training for Disadvantaged Youth in Columbia: A Long-term Follow-up," *American Journal of Applied Economics*, 9 (2), 131–143.

Auerbach, A., 2012, "Budget Rules and Fiscal Policy: Ten Lessons from Theory and Evidence," Working Paper, University of California, Berkeley.

Auerbach, A. and Gale, W., 2015, "The Fiscal Problem: Gone Today, Here Tomorrow," Working Paper, University of California, Berkeley.

Auerbach, A., Gale, W., and Orszag, P., 2004, "Sources of the Long-Term Fiscal Gap," *Tax Notes*, May, 1049–1059.

Auerbach, A., Gokhale, J., and Kotlikoff, L, 1991, "Generational Accounts: A meaningful Alternative to Deficit Accounting," in D. Bradord, ed., *Tax Policy and the Economy*,5, Cambridge, MA: MIT Press, 55–110.

Autor, D., 2014, "Skills, Education, and the Rise in Earnings Inequality among the Other 99 Percent," *Science*, 344, 843–851.

Autor, D., Goldin, C., Katz, L.F. (2020) Extending the Race between Education and Technology. *AEA Papers and Proceedings, 110*, 347–351

Awasthi, R., and Bayraktar, N., 2015, "Can Simplification Lower Corruption," *Eurasian Economic Review*, 5, 297–330.

Bennett, W. and Wilezol, D., 2013, "*Is College Worth It*," Nashville, Tennessee: Thomas Nelson.

Besley, T., Coelhol, M., and Van Reenen, 2013, "Investing for Prosperity: Skills, Infrastructure, and Innovation," *National Institute of Economics and Social Research*, 224(1), 1–13.

Bilgin, M., Gozgor, G., and Rangazas, P., 2019, "Immigration, Innovation, and Economic Growth," *Singapore Economic Review*, (forthcoming).

Bloom, N., Jones, C., Van Reenen, J., and Webb, M., 2020, "Are Ideas Getting Harder to Find?," *American Economic Review*, 110, 1104–1144.

Breslin, B., 2015, "How Bad is Political Corruption in Ireland," *The Outspoken Post*, June 7.

Brynjolfsson, E. and McAfee, A., 2014, *The Second Machine Age: Work, Progress, and Prosperity in a Time of Brilliant Technologies*, New York: WW Norton and Company.

Bueno de Mesquita, B., and Smith, A., 2012, *The Dictator's Handbook*, New York:Public Affairs.

Bustamente, A., Hirsh-Pasek, K., Lowe Vandell, D., and Michnick Golinkoff, R., 2017, "Why DeVos Should Embrace Early Childhood Education," *Education Plus Development*, Brookings Institution.

Butler, S., 2016, Hearing on Congressional Budget: The Need to Control Automatic Spending and Unauthorized Programs, Washington: Brookings Institution.

Caplan, B., 2007, *The Myth of the Rational Voter: Why Democracies Choose Bad Policies*, Princeton: Princeton University Press.

Carnevale, A., Cheah, B., and Hanson, A., 2015, *The Economic Value of College Majors*, McCourt School of Public Policy, Georgetown University.

Carneiro, P. and Heckman, J., 2005, "Human Capital Policy," in J. Heckman and A. Krueger *Inequality in America*, Cambridge, MA: MIT Press.

Carneiro, P., Heckman, J., and Vytlacil, E., 2011, "Estimating Marginal Returns to Education," *American Economic Review*, 101, 2754–2781.

Center on Budget and Policy Priorities, 2016, "Federal Tax Expenditures," *Policy Basics*, February 23, www.cbpp.org

Cingano, F., 2014, "Trends in Income Inequality and Its Impact on Economic Growth," OECD Social, Employment and Migration Working Papers, No.163, Paris: OECD Publishing.

Clarke, B. and Hardiman, N., 2012, "Crisis in the Irish Banking System," in Konzelmann, S. and Fouvargue-Davies, M. (Eds.) *Banking Systems in the Crisis: the Faces of Liberal Capitalism*. Oxford, Routledge, 107–133.

Clarke, L., Horst, R., Izuchukwu, K., Lunderville, C., Prasanna, S., 2015, "Reducing Obesity in Los Angeles County: Toward a Tax on Sugar-Sweetened Beverages," *An Applied Policy Project*, UCLA Luskin School of Public Affairs.

Clemens, M., and Kremer, M., 2016, "The New Role for the World Bank," *Journal of Economic Perspectives*, 30, 53–76.

Coile, C. and Gruber, J., 2007, "Future Social Security Entitlements and the Retirement Decision," *Review of Economics and Statistics*, 89(2), 234–246.

Collier, P., 2009, *War, Guns, and Votes,* New York: Harper Collins.

Collins, C., 2018, "My Advice for High School Graduates: Learn a Trade," May 2, otherwords.org

Corak, M., 2014, "Income Inequality, Equality of Opportunity, and Intergenerational Mobility," *Journal of Economic Perspectives*, 27, 79–102.

Cost, J., 2015, *A Republic No More*, NewYork: Encounter Books.

Coster, H., 2010, "The 10 Hardest Jobs to Fill in America," *Forbes* 5/28.

Dave, D. and Kaestner, R., 2006, "Health Insurance and Ex Ante Moral Hazard: Evidence from Medicare," *International Journal of Health Care, Finance, and Economics*, 9, 367–390.

Dave, D., Kaestner, R., and Wehby, G., 2015, "Does Medicaid Coverage for Pregnant Women Affect Prenatal Health Behaviors?," *NBER Working Papers* 21049.

Das, S., Mourmouras, A., and Rangazas, P., 2018, *Economic Growth and Development: A Dynamic Dual Economy Approach*, New York: Springer

Delisle, J., 2017, "The Disincentive Hypothesis: Don't Blame State Budgets Cuts for Rising Tuition at Public Universities," *Report*, Washington: Brooking Insitution.

DeVries, P., Guajardo, D., Leigh, D., and Pescatori, A., 2011, "A New Action-based Dataset of Fiscal Consolidation," *IMF Working Paper* 11/128, International Monetary Fund.

Dobrescu, Loretti I., Kotlikoff, Laurence J. & Motta, Alberto, 2012. "Why aren't Developed Countries Saving?," *European Economic Review*, 56(6), 1261–1275.

Duncan, A., 2017, "Education Equality and Excellence will Drive a Strong Economy," *Brown Center Chalkboard*, Washingtion: Brookings Institution.

Drazen, A., 2000, *Political Economy in Macroeconomics*, Princeton: Princeton University Press.

Easterly W., Levine R., Roodman D., 2004, "Aid, Policies, and Growth," *American Economic Review*, 94(3), 774–780.

Emont, J., 2020, "Singapore Isn't Kidding When It Comes to Fostering Fertility," *Wall Street Journal*, February 22.

European Commission, 2011, *Corruption Report*, Special Eurobarometer 374, Brussels.

Friedman, T. and Mandlebaum, M., 2012, *That Used to be Us*, Picodar: New York.

Gale, D., 2019, *Fiscal Therapy*, Oxford: Oxford University Press

Garcia, J., Heckman, J., Leaf, D., and Prados, M., 2020, "Quantifying the Life-Cycle Benefits of an Influential Early Childhood Program," *Journal of Political Economy*, 120, 2502-2541.

Gokhale, J., Kotlikoff, L., and Sabelhaus, J., 1996, "Understanding the Postwar Decline in U.S. Saving: A Cohort Analysis," *Brooking Papers on Economic Activity*, 1, 315–390.

Goldin, C. and Katz, L., 2008, *The Race between Education and Technology*, Cambridge MA: Harvard University Press.

Galor, O., 2011, *Unified Growth Theory*, Princeton: Princeton University Press.

Ginsberg, B., 2011, *The Fall of the Faculty: The Rise of the All-Administrative University and Why it Matters*, New York: Oxford University Press.

Gokhale, J., 2014, "Kicking the Social Security Can Down the Road," *Investor's Business Dailey*, August 5.

Gordon, G. and Hedlund, A., 2016, "Accounting for the Rise in College Tuition," *NBER Working Paper* 21967.

Gordon, M., 2018, "Why Do Doctors Overtreat?" *Shots—Health News*, National Public Radio.

Gordon, R., 2016, *The Rise and Fall of American Growth: The U.S. Standard of Living since the Civil War*, Princeton University Press: Princeton.

Gruber, J., 2011, "The Tax Deduction for Employer-Sponsored Health Insurance," in J. Poterba, editor, *Economic Analysis of Expenditures*, *National Tax Journal* v.64 (2), National Tax Association.

Gruber, J. and Mullainathan, S., 2005, "Do Cigarette Taxes Make Smokers Happier," *B.E. Journal of Economic Analysis and Policy*, 5, 1–45.

Gruber, J. and Wise, D., 2004, *Social Security Programs and Retirement around the World: Micro-Estimation*, Chicago: University of Chicago Press.

Gustman, A. and Steinmeier, T., 2015, "Behavioral Effects of Social Security Policies on Benefit Claiming, Retirement, and Saving," *Journal of Public Economics*, 129, 51–62.

Hanushek, E., 2005, "Comments," in J. Heckman and A. Krueger *Inequality in America*, Cambridge, MA: MIT Press.

Hardiman, N., 2015, "Good Governance: A Political Science Perspective," *Joint Committee of Inquiry into the Banking Crisis*, March 10.

Heckman, J, Moon, S., Pinto, R., Savelyev, P., and Yavitz, 2010, "The Rate of Return to the HighScope Perry Preschool Program," *Journal of Public Economics*, 94, 114–129.

Heckman, J., Pinto, R., and Savelyev, P., 2013, "Understanding the Mechanisms Through Which an Influential Early Childhood Program Boosted Adult Outcomes," *American Economic Review*, 103, 2052–2086.

Henriksson, J., 2007, "Ten Lessons about Budget Consolidation," *Bruegel Essay and Lecture Series*, Brussels: Belgium

Ho, V., 2014, "Discussion on Medical Spending Reform and the Fiscal Future of the United States," in J. Diamond and G. Zodrow editors, *Pathways to Fiscal Reform in the United States*, Cambridge, MA: MIT Press.

Hoffman, N., 2011, *Schooling in the Workplace*, Cambridge, MA: Harvard University Press.

Holzer, H., and Lerman, R., 2009, "The Future of Middle-Skill Jobs," CCF Brief #41, Center for Children and Families, Washington: Brookings Institution.

Hunt, J., and Gautheir-Loiselle, M., 2010, "How Much Does Immigration Boost Innovation," *American Economic Journal: Macroeconomics*, 2, 31–56.

Ingram, G., 2016, "Congress finds Bipartisan Support for Foreign Aid and Aid Reform," *Future Development: Economics to End Poverty*, Washington: Brookings Institution.

Ivanyna, M., Mourmouras, A, and Rangazas, P., 2016, "The Culture of Corruption, TaxEvasion, and Economic Growth," *Economic Inquiry*, 54, 520–542.

Jacob, B., 2017, "What we Know about Career and Technical Education in High School," www.brookings.edu/research

Jones, C., 2015, "Bridging Corruption and Legitimacy: *Amakudari*," *Community: The Japan Times*, April 12.

Jones, C., 2002, "Sources of U.S. Economic Growth in a World of Ideas," *American Economic Review*, 92, 220–239.

Joyce, P., 2011, *The Congressional Budget Office: Honest Numbers, Power, and Policy Making*, Washington, D.C.: Georgetown University Press.

Katz, L., 2005, "Comments," in J. Heckman and A. Krueger *Inequality in America*, Cambridge, MA: MIT Press.

Kotlikoff, L., 2019, "The Best Healthcare Plan is Already in Place," *The Hill*, September 8.

______, 2015, "America's Fiscal Insolvency and its Generational Consequences," Testimony to the Senate Budget Committee, February 25, 2015.

______, 2010, *Jimmy Stewart is Dead: Ending the World's Ongoing Financial Plague with Limited Purpose Banking*, Hoboken, New Jersey: Wiley.

______, 2007, *The Healthcare Fix*, Cambridge, MA,: MIT Press.

______, 2003, *Generational Policy*, Cambridge, MA,: MIT Press.

Kotlikoff, L. and Burns, S., 2012, *The Clash of Generations*, Cambridge, MA: MIT Press.

Lemieux, T., 2010, "What Do We Really Know about Changes in Wage Inequality?," in K. Abraham, M. Harper, J. Spletzer (eds.), *Labor in the New Economy*, University of Chciago Press, 17–59.

______, 2014, "Occupations, Fields of Study, and Returns to Education," *Canadian Journal of Economics*, 47(4), 1047–1078.

Lerman, R., 2012, "Can the U.S. Expand Apprenticeships? Lessons from Experience, IZA Policy Paper #46.

Lindert, P., 2004, *Growing Public*, Cambridge, UK: Cambridge University Press.

Lynch, L., 2005, "Comments," in J. Heckman and A. Krueger *Inequality in America*, Cambridge, MA: MIT Press.

Lucca, D., Nadauld, T., and Shen, K., 2015, "Credit Supply and the Rise in College Tuition: Evidence from the Expansion in Federal Student Aid Programs," *Federal Reserve Bank of New York Staff Reports* No. 733.

Malinovskaya, A., and Wessel, D., 2017, "The Hutchins Center Explains: Public Investment," *Upfront*, Washington: Brooking Institution.

Mankiw, G., 2009, "Smart Taxes: An Open Invitation to Join the Pigou Club, *Eastern Economic Journal*, 35, 14–23.

Murray, C., 2008, *Real Education*, New York: Three Rivers Press.

National Center for Education Statistics, 2015, "Immediate Enrollment Rates," *The Condition of Education 2015*, Washington: U.S. Department of Education.

Newman, K. and Winston, H., 2016, *Reskilling America: Learning to Labor in the Twenty-First Century*, Metropolitan Books: New York.

NSC Research Center, 2015, "Fall Term Enrollments Rates 2015," National Student Clearinghouse.

OECD, 2014, *Policy Challenges for the Next Fifty Years*, Economic Policy Paper No. 9, Paris: OECD Publishing.

OECD, 2015, *The Future of Productivity*, Paris: OECD Publishing.

Pauly, M., 2014, "Medical Spending Reform and the Fiscal Future of the United States, in J. Diamond and G. Zodrow, editors, *Pathways to Fiscal Reform in the United States*, Cambridge, MA: MIT Press.

Penner, R., 2014, "Discussion on Federal Budegt Reform: Lessons from State and Local Governments," in J. Diamond and G. Zodrow editors, *Pathways to Fiscal Reform in the United States*, Cambridge, MA: MIT Press.

Perry, S., 2013, "Mayo Doctors Propose Higher—and New—"Sin Taxes"," *MinnPost*, June 15.

Putnam, R., 2015, *Our Kids*, New York: Simon and Schuster.

Raghuram R. and Subramanian, A., 2011, "Aid, Dutch disease, and Manufacturing," *Journal of Development Economics*, 94(1),106–118.

______, 2008, "Aid and Growth: What does the Cross-Country Evidence Really Show?" *Review of Economics and Statistics*, 90(4), 643–665.

______, 2005, "What Undermines Aid's Impact on Growth? *IMF Working Paper 05/126*. http://www.imf.org/external/pubs/ft/wp/2005/wp05126.pdf.

Ravallion, M., 2016, "The World Bank: Why it is Still Needed and Why it Still Disappoints," *Journal of Economic Perspectives*, 30, 77–94.

Riedl, B., 2018, "A Comprehensive Federal Budget Plan to Avert a Debt Crisis," Manhattan Institute.

Romer, C. and Romer, D., 2010, "The Macroeconomic Effects of Tax Changes: Estimates using a New Measure of Fiscal Shocks," *American Economic Review*, 100, 763–801.

Rothwell, J., 2016, "The Declining Productivity of Education," *Social Mobility Memo*, Washington: Brooking Institution.

Schwartz, N., 2018, "As Debt Rises, the Government Will Soon Spend More on Interest than on the Military," September 25, *The New York Times*.

Sheiner, L, 2014, "Perspective on Health Care Spending Growth," *Future of U.S. Health Care Spending Conference*, Washington: Engelberg Center for Health Care Reform.

Simpson-Bowles Comission, 2010, *The Moment of Truth*: Report of the National Commission on Fiscal Responsibility and Reform, Washington D.C.

Skinner, J., 2013, "The Costly Paradox of Health-Care Technology," November/December, *MIT Technology Review*.

Stanciole, A., 2008, "Health Insurance and Lifestyle Choices: Identifying Ex Ante Moral Hazard in the US Market," *Geneva Papers*, 33, 627–644.

Steuerle, C., 2014, *Dean Men Ruling*, New York: Century Foundation Press.

Stiglitz, J., 2013, *The Price of Inequality*, New York: Norton.

Stupak, J., and Marples, D., 2016, "Consumption Taxes: An Overview," *Congressional Research Service*, 7-5700, www.crs.gov

Trines, S., 2018, "Could Germany's Vocational Education and Training System be a Model for the U.S.?," June 12, *World Education News and Reviews*.

Tully, S., 2018, "Can America Keep Up with Its Debt?" February 16, *Fortune*.

______, 2018, "How Debt Could Blow up the Trump Economy," March 15, *Fortune*.

Turner, Sarah. 2004. "Going to College and Finishing College: Explaining Different Educational Outcomes." In *College Decisions: How Students Actually Make Them and How They Could*, ed. Caroline Hoxby. Chicago: University of Chicago Press for NBER.

Vijg, J., 2011, *The American Technological Challenge*, New York: Algora Press

Walters, C., 2015, "Inputs in the production of Early Childhood Human Capital: Evidence from Head Start," *American Economic Journal: Applied Economics*, 7(4), 76–102.

Wadhwa, V., 2012, *The Immigrant Exodus*, Philadelphia: Wharton Digital Press.

Wessel, D., 2012, *Red Ink*, New York: Crown Business.

Wessel, D., 2017, "Three Things to Tackle Now before the Economy's Next Slump," *Wall Street Journal*, 9, 2017, and *Brooking Institution Op-Ed*.

Woessman, L., 2015, "Single-Parent Families and Student Achievement: An International Perspective," Ifo Institute at the University of Munich

Zimmerman, S., 2014, "The Returns to College Admission for Academically Marginal Students," *Journal of Labor Economics*, 32, 711–754.

9 Conclusion

We have offered an introduction to the political economy of fiscal policy in a macroeconomic context where the main focus is long-run economic growth and prosperity. The models developed were applied to important real-world issues such as economic development, income inequality, and fiscal crises. This final chapter summarizes the main results of the analysis by discussing how fiscal policy contributes to answering the five overriding questions provided in the introduction. We also suggest that the problem of good governance has always been with us, driven throughout history by a common set of human characteristics. The challenge of enduring success is to first recognize these human failings and then to create institutions that provide the needed checks on behavior.

9.1 Summary

9.1.1 Why Does Sustained Modern Economic Growth Fail to Take-Off?

Many poor countries have unusually large governments relative to the size of their economies. Tax rates are high and a large fraction of the budget is devoted to government consumption, as exhibited in Table 1.1 of Chap. 1. Econometric studies, using large samples of countries, consistently show that the government consumption share of GDP is negatively correlated with economic growth (see, for example Barro 1997b).

In Sect. 6.1 of Chap. 6, large government consumption shares are due to the small weight placed on the welfare of private sector households relative to the welfare of government officials and their collection of close supporters, as is typically the case in autocratic regimes. High taxes are needed, not only to generate revenue used to reward supporters, but also to punish rivals. In some extreme cases this causes tax rates to be set above the level that maximizes government revenue. See Sect. 6.2 for an example of how this can occur.

M. Ivanyna et al., *The Macroeconomics of Corruption*, Springer Texts in Business and Economics, https://doi.org/10.1007/978-3-030-67557-8_9

Interest groups in early development, such as large landowners, push for high tax rates and low infrastructure spending in order to suppress the urban manufacturing demand for labor. This serves to raise land rents by reducing labor costs in agriculture and primary product sectors. As a result, the structural transformation is slowed and growth in the economy as a whole remains weak. Owners of the scare physical capital used in manufacturing, another potentially powerful interest group, lobby for policies that block the foreign physical capital inflows that help jump-start aggregate growth but would also serve to lower private returns on capital. Unless the vested interests of these potentially powerful groups are resisted by pro-growth leadership, sustained modern growth fails to occur.

9.1.2 Why Does Foreign Aid to Governments of Developing Countries Fail to Generate Growth?

Unconditional aid or "budget support," including conditional aid where the conditions are not adequately enforced, does not deliver lasting growth effects for a variety of reasons (Sects. 3.4, 3.6, and 6.1). The increase in revenue is temporary and is mostly transferred to households for private consumption or directly consumed by governments that are not concerned with aggregate economic growth. Even if some of the aid is invested, without change in the domestic government's fiscal policy, the country will revert back to its original steady state equilibrium when the aid stops flowing. If the aid comes in the form of loans, there is also the danger that the higher taxes needed to repay the debt will discourage future productive activity, possibly resulting in lower long-run output.

Various conditions tied to the aid have the potential to channel the funds to investment. However, conditions are very difficult to monitor and enforce because aid revenue is fungible and accounting systems lack transparency. To help speed economic development, the best strategy is to invoke a *pre-condition* or *selection criterion* that requires developing countries to exhibit a sufficient track record of pro-growth policies before the supporting foreign aid is extended (Sect. 8.4).

9.1.3 Why Does Long-Run Growth Eventually Slow?

Sections 2.11, 3.6, 4.3, 4.5, 5.2, and 8.1.3 address this question. The first source of the growth slowdown is the diminishing returns to all types of investment—physical capital, human capital, and government capital. Some also believe that investment in research and development of new technologies is subject to diminishing returns—more recent inventions lack the productivity impact of their predecessors.

Then there is the leveling and, in some cases reduction, in the *rates* of investment as countries develop. Aggregate savings rates fall and consumption rates rise, reducing funds for private capital investment. The ability of a nation to push larger fractions of the population through higher education stalls because the majority of the population lacks the aptitude and attitude to complete college. The allocation of government revenue to basic research and infrastructure investment is cut in favor of transfers programs.

In part, the reduction in investment rates may be caused by the falling rates-of-return that serve to lower the reward and incentive to investment. However, much of the reduction is due to government policy. The rise in intergenerational redistribution to the elderly causes a fall in national saving, as well as a reduction in government funding for investment. Within the portions of government budgets allocated for education, unrealistic elitism has created a bias toward higher education that has the unintended consequence of primarily benefiting the rich and widening income inequality. Too much is spent on tuition subsidies for higher education and student loans, and too little is spent on investments in young children from lower-income families and in well-designed vocational training for teenagers. More generally, politics often favors the allocation of public investment projects to richer and more powerful regions of the nation, despite the likelihood of higher rates of return in neglected communities where public capital is scarce.

9.1.4 Why Is Income Inequality on the Rise?

As economies develop there is a natural rise in the relative demand for skilled labor. A succinct description of this tendency is provided by Autor (2014, p. 845).

> A technologically advanced economy requires a literate, numerate, technically and scientifically trained workforce to develop ideas, manage complex organizations, deliver health care services, provide financing and insurance, and operate critical infrastructure. As physical labor has given way to cognitive labor, the labor markets demand for formal analytical skills, written communication, and specific technical knowledge—what economists often loosely term cognitive skills—has risen spectacularly.

The rise in the demand for skilled, highly educated workers has increased the labor market *skill premium*—the wage of skilled workers relative to unskilled workers.

In Sect. 2.4, we analyzed the consequences of a rising skill premium. A higher skill premium has increased the demand for education and caused a rise in the relative price of college. In richer families, the children are well-prepared for college and the parents can afford the rising cost. These children not only go to college, but also graduate—ultimately receiving high returns on their human capital investments. In households below the mean, college-preparedness is poor and parents cannot afford to help much with the rising cost of tuition. For these reasons, large fractions of the population do not even attempt college and many of those that do, fail to graduate.

The policies designed to push greater fractions of young people through college have failed because of a lack of investment early in children's lives and because many students simply do not have a taste for academics. Government subsidies are predominately helping rich families whose children would have attended and graduated from college anyway. Given that the supply of skilled workers has not kept pace with the demand, the skill premium has only risen over time.

Furthermore, college graduates as a group have not fared well in the labor market—seeing at most modest increases in real wages for decades. This has contributed to a rise in "residual" wage inequality, i.e. a rise in wage inequality *among* college graduates. Only graduates with quantitative majors or ones that continue on to receive advanced degree obtain high wages. Many college graduates would have better market outcomes if they had received quality vocational training in high school.

9.1.5 Why Have Fiscal Crises Become Commonplace, Threatening the Prosperity of most Developed Countries?

The large unfunded government liabilities are primarily associated with the rise in intergenerational transfers to the elderly. Population aging, combined with the rise in medical costs and the PAYG financing of social programs, have generated rapidly growing intergenerational transfers (Sects. 5.3, 5.5, 5.6, and 8.1.1).

However, this does not explain why the broad middle class is relatively comfortable with intergenerational redistribution and rising debt. Section 2.4 offers one reason. Discretionary household consumption has become increasingly constrained by (i) the lack of median real income growth and (ii) the rise in the cost of required investments in health and education. Families needing to make the health and education investments that give their children a chance at success, have become increasingly willing to use the government to transfer the financial burden of these investments to future generations. In addition, the negative economic consequences of growing public debt have not yet been realized because international credit markets have provided funding to high-borrowing countries such as the United States.

As discussed in Sects. 3.5, 3.6, 5.5, and 8.2, politics also pays a role in the fiscal crisis. Special interest groups tend to accumulate in democracies. Politicians respond to the interest groups for political support. Driven by the perverse incentives of the common pool problem, the natural political response results in more spending and a larger and more complex government where advantages and favors to special interest groups are less transparent.

Federal government spending is dominated by mandatory "entitlement" programs, in particular Social Security, Medicare, and Medicaid. These programs are written into law and are largely protected from the annual discussion of the discretionary components of the budget. Interest groups representing the elderly, the medical profession, drug companies, and the poor have rewarded politicians with support as a result of their protection and expansion of entitlement programs. Another contributor to the fiscal crisis are the "tax expenditures," that politicians have increasingly given out in the form of tax allowances and deductions to interest groups that include homeowners, firms that provide health insurance, and rich asset holders. The frustration of the middle class has likely contributed to the increased polarization of politics that makes it difficult to reconcile the financial inconsistency of the government's policies. The result is a growing gap between spending and tax collection summarized by the fiscal gap (Sects. 5.1, 5.3, 5.5, and 5.6).

In countries at all levels of income, corruption remains a significant problem. Chapter 7 highlights the fact that corruption is particularly problematic when the country's government is able to borrow. Corruption and government debt are each higher when in the presence of the other and their interaction has a significant negative effect on economic growth. Many of the high-debt developed countries have a corruption problem that has contributed to their fiscal crisis.

9.2 The Big Four?—Climate Change

We have focused on three big problems facing the economies of developed countries over this century: the fiscal crisis, slowing economic growth, and widening wage inequality. However, there are other big-problem candidates, one of which is the economic impact of climate change.

9.2.1 The Science

The climate is changing and mostly due to human activity. The change is the result of an accumulation of several gases in our atmosphere such as water vapor, methane, nitrous oxides, chlorofluorocarbons and carbon dioxide (CO_2). These "greenhouse" gases absorb and emit radiation that heats the earth surface. The greenhouse gas with the greatest impact on the warming of the earth is CO_2, a gas that results from the burning of fossil fuels (coal, oil, and natural gas).

Increasing population and worker productivity for more than two centuries has raised GDP and the burning of fossil fuels. For example, in the US, GDP grew about 3 percent annually over the twentieth century and as result emitted 1.5 percent more CO_2 into the atmosphere every year (Nordhaus 2013, pp. 19–23). The emissions of CO_2 grew more slowly than GDP because for most of the twentieth century the CO_2-intensity of our economy (CO_2/GDP) has fallen. This means the efficiency of our energy use has improved but not enough to keep emissions from rising.

Scientists form baseline projections of the CO_2 growth over the twenty-first century based on the counterfactual assumption (we hope) that no policies will be passed to limit or constrain CO_2 emissions. This approach to forming projections is needed to inform and inspire the need for policy action, in the same way, and for the same reasons, that forecasts of the fiscal gap and public debt ratios are made. The projections estimate a continued annual growth of CO_2 emissions in a range between 0.5 and 2 percent annually (Nordhaus 2013, p. 33).

The consequences of the accumulation of greenhouse gases stem from their effect on the warming of the earth's temperature. Projections based on climate models suggest the average surface temperature of the earth will rise between 3 and 7 degrees Fahrenheit or 1.7 and 4 degrees Centigrade (Emanuel 2012, p. 53). Some argue that the climate models are likely to be too conservative because they are based on gradual patterns taken from past data. They omit the effects of melting large ice sheets, disproportionate warming over the poles, and the potential warming effects of all the different pollutants that we emit (Wagner and Weitzman 2015, pp. 11–15).

The warming is predicted to cause rising sea levels, larger and more frequent extreme weather events (floods, droughts, and hurricanes), and increased acidity of the oceans. Just how significant these changes will be is difficult to determine especially if temperatures hit the upper range of the projections or beyond. Most agree that the magnitude of these climate disruptions increase at an increasing rate as temperature rises. The economic effects we discuss below are for what is believed to be the "most likely" rise in temperature, but the costs could jump sharply if temperature rises beyond that range.

9.2.2 Economic Effects

The difficult job of estimating the economic consequences of climate change requires linking the predictions about temperature change to the impact on the natural world and then relating those physical changes to effects on human welfare. The human effects arise from changes in agricultural output, the health environment, property values, and the wildlife that people value. A dollar value is attached to each of these human effects and the total dollar loss is expressed as a fraction of GDP. In short, the challenging exercise involves calculating the dollar valuation of the permanent loss in welfare caused by a given increase in temperature. The economic effects of climate change are much more uncertain than the physical effects, which are quite uncertain in their own right (Nordhaus 2018).

An oft-quoted estimate is that a 4.5°F rise in temperature, a mid-range prediction for warming, is estimated to cause a permanent annual loss equal to 1.5 percent of global GDP. This is a counterfactual calculation that attempts to answer the question, "How much lower would GDP be if we lived in a world that was 4.5°F warmer?" As temperature gradually increases over several decades to the ultimate 4.5°F rise, the loss in each decade would be increasing but would be smaller than the estimated 1.5 percent loss in global GDP. However, the estimated losses rise sharply with further increases in temperature. Because of the significant uncertainties associated with climate change, the policy response to global warming should be aggressive to provide some *insurance* against the possibility of quite large losses if temperature increases toward the upper range of estimates or beyond.

It is also important to note that the costs of global warming vary significantly across geographical location and a country's stage of development. The climate in many places on earth is already too warm and volatile, resulting in low agricultural productivity and unhealthy environments. Further increases in temperature will create larger losses in these areas than in location with colder climates. In addition, richer and technologically advanced economies can more easily adapt to rising temperatures in ways that minimize the cost—changes in farm technologies, preventive health care responses, more air conditioning at work and home, migration of businesses and residents away from coastal areas, and creation of flood barriers. The welfare loss will be a much larger percent of GDP in the developing countries of Africa, Asia, and South American than in Europe and the Unites States. This suggests that increasing economic development of poor countries is one way of reducing the global cost of climate change.

9.2.3 The Policy Response

The insights of economic theory are fundamental to understanding the reasons for climate change and its potential remedy. Introductory economics teaches us that markets fail to efficiently allocate resources in the presence of *externalities*—byproducts of economic activity that cause benefits or damages to those not directly involved in the market transactions. Negative externalities are external damages or social costs that are not included in the market prices that reflect only the private costs associated with producing a good or service. Market prices are too low from a social perspective causing too much of the good to be produced and traded; a misallocation of resources that lowers overall welfare.

Climate change is associated with particularly difficult externalities. First, the totality of the damages caused by climate change is hard to estimate, or even imagine. Second, the worst damages will occur far into the future, impacting all young and unborn generations. Third, the damages escape not just economic transactions or local communities but entire countries, affecting everyone on earth with disproportionate damages occurring in poor countries that do not generate most of the CO_2 emissions.

Economic theory tells us that we can efficiently reduce the pace of global warming by internalizing the social cost associated with CO_2 emissions. Economic activity that generates these emissions needs to confront not only the private resource cost of the activity but also the social cost. This can in principle be done by levying a sales tax equal to the marginal social cost (MSC) caused by the CO_2 emitted when one unit of the good is produced and used. This way the market price (P) will reflect both the marginal private resource cost (MPC) and the marginal social cost, $P = MC = MPC + MSC$.

Estimating the MSC of a given amount of CO_2 emissions is even harder than the job of answering the static counterfactual question of how much lower our GDP would be if we lived in a world with higher temperatures. This is because the MSC is the present value of the rise in social costs at every point in time into the indefinite future. The precise path of the rise in costs and the discount factor used to compute the present value of those costs matters quite a bit, creating more sources of debate.

Economists typically think of the discount factor as being determining by the opportunity cost of funds. For example, the fundamental value of a stock is estimated by discounting the expected stream of dividends from owning the stock. For the discount rate you might use the interest rate on long-term corporate debt that you could purchase instead of the stock. In the climate change context you can think of investing a dollar of current resources to raise the real income of future generations by lowering current CO_2 emissions and the related future economic damages. Alternatively you could invest that same dollar of resources into physical or human capital that would also raise the income of future generations. From this perspective, you should use the rate of return to investment in physical or human capital, typically thought to be between 5 and 10 percent annually, to form the discount rate. Others argue that it is unethical to discount the damages to future generations at all, calling for a discount rate closer to zero. Even if you could reliably estimate the rise in temperature cause by additional CO_2 emitted today, and the associated damages caused over time, you could still debate the value for the discount factor.

William Nordhaus, the Nobel Prize winning economist, has used discount rates of 4 percent (Nordhaus 2013) and 6 percent (Nordhaus 2008) based on conservative estimates of the annualized rate of return to physical capital, the annualized $r - \delta$ from earlier chapters. In 2005-dollars, his models generate a \$28 marginal social cost from one additional ton of CO_2 emissions (Nordhaus 2008, Table 5-1). He cites a more recent government study that argues for a similar MSC of \$25 (Nordhaus 2013, p. 228). He also notes that a carbon tax of this magnitude is a good starting point if the goal is to keep the rise in global temperatures to about 4.5° over this century.

However, as CO_2 continues to accumulate in the atmosphere, the MSC and the carbon tax needed to maintain the 4.5° temperature increase will both rise. By mid-twenty-first century the carbon tax needs to be about \$160 to stay on target. This tax rate is also close to the estimated MSC at that time, implying that the 4.5° target is roughly consistent with the socially optimal level of emissions that satisfies P = MPC + MSC. Trying to target a significantly smaller temperature rise would be inefficient because the tax rate would have to be higher, causing market prices to be higher than marginal costs, i.e. P = MPC + Carbon Tax > MPC + MSC.

To get a feel for how the carbon tax would affect familiar prices, note that 0.00889 tons of CO_2 is emitted per gallon of gas burned. So, if the carbon tax is \$100, the marginal costs of using gas would be 88 cents higher.

The numbers discussed above are conditional on another big assumption—full international participation. In other words, the statement that a schedule of carbon taxes starting at \$25 now and rising to \$160 by mid-century will be consistent with a 4.5° temperature increase over the century assumes that *all countries simultaneously* impose the carbon tax. If there are important "free-riding" countries that fail to tax CO_2 emissions, then the tax that participating countries will have to levy to stay on target increases.

9.2.4 The Climate Crisis and the Fiscal Crisis

The problem of climate change and the likelihood of a prompt policy response to it bears some resemblance to the fiscal crisis. Both problems have been a long time in the making: decades of greenhouse gas accumulation for climate change and decades of population aging and expanded transfer payments to retirees for the fiscal crisis. The necessary policy responses will be costly, creating an incentive for politicians and the public to ignore the problems. Ignoring the problems means their burden will be felt mostly by young and unborn generations. Inaction also increases the chance of sudden and dramatic increases in their social costs, stemming from "tipping point" and "crisis of confidence" effects when temperature change and government debt ratios exceed looming thresholds. There is an important international dimension at play in both cases. International cooperation is crucial in lowering the shared cost of slowing global warming and the limits of continued international lending to the US will determine the timing of the fiscal crisis fallout.

As mentioned in Chap. 8, the problems are related in another way. Imposing a significant carbon tax will discourage activities that cause greenhouse gas accumulation and encourage the development and use of cleaner energy sources. In addition, the revenue collected from the carbon tax would be one step toward reducing government budget deficits.

9.2.5 Summary

For the US, it is likely that the fiscal crisis will be the first problem to impose severe costs in the form of a major economic recession, higher taxes, and reduced government support for retirees. The policies that created the fiscal crisis have already contributed to the long-run growth slowdown by favoring consumption of current generations over various investments in the future. There are more uncertainties about the path and costs of climate change. These uncertainties include the chance of catastrophic loses as the century unfolds, suggesting a significant policy response is needed now to insure against them.

The economics of climate change is important, challenging, and interesting. It deserves at least a mention in this book because government failure is at the dead center of the issue. An entire course would be required to delve into climate change properly. Here are some recommendations on how to begin a self-study. Comfortable but authoritative starting points are Emanuel (2012) and Nordhaus (2013). Recent surveys on the economic effects of climate change that could be used in introductory economics courses include McKitrick (2016) and Harris et al. (2017). More details on the assumptions and models used to estimate the effects of climate change can be found in Tol (2009) and in Nordhaus (2008, 2018). Wagner and Weitzman (2015) warn about the chances for catastrophic losses. Kotlikoff et al. (2019) examine how the net gain of slowing climate change can be shared across generations.

9.3 The Big Four?—Robots

Automation of production is another change facing economies of the developed world that many see as having potentially problematic side-effects. The pace of digital innovations and their diffusion throughout the economy has accelerated in recent years, driven by the widespread adoption of the mobile Internet in the last decade. There are now several billion connected handheld computer devices globally, greatly facilitating e-commerce and the migration of market and non-market activity to the cloud. This is the third wave of digitalization, following the second wave (the PC era from the 1970s to mid-2000s) and the first wave which came after the invention of the digital Computer in the 1940s. As discussed in Sect. 8.1.2, it is currently unclear how important these innovations will be in rescuing the decline in worker productivity growth. However, it does seem clear that the digital age is creating significant structural transformations throughout the economy.

New digital, internet- based ways of organizing production of existing and new goods and services affect broad swaths of the economy, both in industry and services. Amazon and Alibaba have greatly expanded e-retail, disrupting bricks and mortar retailers in the process. Uber and Lyft pioneered shared cars; autonomous, connected, shared cars full of software and resembling moving robots are transforming the car industry. Airbnb likewise is changing the hospitality industry. Numerous startups in the financial sector, *fintech* companies like Lending Tree and Mint, are changing the financial services industry with peer to peer lending and investment services offered by robo-advisors. The health and education sectors are teeming with startups to deliver services in new ways. Even the nature of money is changing, with the emergence of so-called cryptocurrencies, such as bitcoin, which are forms of digital private money. The Internet of Things will connect billions of machines and generate huge amounts of data which will be monetized the way Facebook and Google monetize data for people using their platforms.

The latest wave of advances in the digital economy is about 10 years old and is based on the availability of low cost, high speed, mobile computer devices like the iPhone that connect hundreds of millions of users. The Internet of Things promises to connect more and more elements of our fixed and mobile infrastructure. Data has been called the currency of the new digital economy. In addition to the migration of market activity to the cloud, firms like Google and Facebook offer valuable search and social networking services to people at no charge. In the process, they also collect large quantities of data from users of their platforms. The data can then be analyzed to ascertain the preferences and characteristics of users (data analytics). Crunching big data allows firms to make better decisions about what ads to target to which consumers and to assess risks of various kinds, ranging from credit and disease risks to the risk of jet engine failure. Artificial Intelligence of this type requires both vast quantities of digital data and high speed computers to analyze it. Algorithms sift through this data and make possible the automation of tasks that previously only humans could perform, such as driving cars, perform natural language translation, providing financial advice, and helping detect cancer or other diseases.

Professor Schwab, the president of the World Economic Forum, calls these exciting developments the fourth industrial revolution. Like electricity and the internal combustion engine in earlier eras, the new digital ways of doing things are the manifestation of a "general purpose technology" that will permeate the entire economy, reduce transactions costs and simplify trade, improve the matching of buyers and sellers, cut out the middleman, and offer lower cost and superior value to consumers.

9.3.1 Smart Machines and the Future of Work

There are concerns about a darker side of the new technologies. To begin with, some worry about market concentration and abuse of monopoly power (Brynjolfsson and McAfee 2014). Digital goods and services can be produced and delivered at low marginal costs, eliminating the capital capacity constraints and transportation costs that limit the scale of a company's operations. Selling products on the Internet also has the advantage of creating networks that allow for the rapid expansion of demand. The more people use a network, the more valuable the network is, which helps attract new users. Incumbents may steer people to their proprietary goods and services. Disadvantaged late comers and outsiders could call for government regulation. The collection of large quantities of data likewise gives rise to privacy concerns.

Then there are concerns about smart machines replacing people. Machines replacing workers have been an issue for centuries. In early nineteenth century England, during the original industrial revolution, textile workers threatened by the adoption of new technologies sabotaged weaving machines in protest. The rebellion was put down by the British Army, allowing the new technologies to dominate modes of production. Similarly, the new wave of automation is changing the shape of the workplace. Self-driving cars and trucks could endanger the jobs of millions of taxi and truck drivers. Developing countries in Asia that depend on labor intensive manufacturing could see hundreds of thousands of textile and shoe making jobs disappear. Higher wages in these countries could soon combine with declining cost of robots and improvements in their dexterity to incentivize multinational companies to automate their operations. Service jobs are also being transformed. Already tasks previously performed by paralegals have been automated. Sports writers face competition from computer systems that can write the story of a ball game once they receive data about it. Routine accounting and economic teaching and forecasting tasks are being automated. The emergence of Artificial Intelligence systems, like IBM's Watson, could threaten the jobs of skilled workers. In a much-cited article, Frey and Osborne (2017) estimate that almost 50 percent of jobs will be threatened by 2025. Studies for South East Asian countries by the International Labor Office (ILO) come to similar conclusions. Acemoglu and Restrepo (2017) find that are already negative effects of robots on employment and wages in the U.S.

Other authors dispute these findings. Bessen (2015) looks at the connection between digital innovation, wages, and wealth using case studies. He concludes that in sectors that underwent computer automation jobs grew and wages increased. For example, typesetters were replaced by graphic designers and the expansion of ATMs lowered the cost of banking, which allowed expansion of bank branches and bank employment. A recent OECD study finds the effects of computers on jobs will be much less dire than predicted by Frey and Osborne (see Nedelkoska and Quintini 2018). Due to the innovations of today, large numbers of new occupations and jobs will be created. As was the case in the past, new technology destroys some jobs but creates others.

9.3.2 A Model with Robots

We assess the concerns about automation and possible policy responses with the help of a variant of our overlapping-generations model developed by Sachs and Kotlikoff (2012). As in our model, it features people who live for two periods and have logarithmic utility. An important twist in their model is that there are now *three* factors of production: unskilled labor, H^u, skilled labor, H^s, and machines, K. We can now think of capital or machines as "robots" because we will assume that capital substitutes (replaces) unskilled labor. Young workers supply one unit of unskilled labor inelastically that is a perfect substitute for K in the production of an intermediate input, Q, which is then combined with skilled labor to produce the final good.

Young workers use their unskilled wage for three purchases: consumption goods, physical capital, as before, and now also training courses that result in enhanced job skills. The training courses are purchased when young and the resulting human capital is not used until the following period. In practice, the training could be provided on the job, financed by firms via a reduction in the wage a worker would have otherwise received—what is referred to as "on-the-job" training. So, in the Sachs-Kotlikoff model, there is no retirement period and only the old workers are skilled.

The new production functions with three inputs is an adjusted version of the Cobb-Douglas production function,

$$Y_t = Q_t^{\alpha}\left(H_t^s\right)^{1-\alpha},$$

where $Q_t = \theta H_t^u + (1-\theta)BK_t$. The technology parameters now include θ, the relative productivity of unskilled labor compared to machines, and B, which captures innovations in the type or effectiveness of machines. The parameter B is similar to TFP but applies only to the productivity of machines. Increases in B capture the new technologies discussed above in our description of digital innovations.

An increase in B affects the marginal productivity of unskilled and skilled labor very differently because unskilled labor is assumed to be a *substitute* for machines and skilled labor a *complement* with machines in production. The marginal products of the two types of labor are

$$\frac{\partial Y_t}{\partial H_t^u} = \alpha\theta\left(\frac{H_t^s}{Q_t}\right) \text{ and } \frac{\partial Y_t}{\partial H_t^s} = (1-\alpha)\left(\frac{Q_t}{H_t^s}\right)$$

An increase in B increases Q, lowering the marginal product of unskilled labor and raising the marginal product of skilled labor. Thus, machine innovations widen the inequality between skilled and unskilled labor.

There is a long-run negative consequence to the fall in the marginal product and wages of unskilled labor when machine innovations occur. Young workers use their wages to finance saving and investment in human and physical capital. An event that lowers the unskilled wage this period will lower the accumulation of human and physical capital for the next period, serving to weaken economic growth.

9.3.3 Comments

1. First, the assumption that younger workers are *substitutes* for smart machines is not generally true. The advance of smart machines creates new jobs for workers with the right vocational training. Countries with better vocational education in high school could prepare young workers to *complement* the new technologies by, for example, learning to operate and maintain the new machines.
   At present, skills mismatches and skills shortages exist in many occupations related to the new digital technologies. Robot operators and software engineers are among the skills in short supply. Broad-based vocational education and training must be upgraded to equip the working population with the skills demanded by industry and help it adapt to automation. A three-way partnership between educational institutions, government, and industry is needed to reexamine core education in high school and college, strengthen the STEM fields and upgrade educational priorities for the digital age. Innovations in technologies and physical capital will benefit young workers if complementarities can be created through vocational training early in life.
   Fear of "robots" creates yet another argument, adding to those discussed in Sect. 8.1.4, for greater focus on developing well-designed vocational training in high school.
2. The rise in wage inequality, seen in most developed countries over the last 30 to 40 years, is one of our Big Three economic problems of this century (see Sects. 1.8, 2.4, and 8.1.3). Much of the rise in inequality stems from a growing gap in years of schooling between those with at least a 4 year college degree and the majority of workers without a college degree. In addition, the return to education has never been higher. The wage premium for a college educated worker is almost twice that of a high-school educated worker in the United States because the supply of college-educated workers has not kept pace with the demand. The years-of-education gap and the growing college wage premium are relevant for the *lifetime wages* of workers from a *common birth-cohort* and thus are not related to the mechanism that Sachs and Kotlikoff have in mind.
   However, Sachs and Kotlikoff do provide some evidence that a steepening of the *life-cycle wage profile* has occurred over the Post WWII period that may have contributed to measures of wage inequality across households that do not adjust for worker age. They look at the median income of men aged 45-54 compared to those aged 25-34 and find the ratio was just 1.04 in 1950 but grew dramatically to 1.41 by 2011. Since the growth in average years of schooling over this period, albeit weak, would serve to *lower* the income ratio (older workers have, on average, fewer years of schooling than younger workers), we can conclude that there has been a significant steepening in the life-cycle wage profile of an individual worker. This could be because the shift in occupations toward the service sector and away from manufacturing increases the importance of on-the-job training, which is quite consistent with the Sachs-Kotlikoff story. Smarter

machines, an increase in B, raises the relatively productivity of skilled labor and the "on-the-job training premium" as described in their model.

3. Beyond creating greater wage inequality between younger and older workers, the Sachs-Kotlikoff model predicts that a rise in B would slow saving and investment by young workers in human and physical capital. A windfall from an improvement in the marginal product of capital is all consumed by the generation that owns the capital. The return of skilled labor also goes up. The generation that owns the capital stock is therefore better off. However, the young see their wages decline, which makes them unable to invest as much, leaving them and all other future generations worse off.

   Sachs and Kotlikoff suggest that the government can ameliorate this intergenerational injustice by nationalizing part of the capital stock and using the permanent income from its wealth to run a large welfare scheme (a universal basic income) across all generations. This helps all generations benefit from the improvement in technology.

   Alternatively, *private* intergenerational transfers could break this underinvestment result and remove their poverty trap. Both the altruistic and the warm-glow motives for intergenerational transfers (see Das et al. 2018, Chapter 2) imply that when one generation experiences an exogenous gain in income, some of the gain will be transferred to their children. Bequests allow the young to benefit from the windfall, lessening any negative effect from the drop in unskilled wages.

4. The Sachs-Kotlikoff model offers a possible explanation for the rise in the capital share of income that was documented in Chap. 4. In their model the marginal product of capital is

$$\frac{\partial Y_t}{\partial Q_t}\frac{\partial Q_t}{\partial K_t} = \alpha Q_t^{\alpha-1}(1-\theta)B\left(H_t^s\right)^{1-\alpha} = \alpha(1-\theta)\left(\frac{H_t^s}{Q_t}\right)^{1-\alpha}.$$

   As in the basic overlapping-generations model, the marginal product of capital is equated to the market rental rate paid to capital owners, r_t. The capital share of income can then be written as

$$\frac{r_t K_t}{Y_t} = \frac{\alpha(1-\theta)BK_t\left(H_t^s/Q_t\right)^{1-\alpha}}{Q_t^\alpha\left(H_t^s\right)^{1-\alpha}} = \frac{\alpha(1-\theta)BK_t}{Q_t} = \frac{\alpha}{1+\left(\frac{\theta}{(1-\theta)B}\right)\left(\frac{H_t^u}{K_t}\right)}.$$

   Note that if $\theta = 0$, then $Q_t = BK_t$, and the capital share is once again the constant α. In this case, an increase in B raises the marginal product of capital and output proportionately, leaving the capital share unchanged. If $\theta > 0$, an increase in B causes a rise in the productivity of capital relative to unskilled labor (whose productivity is unaffected by B) and increases the capital share because the marginal product of capital increases more than total output. Thus, technological innovation in machines and machine productivity can explain a rise in the capital share if machines and unskilled labor are substitutes in production.

However, there are other explanations for the rising capital share that are unrelated to technological innovations that cause physical capital to substitute for unskilled labor in firms. For example, most of the rise in the capital share is due to a rise in the rental income from housing capital not firm-based capital (Furman and Orzag 2015; Rognlie 2015).

9.4 The Big Four?—Pandemics

The coronavirus disease (COVID-19) was first identified in Wuhan China during December of 2019. The virus spreads quickly and has potentially dangerous effects on human respiratory functioning that can lead to long-term damage and death. The World Health Organization (WHO) declared COVID-19 a public health emergency of international concern on January 30, 2020. To emphasize the gravity of the situation, the WHO declared the outbreak a pandemic in March 2020. Pandemics of this nature may become more common in the twenty-first century because humans are encroaching on animal habitats, where many of the viruses originate, and because the world has become more globalized, allowing contagious disease to travel more quickly from country to country.[1]

Contagious diseases are a major public health issue that require a coordinated government response to control. The justification for government intervention is based on negative externalities associated with individual choices and actions, similar to those caused by various kinds of pollution including the CO_2 emissions we discussed in Sect. 9.2. If individuals fail to take action to avoid transmission of the virus, they not only endanger themselves but everyone they come into contact with as well. Natural and health environments are both public goods that need government intervention to create socially optimal investment in their protection. Of course, there can be differences of opinion on the extent of the intervention based on different valuations of the public good being protected and different assessments of the government's ability to devise and carry out appropriate policies. However, no government intervention is clearly a suboptimal approach.

The US provides an example where the government response was sub-optimal. In mid-February 2020 the virus landed in Washington State causing the first outbreak. Past neglect of the public health system for dealing with pandemics, along with government leadership that downplayed the risks, gave the virus a chance to take hold and spread. Masks and other protective equipment for frontline nurses were insufficient until well into the spring. Lacking a coordinated national approach, the availability of protective equipment for nurses and treatments for patients was drastically different across the country. The differences resulted from variation in

[1]Governments have been warned about their lack of preparedness for pandemics and the likely consequences for the economy and human welfare. See Garrett (2007) for such a discussion based on lessons learned from the 1918 flu pandemic.

the capabilities of local communities and their hospitals to find suppliers and afford procurements.

As the virus spread, government advocacy for social distancing and mask-wearing by the general public was conflicted and confused. The relatively minor act of wearing a mask was turned into a fiercely combative political football match. The development of testing was slow relative to other countries with less wealth and less human capital expertise. In many places where the rise in cases was eventually abated, the local and national governments were too quick to encourage people to interact as before, leading to a dramatic resurgence in cases and deaths. As a consequence, the richest and most powerful country in the world experienced a disproportionate number of cases and deaths, even after scaling for the size of its population.

9.4.1 Short-Run Economic Effects

The economic effects of a pandemic result from the interplay of three important responses. First, production and trading are restricted, either by government decree or the private decisions of managers and workers to safeguard themselves from a contagious work environment. The switch to a second-best technology for production and trade amounts to a pure supply-side shock, a decrease in the value of TFP below that associated with first-best practices. Second, the fear of contracting the disease causes customers to pull back on trading and spending, independent of the situation on the supply side (i.e. even if no restrictions were imposed on production and trading technologies). This negative demand-side shock is partly due to people not purchasing goods and services that require face-to-face contact with suppliers and other customers and partly due to fear of income loss associated with voluntary or involuntary layoffs from work. Finally, there is fiscal and monetary response of the government authorities as they try to replace the drop in private income with transfers and loans.

In the US the net effect of these three responses was dramatic. After a historical record of 128 straight months of uninterrupted growth in real GDP, beginning with the initial recovery from the Great Recession in June 2009, COVID 19 caused a sharp contraction in real GDP during the first two quarters of 2020—an annualized decline of 5% in the first quarter followed by an astounding 33% decline in the second quarter. The unemployment jumped from about 3.5% at the end of February to above 14% for the period March to June.

Several studies have already been conducted to try to identify whether the collapse in economic activity was due to *voluntary* choices by customers, workers, and businesses to avoid social interaction ("fear") or due to government *mandates* to social distance ("lockdowns"). Most of the studies indicate that fear contributed more to the reduction in customer mobility and job loss than the lockdowns themselves. Some indicate that the biggest effect of the lockdowns was to redirect activity away from nonessential business in more crowded areas (e.g. restaurants, bars, gyms, and other in-person services) and toward grocery stores. By altering the allocation of spending, the lockdowns could have reduced the spread of the virus even if they did not contribute to the majority of the decline in overall economic activity.

In addition, it appears that the timing of the lockdowns matter. If the lockdowns come late, after infections have become widespread, then even relatively small increases in overall mobility when lockdowns are eased can cause infections to jump. A late lockdown that is eased too early is a bad recipe for controlling the spread of a contagious virus.[2]

The US recession caused by COVID-19 would have been much worse if not for a massive policy response on the part of the federal government and the central bank (the "Fed," short for the Federal Reserve). In quick fashion, the federal government passed the CARES Act to bolster incomes of the many households and small businesses. The combined effect of the new legislation, the loss of tax revenue due to the shrinking tax base, and the automatic increases in spending that occur when incomes fall (such are Medicaid and Food Stamps) caused 2.5 trillion dollars in federal government debt to be issued from the beginning of March to the beginning of June. Even without additional government stimulus, in the form of further spending programs and cuts in taxes, the federal deficit is projected to approach 4 trillion dollars in 2020 (depending on the size of the continued stimulus response and tax losses from a stubborn recovery) or about 18 percent of GDP. The pre-COVID projection for 2020 was a 1 trillion dollar deficit. Currently, negotiations are underway to legislate new stimulus legislation that will raise the 2020 deficit further.

The Fed's actions have been even more dramatic. It has ramped up its usual practice of increasing private bank reserves to lower the Federal Funds interest rate in the overnight credit market used by bankers. It has also taken the bigger steps of lowering the discount rate they charge to private banks when they borrow from the central bank and reducing private bank capital requirements to encourage the private banks to lend more. Deviating from business as usual, the Fed has become very active as the "lender of last resort" in all sorts of credit markets. In the government bond market, the Fed purchased 1.6 trillion dollars of government debt, out of the 2.5 trillion issued to finance the deficit as of mid-year 2020. Thus, well over half of the rise in the government deficit is being financed by "printing money" rather than by borrowing from the private sector and foreign sources. This is because when the Fed purchases newly issued debt it gives the government cash, not previously in circulation, to spend on their programs. In addition, the Fed has setup special facilities allowing them to directly lend to virtually everyone: corporations, mid-size businesses, nonprofits, state and local governments, as well as international central banks.

The large spending stimulus provided by fiscal and monetary policy has been widely supported by politicians, economists, and the general public. The policy

---

[2]See Goolsbee and Syverson (2020), and the studies they reference, for examples of early research efforts using cell phone data. The "Geometry of the Pandemic" in *The Economist* July 25, p. 19 discusses research associated with the timing of lockdowns. Correia et al. (2020), using data from the US flu pandemic of 1918, find that cities that locked down earlier and longer had better long-run economic outcomes.

response was necessary to help minimize the sharp drop in economic activity beginning in March 2020. Much uncertainty remains over the exact path of the virus and it is appropriate that central authorities do what they can to limit the economic damage. However, this does not preclude the possibility of longer run negative consequences associated with the massive increases in government debt and the money supply.

9.4.2 Long-Run Economic Effects

The large stimulus needed to keep economies afloat during the pandemic has worsened an already precarious long-run fiscal position in many countries.[3] Before the pandemic, the US Debt to GDP ratio was projected to rise from a value of approximately 80 percent in 2020 to 100 percent by 2030. Due to the appearance of COVID-19, the projection for 2030 has jumped to the 110 to 120 percent range (a historical high including the WWII period).

As we have previously discussed, the US has been fortunate to service its public debt in recent decades at very low interest rates. Despite its anemic national saving rate, the US has expanded its debt at low interest rates because foreign lending has also expanded. Currently foreigners hold about 40 percent of outstanding US debt. However, there are reasons to believe that the US will finally be reaching the limit of its cheap funding. Foreigners have only financed 20 percent of newly issued government debt over the last decade, causing the fraction of total government debt held by foreigners to dip from 50 percent to the current value of 40 percent. The contribution from our previously large lenders, China and Japan, has barely increased over this period. The largest international lenders to the US over the decade have been the UK and Ireland.

The increasingly poisoned relations with China suggests that they will now lend less to the US and the large European stimulus response to the pandemic has reduced their ability to lend abroad. The US has been able to absorb the sharp increase in debt during 2020 in part because of a dramatic rise in precautionary saving by its own households and firms. However, once the pandemic subsides and the recovery strengthens, the saving rate will likely decline back to its low long-run level. It should also be remembered that the largest source of the long-run fiscal crisis comes from the unfunded social programs of advanced economies. The drop in payroll tax revenue because of the pandemic in the US has moved up the projected date, by 2–3 years—to as early as 2031 for Social Security and 2023 for Medicare, when entitlement program trust funds will be exhausted. At these dates, benefits would have to be significantly cut unless payroll tax rates were raised.

[3]For data sources and discussions of the impact of the pandemic on the fiscal crisis see Brian Riedl, "Who Will Fund the $24 trillion in New Debt," *National Review*, July 28, 2020, "How Much is the National Debt? What are the Different Measures Used?," *Peter G. Peterson Foundation*, June 5, 2020, "Updated Budget Projection Show the Fiscal Toll of the COVID-19 Pandemic," *Committee for a Responsible Budget*, June 24, 2020.

This scenario means the Fed and other central banks will have to continue their roles as the lenders of last resort. Even after economies recover, the shortages of funds will put pressure on central banks to purchase government debt and essentially money-finance deficits as we move into the middle of this century. Large money supply increases across the globe during time of normal economic activity will lead to higher inflation. However, a return of inflation may be viewed as the least costly way to deal with the fiscal crisis.

9.4.3 New Generational Tensions

The generational conflict associated with the fiscal crisis has worsened because of the pandemic. Reduced economic activity, due to voluntary and involuntary attempts to increase social distancing and suppress the virus, disproportionately benefits older retired households and disproportionately hurts younger working households and students. The extra debt associated with the government stimulus will also disproportionately burden younger generations as government programs are cut and taxes are increased in the future to service the new debt and prevent additional borrowing.

These generational considerations increase the pressure on central bankers to continue to buy government debt and increase the money supply even after the virus dissipates and economies begin to recover. As mentioned, continued money growth after economies start growing will increase inflation rates. Currently, inflation and inflationary expectations are very low, so any rise in inflation will be unanticipated. This means older households will be hurt by inflation because they are locked into the low-interest government bonds purchased over recent years. The accommodating monetary stance will help the government repay debt because tax revenue increases as inflation pushes nominal incomes higher, while the interest expenses on bonds issued before the rise in inflationary expectations stay fixed. The more inflation is used to repay debt, the fewer tax rate increases or spending cuts will be needed, which helps younger generations that have not yet built up their retirement savings and are not currently holding much low-interest government debt.

The ability to use inflation as a way of reducing debt burdens is partly a function of the types of government securities outstanding. Inflation is most effective when the outstanding debt is composed of securities with longer maturity because the asset holder is then locked into low-interest rates for a longer period of time before the government would have to refinance with newly issued debt (at higher interest rates that reflect the rise in inflationary expectations). The average maturity of US debt is currently about 5 years, so there is some scope for using inflation as a substitute for tax rate increases or spending cuts to service debt obligations.

While inflation could be used to reduce repayment of outstanding debt, it will do nothing to reduce the burden of the government's unfunded liabilities under its entitlement programs. The benefits under Social Security, and effectively under Medicare insurance as well, are indexed to the rate of inflation. Thus, as nominal tax revenue rises with inflation, so will the nominal payments under the large transfers programs.

Using monetary policy and inflation to finance government debt is very common in middle income countries where central banks are more directly tied to the government. Central banks in advanced economies have become more independent from their governments over the twentieth century and have not typically been willing to use money creation to finance government budget deficits. However, central bank behavior during the pandemic has shifted dramatically and these generational considerations provide another reason to believe that a large dose of money financing of government deficits may continue over this decade.[4]

There are alternatives to inflation that the government could use to shift the burden of its public debt to older households. The first is to institute or increase a federal consumption tax. While retired households can avoid wages taxation from payroll and income taxes, this is not true of a consumption tax. The more dramatic alternative, which has actually been threatened in recent years, is to simply default on interest or principle repayments to public debt holders. Recall from our discussion in Chap. 2 that default is a risky approach because if the market senses this as even a possibility it could force the government's hand by selling off government debt and driving interest rates up to the point that default is the government's only practical alternative.

9.5 Is Government Failure Inevitable?

This book is about government failure. Government leadership in creating public capital, laws, and services that facilitate private enterprise is necessary to initiate and sustain growth. In many societies around the world, the public interest that motivates good governance is dominated by private interest of those in power to such an extent that modern sustained growth is never achieved. Perhaps more difficult to understand is why governments, that at one time did provide the necessary leadership, begin to fail, contributing to an economic growth slowdown that prevents successful societies from progressing.

The issue of government failure is connected to the broader question of why successful societies slip back, often quite dramatically. There are general theories of decline that claim failure is inevitable—fundamental flaws in human nature interact with success in a way that leads to a reversal of fortune.[5] Government failure in successful societies can be thought of as a reflection of these underlying fundamental flaws. Why can't we learn from past failures and use the government to help discipline human weakness?

[4]A discussion of post-pandemic inflation can be found in L. Pastor, "Why Inflation Could Follow the Crisis," *Chicago Booth Review*, June 8, 2020.

[5]See a survey of these theories by Ophlus (2012).

As mentioned earlier, there are reasons for growth slowdowns that are independent of human behavior per se. Limits in resources and human abilities create diminishing returns to investment in physical and human capital—a basic assumption of economic analysis. But how societies respond to diminishing returns determines *how much* growth declines. Humans are hardwired, from their long evolution as hunter-gathers, to survive day-to-day. This causes us to focus much more on the present than the future. The recent research in behavioral economics argues the pull of present consumption is so strong it causes us to behave "irrationally." We save and exercise less, and smoke and eat more, than we really want to (see Thaler 2015 for a discussion of self-control). Diminishing returns, that weaken the payoffs to investment, nudge us toward our natural instincts to consume at high rates.

The accumulated wealth from past investments also naturally causes hunter-gathers to conserve energy by focusing on easy pickings. Why not become better-off by arguing that we deserve a bigger share of all this wealth? The existing wealth of rich societies creates its own force to favor redistribution over production, similar to the natural resource curse that plagues some developing countries. A growing sense of entitlement causes the proliferation of interest groups in successful societies, as noted by Olson (1982). The proliferation of interest groups creates factions that compete for the nation's wealth. Again the situation resembles that in poor countries that fail to develop because of factious conflict that undermines the national interest needed to form pro-growth policies. Lack of national interest is a problem that can affect growth at the earliest and latest stages of development.

The interest groups in the rich countries of the twentieth century began asking more of government to make life easier, safer, and fairer. The well-intended response of governments is to create more laws and provide more transfers and services—serving to promote rents over growth. This trend leads to another one of the general sources of decline in successful societies—growing complexity. Complexity is the enemy of the transparency needed to keep government honest. Complexity is also bad for growth because it forces societies to devote more resources to simply maintaining the system—a depreciation cost associated with large institutional capital. Growing complexity means more politicians, officials, bureaucrats, lawyers, analysts, lobbyists, and the professors needed to train them all. Complexity results in a myriad of unintended consequences such as greater costs of production, declining transparency, and growing income inequality because of an increased demand for highly skilled labor needed to maintain the system. Complexity biases investments away from productive skills and towards rent-seeking skills, reinforcing the "wealth curse" that created the complexity to begin with.

Success also naturally leads to complacency and hubris that takes attention away from domestic improvement and undermines international relations. The citizens, especially the key decision-makers, begin to feel content and superior. The successful country becomes defensive and fails to acknowledge and address its most important shortcomings. Uncomfortable trends that do not have immediate consequences are dismissed. Overconfidence causes policymakers to believe that all problems will eventually be solved; "perhaps not now but later, when the problem really needs to be addressed." The same sense of superiority can also cause interest in and respect for other countries to wan, making mutually advantageous economic and political international exchanges more difficult.

9.6 Historical Lessons?

> Have you derived from history any illumination of our present condition, any guidance for our judgements and policies, any guard against the rebuffs of surprise or the vicissitudes of change? Have you found any regularities in the sequence of past events that you can predict the future actions of mankind or the fate of states? Is it possible that, after all, history has no sense, that it teaches us nothing, and that the immense past was only the weary rehearsal of mistakes that the future is destined to make on a large stage and scale. — Will and Ariel Durant, *The Lessons of History*, p. 11.

One of our favorite quotes is from Harry Truman, "the only thing new in the world is the history you never learned." When pondering the fate of successful countries, it is natural to turn to the grand societies of history—the empires. Empires are extreme cases of ambitious governance that should clearly exhibit the determinants of the inevitable decline. Parsons (2010) argues that all empires are unsustainable because their conquered subjects find them intolerable. Alexander the Great perhaps sensed this source of failure. Although the exact motives are unclear, he promoted a homogenizing culture that would blur the lines between the conquerors and their subjects. His untimely death took with him the chance of a stable nation state. His empire quickly dissolved into a factious pursuit of power that led to decades of revolts, constantly shifting alliances, and civil war (Romm 2010).

In the more long-lasting empires, there may be some lessons about institutions and laws that address the human failings—hubris, concerns over income and wealth distribution, inability to deal with complexity, diminished national identity, and lack of focus on the future—that limit sustained progress. Thucydides, one of the world's first historians, believed that, because of the enduring common characteristics of human nature, the lessons from history are potentially valuable to the societies of the day.[6] We agree with Thucydides but, as suggested by Truman's quote, the lessons of history are typically ignored.

---

[6]Woodruff (1993) offers an introduction to the work of Thucydides.

[7]For a history of the Western Roman Empire see, for example, Ward-Perkins (2005), Woolf (2012), Beard (2015), or the classic by Gibbon, perhaps in abridged form: Gibbon (2003). For comparisons to the United States, see Murphy (2007), Smil (2010), and Hubbard and Kane (2013). Beard (2015), Holland (2016) and Strauss (2019) discuss how Augustus and Tiberius, Rome's first emperors, limited conflict within and outside the Empire.

9.6.1 Is the United States, Rome?

The Roman Empire, often viewed as the leading example of a lasting and successful empire, has been the subject of an immense literature, including works that draw comparisons to the United States today.[7] The Roman Empire formed over the course of several centuries. The creation and expansion of the Empire was not initially due to any grand plan. Its expansion was more the result of a struggle over resources by neighboring conquest states. Over the third century BC, the Romans achieved significant success in the struggle for resources. Roman dominion over territory and peoples expanded to include much of the area surrounding the Mediterranean Sea.

However, the success was not evenly shared across the population and served to widen wealth inequality between the aristocracy and the common people. Growing population, natural resource devastation from wars, and a large influx of slave labor eroded the economic position of small farmers and urban workers, further widening inequality. The general population of Roman citizens and their newly formed Italian allies outside of Rome became increasingly frustrated with their economic and political standing.

In the middle of the second century BC, some members of the aristocracy responded to, or perhaps fed on, the frustration by developing a "populist" platform that addressed the concerns of citizens and allies within the empire. The populists attempted to push through aggressive policies such as land redistribution and expanded citizenship by circumventing the generally resistant aristocracy of the Roman Senate—breaking formal and informal procedures that had previously created the bonds of trust and mutual interest needed to hold the Republic together. The breakdown in the spirit of compromise and respect led to many violent confrontations. The situation was summarized in a brief history of Rome written by Velleius Paterculus around AD 30.

> This was the beginning in Rome of civil blood-shed, and the license of the sword. From this time on right was crushed by might, the most powerful now took precedence in the state, the disputes of citizens which were once healed by amicable agreements were now settled by arms, and wars were now begun not for good cause but for what profit there was in them. Nor is this to be wondered at; for precedents do not stop where they begin, but, however narrow the path upon which they enter, they create for themselves a highway whereon they may wander with the utmost latitude; and when once the path of right is abandoned, men are hurried into wrong in headlong haste, nor does anyone think a course is base for himself which has proven profitable to others (pp. 53–54).

Paterculus hinted at factors that accelerated the violence and eventually destroyed the Republic. The initial success of Rome bred two human reactions that led to further expansion, now more by design than necessity. First, Romans began to feel superior and even chosen—because of their success the gods must favor them over others. It became their right and duty to continue to expand. Second, conquest became a necessity for the politically ambitious. The public supported successful generals, who brought glory and resources home to Rome, for high office. Gaining support of the general population was important at this time because Rome was still a *republic*, with government officials that were elected. However, an unintended consequence of joining military with political campaigning was a series of destructive civil wars during the first century BC, as politically ambitious generals raised their own armies and began competing with each other.

Octavian/Augustus, the primary political leader that survived the last of the civil wars during first century BC, became Rome's first emperor in 27 BC. Rome had become an absolute monarchy. Augustus recognized that significant changes were needed to create political stability. He nationalized the army, to eliminate private recruiting of legions by ambitious military leaders, and emphasized negotiation rather than conflict with Rome's major competing states. Tiberius, Augustus' chosen successor, further limited the political competition of generals by putting the brakes on the culture of aggressive expansion and conquest. This overall strategy meant converting Rome from a *conquest state*, where resources were seized from defeated foreign states, to a *tributary state* that generates resources from its core and the previously dominated outer regions of the Empire. Similar to modern states, a successful tributary state raises tax revenue to provide public services in a way that defends the empire from invaders and prevents revolt from within. This is no easy task, especially for former conquest states. As put by Woolf (2012):

> Conquest states needed to transform themselves into stable structures of domination. Their rulers came to depend not only on the use of threat of violence, but also on the tacit support of local elites of various kinds. Through their help levies, tithes, taxes, or some combination of these was extracted. Local rulers took a portion but most of the surplus was put to the task of maintaining order and defending the empire (p. 26).

> Roman history is, in some sense, the story of unending struggles to balance the imperial budget (p. 185).

For almost two centuries, the cultural and institutional shift initiated by Augustus and Tiberius worked for Rome—creating a period of relative peace and prosperity.[8] Toward the end of the second century AD, Rome was hit with the confluence of several bad shocks: weak and selfish emperors, disease, famines, and several invasions. Economic activity and population size peaked out and began to decline.[9] Around AD 250, Rome began to lose substantial portions of its territory to enemies and their ability to collect taxes also weakened.[10] Financial stress was further seen in the debasement of Roman coinage—monetary financing of government budget deficits.[11] The debasement became severe in the third century. While there was some economic recovery in the fourth century, it was limited and short-lived. The

[8]The two major exceptions was some expansion into Britain—its proximity to the coast of the Roman province of Gaul made it just too tempting—and Dacia (Romania)—when emperor Trajan just had to prove himself to be like his hero Alexander the Great.

[9]See Smil (2010, pp. 139–140) and Woolf (2012, pp. 190–191).

[10]See MacMullen (1988, pp. ix and 42).

[11]See Hubbard and Kane (2013, p. 102).

decline of the Western Roman Empire, including the city of Rome, was well under way.

It is widely agreed that the decline of Rome was caused by many factors. One of the contributing factors was the corruption of government that limited tax collection and military effectiveness. The main proponent of corruption as a significant causal factor in the decline is MacMullen (1988). He argues that *decurions*, the informal network of local officials referred to in the quote above from Woolf, were generally effective in raising tax revenue in the early years of the Empire. They skimmed their share, but consistently passed revenue up the chain because they were generally loyal to the Empire and were motivated to win favor with the central government in Rome. In addition to collecting taxes, decurions were important in the local governance of communities and were regarded as the "backbone" of the Empire. The decurions shared in Rome's national identity.

The financial strains of maintaining the military and building public infrastructure, especially during times when the economy was weak, put pressure on the decurions to satisfy increasing revenue demands. Decurions began to withdrawal from public service for an easier and less stressful life. They were replaced by a bureaucracy that grew out of the central government. The large professional class of government bureaucrats was difficult for Rome to monitor and control. The professional bureaucrats lacked the pride in the Empire possessed by the decurions, who had seen themselves as an integral part of the ruling class. Corruption among the bureaucrats began to mount, causing the loss of tax revenue.

The inability to collect revenue weakened financial support for the military. Low pay and insufficient supplies, created incentives for the military to extort the communities they were sent to defend. While some extortion by the military was always present, it intensified and began to creep up the ranks. Similar to the reasons that decurions gave up public service, so did the best military leaders, who lost pride in military service and saw other occupations as more attractive.

> The principle commands of the army were filled by men who had received a liberal education, were well instructed in the advantages of law and letters, and who had risen, by equal steps, through the regular succession of civil and military honors. To their influence and example we may partly ascribe the modest obedience of the legions during the first two centuries of the Imperial history.
>
> But when the last enclosure of the Roman constitution was trampled down by Caracalla, the separation of professions gradually succeeded to the distinction of ranks. The more polished citizens of the internal provinces were alone qualified to act as lawyers and magistrates. The rougher trade of arms was abandoned to the peasants and Barbarians of the frontiers, who knew no country but their camp, no science but that of war, no civil laws, and scarcely those of military discipline. (Gibbon 2003, p. 103).

Commanders, who were no longer loyal to the heroic generals of the past nor to the central government of Rome, often used soldiers as extortion gangs to collect money and goods from the villages and cities near where they were stationed. Less time and effort was devoted to training, discipline was eroded, and willingness to engage the enemy lessened. Corruption of the government and the military weakened the defenses along the frontier and allowed for more successful invasions into Roman territory.

In summary, the Western Roman Empire can be viewed as an example of the general theory of societal failure. Over confidence, lack of foresight, and ambition caused the Empire to expand before Augustus and Tiberius had the wisdom, motivated also by their own selfish interest to prevent further civil war and remain in power, to recognize the diminishing returns to violent conquest and the growing depreciation cost associated with maintaining a large empire. They saw that Rome had "much less to hope than to fear from the chance of arms, and that, in the prosecution of remote wars, the under taking became every day more difficult, the event more doubtful, and the possession more precarious, and less beneficial," (Gibbon 2003, pp. 11–12). In the end, the possession was in fact too precarious as the Romans could not create a successful tributary state over their dominion.

Success made leaders and citizens inherently more selfish. Pride and devotion to Rome weakened over time and its dedicated civil servants began slipping away to easier private pursuits. Decius, who was pressed to become emperor during a time of crisis in AD 249, thought hard about how Roman greatest could be restored. He concluded that restoring greatness would require restoring public virtue and a consistent rule of law. He encouraged the senate to revive the office of the *censor*, a formal check on bad governance. The senate elected the highly respected Valerian to the office. Unfortunately, Decius was soon killed battling a Goth invasion and Valerian, who eventually became emperor himself, was too old be effective for long. Valerian made a bad choice, following the now established tradition of his time, and he turned things over to his son, Gallienus, who was not up to the task (Gibbon 2003, pp. 143–152).

With fewer dedicated public servants, monitoring of government bureaucrats became more important. However, the system for collecting taxes was too large and complex to monitor effectively, allowing corruption to run wild. A culture of corruption became pervasive even among high level civil servants and military leaders. Tax collection could not keep up with the spending of undisciplined Emperors and the needs of a large, and now more selfish, military. The insufficiently supplied and corrupted military could no longer provide an effective national defense over the Empire. Combine this with the fact that Rome was an imperial empire that was overly dependent on the strengths, limitations, and personal ambitions of its leaders, it is remarkable that the Western Roman Empire survived as *the* regional superpower for about 400 years, approximately 200 BC to AD 200, without clear signs of decline.

[12]References for the Byzantine Empire include Norwich (1999), Brownsworth (2009), and Wickham (2009).

9.6.2 Other Empires

Some argue that the Eastern Roman Empire, which evolved into the Byzantine Empire, was a prominent regional super power for 1000 years, much longer than the Western Roman Empire.[12] Was Byzantium particularly successful at checking societal decline created by human failings? Not really. It is much too generous to argue that the Byzantine Empire was a regional superpower for such an extended period. When the Western Empire was in decline during the fourth and fifth centuries, the Eastern Empire was also in a vulnerable state. Both Empires were suffering from the same human failings that come with success and over-expansion. In the mid-fourth century, the Eastern Roman Emperor Julian saw the same issues that undermined Western Roman society.

> The view from the throne, however, wasn't quite so rosy. Everywhere he looked that bright December day Julian saw vice, debauchery, and unrestrained decay. The reign of Constantine's sons seemed to have unleashed bribery, gluttony, and every kind of corruption. Imperial offices were bought and sold with alarming ease, and even the army had grown soft and undisciplined. Ostentatious displays of wealth hid the decay under a glittering façade, and extravagance seemed to replace governance. (Brownsworth 2009, p. 32)

The weakening Eastern and Western Empires faced plenty of external threats as well. Both Empires were losing ground and appeasing the invasions of barbarian tribes by giving up territory, incorporating barbarians into the army, and paying tribute to barbarian leaders to hold them off. This policy of appeasement led to further decline in Rome's national identity.

As Rome was falling to barbarian rule in the early fifth century, the Eastern Emperor Theodosius II carried out the most important public infrastructure project in Byzantine history—a walling off of the Eastern capital in Constantinople. Theodosius II, who was and still is generally regarded as a weak and passive leader, let discretion be the better part of valor (or more likely his advisors did—Theodosius was very young at the time). Constantinople was already located in a highly advantageous geographic position and Theodosius made it impenetrable. More than anything else, it is the long-life of this remarkable city that gives the Eastern Empire its reputation for endurance.

From 527 to 565, under the reign of Justinian, and his famous general Belisarius, the Byzantine Empire briefly achieved the status of a true regional superpower. Former territory of the Western Roman Empire was reacquired, the economy did well, cities grew in population, and public investments rebuilt the Empire's glory. Once again aggressive and daring leadership overreached. Large cities were a symbol of success but they were also a death trap. The insufficient public health infrastructure and technologies of the ancient world made large cities such as Rome and Constantinople very susceptible to the spread of disease. The Black Death appeared and ravaged the reconquered Eastern Empire, particularly the cities. Tax revenue declined and the army weakened from the lack of population and funds. The Empire was too large to hold together and by 600 it was in retreat on all fronts. The Lombards seized Italy. The Balkans broke free from Byzantine control. Persian and then Arab armies gained control of the Middle Eastern territories, crossed into Spain, and frequently besieged Constantinople. By the early 700 s, while the city of Constantinople continued to hold, most of the former Eastern Roman Empire was under Arab control.

However, the common pattern of overly ambitious and aggressive leadership applies to all peoples. The Arab Empire also became too large to hold together. Revolts and religious divisions mounted that weakened the Arab hold on the Mediterranean. Lucky for Byzantine, there was a run of good leadership that could take advantage of this opportunity. The so-called Macedonian Dynasty led a resurgence that restored Byzantium to superpower status from 867 to 1025—considered by many the golden age of the Empire. The success of the revival culminated under perhaps the single greatest Byzantine leader—Basil II, an exceptionally effective military and political leader, who ruled from 976 to 1025.

It takes strong leadership, or effective institutional checks, to sustain success. When Basil II died, the Byzantine Empire had neither. The ruling elite that replaced Basil conducted highly extractive and destructive policies. Taxes, concentrated on the poor general population, increased. The property rights established under the laws of Macedonian Dynasty were ignored and the elite seized and concentrated land-holdings. The small farmer-peasant society, that also supplied the military, collapsed. The army became increasingly reliant on the use of mercenaries. As the tax base shrunk and spending jumped, the ruling elite again resorted to devaluation of coins, leading to inflation. The Empire was weakened and ready to lose ground to the next external threats—which this time took the form of Normans from the north and the Seljuk Turks from the east. The decline was underway with some cycles of success and failures, but the trend was downward.

Eventually, even Constantinople fell for good—unable to withstand the bombardment of a bronze monster cannon, invented by a Hungarian and sold to the Turkish leader Mehmed II. Constantinople became capital of the Ottoman Empire in 1453. Seizing control of Constantinople had long been a goal of the Ottoman Turks who, for the two prior centuries, struggled for regional dominance against not only the Byzantines, but also against other Turkic tribes, Venice, Hungary, and Serbia. The conquest of Constantinople propelled them, under the rule of Mehmed II (1451–1481), to become an empire that rivaled ancient Rome.

The Ottoman Empire lasted as a true regional power for about two centuries, roughly 1450 to 1650, before it began to slowly unravel.[13] It suffered from the main problems of all ancient empires, the inability to maintain a military force capable of fighting on several fronts against invaders and provinces seeking independence, coupled with unstable politics and constant fiscal crises—a repeat of Roman and Byzantine history. The continual conflict associated with maintaining an empire creates at the same time a desperate need for funds and a significant difficulty in raising the funds.

[13]For an account of the Ottoman Empire see Finkel (2005).

In addition, we have the standard political conflict over the control of the wealth accumulated by successful societies—the "accumulated wealth curse." During the seventeenth century the sultan became more of a figure-head, creating a power vacuum among those looking to better their position: the royal dynasty, their advisors and servants, the janissaries (an elite military group, sometimes in concert and sometimes in opposition with a rival military group—the cavalry), provincial leaders, and guild members. Those who temporarily seized power tended to drain the treasury of resources for their own purpose, resulting in attempts to raise funds through large tax levies on other groups and coin debasement that just added to the political instability.

The formation and maintenance of ancient empires were only temporarily possible due to unique leadership, extraordinary national or religious pride that make a loyal population willing to sacrifice for glory, and military effectiveness mixed with a good deal of luck. Once the main conquest stage is over, the overly ambitious task of controlling a large and complex state gradually gives way to human failings and to the upstart ambitions of foreign invaders and disgruntled subjects.

The Ottoman Empire officially came to an end when it was defeated by the French and the British in World War I. At the end of the War, the British Empire, by far the largest in history, reached its peak. The British Empire that had been forming since the late seventeenth century, then began its dramatic decline.

The British Empire was created using a two-pronged strategy.[14] First, there were public-private joint ventures that created the monopoly rents needed to justify risky explorations and investments. Second, the government seized and then provided land to British migrants in order to populate the colonies with loyal subjects. As the Empire expanded, the primary beneficiaries were wealthy private investors and the banks that intermediated their financing, as well as many of the British immigrants that filled the colonies. From the beginning, there were concerns that leading politicians also benefited from their (too) close relations with wealthy investors and bankers. The bankers guided and facilitated the politicians' personal investment in imperial activity in exchange for policies that secured those investments.

Early on, there were those back home in England who thought it would be more ethical, economical, and politically sustainable to turn the Empire into a loose federation of states run primarily by locally elected representatives. The ambitious and hubristic hard-liners, generally won out, largely because even the more moderate politicians were concerned about competition for control of developing regions with other European powers.[15] However, before World War I the liberal critics of the Empire made political headway by continuing to question the morality of the Empire

[14]Ferguson (2002) offers a history of the British Empire the blends the economic and political dimensions.

[15]See Fieldhouse (1973) for an account of how Europeans were compelled, often reluctantly because of the expense, to formally colonize countries because of competition over control and power.

and its burden on taxpayers who were sacrificing to help finance the profits of a small elite group. The greed of a powerful few had caused the Empire to overreach in a way that provided, at best, very limited benefit to the general public. Eventually, the "pride and glory" of the Empire was unable to sustain public support at home. The effect of the two World Wars was only to provide the external shocks that sped the Empire's inevitable collapse.

The British spent more on World War I than any other combatant and the War left them with a yet larger territory to manage. A clear consensus formed that the costs of the Empire now far exceeded the narrowly gained benefits. The large national debt accumulated to finance the War constrained Britain's ability to rebuild its defense, causing it to enter World War II in a vulnerable position. Britain needed to make heavy appeals to the United States for supplies and funds.

The United States was quite hostile to Britain's imperialism and was not particularly sympathetic to its now weakened position. They drove a hard bargain, both politically and economically, for providing Britain with aid. At the end of World War II, Britain was left with extremely heavy debts and was no longer able to hold on to its Empire. As with all Empires in history, the British Empire was overly ambitious, generated imperial benefits that were too narrowly enjoyed, and created too much resentment from within and outside its borders.

After World War II, the United States emerged as the world's economic and military superpower. By any reasonable definition, however, the United States is not an empire. The United States has not consistently exerted final authority on the political decisions of another country—including even those that it has invaded. Nevertheless, it does exert considerable indirect influence around the world.

Despite not fitting the strict definition of an empire, the United States exhibits many of the signs of decline displayed by the powerful societies from history. In the United States these failings take the form of increasingly favoring consumption over investment, creating overly complex laws and institutions that generate a myriad of unintended consequences and that foster rent seeking, policies that favor the elite or special interest at the expense of the national interest, complacency and arrogance in dealing with domestic problems and international relations. As suggested by Thucydides in the fifth century BC, confronting these common sources of decline begins with a better understanding of history and a self-critical recognition of human limitations. It remains to be seen whether this knowledge would be sufficient to generate the reforms needed to simplify its society, make its government more transparent, focus on the long-term consequences of policy, and become more informed about the culture and politics of other countries. Based on a reading of the history since Thucydides, one cannot be optimistic.

The Durants, whose quote begins this section, place blame for the decline in societies on the failure of political and intellectual leaders to meet the challenges of change (Durant and Durant 1968, p. 92). The two largest challenges of change for current advanced countries are aging and growing wage inequality. Dealing with both challenges starts with more realistic expectations. Government policy cannot continue to be as generous to the entire population of older households as did in the past when their relative numbers were lower. The Durants see the second current challenge as a common endogenous symptom of developing economies—the majority of households will not benefit proportionally from technological progress and increased complexity of institutions. As a result, resentment builds and the majority becomes "a cultural drag upon the minority"—"the price the minority pays for control of educational and economic opportunity." To mediate the problems caused by the second challenge, a more realistic and egalitarian education policy is needed that reduces subsidies of 4 year college in favor of pre-school investment for children from disadvantaged families and quality vocational training for the broad middle class.

9.7 Suggestions for Further Reading and Study

For those that found the two-period model useful, see Obstfeld and Rogoff (1996) for applications to international economics and Persson and Tabellini (2000) for applications in political economy.

The first two-period overlapping generations model with physical capital and production was due to Diamond (1965). It has become one of the two workhorse models of macroeconomics. Unfortunately, most students are not exposed to this model, or any other model built on microeconomic foundations, as undergraduates. If the model does not sound familiar or was difficult to grasp in your first attempt, you may want to read a somewhat less ambitious introduction alongside of this book. An excellent intermediate undergraduate textbook treatment of the overlapping-generations model is provided by Auerbach and Kotlikoff (1998). Farmer and Schelnast (2013) provide a graduate-level treatment of the overlapping-generations model, with a special focus on international trade. Das et al. (2018) use the overlapping-generations model to discuss development economics. More advanced and more general treatments of the overlapping-generations model can be found in Azariadis (1993) and de la Croix and Michel (2002). These are important books for graduate students who want to concentrate on theoretical work.

The overlapping generation model was extended to include altruistic intergenerational transfers by Barro (1974), Drazen (1978) and Becker (1981, 1988). If the nonnegativity constraint on financial transfers is ignored, altruism provides a justification for infinitely lived agent model, the other workhorse model of macroeconomics. Barro (1997a) provides an intermediate undergraduate treatment of macroeconomics using the infinitely-lived agent model. A more advanced undergraduate textbook that covers the overlapping-generations model and the extension to include intergenerational transfers is Lord (2001). Graduate treatments of the infinitely lived agent model include Romer (2001) and Acemoglu (2009).

Calibrated dynamic general equilibrium models were first used in public finance to examine the effects of tax reform (Summers (1981) and Auerbach et al. (1983)) and in macroeconomics to explain business cycles (Kydland and Prescott (1982) and McCandless (2008)). Calibration methods have since been extended to every area of macroeconomics. For a general discussion of the approach, including additional applications, see Kydland and Prescott (1996), followed by a critique from Hansen and Heckman (1996). The calibration experiment we presented to test the importance of physical capital accumulation to economic growth, is based on King and Rebelo (1993). An extension to include human capital can be found in Rangazas (2000, 2002). Córdoba and Ripoll (2013) and Manuelli and Seshadri (2014) offer quantitative theories where human capital accumulation is the dominant determinant of an economy's labor productivity. An alternative approach that stresses the connection between TFP and *broad notions* of capital, emphasizing the knowledge embodied in firms rather than individuals, has been developed by Parente and Prescott (2000).

Some may want to focus future study on governance issues and fiscal policy. Two excellent places to start if you want to think more about interest groups, elections, and politicians' behavior are Belsey (2005) and Bueno de Mesquita and Smith (2011). Belsey is more theoretical and Bueno de Mesquita and Smith more empirical. Kotlikoff (2003) provides a more advanced discussion of the generational impacts of fiscal policy. Alesina and Passalacqua (2015) give a recent survey of the political economy of debt financing. For a serious introduction to the theory of distortionary taxation, which we have largely ignored, see Salanie (2011). More on regional fiscal policy and fiscal federalism can be found on the recent volume edited by Ahmad et al. (2016). Chapter 8 contains an extensive list of references for those interested in the current fiscal crisis and possible reforms.

References

Acemoglu D, 2009, *Introduction to Modern Economic Growth*, Princeton, New Jersey : Princeton University Press.

Acemoglu, D. and Restrepo, P., 2017, "Robots and Jobs: Evidence from U.S. Labor Markets," *NBER Working Paper* no. 23285, Cambridge, MA: National Bureau of Economic Research.

Ahmad, E., Bordignon, M., and Borsio, G., 2016, *Multi-level Finance and the Euro Crisis*, Cheltenham, UK: Edward Elgar

Alesina, A., and Passalacqua, A., 2015, "The Political Economy of Government Debt," in Taylor, J., and Uhlig, H. (editors), *Handbook of Macroeconomics*, Amsterdam: North Holland.

Auerbach A, Kotlikoff L, 1998, *Macroeconomics: An Integrated Approach*, Cambridge, Massachusetts : MIT Press.

Auerbach A, Kotlikoff L, Skinner J, 1983, "The Efficiency Gains from Dynamic Tax Reform," *International Economic Review* 24(1):81–100.

Autor, D., 2014, "Skills, Education, and the Rise in Earnings Inequality among the Other 99 Percent," *Science*, 344, 843-851.

Azariadis C, 1993, *Intertemporal Macroeconomics*, Oxford, UK: Blackwell,.

Barro R, 1974, "Are Government Bonds Net Wealth? " *Journal of Political Economy* 82 (6):1095–1118.

Barro R, 1997a, *Macroeconomics*, Cambridge, Massachusetts :MIT Press.

Barro, R., 1997b, *Determinants of Economic Growth*, Cambridge, Massachusetts: MIT Press.

Beard, M., 2015, *SPQR A History of Ancient Rome*, New York: Liveright Publishing.

Becker G., 1981, *A Treatise on the Family*, Cambridge, Massachusetts : Harvard University Press.

Becker G., 1988, "Family Economics and Macro Behavior," *American Economic Review* 78 (1):1–13.

Belsey, T., 2005, *Principled Agents*, Oxford: Oxford University Press.

Bessen, J., 2015, "Toil and Technology," *Finance & Development*, 52, Washington DC: International Monetary Fund.

Brownsworth, L., 2009, *Lost to the West: The Forgotten Byzantine Empire that Rescued Western Civilization*, New York: Three Rivers Press.

Brynjolfsson, E. and McAfee, A., 2014, *The Second Machine Age*, New York: W.W. Norton

Bueno de Mesquita, B., and Smith, A., 2011, *The Dictator's Handbook*, New York: Public Affairs.

Córdoba J, Ripoll M, 2013, "What explains schooling differences across countries?" Journal of Monetary Economics 60(2):184–202.

Correia, S., S. Luck, and E. Verner, 2020, "Pandemics Depress the Economy, Public Health Responses Do Not: Evidence from the 1918 Flu," Federal Reserve Bank of New York.

Das, S., Mourmouras, A., Rangazas, P., 2018, *Economic Growth and Development*, New York: Springer

de la Croix D, Michel, P, 2002, *A Theory of Economic Growth: Dynamics and Policy in Overlapping Generations*, Cambridge, UK :Cambridge University Press,.

Diamond P., 1965, "National Debt in a Neoclassical Growth Model," *American Economic Review* 55(5):1126–1150.

Drazen A., 1978, "Government Debt, Human Capital, and Bequests in a Life-Cycle Model," *Journal of Political Economy*, 86(3):505–516.

Durant, W., and Durant, A., 1968, *The Lessons of History*, New York: Simon and Schuster.

Emanuel, K., 2012, *What We Know About Climate Change*, Cambridge, MA.: MIT Press.

Farmer K, Schelnast M., 2013, *Growth and International Trade: An Introduction to the Overlapping Generations Approach*, Berlin :Springer-Verlag,.

Ferguson, N., 2002, *Empire: The Rise and Demise of the British World Order and the Lessons for Global Powers*, New York: Basic Books.

Fieldhouse, D., 1973, *Economics and Empire 1830-1914*, Ithaca, N.Y.: Cornell University Press.

Finkel, C., 2005, *Osman's Dream: The History of the Ottoman Empire*, New York: Basic Books.

Frey, C. and Osborne, M., 2017, "The Future of Employment: How Susceptible are Jobs to Computerisation?" *Technological Forecasting and Social Change*, 114, 254–280.

Furman, J. and Orzag, P., 2015, "A Firm-Level Perspective on the Role of Rents in the Rise in Inequality," paper presented at "A Just Soceity," Centennial Event in Honor of Joseph Stiglitz, Columbia University, New York, October 16, 2015.

Garrett, T., 2007, "Economic Effects of the 1918 Influenza Pandemic," Federal Reserve Bank of St. Louis.

Gibbon, E., 2003, *The Decline and Fall of the Roman Empire*, New York: The Modern Library.

Goolsbee, A., and Syverson, C., 2020, "Fear, Lockdown, and Diversions: Comparing Drivers of the Pandemic Economic Decline 20202," Becker-Friedman Institute Working Paper No. 2020-80, University of Chicago.

Hansen L, Heckman J., 1996, "The Empirical Foundations of Calibration," *Journal of Economic Perspectives* 10(1):87–104.

Harris, J., Roach, B., and Codur, A., 2017, *The Economics of Global Climate Change,* Medford, MA: Global Development and Environmental Institute, Tufts University.

Holland, T., 2016, *Dynasty: The Rise and Fall of the House of Caesar*, London: Abadus.

Hubbard, G. and Kane, T., 2013, *Balance: The Economics of Great Powers*, New York: Simon and Schuster.

King R, Rebelo S., 1993, "Transitional Dynamics and Economic Growth in the Neoclassical Growth Model," *American Economic Review* , 83:908–931.

Kotlikoff, L., 2003, *Generational Policy*, Cambridge, Mass: MIT Press.

Kotlikoff, L., Kubler,F., Polbin, A., Sachs, J., and Scheidegger, S., 2019, Making Carbon Taxation a Generational Win Win," NBER Working Paper 25760, Cambridge, Mass.

Kydland F, Prescott E., 1982, "Time to Build and Aggregate Fluctuations," *Econometrica* 50(6): 1345–1370.

Kydland F, Prescott E., 1996, "The Computational Experiment: An Econometric Tool," *Journal of Economic Perspectives* 10(1):69–86.

Lord W., 2001, "Household Dynamics, Policies, and Economic Growth," New York: Oxford University Press.
MacMullen, R., 1988, *Corruption and the Decline of Rome*, New Haven: Yale University Press.
Manuelli R, Seshadri A., 2014, "Human Capital and the Wealth of Nations," *American Economic Review*, 104 (9):2736–2762.
McCandless, G., 2008, *The ABCs of RBCs*, Cambridge, MA: Harvard University Press.
McKitrick, R., 2016, *A Practical Guide to the Economics of Carbon Pricing*, University of Calgary School of Public Policy Research Papers, V9, Issue 28.
Murphy, C., 2007, *Are We Rome? The Fall of an Empire and the Fate of America*, Boston: Houghton Mifflin.
Nedelkoska, L., and Quintini, G., 2018, "Automation, Skills Use, and Training," OECD Working Paper No. 202
Nordhaus, W., 2008, *A Question of Balance*, New Haven; Yale University Press.
______, 2013, *The Climate Casino*, New Haven: Yale University Press.
______, 2018, "Projections and Uncertainties about Climate Change in an Era of Minimal Climate Policies," *American Economic Journal: Economic Policy*, 10(3), 56–360
Norwich, J., 1999, *A Short History of Byzantium*, New York: Vintage Books.
Obstfeld, M., and Rogoff, K., 1996, *Foundations of International Macroeconomics*, Cambridge, Mass: MIT Press
Olson, M., 1982, *The Rise and Decline of Nations: Economic Growth, Stagflation and Social Rigidities*, New Haven: Yale University Press.
Ophlus, W., 2012, *Immoderate Greatness*, Charleston: Create Space Independent Publishing.
Parente S, Prescott E., 2000, *Barriers to Riches*, Cambridge, Massachusetts: MIT Press,.
Parsons, T., 2010, *The Rule of Empires*, Oxford: Oxford University Press.
Rangazas P., 2000, "Schooling and Economic Growth: A King-Rebelo Experiment with Human Capital," *Journal of Monetary Economics*, 46(2):397–416.
Rangazas P., 2002, "The Quantity and Quality of Schooling and U.S. Labor Productivity Growth (1870-2000)," *Review of Economic Dynamics*, 5(4): 932–964.
Rognlie, M., 2015, "Deciphering the Fall and Rise in the Net Capital Share," Brookings Papers on Economic Activity, BPEA Conference Draft, March 19–20.
Persson, T., and Tabellini, G., 2000, *Political Economics*, Cambridge MA: MIT Press
Romer D. 2001, *Advanced Macroeconomics*, New York: McGraw-Hill.
Romm, J. 2010, *Ghost on the Throne,* New York: Vintage Books.
Sachs, J. and Kotlikoff, L., 2012, "Smart Machines and Long-term Misery," *NBER Working Paper* no. 18629, Cambridge, MA: National Bureau of Economic Research.
Salanie, B., 2011, *The Economics of Taxation*, Cambridge, Mass.: MIT Press.
Smil, V., 2010, *Why America is Not Rome*, Cambridge, Massachusetts: MIT Press.
Strauss, B., 2019, *Ten Caesars: Roman Emperors from Augustus to Constantine*, New York: Simon and Schuster.
Summers L., 1981, "Capital Taxation and Capital Accumulation in a Life-cycle Growth Model," *American Economic Review*, 71(4):533–544.
Thaler, R., 2015, *Misbehaving: The Making of Behavioral Economics*, New York: W.W. Norton.
Tol, R., 2009, "The Economic Effects of Climate Change," *Journal of Economic Perspectives*, 23 (2), 29–51
Wagner, G., and Weitzman, M., 2015, *Climate Shock*, Princeton: Princeton University Press.
Ward-Perkins, B., 2005, *The Fall of Rome and the End of Civilization*, Oxford: Oxford University Press.
Wickham, C., 2009, *The Inheritance of Rome*, New York: Penguin Books.
Woodruff, P., 1993, *Thucydides on Justice, Power, and Human Nature*, Indianapolis: Hackett Publishing Company.
Woolf, G., 2012, *Rome: An Empire's Story*, Oxford: Oxford University Press.

A. Technical Appendix

This appendix gives a quick refresher of the topics in college algebra and basic calculus, and their extension to optimization theory, that are used in the models of the text. To see the different concepts in action, we have included EXAMPLES FROM THE TEXT as each topic is reviewed.

A.1 Two Useful Functions

We use two types of functions frequently in the text.

Power Functions

A power function has the general form

$$y = f(x) = Ax^a,$$

where x is a nonnegative variable and a and A are positive constants, or *parameters*. In words, the function says that y is an increasing function of x, but the relationship between the two variables can have a variety of characteristics depending on the precise value of a.

For,

$0 < a < 1$	$f(x)$ is a concave function of x
$a = 1$	$f(x)$ is a linear function of x
$a > 1$	$f(x)$ is a convex function of x

If these shapes are not familiar, set $A = 1$ and plot $f(x)$ for different values of x, given a value of a that satisfies each of the three different cases above.

When dealing with power functions you need to remember some of the algebra associated with expressions that are raised to a power. Here are some important algebraic results for such expressions, where a and b are positive parameters.

M. Ivanyna et al., *The Macroeconomics of Corruption*, Springer Texts in Business and Economics, https://doi.org/10.1007/978-3-030-67557-8

(i) $x^a x^b = x^{a+b}$
(ii) $(x^a)^b = x^{ab}$
(iii) $(x^a)^{1/b} = x^{a/b}$
(iv) $x^{-a} = \frac{1}{x^a}$
(v) $\frac{x^a}{x^b} = x^a x^{-b} = x^{a-b}$
(vi) $(xz)^a = x^a z^a$, where z is another nonnegative variable

We also need to remember the rules for differentiating a power function with respect to x.

(i) First derivative

$$f'(x) = aAx^{a-1}$$

(ii) Second Derivative

$$f''(x) = (a-1)aAx^{a-2}$$

Note that, given our assumptions, $f'(x) > 0$. However, the sign of $f''(x)$ depends on the precise value of a. The sign of the second derivative is important because it offers a way of identifying the shape of the function without the need to form plots.

For,

$0 < a < 1$	$f''(x) < 0 \Rightarrow f(x)$ is a concave function of x
$a = 1$	$f''(x) = 0 \Rightarrow f(x)$ is a linear function of x
$a > 1$	$f''(x) > 0 \Rightarrow f(x)$ is a convex function of x

A way of understanding the connection between the second derivative and the shape of $f(x)$ is to note that the second derivative tells us what is happening to the *slope* of $f(x)$, i.e. it gives us the change in the first derivative, when there is an increase in x.

For,

$0 < a < 1$	$f'(x)$ is *falling* as x increases, so the graph becomes flatter
$a = 1$	$f'(x)$ is *constant* as x increases, so the graph remains linear
$a > 1$	$f'(x)$ is *increasing* as x increases, so the graph becomes steeper

Examples from the Text

In Sect. 2.2 of Chap. 2, we use the following power function for second period worker productivity and income,

$$y_2 = Ag_2^{\mu}.$$

Worker productivity is an increasing concave function of public capital per worker because $A > 0$ and $0 < \mu < 1$. The first and second order derivatives of the function are

$$\mu A g_2^{\mu-1} = \frac{\mu A}{g_2^{1-\mu}} > 0 \text{ and } (\mu - 1)\mu A g_2^{\mu-2} = \frac{(\mu - 1)\mu A}{g_2^{2-\mu}} < 0.$$

In Sect. 2.6 of Chap. 2, we consider the idea that public capital is an imperfect public good,

$$y_2 = A\left({}^{G_2}\!/_{N^{\xi}}\right)^{\mu},$$

with $0 \leq \xi \leq 1$. To simplify the production function, and relate it to the production function we started with, we needed do some algebra with expressions involving exponents

$$y_2 = A\left(\frac{G_2}{N^{\xi}}\frac{N}{N}\right)^{\mu} = A\left(g_2 N^{1-\xi}\right)^{\mu} \equiv \overline{A} g_2^{\mu}, \quad \text{where } \overline{A} \equiv N^{(1-\xi)\mu}.$$

(Natural) Logarithmic Function

Our other special function is the natural logarithmic function, which we refer to as just the log function. The log function is an increasing concave function of the form,

$$y = f(x) = A \ln x,$$

where x is a positive variable and A is a positive parameter. As with the power function, if you are not familiar with the shape of the log function you should set $A = 1$ and plot the function for different values of x.

Alternatively, we can learn about its shape by recalling the rules of differentiation for log functions,

(i) First Derivative

$$f'(x) = \frac{A}{x} > 0$$

(ii) Second Derivative

$$f''(x) = -\frac{A}{x^2} < 0$$

As with the power function when $a < 1$, the derivative of the logarithmic function is positive and decreasing as x increases, i.e. its slope becomes flatter at higher values of x.

The following results will be useful when doing algebra with expressions involving logs. The parameter a and the variable z are both positive values.

(i) $\ln(xz) = \ln x + \ln z$

(ii) $\ln\left(\frac{x}{z}\right) = \ln x - \ln z$

(iii) $\ln(x^a) = a \ln x$

Examples from the Text

The single period utility function we use throughout the text takes the natural log form, $u = \ln c$. The marginal utility of consumption is the derivative of u with respect to c, $1/c > 0$. The marginal utility of consumption is clearly decreasing in c. This can also be verified by taking the second derivative with respect to c, $-1/c^2$, which tells us how the marginal utility of consumption changes with c.

In Sect. 2.2 of Chap. 2, we encountered a situation where second period consumption is determined by government capital

$$\ln(c_2) = \ln(y_2) = \ln\left(Ag_2^{\mu}\right).$$

Using the algebra rules for taking logs, we can write the last expression above as

$$\ln(A) + \mu \ln(g_2).$$

A.2 Optimization

Single Choice Variable

The two special functions discussed in the previous section are increasing in x. This means that they have no maximum value. In economic terms, if these functions represent output or utility, as x increases there is always a marginal benefit. However, because of scarcity, there is typically also a cost to increasing x. For simplicity, suppose the scarcity is reflected in the fact that sellers of x charge a price, p, for its use. Also assume the market for x is competitive, so individual agents take the value of p as given (unaffected by their actions).

The *rationality* assumption in neoclassical economics says that agents will assess both the benefits and costs of making a decision and make choices that do not systematically deviate from the choice that maximizes the net benefit. To illustrate how this assumption works, we create a new function that reflects both the benefit and the cost of choosing x. The simplest function that illustrates this idea is the *profit function*. Let the profit function be defined as,

$$\tilde{f}(x) = Ax^a - px,$$

where $A > 0$, $p > 0$, and $0 < a < 1$. The first and second derivatives of the profit function are

$$\tilde{f}'(x) = aAx^{a-1} - p$$

$$\tilde{f}''(x) = (a-1)aAx^{a-2} < 0.$$

Note that the second derivative is negative, so the profit function is concave. This also tells us that the first derivative is decreasing. However, the first derivative can have any sign. When x is low it is more likely to be positive. A positive derivative indicates that total profit increases as x increases. As x increases the value of the first derivative falls, the marginal profit becomes smaller, until it reaches zero. At this point, further increases in x will lower total profit. So, the rule for finding the highest profit is to choose x such that the first derivative is zero.

The previous paragraph exemplifies a general and very important result for economics, known in mathematics as *Fermat's Theorem*. For a strictly concave function, $\tilde{f}(x)$, the value of x that maximizes $\tilde{f}(x)$, satisfies the *first order condition*, $\tilde{f}'(x) = 0$. In the profit function example above, we can find the profit maximizing value of x explicitly by solving, $\tilde{f}'(x) = aAx^{a-1} - p = 0$, for x to get $x = (aA/p)^{1/(1\ -\ a)}$.

Examples from the Text

In Sect. 2.2 from Chap. 2, we wrote the life-time utility of the household as a function of public capital, g_2,

$$U = \tilde{f}(g_2) = \ln(y_1 - g_2) + \beta \ln\left(A g_2^{\mu}\right) = \ln(y_1 - g_2) + \beta \ln(A) + \beta\mu \ln(g_2).$$

The cost of choosing g_2 is the loss in utility from less first period consumption and the benefit of g_2 is the gain in utility from greater second period consumption.

The first and second derivatives with respect to g_2 are

$$f'(g_2) = -\frac{1}{y_1 - g_2} + \beta\mu\frac{1}{g_2}$$

$$f''(g_2) = -\frac{1}{(y_1 - g_2)^2} - \beta\mu\frac{1}{g_2^2} < 0,$$

so, lifetime utility is a strictly concave function of g_2. Solving the first order condition for $g_2, \tilde{f}'(g_2) = 0$, gives the public capital that maximizes the household's lifetime utility. The solution is given in Eq. (2.4a) from Chap. 2.

Multiple Choice Variables

Often economic agents are modelled as attempting to "do the best they can," more formally as maximizing some objective function, by choosing more than one variable. The basic approach when there is more than one choice variable is analogous to the one variable case. We illustrate the approach in the situation where there are two choice variables. In this case, the net benefit function has two arguments, x_1 and x_2, and is written as $\tilde{f}(x_1, x_2)$. The derivative of $\tilde{f}(x_1, x_2)$ with respect to *each* choice variable can be taken, one at a time. These types of derivatives are called *partial derivatives*—they give the change in the function due to a change in one of the arguments, *holding all other arguments constant*.

One way of reinforcing the notion and the mechanics of taking a partial derivative is to think of a function with a *single argument* created from $\tilde{f}(x_1, x_2)$. This is done by holding x_2 constant. When x_2 is fixed at a certain value, it simply becomes a constant part of the newly defined function. For example, if we think of x_2 as fixed at the value $\bar{x}_2$, we can define the new function $h(x_1) \equiv \tilde{f}(x_1, \bar{x}_2)$. The partial derivative of $\tilde{f}(x_1, x_2)$ with respect to x_1 is then defined as $\tilde{f}_{x_1} \equiv h'(x_1)$ or, using a different notation, as $\frac{\partial \tilde{f}}{\partial x_1} \equiv h'(x_1)$. The second notation is a bit clumsy, but it is clearer in dynamic models where subscripts are used to denote time periods. Both types of notation are frequently used. Of course, the same procedure can be used to define the partial derivative with respect to x_2.

The partial derivatives are themselves typically functions of x_1 and x_2 and so they can be differentiated to get the *second partial derivatives*. There is a way of checking for the concavity of $\tilde{f}(x_1, x_2)$ that involves the second partial derivatives. This check is a bit complicated, so you need to trust that when we do maximization problems in the text, that we are using concave functions. However, if you build your own original models, you need to research the different ways of checking for concavity of functions with multiple choice variables.

If you are sure that $\tilde{f}(x_1, x_2)$ is a strictly concave function of x_1 and x_2, then you can identify the maximizing choices of x_1 and x_2 using the first order conditions in a manner perfectly analogous to the case with a function of just one variable. The first order conditions simply set the partial derivatives equal to zero,

$$\frac{\partial \tilde{f}}{\partial x_1} = 0 \text{ and } \frac{\partial \tilde{f}}{\partial x_2} = 0.$$

Examples from the Text

In Chap. 4, the Cobb-Douglas production function is introduced,

$$Y_t = AK_t^{\alpha} L_t^{1-\alpha},$$

where Y denotes output, K denotes the capital stock rented, L denotes the hours of work hired, and where $A > 0$ and $0 < \alpha < 1$ are technological parameters.

The marginal product of an input is the increase in output that results from an increase in the use of an input. Formally, it is the partial derivative of the production function with respect to a particular input, holding other inputs constant. For a Cobb-Douglas production function, the marginal product of labor and the marginal product of capital are $\frac{\partial Y_t}{\partial L_t} = (1-\alpha)AK_t^{\alpha}L_t^{-\alpha}$ and $\frac{\partial Y_t}{\partial K_t} = \alpha AK_t^{\alpha-1}L_t^{1-\alpha}$ (see the rules for differentiating power functions given above). These expressions can be simplified somewhat by using the algebra to write them in terms of the *capital intensity*, $k_t \equiv K_t/L_t$. The simplified expressions for the marginal products are, $\frac{\partial Y_t}{\partial L_t} = (1-\alpha)Ak_t^{\alpha}$ and $\frac{\partial Y_t}{\partial K_t} = \alpha Ak_t^{\alpha-1}$ (see the algebra rules for manipulating expressions with exponents given above).

We assume that markets are perfectly competitive in our production economy. As discussed in elementary economics, the notion of competitive markets applies not only to the markets for goods but also to the factor markets for labor and capital. The competitive assumption applied to the factor markets means that firms demand inputs to maximize profits taking as given the market prices of the inputs: the wage rate paid to labor (w) and rental rate on physical capital (r). No single firm is large enough to be able to influence market prices when they unilaterally change their production or input levels. The price of the economy's single output good is taken to be one. So we can think of output and revenue as being the same.

Given the competitive assumptions, the profit function can then be written as $Y_t - w_t L_t - r_t K_t$. Just as in the one-variable case, maximizing profits requires that firms hire capital and labor as long as the marginal benefit (marginal product) exceeds the marginal cost (factor price). Formally, the necessary first order conditions for profit maximization are

$$\alpha A k_t^{\alpha-1} = r_t$$
$$(1-\alpha) A k_t^{\alpha} = w_t.$$

Constrained Maximization with Multiple Choice Variables

Let's extend the discussion from the previous section to the case where $f(x_1, x_2)$ is a strictly concave function of x_1 and x_2, but where the choice variables have to satisfy a resource constraints of the general form $F(x_1, x_2) = E$, where E is a positive constant. When resource constraints are present, there is a very important method that generates the first order conditions for the maximizing values of x_1 and x_2. It is called the *Lagrangian Method*, named after its inventor, the mathematician Joseph-Louis Lagrange. He showed that the first order conditions that must be satisfied by the maximizing values of x_1 and x_2 are

$$\frac{\partial f}{\partial x_1} = \lambda \frac{\partial F}{\partial x_1}, \ \frac{\partial f}{\partial x_2} = \lambda \frac{\partial F}{\partial x_2}, \ \text{ and } F(x_1, x_2) = E,$$

where λ is a variable called the *Lagrange multiplier.*

The first order conditions are easy to remember because they can reproduced by maximizing the *Lagrangian function*, $L(x_1, x_2, \lambda) = f(x_1, x_2) + \lambda[E - F(x_1, x_2)]$ with respect to x_1, x_2, λ. In other words, treat L as any other function and find the maximizing values by setting the partial derivatives of L to zero,

$$\frac{\partial L}{\partial x_1} = 0, \ \frac{\partial L}{\partial x_2} = 0, \ \text{ and } \ \frac{\partial L}{\partial \lambda} = 0.$$

These three equations, when written out and rearranged algebraically, are exactly the three equations stated above.

Examples from the Text

In Sect. 2.3 from Chap. 2, households maximize their lifetime utility by choosing the optimal consumption path over their two periods of life subject to their lifetime budget constraint. Matching the household's problem with the general set-up above we have

$$f(x_1, x_2) \equiv \ln(c_1) + \beta \ln(c_2), F(x_1, x_2) \equiv c_1 + \frac{c_2}{1 + r*}, \text{ and } E \equiv y_1$$

where we have set $y_2 = g_2 = 0$ only for simplicity; we could have proceeded just fine by defining $E = y_1 + \frac{y_2}{1+r*} - g_2$, as in the text. The Lagrangian function in our application is.

$$L(c_1, c_2, \lambda) = \ln(c_1) + \beta \ln(c_2) + \lambda \left(y_1 - c_1 - \frac{c_2}{1 + r*} \right).$$

Differentiating and setting the partial derivatives equal to zero, gives us

$$\frac{1}{c_1} = \lambda, \frac{\beta}{c_2} = \frac{\lambda}{1 + r*}, \text{ and } c_1 + \frac{c_2}{1 + r*} = y_1,$$

(see the rules for differentiating the natural log function given above). Solving these three equations for the three unknowns (c_1, c_2, λ), yields the optimal consumption demand functions and a value for the Lagrange multiplier,

$$c_1 = \frac{y_1}{1 + \beta}, c_2 = \frac{\beta(1 + r*)y_1}{1 + \beta}, \lambda = \frac{1 + \beta}{y_1}.$$

A.3 Nonnegativity Constraints and Corner Solutions

The choice variables of economic agents are often restricted to be nonnegative values. The optimization approach taken in Sect. A.2 does not explicitly acknowledge this type of constraint on the choice variables. In many situations this is not a problem because, given the choice variables and the particular functions chosen, the optimal solutions naturally come out to be positive values. However, in some applications it is quite possible that some of the unconstrained optimal choice variables may take on negative values. This is not the proper solution if there are economic constraints preventing that possibility.

Fortunately, the Lagrangian method can be modified to account for nonnegativity constraints. The first order conditions with nonnegatvity constraints on x_1 and x_2 are

(i) $\frac{\partial L}{\partial x_1} \leq 0, x_1 \geq 0,$
(ii) $\frac{\partial L}{\partial x_2} \leq 0, x_2 \geq 0,$

and

(iii) $\frac{\partial L}{\partial \lambda} = 0.$

where in (i) and (ii), *at least one* of the inequalities must be a strict equality. In the situation where the optimal values of both choices variables is strictly positive, then

$x_1 > 0$ and $x_2 > 0$, so by the rule just stated $\frac{\partial L}{\partial x_1} = 0$ and $\frac{\partial L}{\partial x_2} = 0$, exactly as in the case where nonngegativity constraints are not accounted for. However, if an unconstrained choice of, say x_1, turns out to be negative, then the nonnegativity constraint binds and we have

$$\frac{\partial L}{\partial x_1} < 0, x_1 = 0.$$

This condition can be interpreted intuitively in the following way. Begin by thinking of $\frac{\partial L}{\partial x_1}$ as the marginal net benefit of increasing the value of x_1 (note that the Lagranian function incorporates both benefits and costs). If at $x_1 = 0$, $\frac{\partial L}{\partial x_1} > 0$, then the marginal benefit is positive and it is rational to increase x_1 above zero. However, if $\frac{\partial L}{\partial x_1} < 0$, then it is rational to *reduce* x_1 below zero in order to cause the total net benefit to rise. If this is not permitted, then the best the decision maker can do is set $x_1 = 0$. Because $x_1 = 0$ is at the end or at the "corner" of the permissible choices for x_1, this is referred as a *corner solution.*

Examples from the Text

In Sect. 2.2 from Chap. 2, we consider the possibility of borrowing constraints, which are nonnegativity constraint on asset accumulation. We assume that the market for private international loans does not exist and then consider situations where the government may or may not be able to borrow and lend in international markets. In this situation the household would like to set $s < 0$. i.e. they would be better off choosing negative saving but are restricted from doing so. They are at a corner solution with $s = 0$.

The single-period private budget constraints of the *credit-constrained* household are,

$$c_1 = (1 - \tau_1)y_1 = y_1 - g_2 + b_2$$
$$c_2 = (1 - \tau_2)y_2 = y_2 - (1 + r^*)b_2,$$

where we have used the government budget constraints in each period to express the private budget constraints in terms of g_2 and b_2.

The government may be able to relieve the credit constraint if they can borrow in international loan markets, i.e. if they are able to choose a positive value of government debt, $b_2 > 0$. To make the government's problem fit the theory of optimization with nonnegativity constraints, let's introduce government saving, $s_2^g = -b_2$. If the government lends in international markets, then $b_2 < 0, s_2^g > 0$ and if they borrow in international markets, then $b_2 > 0, s_2^g < 0$. The household budget constraints can be rewritten in terms of government saving as

$$c_1 = (1 - \tau_1)y_1 = y_1 - g_2 - s_2^g$$
$$c_2 = (1 - \tau_2)y_2 = y_2 + (1 + r^*)s_2^g.$$

The benevolent government chooses g_2 and s_2^g to maximize $U = \ln\left(y_1 - g_2 - s_2^g\right) + \beta \ln\left(y_2 + (1 + r^*)s_2^g\right)$. If other countries will *accept loans from* the government but will *not lend to* the government, then the government faces the nonnegativity constraint, $s_2^g \geq 0$. The first order conditions for the government problem are,

$$\frac{\beta\mu A g_2^{\mu-1}}{c_2} - \frac{1}{c_1} = 0$$

$$\frac{\beta(1 + r*)}{c_2} - \frac{1}{c_1} \leq 0, s_2^g \geq 0.$$

If $b_2 < 0, s_2^g > 0$, the government is a lender, and we get the efficient solution given by (13) from the text,

$$\mu A g_2^{\mu-1} = 1 + r^*$$

$$\frac{c_2}{c_1} = \beta(1 + r^*).$$

This would also be the solution if the government could freely borrow and thus doesn't confront the nonnegativity constraint.

If, however, the government would prefer $b_2 > 0, s_2^g < 0$, but no country or international institution will lend to it, then we have the constrained solution

$$\frac{\beta\mu A g_2^{\mu-1}}{c_2} - \frac{1}{c_1} = 0$$

$$\frac{\beta(1 + r*)}{c_2} - \frac{1}{c_1} < 0, \quad s_2^g = 0,$$

which implies $\mu A g_2^{\mu-1} > 1 + r^*$. Government *investmentis inefficiently low* because the marginal product of public capital is greater than the cost of borrowing.

A.4 Total Differentials and Linear Approximations

If $y = f(x_1, x_2)$ is a differentiable function of x_1 and x_2, one can define the *total differential* of f as

$$dy = \frac{\partial f}{\partial x_1} dx_1 + \frac{\partial f}{\partial x_2} dx_2,$$

where dy, dx_1, and dx_2 are real variables that are interpreted as "changes" in the original variables. The concept of the total differential extends naturally to the case where the function has many arguments or independent variables.

If one imagines that the total differential is taken at a particular point where $x_1 = \bar{x}_1$ and $x_2 = \bar{x}_2$, then it can be related to the notion of a *linear approximation* of $f(x_1, x_2)$,

$$y = f(\bar{x}_1, \bar{x}_2) + \frac{\partial f}{\partial x_1}(\bar{x}_1, \bar{x}_2)dx_1 + \frac{\partial f}{\partial x_2}(\bar{x}_1, \bar{x}_2)dx_2,$$

where dx_1 and dx_2 are interpreted as deviations from the values $x_1 = \bar{x}_1$ and $x_2 = \bar{x}_2$, and the partial derivatives are evaluated at the point $(\bar{x}_1, \bar{x}_2)$. Note that, analogous to the interpretations of dx_1 and dx_2, it is natural to think of dy as $y - f(\bar{x}_1, \bar{x}_2)$.

Examples from the Text
In Sect. 5.3 from Chap. 5, we analyze the nonlinear transition function for private capital accumulation

$$k_{t+1} = (1 - \tau_t)\mathrm{w}_t - \frac{(1 - \tau_t)\mathrm{w}_t + z_{t+1}/R_t}{1 + \beta} - b_{t+1}.$$

The transition equation cannot be solved explicitly for k_{t+1} because of the nonlinear effect of k_{t+1} on R_t. However, we can easily do a qualitative analysis of how introducing different fiscal policies affect capital accumulation by taking the total differential of the transition equation from an initial position with $z_t = 0$, so that a small change in R_t has no effect on the right-hand-side.
Begin by thinking of the transition equation as being a function of the fiscal variables, τ_t, z_{t+1}, b_{t+1}. Now take the total differential with respect to the fiscal variables,

$$dk_{t+1} = -\mathrm{w}_t d\tau_t - \frac{-\mathrm{w}_t d\tau_t + dz_{t+1}/R_t}{1 + \beta} - db_{t+1},$$

for a given value of w_t and where the initial value of z_{t+1} is zero. The total differential can be used to examine the qualitative effects of small changes in fiscal policy from this particular initial position.

A.5 L'Hospital's Rule

On occasion one encounters a ratio of functions or expressions that take on an *indeterminate form* at a point of interest. An indeterminate form is one where the ratio becomes $\frac{0}{0}$ or $\frac{\infty}{\infty}$. In some cases indeterminate forms actually do have a determinate value that is simply not immediately obvious. *L'Hospital's Rule* indicates when this might be true.

The rule says that if you have two differentiable expressions, $f(x)$ and $h(x)$, and at a particular value of x, say $x = x_0$, the ratio $\frac{f(x)}{h(x)}$ takes an indeterminate form, then $\lim_{x \to x_0} \frac{f(x)}{h(x)} = \lim_{x \to x_0} \frac{f'(x)}{h'(x)}$. The result is useful because sometimes the ratio of derivatives has a determinate form.

Examples from the Text

In Sect. 2.10 of Chap. 2, we introduced a more general lifetime utility function with a single period utility flow from consumption of the form,

$$u_t = \frac{\left(c_t^{1-1/\sigma} - 1\right)}{(1 - 1/\sigma)}.$$

The motivation for needing a more general utility function is provided in the text, but part of the reason for its unusual form is to allow the logarithmic utility function, that we use in most of our models, to appear as a special case. Using L'Hospital Rule one can show that $u_t = \ln c_t$, when $\sigma = 1$.

To see this, first note that when $\sigma = 1$, the utility function has the indeterminate form $\frac{0}{0}$. Second, we need to use the result that the exponential function and the natural log functions are inverses of each other, i.e. $x^a = e^{a \ln x}$. This means we can write $c_t^{1-1/\sigma}$ as $e^{(1-1/\sigma)\ln c_t}$. Third, the rule for differentiating the exponential function $f(x) = e^{ax}$, is $f'(x) = ae^{ax}$. Finally, to apply the result, think of the expressions in the numerator and the denominator as functions of σ.

Now, we can write utility as

$$u_t = \frac{\left(e^{(1-1/\sigma)\ln c_t} - 1\right)}{(1 - 1/\sigma)}.$$

Differentiating the numerator and the denominator with respect to σ and then taking the ratio of the two derivatives gives

$$\frac{\frac{1}{\sigma^2} \ln c_t e^{(1-1/\sigma)\ln c_t}}{\frac{1}{\sigma^2}} = \ln c_t e^{(1-1/\sigma)\ln c_t}.$$

At $\sigma = 1$, the ratio is $u_t = \ln c_t$, because $e^0 = 1$.

A.6 Expected Utility

In applications where the future is uncertain, economists often take an *expected utility approach.* For concreteness in developing this concept, suppose there are m possible states of nature in the future that affect the level of income and consumption possibilities of our two-period households. From the perspective of the current period, period 1, the expected lifetime utility is

$$EU = \ln c_1 + \beta E \ln c_2,$$

where E is the *expectation operator* that indicates an expected value is being taken over all possible future values of second period consumption. To be even more explicit, let π_i denote the probability that state i occurs. Define c_2^i as the value of consumption in state i. We can then write

$$E \ln c_2 = \sum_{i=1}^{m} \pi_i \ln\left(c_2^i\right).$$

Given this definition, the household or government can choose variables in period 1 (e.g. household saving, government investment, or government borrowing) knowing that there is also some random variable that affects the resulting value of future consumption (e.g. the interest rate on saving or the return to government investment). Essentially the same optimization procedure can be used as in the certainty case, with the complication that the return to the first period choice will vary across the different states of nature.

Examples from the Text

Section 3.5 contains a model where the current government makes transfers of income to two different household types, labeled P and R. The government is altruistic in the sense that it values, possibly differently, the utility of the two household types. Uncertainty enters because the current government is unsure that it will be re-elected to serve in the future period. The uncertainty matters because the government must decide how much to borrow in the current period and its choice will impact the ability to finance transfers in the future (the more that is borrowed, the more funds that must be used to repay debt in the future). So, the government makes its current period transfers, and the associated debt policy, based on the expected consequences of its actions into the future.

In the text, we focus on the case where there is complete political polarization. One party cares only about the R-households and the other party cares only about the P-households. If the party supporting the R-households is currently in power, its expected utility function is

$$\ln c_1^R + \beta E \ln c_2^R,$$

where the expectation is taken over the two political states of nature—the current party is re-elected or not. For example, if the probability of being re-elected is ½, we have

$$\ln c_1^R + \beta E \ln c_2^R = \ln c_1^R + \frac{\beta}{2} \ln c_2^R.$$

The choices of the R-government in the current period are modeled to maximize this objective function using the same optimization approach as in the certainty case.

A.7 Game Theory and Nash Equilibrium

There are (*game theoretic*) settings where an individual agent's (*player's*) optimal choice (*action*) depends on the optimal choice of others in a direct way, rather than simply indirectly through the competitive market price. In this case, each agent must form an optimal choice function that is contingent on the choices of others (a *best response function*). In addition, it is often assumed that there is no cooperation between agents. Each agent arrives at his choice without bargaining or colluding with other players (a *non-cooperative game*).

A commonly used equilibrium notion in this type of *non-cooperative game* is one where (i) each player simultaneously forms a best response based on beliefs about what other players choose and (ii) those beliefs turn out to be correct. This type of equilibrium is called a *Nash Equilibrium*, named after the Nobel Prize winning mathematician, John Nash.

Examples from the Text

Section 3.6 contains a model where different interest groups lobby the government for transfers. The groups do not coordinate their decisions, i.e. each group chooses its rent-seeking activity taking the others' behavior as given. The central government and the different interest groups play a non-cooperative Nash game, where all actions are taken independently and simultaneously.

The economic problem with this type of uncoordinated equilibrium is that households act under the belief that most of the marginal tax burden of raising their transfers can be passed off to other groups. So, each group acts like the financing of a marginal dollar of transfers is less expensive than it actually is. In the end, the tax rate must adjust to reflect all the transfer requests. This is known as the *common pool* (of tax revenue) problem.

A.8 Quadratic Equations

Some equations in the unknown variable x can be written in the following quadratic form

$$ax^2 + bx + c = 0,$$

where $a \neq 0$. Mathematically, there are two solutions for x that satisfy the equation, although one or both may not make sense as solutions to an economic problem. The mathematical solution are given by the *quadratic formula*,

$$x = \frac{-b \pm \sqrt{b^2 - 4ac}}{2a}.$$

Examples from the Text

Section 2.10 derives a transition equation for government capital,

$$g_{t+1}\left(\Gamma + g_{t+1}^{(\sigma-1)(1-\mu)}\right) = \Gamma y_t = \Gamma A g_t^{\mu},$$

where $\Gamma \equiv (\beta\mu)^{\sigma} A^{\sigma-1}$.

In general, there is no explicit solution for g_{t+1}. One of the situations where an explicit solution is available, is when $\sigma = (2-\mu)/(1-\mu)$. In this case, the transition equation becomes a quadratic equation in g_{t+1} because $g_{t+1}^{(\sigma-1)(1-\mu)} = g_{t+1}$. The transition can then be written in quadratic form as

$$g_{t+1}^2 + \Gamma g_{t+1} - \Gamma A g_t^{\mu} = 0.$$

The solutions from the quadratic formula are

$$g_{t+1} = \frac{-\Gamma \pm \sqrt{\Gamma^2 + 4\Gamma A g_t^{\mu}}}{2},$$

but clearly there is only one positive solution that makes sense in the economic application.

Solving for the only positive root gives us the following transition equation,

$$g_{t+1} = \frac{\Gamma}{2}\left(\sqrt{1 + 4Ag_t^{\mu}/\Gamma} - 1\right).$$

A.9 Infinite Series

A *sequence* is an ordered list of terms, $a_0, a_1, a_2, \cdot, \cdot, \cdot, a_n$. A special case of a sequence is one where consecutive terms have the same ratio, known as a *geometric sequence*. This is possible when the terms of the sequence have a common base value that is raised to an increasing power as follows:

$a_0 = a^0 = 1,\ a_1 = a^1 = a,\ a_2 = a^2,\ a_3 = a^3, \cdot, \cdot, \cdot, a_n = a^n$. So the ratio of consecutive terms is always a.

Of more direct interest to us is the *sum* of a geometric sequence known as a *geometric series*, defined as

$$S_n = \sum_{i=0}^{n} a^i = 1 + a + \cdots + a^n.$$

Note that $S_n - aS_n = 1 - a^{n+1}$, so

$$S_n = \frac{1 - a^{n+1}}{1 - a}.$$

Finally, note when $0 \le a < 1$, then if $n \rightarrow \infty$, the *infinite geometric series* is

$$S_\infty = \frac{1}{1 - a}.$$

Examples from the Text

In the solution to *Problem* 2 from Chap. 5, we use the formula for a geometric series twice.

First, remember that $R = 1 + r - \delta$ and because we assume a positive interest rate, $0 < \frac{1}{R} = \frac{1}{1+r-\delta} < 1$. In part (a) of *Problem* 2, we then have $\frac{1}{R}\sum_{i=0}^{\infty}\left(\frac{1}{R}\right)^i = \frac{1}{R} \times \frac{1}{1-\frac{1}{R}} = \frac{1}{R}\frac{R}{R-1} = \frac{1}{r-\delta}$ and in part (b) of *Problem* 2, we have $B_t = \sum_{i=0}^{\infty}\frac{-PD_{t+i}}{\prod_{j=0}^{i} R_{t-1+j}} = (-PD)\sum_{i=0}^{\infty}\frac{1}{R^{i+1}} = \frac{-PD}{R}\sum_{i=0}^{\infty}\frac{1}{R^i} = \frac{-PD}{r-\delta}$.

Index

M. Ivanyna et al., *The Macroeconomics of Corruption*, Springer Texts in Business and Economics, https://doi.org/10.1007/978-3-030-67557-8

The manufacturer's authorised representative in the EU is Springer Nature Customer Service Centre GmbH, Europaplatz 3, 69115 Heidelberg, Germany. If you have any concerns regarding our products, please contact ProductSafety@springernature.com

Printed and bound by CPI Group (UK) Ltd, Croydon, CR0 4YY
30/09/2026
02225494-0016